Islandica

A Series in Icelandic and Norse Studies

Cornell University Library

PATRICK J. STEVENS, MANAGING EDITOR

VOLUME LIV

Romance and Love
in Late Medieval and Early Modern Iceland

Essays in Honor of Marianne Kalinke

EDITED BY KIRSTEN WOLF AND JOHANNA DENZIN

Romance and Love in Late Medieval and Early Modern Iceland

Essays in Honor of Marianne Kalinke

EDITED BY

KIRSTEN WOLF AND JOHANNA DENZIN

ISLANDICA LIV

CORNELL UNIVERSITY LIBRARY
ITHACA, NEW YORK
2008

Copyright © 2008 by Cornell University Library

All rights reserved. Except for brief quotations in a review, this book, or parts thereof, must not be reproduced in any form without permission in writing from the publisher.

First published 2008 by Cornell University Library

Printed in the United States of America
Design and composition: Jack Donner, BookType

A complete version of this book is available through open access at http://cip.cornell.edu/Islandica

Cloth printing 10 9 8 7 6 5 4 3 2 1

CONTENTS

Acknowledgments vii
Tabula Gratulatoria ix
Preface xi

Introduction 1

Gunnarr and Hallgerðr: A Failed Romance 5
ROBERT COOK

The Native Romance of Gunnlaugr and Helga the Fair 33
THEODORE M. ANDERSSON

Romance, Marriage, and Social Class in the Saga World 65
JENNY JOCHENS

The Anomalous Pursuit of Love in *Kormaks saga* 81
MARGRÉT EGGERTSDÓTTIR

Sturla Þórðarson on Love 111
ÚLFAR BRAGASON

Klári saga as an Indigenous Romance 135
SHAUN F. D. HUGHES

When Skaði Chose Njǫrðr 165
JOHN LINDOW

Enabling Love: Dwarfs in Old Norse-Icelandic Romances 183
ÁRMANN JAKOBSSON

Hrólfs saga kraka: A Tragedy, Comedy, History, Pastoral, 207
Pastoral-Comical, Historical-Pastoral, Tragical-Historical,
Tragical-Comical-Historical-Pastoral . . . Romance
JOHANNA DENZIN

"The Best Medicine in the Bitterest of Herbs": 231
An Eighteenth-Century Moral Tale
M. J. DRISCOLL

On the Transmission of the Old Norse-Icelandic Legend 257
of Saints Faith, Hope, and Charity
KIRSTEN WOLF

Arctic Garden of Delights: The Purpose of the Book 279
of Reynistaður
SVANHILDUR ÓSKARSDÓTTIR

Love in a Cold Climate—With the Virgin Mary 303
MARGARET CLUNIES ROSS

Mírmanns saga: The First Old Norse-Icelandic 319
Hagiographical Romance?
SVERRIR TÓMASSON

Contributors 337

ACKNOWLEDGMENTS

All the articles in this book have been written with the standards and example of Marianne Kalinke in mind. The editors wish to thank Patrick Stevens, Curator of The Fiske Icelandica Collection at Cornell University Library, for his enthusiam for this project, which he saw as a fitting tribute to Marianne. We are grateful to him for agreeing to accept this book for publication in the *Islandica* series. We have had ongoing editorial help from the able project assistant Natalie Van Deusen of the University of Wisconsin-Madison. We wish to thank all the contributors for their learning, assistance, and patience during the long process from abstracts to print.

KW and JD

TABULA GRATULATORIA

Sarah M. Anderson
Theodore M. Andersson
The Arnamagnæan Institute
 and Dictionary
Ármann Jakobsson
The Árni Magnússon Institute
Ásdís Egilsdóttir
Aðalheiður Guðmundsdóttir
Bergljót Soffía Kristjánsdóttir
Ingvil Brügger Budal
Michael Chesnutt
Carol J. Clover
Margaret Clunies Ross
Robert Cook
Margaret Cormack
Helen Damico
Helle Degnbol
Johanna Denzin
Matthew James Driscoll
Einar G. Pétursson
Eiríkur Rögnvaldsson
Anthony Faulkes
Gillian Fellows-Jensen
Fiske Icelandic Collection,
 Cornell University Library
Roberta Frank
R. D. Fulk
Kari Ellen Gade
Gísli Sigurðsson
Gottskálk Jensson

Arthur Groos
Stefanie Gropper
Terry Gunnell
Guðrún Hólmgeirsdóttir
Guðrún Ingólfsdóttir
Guðvarður Már Gunnlaugsson
Guðrún Þórhallsdóttir
Jan Ragnar Hagland
Tom Hall
Richard L. Harris
Odd Einar Haugen
Wilhelm Heizmann
Shaun F. D. Hughes
Institut für Nordische
 Philologie, Ludwig-Maximi-
 lians-Universität München
Institut für Nordische Philologie,
 Westfälische Wilhelms-
 Universität Münster
Tatjana N. Jackson
Judith Jesch
Jenny Jochens
Vera Johanterwage
Peter A. Jorgensen
Jon Gunnar Jørgensen
Hildegard Elisabeth Keller
John Kennedy
Gert Kreutzer
Hans Kuhn
Beatrice La Farge

Carolyne Larrington
Annette Lassen
Anatoly Liberman
John Lindow
Bernadine McCreesh
John McKinnell
Rory McTurk
Mats Malm
Margrét Eggertsdóttir
Andrea Meregalli
William Ian (Bill) Miller
Stephen A. Mitchell
Else Mundal
Ólafur Halldórsson
Ólöf Benediktsdóttir
Andy Orchard
Kjartan Ottósson
Louis A. Pitschmann
Eva Rode
Elizabeth Ashman Rowe
Christopher Sanders
Jens Eike Schnall
Sigurgeir Steingrímsson
Eckehard Simon

Peter Springborg
Svanhildur Óskarsdóttir
Sverrir Tómasson
Karen Swenson
Timothy R. Tangherlini
Torfi H. Tulinius
Jeffrey Turco
Þórunn Sigurðardóttir
University Library of
 Southern Denmark
Fjodor Uspenskij
Úlfar Bragason
Vésteinn Ólason
Andrew Wawn
Jonas Wellendorf
Lars van Wezel
Henrik Williams
Tarrin Wills
Kendra J. Willson
Kirsten Wolf
Charles D. Wright
Yelena Sesselja Helgadóttir
 (Yershova)

PREFACE

The Cornell University Library published the first volume of the *Islandica* series, a *Bibliography of the Icelandic Saga and Minor Tales*, compiled by Halldór Hermannsson, in 1908. The series, initially conceived as "an annual relating to Iceland and the Fiske Icelandic Collection," has evolved during its century of existence. Over the years, it has included a number of scholarly monographs while maintaining its tradition of publishing learned bibliographies. Now, *Islandica* no longer appears solely in print. Commencing with volume LIII, a version of each series volume is available online at http://...library.cornell.edu/islandica.

Professor Marianne Kalinke retired from the University of Illinois at Urbana-Champaign in May 2006 after a distinguished career of teaching and writing. Acclaimed for her work on Old Norse-Icelandic Arthurian romances, she is perhaps best known in the scholarly community for her *Bridal-Quest Romance in Medieval Iceland* (Ithaca and London: Cornell University Press, 1990; *Islandica* XLVI).

It is therefore a profound pleasure to offer this Festschrift, *Romance and Love in Late Medieval and Early Modern Iceland*, in honor of Marianne's remarkable contributions during *Islandica*'s centennial year. Fourteen authors have graced this volume with contributions that reflect, in their own lively way, Marianne's brilliant influence on the modern study of Old Norse-Icelandic literature.

Professor Kirsten Wolf of the University of Wisconsin-Madison and Professor Johanna Denzin of Columbia College, Missouri, proposed this Festschrift as a tribute to their teacher, friend and fellow scholar, knowing they would be far from alone in wanting to have the opportunity to honor her. Kirsten and Johanna have done remarkably in bringing this expression of esteem from all the contributors to fruition.

The Cornell University Press has been graciously forthcoming in its collaboration on the publication process. This volume, and the new electronic home of the *Islandica* series, would not have been possible without the enthusiasm and wisdom of my library colleague, Teresa Ehling, Director of the Center for Innovative Publishing in the Cornell University Library. I am also pleased to acknowledge Elaine Engst, Director of the Division of Rare and Manuscript Collections, for her counsel regarding the future of our venerable series.

Patrick J. Stevens
Curator, the Fiske Icelandic Collection
and Managing Editor, *Islandica*

INTRODUCTION

This volume has been conceived to honor Marianne Kalinke upon her retirement from teaching at the University of Illinois at Urbana-Champaign in May 2006.

Marianne started her teaching career in 1969 at Albertus Magnus College. Two years later, in 1971, she accepted a position at the University of Rhode Island, where she taught for eight years. In 1979, she began her tenure at the University of Illinois in the Department of Germanic Languages and Literatures, where in 2003 she was elected to the Center for Advanced Study and in 2005 named Trowbridge Chair in Literary Studies. Marianne has a distinguished record of service to both the department and the university. On two separate occasions, she served as department chair; twice, she acted as graduate advisor; and during her twenty-seven years of teaching at Illinois she served on every possible department committee. She also participated in almost forty different university committees, while at the same time mentoring scores of students, from undergraduate to graduate, developing new courses, and serving as a managing editor of the *Journal of English and Germanic Philology*, a position she has held since 1981.

Marianne's scholarship began with her doctoral dissertation on *Erex saga* at Indiana University. She and Foster Blaisdell, her advisor, subsequently published a translation of *Erex saga* and *Ívens saga* in 1977. Her work on these two texts set the course for her interest in Old Norse-Icelandic Arthurian romances and led to a stream of publications on this topic: *King Arthur, North-by-Northwest: The matière de Bretagne in Old Norse-Icelandic Romances* (1981); *Bibliography of Old Norse-Icelandic Romances* (1985), which she compiled in collaboration with P. M. Mitchell; *Möttuls saga* (1987), which she edited and published under the auspices of the Arnamagnaean Institute in Copenhagen; and *Bridal-Quest Romance in Medieval Iceland* (1990), her seminal work on the Old Icelandic bridal-quest stories. Marianne also served as an associate editor of *The Arthurian Encyclopedia* (1986) and *The New Arthurian Encyclopedia* (1996) and as the general editor of a three-volume series of editions and translations of the Old Norse-Icelandic Arthurian corpus: *Norse Romance I: The Tristan Legend*, *Norse Romance II: The Knights of the Round Table*, and *Norse Romance III: Hærra Ivan* (1999); she herself edited and translated *Möttuls saga*, *Ívens saga*, and *Erex saga* for the second volume. During this time, the mid-1990s, Marianne also began important new work on medieval saints' lives, examining the narratives, in part, as sacred romances, which resulted in *The Book of Reykjahólar: The Last of the Great Medieval Legendaries* (1996) and *St. Oswald of Northumbria: Continental Metamorphoses. With an Edition and Translation of* Ósvalds saga *and* Van sunte Oswaldo deme konninghe (2005).

Reviewing Marianne's career and scholarship, it becomes clear why the theme of romance and love (both secular and sacred) has been chosen as the central focus of a Festschrift to honor her. Both concepts are, however, difficult to define, and when romance is extended to designate also a genre, it becomes even more difficult to come up with a suitable definition. This volume does not reflect any one theoretical paradigm on romance. Rather, the articles approach the theme of Old Norse-Icelandic romance and love from a variety of perspectives.

Several articles in the volume examine the dichotomy of love between a man and a woman. Robert Cook looks at the failed romance of Gunnarr and Hallgerðr in *Njáls saga* and comments on the difference between the depiction of love in the world of courtly romances and the Sagas of Icelanders. Theodore Andersson, in turn, analyzes the romance of Gunnlaugr and Helga the Fair in *Gunnlaugs saga ormstungu*, arguing that while the saga has traditionally been regarded as a late text influenced by *Hallfreðar saga*, *Bjarnar saga Hítdœlakappa*, and *Egils saga Skallagrímssonar*, it is actually an early production that served as a source for these other sagas. Jenny Jochens examines *Vatnsdœla saga* and *Hallfreðar saga* in an attempt to explicate the tribulations that the couples Ingólfr and Valgerðr and Hallfreðr and Kolfinna encounter in their romantic and married lives. Margrét Eggertsdóttir considers the tragic and comic elements that coexist in *Kormáks saga* and explores the themes of love and honor and the differing societal roles of women and men. Úlfar Bragason analyzes the emotional and intellectual relationship of Sturla Þórðarson with those closest to him, especially the women in his life, as this is presented in *Íslendinga saga*. Shaun F. D. Hughes discusses *Klári saga* and argues that the saga is not translated from a continental model, but is an indigenous composition composed by Bishop Jón Halldórsson. He identifies strong influence from Middle Low German in the language of *Klári saga* and sees the saga as a pastiche of romance and *exemplum* elements.

There are also articles that explore the intersection of folklore, mythology, and romance. John Lindow examines the tale of Skaði's choice of Njǫrðr as her husband, and to illuminate the story he analyzes the mythic parallel to this episode in the account of Freyr's attraction to Gerðr and the "historical" parallel in the account of Kormákr's attraction to Steingerðr, which is triggered by the sight of her feet. Ármann Jakobsson discusses the role of dwarfs in fourteenth-century Icelandic romances, including *Göngu-Hrólfs saga*, *Viktors saga ok Blávus*, *Samsons saga fagra*, and *Sigurðar saga þǫgla*, arguing that the trickster role of the dwarf in these narratives can be interpreted in the light of the dwarf's undefined presence in the eddic material. Johanna Denzin examines how *Hrólfs saga kraka*, traditionally classified as a heroic epic, actually functions as a romance on many levels. She analyzes the four failed romances of the saga and explicates many of the folkloric motifs and romance themes found in the story.

One article in the collection examines the social construction of romance, morality, and gender in a post-medieval text. This is Matthew James Driscoll's analysis of the *Saga of Lucian og Gedula*, which is found transcribed in one of the autograph miscellanies of the Icelandic clergyman Jón Hjaltalín. Driscoll argues that the romance, which tells the tale of a farmer's son and an aristocrat's daughter, who are initially prohibited from marrying because of the differences in their social status, can also be read as a moral tale.

Marianne has herself postulated a similarity between medieval romance and certain saints' lives. Four articles in the volume examine sacred and hagiographic texts. Kirsten Wolf analyzes the transmission of the Old Norse-Icelandic legend of Saints Faith, Hope, and Charity in an attempt to determine with somewhat more precision the complex relationship among the four manuscripts of the legend and, by extension, to assess C. R. Unger's choice of manuscripts for his edition. Saints' lives are also, in part, the topic of Svanhildur Óskarsdóttir's article, though they are here treated in the context of the late-fourteenth-century Reynistaðarbók (AM 764 4to). She demonstrates that the codex represents an attempt at compiling a universal history in Icelandic and notes an endeavor on the part of the compiler to keep women in focus. She speculates that the work may well have been intended for nuns in Iceland in the late Middle Ages. Margaret Clunies Ross examines love in Christian skaldic poetry, arguing that late medieval European vernacular poetry of religious devotion is often characterized by an emotional fervor of great intensity, especially when adressed to the persons of Christ and his mother Mary. She notes that such affective piety appears to only a very limited degree in the Icelandic Marian miracle poems, but demonstrates that they display other qualities of equal interest and are no less concerned with love. Sverrir Tómasson discusses genre classifications with a focus on *Mírmanns saga*, arguing that the saga may well be considered the first Old Icelandic hagiographical romance.

The world of romance, whether secular or sacred, is often fraught with difficulties. Lovers are parted and have to struggle to be reunited, monsters or evil step-mothers have to be defeated, and the strength of one's devotion to God or the Virgin Mary has to be demonstrated. Scholars of medieval romance themselves often encounter a thicket of theoretical or philological thorns to wade through, but as all lovers of a good romance know, the protagonist is always rewarded for his or her kindness, wit, hard work, and perseverance. This collection of articles by a small cohort of Marianne Kalinke's friends and colleagues is offered to Marianne, who has dedicated a large portion of her career to working through the morass of medieval romance in its many different forms and rewarded us with her findings and insight.

Kirsten Wolf   Johanna Denzin

Gunnarr and Hallgerðr:
A Failed Romance

ROBERT COOK

In contrast to the medieval French romances, which are centrally concerned with defining the nature and effects and obligations of love, the Sagas of Icelanders have usually been thought to have feud and honor as their controlling themes. The love stories in the sagas—between Kjartan and Guðrún in *Laxdœla* saga, Gunnlaugr and Helga in *Gunnlaugs saga*, Kormákr and Steingerðr in *Kormáks saga*, to take some of the best known examples—appear mute and truncated in comparison with the fulsome treatment of love and emotions in the French romances, with their extensive authorial comments and internal monologues and direct expressions of love.[1] Accordingly, there has been a tendency to avoid reading love as a central theme in these sagas.[2]

The recent work of the Swedish scholar Daniel Sävborg forces us to rethink the role of emotions and love in the sagas.[3] He shows that the continental literary tradition of courtly love was known and understood in the North and followed in the *riddarasögur* in much the same style. The fact that the Sagas of Icelanders are written in a different

---

1. See, for example, the lengthy passages dealing with the hero's falling in love in Chrétien de Troys, *Yvain (Le chevalier au lion)*, ed. T. B. W. Reid (Manchester: Manchester University Press, 1961), ll. 1356–1406 and 1416–1427 (author's comments), 1428–1506 (Yvain's monologue).
2. M. I. Steblin-Kamenskij, *The Saga Mind*, trans. Kenneth H. Ober (Odense: Odense University Press, 1973), pp. 86–95, is a case in point.
3. Daniel Sävborg, *Sagan om kärleken. Erotik känslor och berättarkonst i norrön litteratur*, Acta Universitas Upsaliensis, Historia Litterarum 27 (Uppsala: Uppsala Universitet, 2007).

and restrained style, however, should not blind us to the presence there too of strong passions. Earlier scholars, such as Vésteinn Ólason and William I. Miller,[4] have pointed to the presence of emotions in the sagas, but Sävborg is the first to provide a meticulously detailed account of the way that brief but loaded formulas such as *sitja á tali (við)* and incidents of exchanges of clothing can add up to a powerful depiction of love, which in some cases becomes a formative element in the sagas.

Sävborg does not analyse, as I propose to do, the Gunnarr-Hallgerðr relationship, and with good reason: it has few of the indicators of an emotionally charged love relationship. And yet, in a saga that is virtually obsessed with sex and marriage and divorce and sexual innuendo and ambiguity and identity,[5] the relationship between Gunnarr and Hallgerðr plays a dominant and to some extent formative role, and deserves analysis on its own terms.

An interest in how people get along (interpersonal relationships)

The author of *Njáls* saga shows more interest in emotional states than we would expect, given the neutral style of the Sagas of Icelanders. He is particularly keen to comment on relations between characters, either through brief statements of his own ("things went well between them") or through utterances of his characters ("Yes, our love goes well"). The persistency of such remarks, which supplement the events themselves, reveals that he was indeed interested in the status of relationships and the emotional state of persons in relationships.

When Hǫskuldr has given Hrútr his first sight of Unnr—without her

---

4. Vésteinn Ólason, "Emosjon og aksjon i *Njáls saga*," *Nordica Bergensia* 3 (1994), pp. 157–172; William I. Miller, "Emotions and the Sagas," in *From Sagas to Society: Comparative Approaches to Early Iceland*, ed. Gísli Pálsson (Enfield Lock: Hisarlik Press, 1992), pp. 89–109.

5. This has been well covered, from different perspectives, in at least three articles: Helga Kress, "'Ekki hǫfu vér kvennaskap.' Nokkrar laustengdar athuganir um karlmennsku og kvenhatur í *Njálu*," in *Sjötíu ritgerðir helgaðar Jakobi Benediktssyni 20. júlí 1977*, ed. Einar G. Pétursson and Jónas Kristjánsson, 2 vols. (Reykjavík: Stofnun Árna Magnússonar, 1977), vol. 1, pp. 293–313; Ursula Dronke, "The Role of Sexual Themes in *Njáls saga*," *Dorothea Coke Memorial Lecture, University College London, 27 May 1980* (London: University College London, 1980); and Ármann Jakobsson, "Masculinity and Politics in *Njáls saga*, " *Viator* 38 (2007), pp. 191–215. I am grateful to Ármann for giving me an early version of his paper and for much useful counsel during this writing.

knowing it—and asks him how he likes this prospective bride, Hrútr replies "Well enough, but I don't know if we're meant to be happy together."[6] At the wedding, which was postponed in order for Hrútr to claim an inheritance in Norway, there is the sudden but somehow not unexpected statement that "the bride had a sad look about her," and shortly after this we read that "there was little intimacy between her and Hrut, and so it went all through the winter." In the spring she went to the Althing to meet her father Mǫrðr; "her spirits were rather heavy"[7] and she soon burst into tears. Mǫrðr finds no evidence of a problem in their relationship and sends her back to continue her life with Hrútr. Here again we are given an inside view: "Then Hrut rode home from the Althing, together with his wife, and things went well between them that summer. But when winter came the difficulty returned, and it became worse as spring drew on."[8] At this point the audience is as ignorant of the underlying problem as Mǫrðr is, but unfortunately for Hrútr, all the embarrassing details of this troubled relationship soon come into the open. This, the first marriage presented in the saga, is unsparingly anatomized.

The relationship between Hrútr and Unnr may be the most exposed in the saga, but the author's interest in personal and marital relationships is seen throughout, from the curt "Thrain had little love for her,"[9] to the elaborate deliberations over Hallgerðr's character and its suitability for the wedded state, to Gizurr hvíti's statement that Mǫrðr (Valgarðsson) loves Gizurr's daughter "like the eyes in his head."[10] One marriage in the saga, that of Hallgerðr and Glúmr, is specifically portrayed as harmonious: "Glum and Hallgerd got along well together, and things went this way for a while."[11] This very positive

---

6. *Brennu-Njáls saga*, ed. Einar Ólafur Sveinsson, Íslenzk fornrit 12 (Reykjavík: Hið íslenzka fornritafélag, 1954), 2.8: "'Vel, ... en eigi veit ek, hvárt vit eigum heill saman.'" All references will be to this edition, by chapter and page. The English is taken from my Penguin Classics translation of 2001.
7. 6.22: "ok var brúðrin dǫpr heldr.... En fátt var um með þeim Hrúti um samfarar, ok ferr svá fram allt til várs.... en henni var skapþungt nokkut."
8. 6.23: "Síðan reið Hrútr heim af þingi ok kona hans með honum, ok var nú vel með þeim um sumarit. En þá er vetraði, þá dró til vanða með þeim, ok var þess verr, er meir leið á várit."
9. 34.87: "Þráinn unni henni lítit." This refers to Þráinn Sigfússon and his first wife Þorhildr skáldkona.
10. 135.355: "... hann ann henni sem augum í hǫfði sér."
11. 14.46: "Þau komu vel ásamt, Glúmr ok Hallgerðr; ok fór svá fram um hríð."

statement is soon reinforced by her response to Þjóstólfr's question; "Yes, our love goes well."[12]

Such pronouncements, whether positive or negative, do not accompany all marriages in the saga, so that their absence is noticeable and itself perhaps significant. Ursula Dronke points out that instead of being told that all went well with Hildigunnr and Hǫskuldr, we learn only that "Hildigunn and Bergthora got along well."[13] Einar Ólafur Sveinsson noticed this, but still wrote of "the affection which is obviously beginning to awaken between her and Höskuldur."[14] This may be reading too much into the story, for the only glimpse we get into the workings of this marriage comes when Hildigunnr whets Flosi to avenge her husband (ch. 116).[15]

An insight into the dynamics of the relationship which concerns us most in this paper is provided during the reciprocal slayings instigated by Hallgerðr and Bergþóra. After Hallgerðr's insulting assertion that both her husband and Njáll are "soft" (blauðr), we read: "Then Gunnar was cold with her for a long time, until she became more yielding."[16] Gunnarr seems to have found a way to tame her, if only temporarily, but the over-riding fact is that in spite of all the hints the author gives about that relationship, there are none to indicate that it is a happy one.

The author's interest in personal relationships is also apparent in comments on how one person influences another. About Þjóstólfr, Hallgerðr's Hebridean foster-father, "It was said that he did nothing to improve Hallgerd's character."[17] Gunnarr warns his kinsman Sigmundr Lambason about his Swedish companion Skjǫldr: "I've been told about him ... that he does not improve your character—and what you certainly need is some improvement."[18] We are soon told that the foolish

---

12. 15.47: "'Vel er um ástir okkrar.'"
13. 97.247: "ok fór allt vel með þeim Hildigunni ok Bergþóru." Dronke, "The Role of Sexual Themes," pp. 4–5.
14. Einar Ólafur Sveinsson, Njáls Saga. A Literary Masterpiece, trans. Paul Schach (Lincoln: University of Nebraska Press, 1971), p. 106; see also p. 112.
15. See Carol J. Clover, "Hildigunnr's lament," in Structure and Meaning in Old Norse Literature, ed. John Lindow et al. (Odense: Odense University Press, 1986), pp. 141–83.
16. 38.102: "Var þá Gunnarr lengi fár við hana, þar til er hon lét til við hann."
17. 9.30: "Þat var mælt, at hann væri engi skapbœtir Hallgerði."
18. 41.106: "'Svá er mér frá honum sagt ... at hann sé þér engi skapbœtir; en þú þarft hins heldr, at bœtt sé um með þér.'"

Sigmundr is falling under the influence of Hallgerðr, who persuades him, together with Skjǫldr, to kill Þórðr leysingjason. Rannveig is aware of the influence of her daughter-in-law and warns Sigmundr that "if you rise to Hallgerd's bait again it will be your death."[19] After Gunnarr has made a settlement with Njáll for the slaying, he repeats the warning and adds a keen analysis of the Sigmundr-Hallgerðr relationship: "you must never rise to Hallgerd's bait again. You're not at all like me: you are given to mockery and sarcasm, while I am not. You get along well with Hallgerd, because you have more in common with her."[20] Inevitably Sigmundr rises to Hallgerðr's bait again, which leads to his death. Hrappr Ǫrgumleiðason is another character who has a malign effect on others, first on Þráinn in Norway and then at Grjótá in Iceland, where in an unusual repetition it is said twice that he had a harmful influence.[21] His role is apparent in the slanders against the sons of Njáll: "Killer Hrapp and Grani were the ones who spoke most abusively about the sons of Njal and they saw to it that there was no offer of compensation."[22]

The most extreme example of a person exerting evil influence is of course Mǫrðr, who ingratiates himself with the sons of Njáll by giving them gifts and telling them lies which rupture their fine relationship with Hǫskuldr Þráinsson, so that eventually they slay him.[23]

It is in keeping with saga style that authorial comments are made by events as well as by words. On this account—turning again to marital relationships—the union of Bergþóra and Njáll must be considered a success, though this is never stated explicitly. Bergþóra's concern for family honor, her gracious acceptance of the grieving Hróðný and her insistence on dying by the side of her man—a noble sacrifice clearly

---

19. 42.109: "'En ef Hallgerðr kemr annarri flugu í munn þér, þá verðr þat þinn bani.'"

20. 44.111: "'... ok skyldir þú nú eigi annarri flugu láta koma í munn þér. Ert þú mér ekki skaplíkr; þú ferr með spott ok háð, en þat er ekki mitt skap; kemr þú þér því vel við Hallgerði, at it eiguð meir skap saman.'"

21. 88.220: "ok bjó Hrappr þar [at Hrappsstaðir]; hann var þó lengstum at Grjótá. Hann þótti þar ǫllu spilla." 91.225: "Hrappr átti bú á Hrappsstǫðum, en þá var hann at Grjótá jafnan, ok þótti hann þar ǫllu spilla."

22. 91.227: "Þeir lǫgðu verst til þeira Njálssona Víga-Hrappr ok Grani ok ollu mest, er þeim var engi sætt boðin."

23. For a fuller and kinder view, see my "Mörður Valgarðsson," *Sagnaheimur. Studies in Honour of Hermann Pálsson*, ed. Ásdís Egilsdóttir and Rudolf Simek (Vienna: Fassbaender, 2001), pp. 63–77.

24. ÍF 3, p. 60: "Helga var svá fǫgr, at þat er sǫgn fróðra manna, at hon hafi fegrst kona

meant to contrast with Hallgerðr's refusal to help her husband at his dying moment—all these define her as a supportive wife, living harmoniously with her husband.

These contrasting couples—Njáll-Bergþóra and Gunnarr-Hallgerðr—are at the heart of the saga. Our task now is to tease from the reticent narrator the nature of the more problematic of these relationships.

Love at first sight

The best part of the Gunnarr-Hallgerðr romance is its beginning. Hallgerðr has been marked as a tall beauty from her first appearance in the saga; her long silk-like hair is described several times (1.6, 13.44, 33.85). It should be noted, however, that she falls short of superlative beauties like Helga Þorsteinsdóttir in *Gunnlaugs saga Ormstungu*, said to be the fairest woman in all Iceland,[24] or Guðrún Ósvífrsdóttir in *Laxdœla saga*, the loveliest woman then growing up in Iceland.[25] If they are Miss Iceland, Hallgerðr is Miss Akureyri; her hair, though long and silky, is no match for Helga Þorsteinsdóttir's, and her dress is emphasized more than her natural beauty. When she is brought out to meet Glúmr she is wearing a woven black cloth, a scarlet tunic and a silver belt (13.44). When she meets Gunnarr at the Althing, she is the best-dressed of a group of well-dressed women[26]—this time she is wearing an ornamented red tunic and a scarlet cloak trimmed with braids[27] down to the hem. He himself is in a company of superlatively dressed men who capture the admiration of everybody, and with the stately garments he received from King Haraldr Gormsson and the gold bracelet from Jarl Hákon (see 31.82–83) he must have been

---

verit á Íslandi. Hár hennar var svá mikit, at þat mátti hylja hana alla, ok svá fagrt sem gull barit...."

25. ÍF 5, p. 86: "hon var kvenna vænst, er upp óxu á Íslandi, bæði at ásjánu ok vitsmunum. Guðrún var kurteis kona ... Allra kvenna var hon kœnst ok bezt orði farin; hon var ǫrlynd kona."

26. 33.85: "þá sá hann [Gunnarr] konur ganga í móti sér ok váru vel búnar. Sú var í ferðarbroddi konan, er bezt var búin."

27. This rendering of *búin hlǫðum* is taken from a 2007 Ph.D. dissertation at University College London by Anna Zanchi, "Dress in the *Íslendingasögur* and *Íslendingaþættir*," p. 80.

---

28. I owe this observation to Anna Zanchi. It may be pointed out that Gunnarr had

by far the best-dressed man at the Althing. He and Hallgerðr are a match for finery, but the origins are different: Gunnarr's are royal gifts in return for exploits abroad; Hallgerðr's have been acquired at home and proclaim her status as a member of a leading family.[28] For personal, physical beauty, Gunnarr is more than a match for her: "He was handsome and fair of skin and had a straight nose, turned up at its tip. He was blue-eyed and keen-eyed and ruddy-cheeked, with thick hair, blond and well-combed."[29]

The meeting between two such paragons of beauty and finery and lineage is bound to be momentous. They were surely the Couple of the Year at that Althing, also because their mutual attraction to each other is immediate and spontaneous. She takes the initiative and greets him; she knows who he is, and indeed, he must have been the talk of the Althing. He, at a disadvantage, has to ask her name. After identifying herself she continues to hold the initiative and suggests a topic of conversation: like Desdemona, she wants to hear about his travels. "She spoke boldly to him and asked him to tell her about his travels, and he said he would not refuse."[30] This appeal to his ego is sure to please Gunnarr, especially after the gloomy reception he received at Bergþórshváll: Njáll listened but was not interested in the adventures themselves, only in their consequences. He predicted trouble from envious men and suggested that Gunnarr would do well to stay away from the Althing (32.84). After such a cold shower, Gunnarr needs comfort, and we may suspect that this discouraging visit to Njáll made him vulnerable to Hallgerðr's feminine glamor at the Althing which Njáll did not want him to attend.

The new friends sit down to talk, and at this point the author delays presenting the dialogue in order to describe their clothing (see above). It is as though he wishes to freeze for a moment a tableau of the two handsome young people getting acquainted at their leisure. He achieves

---

earlier worn gold lace and red cloth and a gold ring underneath his Kaupa-Heðinn disguise (23.64); later, when he comes to the horse-fight, he is wearing a red tunic and a wide silver belt (59.150). The latter are probably not royal gifts, the former certainly not.

29. 19.53: "Hann var vænn at yfirliti ok ljóslitaðr, réttnefjaðr ok hafit upp í framanvert, bláeygr ok snareygr ok roði í kinnunum; hárit mikit, gult, ok fór vel."

30. 33.85: "Hon mælti til hans djarfliga ok bað hann segja sér frá ferðum sínum, en hann kvazk ekki mundu varna henni máls."

31. One might wonder about the possible significance of their talking aloud. Does it

this by placing a six-line description of their attire between "They sat down and talked" (*settusk þau þá niðr ok tǫluðu*) and "They talked aloud for a long time" (*Þau tǫluðu lengi hátt*). By thus freezing the moment for us, giving us a static portrait of their external appearance, the author raises a suspicion that their attraction is superficial. What was said during this long conversation is less important than what they looked like.

As Sävborg has shown us, formulas describing lengthy conversations between a man and a woman are, in the rhetoric of the sagas, an indication of strong attraction. In this case, however, the lack of accompanying formulas and the emphasis on appearance undercut the intimacy of this scene.[31]

When their conversation (was it all devoted to Gunnarr's exploits?) is finally opened up to the reader it proves to be worth examining in detail, if only because there are few developed proposal scenes in the sagas, and because this is the only extended dialogue between Gunnarr and Hallgerðr presented in the saga. After their unrecorded conversation, Gunnarr shows his ignorance once more, asking whether she is married. A simple "no" would do as an answer, but she adds, candidly—and at this point, in the middle of her speech, the dialogue moves into direct discourse—that "there aren't many who would want to take the risk." This is an unexpected response, which Gunnarr has trouble dealing with. If she had said "I don't plan to marry," his next remark would be an appropriate response. But that is not what she said, and a fitting answer to what she actually said would be "Why is that? Why would no one want to take a chance with you?" But that would be an inquiry into her background, of which Gunnarr is ignorant and willing to remain so. This lack of curiosity, combined with a bit of competitiveness, causes him to ask: "Is there no one good enough for you?"[32]

Her response to his question is magnificently ambiguous: "It's not that ... but I'm very demanding when it comes to men."[33] The

---

too suggest a lack of intimacy? Or are we to assume that they spoke audibly during their long unrecorded conversation and then dropped their voices for the exchange that follows? Intimate conversation is sometimes explicitly quiet: in ch. 23 of *Laxdœla saga* Óláfr pái and Þorgerðr talk for a whole day outside the hearing of others.

32. 33.85: "Þykki þér hvergi fullkosta?"

33. 33.85–86: "Eigi er þat ... en mannvǫnd mun ek vera."

34. Suggested by Dronke, "The Role of Sexual Themes," pp. 19–20.

adjective *mannvǫnd* ("demanding") can mean both that she is indeed hard to please (this would answer Gunnarr's question) and that she is very difficult towards men.[34] If he understood the second meaning, Gunnarr pays it no heed and presses on to a proposal of marriage. In both of her complex answers Hallgerðr is offering to open herself up, to explain to Gunnarr why she is a risky marriage bet and what makes her a difficult woman. But Gunnarr, who started this conversation in ignorance, not knowing her name or marital status, continues in blissful ignorance, moved more by the challenge which this enigmatic woman presents than by a concern to understand her. He turns directly—carelessly, we might add—to his proposal, couched hypothetically at first: "How would you answer if I were to propose to you?"[35] She responds, equally coyly, by questioning his seriousness,[36] but he—now in the indicative voice—states that in fact he is serious.[37] She responds by reverting once more to the conditional (is she mimicking him?)—"if this is what's on your mind"[38]—and directs him to her father, like a proper daughter (she was not always so proper).

This dialogue is far from straightforward. Twice the phrase "*Eigi er þat*" (That's not so) is used, once by each of the speakers, to reverse the direction of the previous, negative remark ("*Þykki þér hvergi fullkosta?*", "*Þat mun þér ekki í hug*"). *Duplex negatio affirmat.* Gunnarr's remarks, although not always "correct" according to the rules of discourse, are conventional and predictable. Hallgerðr, with her use of the unexpected and the ambiguous, is the more subtle conversationalist, and it is possible that her gestures at self-revelation (few men would risk marrying her, she is hard on men) are designed to stimulate Gunnarr to rise to the challenge of marrying a difficult woman.

The arrangement with her family is more by concession than by whole-hearted approval. Hǫskuldr, always short of good counsel, wisely refers the matter to Hrútr, who recognizes that Gunnarr has

---

35. 33.86: "Hversu munt þú því svara, ef ek bið þín?" Bolli's initial proposal to Guðrún in *Laxdœla saga* is similarly hypothetical: "Eitt sinn spurði Bolli Guðrúnu, hversu hon myndi svara, ef hann bæði hennar."
36. 33.86: "Þat mun þér ekki í hug."
37. 33.86: "Eigi er þat."
38. 33.86: "Ef þér er nokkurr hugr á ... "
39. 33.86–87: "'Eigi er þat,' segir Hrútr, 'meir er hitt, at ek sé, at þú mátt eigi við

no control over himself and that this is a match based on desire which cannot be prevented.[39] Then, in a way that is not flattering to the bride but is at least an honest attempt to come clean, he points out the weaknesses of Hallgerðr: "Hrut told Gunnar, without being asked, everything about Hallgerd's character, and though it seemed to Gunnar at first that there were many faults, it finally came about that they made an agreement."[40] Hallgerðr's earlier remarks about no one wanting to take a chance with her, and about her being *mannvǫnd*, anticipate Hrútr's warning and rob it of its force: Gunnarr has already heard, from herself, that Hallgerðr is a difficult match, and in both cases he regards the hinted-at or explicit flaws as a challenge rather than as a matter for serious consideration. This comes close to comedy: the prospective bridegroom hears unfavorable information about his chosen one but persists in his determination to ignore negative signals. He is also, of course, likely to distrust Hrútr, whom he had earlier humiliated.

When the terms of the wedding are settled, Gunnarr rides to Njáll at Bergþórshváll, and there is nothing comical about their meeting: Njáll is depressed to hear of the agreement (*Hann tók þungt á kaupum hans*, 33.87) and simply expresses his grim foreboding, without any attempt to advise or plead. Like Hrútr, he is wise enough to know that the marriage is inevitable. His clairvoyance tells him of the evil fate which lies ahead, also inevitable. Taken as a whole, this scene describes a remarkable decline: the romantic aura of the love-at-first-sight meeting, when seen through the eyes of wiser and older men, becomes a blind venture on the part of two glamorous but foolhardy people.

The wedding feast itself is even more pathetic than the betrothal. For some obscure reason, the saga says that the wedding feast is meant to be a secret, but of course this is an impossibility,[41] and although no time lapse is mentioned, the wedding appears to take place that

gera.'" ... "'Veit ek, at svá mun vera, at ykkr er báðum girndarráð, ok hættið þit mestu til, hversu fer.'"

40. 33.87: "Hrútr segir Gunnari allt um skaplyndi Hallgerðar ófregit, ok þótti Gunnari þat fyrst œrit mart, er áfátt var, en þar kom um síðir, at saman fell kaupmáli þeira." Hrútr was similarly frank and cautionary when responding to Glúmr's proposal (13.42).

41. 33.87: "Skyldi þetta boð vera at Hlíðarenda ok skyldi fara fyrst leyniliga, en þó kom þar, er allir vissu." One wonders from whom the wedding is to be kept secret; in ch. 8 of ~~Kormáks saga it is explicit that~~ Kormákr was not to know of Steingerðr's marriage to Bersi.

42. 31.83: "Gunnarr lagði hug á Bergljótu, frændkona jarls, ok fannsk þat oft á, at jarl

same fall. When it does (in ch. 34), we are first introduced to the sons of Sigfúss and then given a description of the seating arrangement. Following that, an unusual event takes place: Þráinn Sigfússon, taken by the beauty of Hallgerðr's fourteen-year-old daughter Þorgerðr, is criticized by his wife for ogling. Þráinn, who did not care much for his wife anyway, leaps across the table and declares himself divorced—not exactly a favorable omen for a wedding feast. Stranger still, he immediately asks for the hand of Þorgerðr, and is approved unquestioningly by both Hrútr and Njáll, the same two men who had recently had doubts about the other wedding, the one supposedly being celebrated at this feast. Now there are two weddings instead of one, and the signs are that the suddenly introduced one will be more successful: approval is gained from all concerned, financial arrangements are worked out, and the ominous final sentences of the chapter tell us that while Hallgerðr was bountiful (*fengsǫm*) and assertive (*atkvæðamikil*) in running the household at Hlíðarendi, Þorgerðr was simply a good housewife (*góð húsfreyja*) at Grjótá. The author makes no further remarks about the Þráinn-Þorgerðr relationship, but it clearly endures, in spite of Þráinn's flaws, and produces the most idealized person in the saga. In every way the Gunnarr-Hallgerðr wedding has been upstaged by that of Þráinn and Þorgerðr.

Woman with a past

Romance marriages often come at the end of the story, after a long series of trials, and the bride is often virginal, though this is by no means always the case in a literature where men tend to fall in love with married women. Laudine, in *Yvain*, is a widow, whose husband is in fact slain by the man who then marries her (cp. the marriage of Kári and Hildigunnr at the end of *Njáls saga*). But no romance heroine—and no saga heroine either—has a past to match that of Hallgerðr, who has been twice married and twice been the cause of her husband's death. Her experience in the erotic realm is much more extensive than Gunnarr's, concerning whom we have only a one-sentence remark about his falling in love with a kinswoman of Hákon jarl: "Gunnar fell in love with Bergljot, the earl's kinswoman, and it was often apparent that the earl would have married her off to Gunnar if he had asked for this."[42] Two of the indications of love that Sävborg analyses appear here, the phrase *leggja hug á* (fall in love with) and the view of others that this is a viable relationship which the earl would have sanctioned. But *leggja hug á* does not necessarily point to a sexual relationship, and in this case the view from outside does not testify to the intensity of their love, but to the earl's attitude.[43] One suspects that the Gunnarr-Bergljót episode, like the Kjartan-Ingibjörg episode in *Laxdæla saga*, chs. 41–43, was innocent.[44] In any case, it is clear that Gunnarr's previous erotic experience was significantly less than Hallgerðr's.

Both of her first two marriages follow the same pattern, which is later repeated in her marriage to Gunnarr: a domestic quarrel leads to the husband slapping his wife, and this leads to the death of the husband.[45] In the first two marriages the slayer is Hallgerðr's foster-father Þjóstólfr, and yet, despite the repeated pattern, the contrast between the marriages could not be greater. Hallgerðr married Þorvaldr against her will and without her consent, never cared for him, and did nothing to stop Þjóstólfr from taking vengeance for the slap. She married Glúmr willingly and by her own consent, loved him, and told Þjóstólfr specifically *not* to take vengeance. When he did so anyway, she took vengeance for her husband and had Þjóstólfr killed.

The contrast between the first two marriages provides us with important information about Hallgerðr's character, by showing us what a different person she can be, depending on how she is treated. The key features of her personality are fixed early in the saga: "she was lavish and harsh-tempered" (*Hon var ǫrlynd ok skaphǫrð*, 9.29), but

---

mundi hana hafa gipta Gunnari, ef hann hefði nǫkkut þess leitat."

43. Contrast *Laxdœla saga*, ÍF 5, p. 112: "Þat var allra manna mál, at með þeim Kjartani ok Guðrúnu þœtti vera mest jafnræði þeira manna, er þá óxu upp." Cited in Sävborg, *Sagan om kärleken*, p. 346.

44. Of the two relationships with Norwegian royal women, Kjartan's has the greater claim to being sexual, to judge from Ingibjörg's parting gift and their heartfelt farewell. I am grateful to Daniel Sävborg for a helpful discussion of this and other matters.

45. Anna Cornelia Kersbergen has shown many parallels between Hallgerðr's first two marriages and those of Guðrún in *Laxdœla saga*, arguing convincingly that *Njáls saga* was influenced by the earlier saga. See *Litteraire motieven in de Njála* (Rotterdam: Nijgh & Van Ditmar, 1927), pp. 90–93. Both first husbands are named Þorvaldr, and both women are free spenders, etc., but their characters are quite different.

46. Dronke, "The Role of Sexual Themes," p. 17; Heather O'Donoghue, "Women in

the precise meaning of the two adjectives is open to conjecture. Ursula Dronke suggests "unyielding" for the second one, while Heather O'Donoghue has "hard-hearted."[46] Translators have been said to be too harsh on Hallgerðr,[47] and I suspect now that "generous and proud" might be closer to the true sense—certainly "lavish" is unfairly severe as a translation of *ǫrlynd*. She is a woman with a sense of her own dignity, and she does not tolerate offense. This, along with her open-handedness, is a fixed part of her being.

When Þorvaldr tells his father of his intention to marry Hallgerðr, Ósvífr warns him that "she's a strong-minded woman, and you're hard and unyielding."[48] Þorvaldr persists, and when he raises the matter with Hǫskuldr he is warned again: "I won't mislead you. My daughter is hard to get along with, but as for her looks and manners you can see for yourself."[49] Even before she has been tested in action, her unyielding character is clearly delineated.

When the first test comes, she considers it offensive to be betrothed to Þorvaldr, both because she had not been consulted and because Þorvaldr, though prosperous, is of an inferior family. And since she is a *skaphǫrð* woman, she does not hesitate to tell her father of her displeasure on both scores. Hǫskuldr says she has too much pride (*ofmetnaðr*), and she retorts that if she does, it comes from her family (10.31).

The marriage develops as can be expected from an open-handed woman of firm character and a miserly, hot-tempered man. When springtime comes and there is a shortage of flour and dried fish, Þorvaldr complains that in the past the same amount of supplies lasted into the summer. He seems to overlook the fact that there are at least two more mouths (Hallgerðr and Þjóstólfr) to feed than before, though

---

Njáls saga," in *Introductory Essays on Egils saga and Njáls saga*, ed. John Hines and Desmond Slay (London: Viking Society for Northern Research, 1992), p. 88.

47. Carol Clover, "Regardless of Sex: Men, Women, and Power in Early Northern Europe," *Speculum* 68 (1993), p. 371, fn. 30. Some other translations: Dasent has "lavish and hard-hearted," N. M. Petersen "rundhaandet, men hæftig af Sind," Andreas Heusler "verschwenderisch und trotzigen Sinnes," Bayerschmidt-Hollander "headstrong and of harsh disposition," Magnusson-Palsson "impetuous and willful." The word *skaphǫrð* is used of two other women in the saga, Bergþóra (20.57) and Hildigunnr (95.239).

48. 9.30: "hon er kona skapstór, en þú harðlyndr ok óvæginn."

49. 9.31: "en ek vil enga vél at ykkr draga, at dóttir mín er hǫrð í skapi. En um yfirlit hennar ok kurteisi meguð þit sjálfir sjá."

50. 11.33: "Hallgerðr var fengsǫm og stórlynd, enda kallaði hon til alls þess, er aðrir

the saga does make a point of her lavishness: "Hallgerðr was bountiful and high-spirited and demanded to have whatever the neighbours had and squandered everything."[50] This is unambiguous and shows how her natural generosity can go too far. When Þorvaldr complains, she responds as we would expect, proudly and insultingly: "It's none of my business if you and your father starved yourselves to get rich."[51] Though the insult was probably deserved, Þorvaldr becomes so angry that he strikes her in the face, drawing blood—and he quickly pays for that with his life.

Hallgerðr's second marriage is a contrast in every way, so much so that one writer, Magnús Sigurðsson, thought that this section, with its markedly changed atmosphere, had a different source from the other stories concerning Hallgerðr.[52] But instead of re-creating another version of the saga, as some writers on Hallgerðr tend to do, we will do better to deal with the saga solely in its present form. It is true that Hallgerðr seems to be another person in her second marriage, but surely the point is that she has more sides than one, that she is capable of change, depending on the way she is treated.

As before with Þorvaldr (and later with Gunnarr), the suitor is not to be put off by bad signs—in this case by his brother's pointing out the fact that she had her first husband killed, and by Hǫskuldr's admission that the first marriage ended in misfortune. Hǫskuldr seems to have learnt from that experience and this time insists that her approval be sought. She is sent for, and appears in her best finery and with lady-like behavior to match it. The entire betrothal scene (13.42–45)—her agreement, the concern for proper legal form, the valuing and determining of property—is carried out with a finesse and politeness unusual in the family sagas. It might be more at home in a romance. Moreover, the new couple live harmoniously: she declines to run the household, and we read that she "controlled herself very well that winter, and people were not displeased with her"[53] an understate-

---

áttu í nánd, ok hafði allt í sukki." Her underlying generosity is evident when she moves back to her father after Þorvaldr's death and first distributes gifts to all the household at Fell (12.36).

51. 11.33: "Ekki fer ek at því, þóttú hafir svelt þik til fjár ok faðir þinn."

52. Magnús Sigurðsson, "Hallgerður í Njálu," *Tímarit Þjóðræknisfélags Íslendinga* 13 (1931), pp. 75–88; see especially pp. 78–9.

53. 14.45: "Hallgerðr sat mjǫk á sér um vetrinn, ok líkaði við hana ekki illa."

54. Anne Heinrichs, "Hallgerðrs Saga in der Njála: Der doppelte Blick," in *Studien zum*

ment that says much. She remains "lavish and bountiful" (ǫrlynd og fengsǫm,14.46), as we have learned to expect, but in the context of a loving marriage her extravagance presents no problem.[54] She yields graciously when Þórarinn proposes to take over the farm at Varmalœkr if Glúmr should die before him (14.47), and, as cited above, both the author and Hallgerðr herself make explicit comments about the strength of the love between Hallgerðr and Glúmr. When an outside force (Þjóstólfr) introduces disharmony, the husband's slap is brought on not by an insult but by her well-intentioned plea for her foster-father.

The blow itself is less violent than the other two she receives from angry husbands: "Glum struck her with his hand"[55] The verb used here, *drepa*, is less strong than *ljósta*, used of the slaps administered by Þorvaldr and Gunnarr, and in addition it is not certain that the blow was directed at the face, as it was explicitly with the other two. Glúmr's gesture may have been little more than a brusque shove.[56] And immediately after the blow, whatever it was, the author states that "she loved him greatly and was not able to calm herself, and wept loudly."[57] Her reaction is that of a woman in love, not that of an abused wife grimly set on vengeance. There are no negative signs in her relationship with Glúmr, and surely the point of the episode is to show this important and positive side of her character.

By the time Gunnarr comes along, Hallgerðr has been run through an emotional mill, first by a wretched marriage, thankfully ended, and then by a harmonious marriage which ended tragically. If, like Guðrún Ósvífrsdóttir, she were to be asked at the end of her life which of her three husbands she loved the most, the answer would have been unambiguous: Glúmr. Her readiness to marry a third time must have more to do with a desire to stabilize her position in society—she is still

---

altgermanischen: Festschrift für Heinrich Beck, ed. Heiko Uecker (Berlin: De Gruyter, 1994), pp. 327–53, points out on pp. 347–8 that the term *fengsǫm* (lavish) is used of Hallgerðr in all three marriages, but coupled differently: with Þorvaldr she is *fengsǫm ok stórlynd* (11.33), with Glúmr she is *ǫrlynd ok fengsǫm* (14.46), and with Gunnarr she is *fengsǫm ok atkvæðamikil* (34.90). Of the three pairs of adjectives, only the one relating to her marriage with Glúmr (*ǫrlynd*) has an unambiguously positive connotation.

55. 16.48: "Glúmr drap til hennar hendi sinni."
56. This point has been anticipated by Heinrichs, "Hallgerðrs Saga in der Njála," p. 348: "Glúmrs Ohrfeige ist, verglichen mit Þorvalds, fast nur ein Streicheln."
57. 16.48: "Hon unni honum mikit ok mátti eigi stilla sik ok grét hástǫfum."
58. 33.86: "hon er blandin mjok, ok vil ek þik í engu svíkja." The term "mixed" may

a fairly young woman, perhaps in her late thirties or early forties and apparently living at Laugarnes with her fourteen-year-old daughter and a small household. She is not poor, but a good marriage would strengthen her social position, and she is sufficiently aware of her attractiveness to know that she can tempt the best catch in Iceland. And so she does, but without any illusions that this will be a love marriage. That part of her life is over.

A compatible couple?

We saw above that two highly-regarded outsiders viewed the sudden engagement of this infatuated couple with some alarm: Hrútr commented on her mixed nature[58] but deferred to the couple's determination, while Njáll's reaction was a simple condemnation: "Every kind of evil will come from her when she moves east."[59] This powerful statement resembles Hrútr's comment in ch. 1 on Hallgerðr's thief's eyes and the great harm which her beauty will cause: both are sweeping, absolute proclamations rather than predictions of specific acts. They anticipate an evil, destructive situation. Unfortunately, Hrútr's comments on her destructive potential and her mixed character and Njáll's anticipation of an evil time prove to be true.

Although there are hardly any direct comments on their incompatibility, the indirect indications are clear, for example in Gunnarr's remarks to Sigmundr cited above: "You're not at all like me: you are given to mockery and sarcasm, while I am not. You get along well with Hallgerðr, because you have more in common with her." Another hint comes in the descriptions of their two children, as unlike each other as their parents. "Gunnar and Hallgerd had two sons. One was called Hogni and the other Grani. Hogni was an able man, quiet, not easily persuaded and truthful."[60] The unexpected silence

best apply to what we have been examining: her variable behavior depending on how she is treated. A different reading is offered by Zoe Borovsky, who examines the use of *blanda* in Eddic poetry, especially in *Lokasenna*, and concludes that "Hallgerðr comes to stand for a 'giant' past that disrupts and 'mixes,' taints, or poisons the new, more peaceful order." See "'En hon er blandin mjök': Women and Insults in Old Norse Literature," in *Cold Counsel. Women in Old Norse Literature and Mythology*, ed. Sarah M. Anderson with Karen Swenson (New York and London: Routledge, 2002), pp. 1–14, citation from p. 11.

59. 33.87: "Af henni mun standa allt it illa, er hon kemr austr hingat."
60. 59.150: "Gunnarr ok Hallgerðr áttu tvá sonu; hét annarr Hǫgni, en annarr Grani. Hǫgni was maðr gerviligr ok hljóðlyndr, tortryggr ok sannorðr."
61. 75.182: "Þeir váru frumvaxta synir Gunnars, Hǫgni ok Grani. Þeir váru menn

about Grani gives rhetorical emphasis to the fact that he is quite a different person from Hǫgni. Later this sharp distinction is specifically related to the parents: "Gunnar's sons, Hogni and Grani, were now young men. They were quite different from each other: Grani had much of his mother's character, but Hogni was a fine person."[61] And shortly afterwards a third gloss is given when Gunnarr, sensing his forthcoming end, asks Njáll to look after Hǫgni: "I want to ask you one thing, though—that you keep an eye on my son Hogni. About Grani I have nothing to say, for he does many things that are not to my liking."[62] Grani is described in these statements primarily in terms of the absence of the good qualities that Hǫgni possesses. The third of these comments, by Gunnarr rather than the narrator, tells us that Grani's character has already led him to commit (unspecified) acts antithetical to Gunnarr's nature—just as Hallgerðr did in her feud with Bergþóra and in the theft at Kirkjubœr. Taken together, these three comments on Grani emphasize the incompatibility between Gunnarr and Hallgerðr.

In contrast to Hallgerðr's firm character stands Gunnarr's softer one.[63] In his opening description (ch. 19) he is first and foremost a superb athlete and warrior, with ideal blond looks; he is also said to be generous and even-tempered and a loyal and judicious friend. His exploits abroad show his fighting skills at their best, and it is significant that his ability to leap both backwards and forwards and to wield his sword so that there seem to be three in the air at once only figure in his battles abroad (see ch. 30), never in his fights in Iceland. His disappointing career at home, consisting of responses to provocations by lessser men (as Njáll predicted, 32.84) may be characterized in part by a statement he makes to Unnr when she asks him to recover her property from Hrútr: "I'm daring enough to try to get the money, but I don't know how to take up the case."[64] Long on courage, short on know-how. At Unnr's prodding, he turns to Njáll, as he will again and again. Although he is fortunate in having

óskapglíkir: hafði Grani mikit af skapi móður sinnar, en Hǫgni var vel at sér."
   62. 75.184: "En þess vil ek biðja, at þér sjáið á með Hǫgna, syni mínum. En ek tala ekki um Grana, því at hann gerir mart ekki at mínu skapi."
   63. In contrast to the adjective *skaphǫrð* used for Hallgerðr, Gunnarr is said by Bergþóra, when she whets her sons, to be *skapgóðr* (44.114).
   64. 21.58: "Þora mun ek ... at heimta fé þetta, en eigi veit ek, hversu upp skal taka málit."
   65. Hans E. Kinck, in *Mange slags kunst* (Kristiania [Oslo]: Aschehoug, 1921), p. 42,

the country's greatest lawyer as his friend, from whom it is natural to seek advice and help, the overall impression is that Gunnarr lacks the intelligence to match his prowess and modest good nature.[65] Comments by characters within the saga point to a general apprehension that if Gunnarr makes an intelligent move, the inspiration must have come from Njáll. [Hǫskuldr:] "Gunnar did not come up with this by himself. Njal must have planned it all." "Valgard said it must have been at Njal's advice and that this would not be the end of the advice Njal had given him."[66] Worse than his dependence on Njáll is that he repeatedly neglects to follow Njall's advice—most crucially the advice about not killing twice in the same family and not breaking a settlement made by good men (see chs. 55, 73, 74)—and this leads to his death.

The true nature of the relationship between Hallgerðr and Gunnarr is defined by Hallgerðr when Bergþóra has treated her insultingly at the feast at Bergþórshváll: "There's little use to me in being married to the most manly man in Iceland if you don't avenge this, Gunnar."[67] She measures Gunnarr by the extent to which he lives up to her notion of how "the most manly man in Iceland" should behave; sadly, he does not always fulfill her expectations, beginning with this very feast at Bergþórshváll. During the ensuing feud between the two wives she is disappointed at Gunnarr's willingness to make a peaceful settlement with Njall for every slaying, and we are even treated to a rare domestic scene on this score:

> Hallgerd was very cross with Gunnar for having settled the slaying peacefully. Gunnar said that he would never turn against Njal or his sons, and she went on raging. Gunnar paid no attention.[68]

stressed Gunnarr's lack of intelligence. See also Matthías Pétursson, "Þrír karlar og þrjár konur í Njálu," *Góðasteinn. Héraðsrit Rangæinga* 42 (2006), pp. 29–45, esp. pp. 29–31, who describes Gunnarr as a figure designed to meet the heroic expectations of young people.

66. 23.65: "... ok mun eigi Gunnarr einn hafa um ráðit. Njáll mun þessi ráð hafa til lagt"; 65.161-2: "Valgarðr kvað þetta vera mundu ráð Njáls ok þó eigi ǫll upp komin, þau sem hann mundi hafa ráðit honum."

67. 35.91: "Fyrir lítit kemr mér ... at eiga þann mann, er vaskastr er á Íslandi, ef þú hefnir eigi þessa, Gunnarr."

68. 37.99: "Hallgerðr leitaði á Gunnar mjǫk, er hann hafði sætzk á vígit. Gunnarr kvezk aldri bregðask skyldu Njáli né sonum hans; hon geisaði mjǫk. Gunnarr gaf eigi gaum at því."

69. 54.138-9: "Hvat ek veit ... hvárt ek mun því óvaskari maðr en aðrir menn sem mér

Slightly later, in a passage already cited, she tells Gunnarr that both he and Njall are "soft," and indeed Gunnarr later reveals that side of himself to Njall in a famous passage: "What I don't know is whether I am less manly than other men because killing troubles me more than it does them."[69] Such speech reveals a sensitivity unexpected in heroic figures, and an uncertainty about himself which is likely to be reflected in other areas, most especially in his role as a husband. Ignoring her ill-tempered raving, turning his back, was probably a typical way of dealing with her. Unfortunately, a man who has to ignore his wife and has no control over her is not fully a man.

Once the deadly feud between Hallgerðr and Bergþóra is over, as well as the episode of the theft at Kirkjubœr, Hallgerðr plays a very small role in Gunnarr's life, only surfacing again when he is under siege at Hlíðarendi. Her only appearances in the events narrated in chs. 52–75, involving antagonists from Kirkjubœr and Þríhyrning and Sandgil, are the following:

- When Gunnarr takes up his halberd and rides off to seek vengeance against Otkell and Skammkel, she says "Good. Now they can find out whether Gunnar will go away from them crying."[70]
- The birth of her grandson is announced, and she proposes the name Hǫskuldr. Her sons Grani and Hǫgni are first mentioned. (59.149)
- When Gunnarr and Kolskeggr return triumphantly to Hlíðarendi after fighting off the ambush at the Rangá, we read that "Hallgerd was pleased at the news and praised them for what they did."[71]
- When Gunnarr changes his mind about going abroad to carry out his sentence of outlawry, "Hallgerd was pleased that Gunnar returned home."[72]

In all of these scenes but the second, Hallgerðr carries out her self-appointed role as the wife of "the most manly man in Iceland," pleased at his seeking revenge, proud of his killings at the ambush (even though killing Þorgeirr Otkelsson means that Gunnarr has killed

þykkir meira fyrir en ǫðrum mǫnnum at vega menn."
    70. 54.136: "Þat er vel. . . . nú munu þeir reyna, hvárt hann gengr grátandi undan þeim."
    71. 72.177: "Hallgerðr fagnaði þessum tíðendum ok lofaði verkit."
    72. 75.183: "Hallgerðr varð fegin Gunnari, er hann kom heim."
    73. Heinrichs, "Hallgerðs Saga in der Njála," pp. 349–50, observes that in each of these

twice within the same family), and happy that he will face his enemies at home rather than go into safe exile (even though this too will mean his death).[73] These reactions define her relationship toward Gunnarr: she does not love or value him for himself, but for the unflinchingly heroic, vengeance-seeking side of his nature. Unfortunately for their marriage, there is more to Gunnarr than that.[74]

More sinned against than sinning

The antipathy of the author of *Njáls saga* for Hallgerðr is obvious: the mention of "thief's eyes" in the opening scene, and the repeated references to her hair are obviously designed to focus attention on the two scenes which most clothe her in shame: the theft at Kirkjubœr and the refusal to give Gunnarr hair for his bowstring. Many writers—more popular than scholarly—have nonetheless tried to redeem Hallgerðr, sometimes by creating an alternate version of the story to the one set down in the only existing version of the saga. Hans Kinck assumed that the author had to adapt his story for an audience that was not capable of a deep understanding of the female psyche. His unprovable assumption was that behind the fictional Hallgerðr stood a different and "real," historical Hallgerðr. The original reason for Hallgerðr's refusal of her hair, for example, stems from her dislike of Gunnarr's mother Rannveig, a constant and oppressive presence in the house at Hlíðarendi. Gunnarr requested that the two women work together at twisting Hallgerðr's hair into a bowstring, but unfortunately—according to Kinck—the idea of cooperating with Rannveig was repugnant to Hallgerðr.[75] To take one other example: Magnús Sigurðsson claimed that Gunnarr bought the slave Melkólfr in order to have him burn down the shed at Kirkjubœr and thus avenge himself on Otkell. He deliberately dishonors and slaps Hallgerðr in front of guests in order to distract attention from himself and place the blame on her.[76]

---

three scenes Hallgerðr's view is contrasted with that of Rannveig, whose maternal concern is for Gunnarr's life, not his heroic status. We might almost guess that Rannveig's role in the saga is to highlight, by contrast, Hallgerðr's one-dimensional view of her husband.
   74. In the terms of Ármann Jakobsson's article on "Masculinity and Politics in *Njáls saga*," Hallgerðr represents the false ideology of masculinity which overshadows the saga.
   75. Kinck, *Mange slags kunst*, pp. 47–9.
   76. Magnús Sigurðsson, "Hallgerður í Njálu," pp. 82–5.
   77. Adeline Rittershaus, *Altnordische Frauen* (Frauenfeld und Leipzig: Huber & Co.,

It is possible, however, without reading things into the text which are not there, to find extenuating circumstances which will at least allow us to understand Hallgerðr, if not to pardon her (the French expression *tout comprendre, c'est tout pardonner* suggests that the two are close together). For one thing, the real cause of Gunnarr's death lies in the conflicts provoked by Otkell and by the men of Sandgil and Þríhyrning, and the devious plotting of Mǫrðr. Hallgerðr was not involved in these events, and her contribution to his death is minimal.

We have seen that Hallgerðr's proud character reacts differently to different circumstances. For some reason which is not altogether clear, the reception she gets from the family at Bergþórshváll is vehement. Njáll's statement to Gunnarr that "Every kind of evil will come from her when she moves east," though based on his gift of foresight, seems a personal and harsh outburst—in contrast, say, to his calm prediction that the cause of his death will be something that people would least expect (55.139). Equally vehement is Bergþóra's hostile and insulting treatment of the new wife of their good friend Gunnarr, when he brings his bride to Bergþórshváll for what will be the last of the winter feasts exchanged by the households. By any fair standard, Hallgerðr's record should be "clean" by now: her first husband's death was amply compensated, and she herself saw to it that the slayer of Glúmr—to whom she was a good wife—was avenged.

Most readers agree that Bergþóra is deliberately offensive when she tells Hallgerðr to give up her seat for the late arrival Þorhalla, but there are different opinions as to why Bergþóra does this. Adeline Rittershaus sees it as the natural antipathy of a simple, solid, hard-working woman for an elegant and indolent younger woman.[77] Ursula Dronke sees a deeper resentment, one based on a conception of a wife's role: "Hallgerðr was a traitor to her first husband, she had him killed. She betrayed the principle that a wife should live by: she did not build her life upon the marital bond."[78]

In more extended form and indeed as a central thesis in her book, Rósa Blöndal has argued that Bergþóra's harsh rudeness towards

1917), p. 159.
78. Dronke, "The Role of Sexual Themes," pp. 22–3.
79. Rósa Blöndal, *Leyndar Ástir í Njálu* (Reykjavík: Vasaútgáfan, 1987). See also her later

Hallgerðr comes from the great disappointment at Bergþórshváll when Gunnarr took a bride from another district rather than from the farm of his best friend.[79] The saga reports in ch. 20 that Njáll had three daughters, without naming them. Later we learn that one of them, Þorgerðr, married Ketill Sigfússon of Mǫrk (34.88), and still later that a second, Helga, married Kári Sǫlmundarson (90.225). According to Rósa, it was the hope at Bergþórshváll that the third, unnamed daughter would marry Gunnarr of Hlíðarendi. When things turned out otherwise, this daughter stayed at home with her grief and disappointment rather than go to the wedding of Gunnarr and Hallgerðr; this explains why only her sisters Þorgerðr and Helga are mentioned as being present (34.88).

There are many useful insights in Rósa's book, but such speculation has little support from the text, where we would in fact expect considerable clarity if the matter were as important as Rósa claims. As things stand, the hostility of the couple at Berþórshváll toward Hallgerðr is one of the many unexplained details in the saga.[80]

Hallgerðr's sharp response to Bergþóra's insult comes as no surprise. She gives a flat "no" to the request to move aside, leading Bergþóra to assert her authority in blunt language more appropriate to a drill sergeant than to a hostess at a feast with old friends: "I decide things here."[81] At this point, a sensitive and loving husband would have noticed the offensiveness of Bergþóra's demand;[82] Gunnarr, on the other hand, remains silent (as does Njáll), and the two women are left to fight it out on their own. We remember that the adjective *skaphǫrð* was used for Bergþóra (20.57) as well as for Hallgerðr; what we are now witnessing is a quarrel between two *skaphardar* women, each bringing out the worst in each other. What follows—Hallgerðr's insults about Njáll's beardlessness and Bergþóra's fingernails, and Bergþóra's

---

article in *Lesbók Morgunblaðsins*, 27. janúar 1996: "Hvað hétu dætur Njáls og Bergþóru?"

80. Some other unanswered questions: Why does Njáll invent the elaborate and unnecessary scheme for summoning Hrútr (ch. 22)? Why doesn't Gunnarr go to Njáll for food and hay, rather than to Otkel? Why does he buy the slave Melkólfr from Otkel (ch. 47)? Why doesn't Skarphéðinn go abroad with his brothers (ch. 75)? Why does Njáll add a silk robe and a pair of boots to the pile of money collected to compensate for the death of Hǫskuldr Þráinsson? Why does he not acknowledge having done so (ch. 123)?

81. 35.91: "Ek skal hér ráða."

82. We recall that in ch. 46 of *Laxdœla saga*, a gentler saga in many ways, Kjartan insists ~~that his wife Hrefna occupy the~~ best seat.

83. 35.91: "en eigi var skegglauss Þorvaldr, bóndi þinn, ok rétt þú honum þó bana."

accusation that Hallgerðr arranged the death of Þorvaldr[83]—is the verbal prelude to the extended bloody feud that follows, in which these women initiate a series of six reciprocal slayings between the two households.

Bergþóra initiated the hostility with her demand that Hallgerðr give up her seat. It is Hallgerðr, however, who initiates the series of killings, by arranging to have Kolr kill Svartr: she believes in vengeance, and in her mind Bergþóra's accusation that she arranged the death of Þorvaldr calls for vengeance. Hallgerðr's immediate response to that accusation was to appeal to Gunnarr, in the lines cited above (see n. 67). Taken literally, the word *hefna* ("avenge") means that she wants Gunnarr to kill her friends, but even the vengeance-minded Hallgerðr cannot mean anything as ludicrous as that. More likely, her utterance reflects her confused and angry state—it is a desperate cry to her husband to support her, in one way or another. But instead of taking her side, or at least trying to mediate between both sides, he chooses unequivocally the side of Bergþóra and Njáll, and even adds to the insults already delivered: "it would be best for you to pick quarrels with your servants, and not in the dwellings of others,"[84] implying that she is a quarrelsome housewife at Hlíðarendi. His foolish and intemperate remarks are accompanied by a dramatic display of agility, leaping across the table. This of course recalls Þráinn's similar acrobatics at the wedding in the preceding chapter, where the leap across the table was followed by a divorce. It is not going too far to say that Gunnarr's is also a divorce-leap, in effect: he has now taken a side firmly against his wife, and so it will remain. From this point on they are at odds, and their marriage is effectively over. Her only remaining pleasure will be the moments when he lives up to her ideal of heroism.

Gunnarr mistreats her again over the matter of the theft of food at Kirkjubœr—this too is a public humiliation, in the presence of guests who have stopped at Hlíðarendi for a meal on their way home from the Althing (ch. 48). This slap is worse than those delivered by her first two husbands, both because it is public rather than private and because it is accompanied by an accusation of thievery. There is no question that

---

84. 35.91: "... ok er þat makligast, at þú sennir við heimamenn þína, en eigi í annarra manna híbýlum."

85. See Theodore M. Andersson, "The Thief in *Beowulf*," *Speculum* 59 (1984), pp.

theft was regarded as a mean and low offense, symptomatic of a flawed character,[85] but the motivation in this case (a wife fighting for her husband's honor) is a noble one. The public humiliation is particularly hard to bear because her act of vengeance against Otkell was intended to make up for the public humiliation that Gunnarr endured at his hands. It must have been particularly galling to this honor-conscious wife that Gunnarr—after his fair offer to buy food and hay was rudely refused, and after determining not to appropriate what he needed (apparently an acceptable procedure in emergencies)—agreed without hesitation to buy an unknown slave from the man who had just humiliated him. Even if Gunnarr could not, she herself could hear, at least in her mind, the guffawing and snickering from Otkell's followers, particularly Skammkell, at this ill-advised move.[86]

Hallgerðr's keen sense of honor, both hers and her husband's, and a willingness to carry out its obligations, led her to a strong response to this third marital slap: "Hallgerðr said she would remember this slap and pay it back if she could."[87] Her opportunity comes when Gunnarr's bowstring breaks; her ensuing behavior has earned her enduring infamy, as both Gunnarr and Rannveig predict (77.189). We must not forget, however, that her action is the fulfillment of the vengeance she swore when Gunnarr slapped her in the presence of their guests. She says so explicitly when Gunnarr asks for two locks of her hair and tells her that his life hangs in the balance: "Then I'll recall the slap you gave me, and I don't care whether you hold out for a long or a short time."[88]

493–508.
86. Gunnarr's purchase of Melkólfr has long been a puzzle—see the "solution" by Magnús Sigurðsson above—but perhaps it was added simply to show how far Gunnarr was ready to be humiliated, and thereby to justify further his wife's honor-motivated retaliation against Kirkjubœr.
87. 48.124: "Hon kvazk þann hest muna skyldu ok launa, ef hon mætti."
88. 77.189: "Þá skal ek nú ... muna þér kinnhestinn, ok hirði ek aldri, hvárt þú verr þik lengr eða skemr." This episode has had more than its share of interpretations; a recent ingenious one is that of Kristján Jóhann Jónsson, *Lykillinn að Njálu* (Reykjavík: Vaka-Helgafell, 1998), pp. 132–3, who places the exchange between husband and wife in the category of the defiant and ironic statements made by heroes who are about to die. Reconciled at last, Gunnarr and Hallgerðr speak to each other with dark humor and nonchalance, both of them pretending that her hair will save him from his fated end, and both of them knowing in fact that it cannot. This is an unlikely inference, though it has been pointed out that Gunnarr's request is unrealistic—hair would not have been suitable in any case. See, for example, Sigurður Guðmundsson, "Gunnar á Hlíðarenda," *Skírnir* 92 (1918), pp. 63–88, 221–51, esp. pp. 85–6.
89. Concerning the settlement which Njáll arranges, the saga reports that "Gunnar

Gunnarr had no chance of surviving the assault, but as a result of Hallgerðr's refusal, his end will come sooner than otherwise. The main difference between "sooner" and "later" is that the slap is now avenged. The troubled life together of Gunnarr and Hallgerðr is over, but at least it ended on a note of honor. She has paid him, as she vowed, for his slap, and he died as a true hero in her view, taking vengeance on those who arranged a sentence of outlawry, a sentence which both husband and wife must have found unfair.[89]

Conclusion

Daniel Sävborg has given us a thorough analysis of how the love between Kjartan and Guðrún (in *Laxdœla saga*) is depicted in the characteristic style of the Sagas of Icelanders.[90] He explicates carefully all the relevant scenes and formulas and demonstrates convincingly that their love is presented as mutual and strong, and that it plays a fundamental role in the saga's plot, initiating its central feud.[91] This view, as stated at the outset of this paper, has not been dominant among saga scholars, who have preferred to see honor and vengeance as the chief motivating forces.

I have attempted to analyse the presentation of another famous, but quite different saga couple. Both relationships have tragic consequences: Guðrún's frustration and bitterness at Kjartan's harassment and her jealousy of Hrefna bring her to arrange his death, which initiates a feud that leads to her husband Bolli's death and that of others.

---

gave no indication that he thought this settlement unfair" ("Gunnarr lét ekki á sik finna, at honum þœtti eigi góð sættin," 74.180). The wording raises and leaves open the possibility that Gunnarr, in his own mind, found the settlement unfair, and this may be the reason he failed to go abroad. After all, he was ambushed by the two Þorgeirs and killed them in self-defense. Njáll could have presented this in Gunnarr's defense, but instead chose to submit the case to arbitration, and the arbitrators decided on exile. One can readily imagine that Hallgerðr, and very likely Gunnarr too, were not happy with this outcome.

90. Sävborg, *Sagan om kärleken*, pp. 340–62.

91. Sävborg, *Sagan om kärleken*, pp. 260–1: "Det är sammanfattningsvis tydligt att kärlek (och därmed relaterade känslor) har fundamental betydelse för konfliktens uppkomst, för kränkningar och motkränkningar, mord och hämnd. Men samtidigt måste man ge Meulengracht Sørensen rätt när han påpekar att det finns fler motiv till konflikten än de erotiska. Stölden av svärdet har således ingen rimlig koppling till Guðrúns och Kjartans kärlek—händelsen tycks vara en konsekvens av Ósvifrsönernas avundsjuka på Kjartans make—til skillnad från stölden av motren... Sagan laborerar med dubbla motiv till konflikten, både erotiska och ickeerotiska."

92. For an analysis of this feud see William I. Miller, "Justifying Skarpheðinn," *Scandi-*

Hallgerðr's frustration and bitterness bring her to initiate the hostility between Þráinn and the sons of Njáll, when she persuades Þráinn to be present at the slaying of their foster-father (41.107); this leads to the central feud of the saga, to the Burning, and beyond.[92] She also contributes to the death of her husband Gunnarr. Both relationships have a powerful effect on the events of their sagas.

As for the internal workings of these relationships, however, the two sagas are totally different. Kjartan and Guðrún were in love and by all rights should have spent their life together; had it not been for Bolli's selfish intervention they would have married and, as the cliché goes, lived happily ever after. As things were, they had to live with the bitterness of seeing their true love married to another. Gunnarr and Hallgerðr, on the other hand, did marry, but they did so rashly, taking no time to develop a viable relationship. They proved to be a seriously incompatible couple. Hallgerðr's bitterness, more evident than Gunnarr's, came from her disappointment in the man she married, because he failed to live up to the social role that she—widowed twice and no longer capable of love—wanted her husband to play. In this sense, *Njáls saga* is an answer to *Laxdœla saga*: it shows that a failed affair, a relationship devoid of love, can be as effective and potent as true love in shaping a saga.

Bibliography

Andersson, Theodore M. "The Thief in *Beowulf*." *Speculum* 59 (1984): 493–508.

Ármann Jakobsson. "Masculinity and Politics in *Njáls saga*." *Viator* 38 (2007): 191–215.

Blöndal, Rósa. *Leyndar Ástir í Njálu*. Reykjavík: Vasaútgáfan, 1987.

———. "Hvað hétu dætur Njáls og Bergþóru?" *Lesbók Morgunblaðsins*, 27. janúar 1996.

Borovsky, Zoe. "'En hon er blandin mjök': Women and Insults in Old Norse Literature." In *Cold Counsel: Women in Old Norse Literature and Mythology*. Ed. Sarah M. Anderson with Karen Swenson. New York and London: Routledge, 2002. Pp. 1–14.

Brennu-Njáls saga. Ed. Einar Ólafur Sveinsson, Íslenzk fornrit 12. Reykjavík: Hið íslenzka fornritafélag, 1954.

Clover, Carol J. "Hildigunnr's lament." In *Structure and Meaning in Old Norse Literature*. Ed. John Lindow et al. Odense: Odense University Press, 1986. Pp. 141–83.

navian Studies 55 (1983), pp. 316-44.

———. "Regardless of Sex: Men, Women, and Power in Early Northern Europe." *Speculum* 68 (1993): 365–88.
Cook, Robert. "Mörður Valgarðsson." In *Sagnaheimur. Studies in Honour of Hermann Pálsson*. Ed. Ásdís Egilsdóttir and Rudolf Simek. Vienna: Fassbaender, 2001. Pp. 63–77.
Chrétien de Troyes. *Yvain (Le chevalier au lion)*. Ed. T. B. W. Reid. Manchester: Manchester University Press, 1961.
Dronke, Ursula. "The Role of Sexual Themes in *Njáls saga*," Dorothea Coke Memorial Lecture, University College London, 27 May 1980. London, 1980.
Einar Ólafur Sveinsson. *Njáls Saga. A Literary Masterpiece*. Trans. Paul Schach. Lincoln: University of Nebraska Press, 1971.
Heinrichs, Anne. "Hallgerðrs Saga in der Njála: Der doppelte Blick." In *Studien zum altgermanischen: Festschrift für Heinrich Beck*. Ed. Heiko Uecker. Berlin: De Gruyter, 1994. Pp. 327–53.
Kersbergen, Anna Cornelia. *Litteraire motieven in de Njála*. Rotterdam: Nijgh & Van Ditmar, 1927.
Kinck, Hans E. *Mange slags kunst*. Kristiania [Oslo]: Aschehoug, 1921.
Kress, Helga Kress. "'Ekki hǫfu vér kvennaskap'. Nokkrar laustengdar athuganir im karlmennsku og kvenhatur í *Njálu*." In *Sjötíu ritgerðir helgaðar Jakobi Benediktssyni 20. júlí 1977*. Ed. Einar G. Pétursson and Jónas Kristjánsson. 2 vols. Reykjavík: Stofnun Árna Magnússonar, 1977. Vol. 1, pp. 293–313.
Kristján Jóhann Jónsson. *Lykillinn að Njálu*. Reykjavík: Vaka-Helgafell 1998.
Magnús Sigurðsson."Hallgerður í Njálu." *Tímarit Þjóðræknisfélags Íslendinga* 13 (1931): 75–88.
Matthías Pétursson. "Þrír karlar og þrjár konur í Njálu." *Goðasteinn. Héraðsrit Rangæinga* 42 (2006): 29–45.
Miller, William I. "Justifying Skarpheðinn." *Scandinavian Studies* 55 (1983): 316–44.
———. "Emotions and the sagas." In *From Sagas to Society: Comparative Approaches to Early Iceland*. Ed. Gísli Pálsson. Enfield Lock: Hisarlik Press, 1992. Pp. 89–109
Njal's saga. Trans. Robert Cook. London: Penguin, 2001.
O'Donoghue, Heather. "Women in *Njáls saga*." In *Introductory Essays on Egils saga and Njáls saga*. Ed. John Hines and Desmond Slay. London: Viking Society for Northern Research, 1992. Pp. 83–92
Rittershaus, Adeline. *Altnordische Frauen*. Frauenfeld and Leipzig: Huber & Co., 1917.
Sigurður Guðmundsson. "Gunnar á Hlíðarenda." *Skírnir* 92 (1918): 221–52.
Steblin-Kamenskij, M.I. *The Saga Mind*. Trans. Kenneth H. Ober. Odense: Odense University Press, 1973.
Sävborg, Daniel. *Sagan om kärleken. Erotik, känslor och berättarkonst i norrön litteratur*. Acta Universitatis Upsaliensis. Historia Litterarum 27. Uppsala: Uppsala Universitet, 2007.
Vésteinn Ólason. "Emosjon og aksjon i *Njáls saga*." *Nordica Bergensia* 3 (1994): 157–72.
Zanchi, Anna. *Dress in the Íslendingasögur and Íslendingaaþættir*. Ph.D. dissertation. University College London, 2007.

The Native Romance of Gunnlaugr and Helga the Fair

THEODORE M. ANDERSSON

It is commonly held that *Gunnlaugs saga ormstungu* is a late text that partakes of the romantic tonalities which accrued in Iceland from foreign models during the thirteenth century. This view goes back to a study by Björn M. Ólsen, who not only emphasized the romantic components but provided a detailed comparison of the text to other sagas, notably *Hallfreðar saga*, *Bjarnar saga Hítdœlakappa*, and *Egils saga Skallagrímssonar*. He concluded that the author of *Gunnlaugs saga* made use of these and other sagas in his composition, which must therefore be a relatively late phenomenon in the literary chronology. As far as I can determine, Björn M. Ólsen's analysis has gone largely unchallenged and has now enjoyed widespread acquiescence for nearly a century. In this paper I undertake a belated critique of his view, arguing that *Gunnlaugs saga* is more likely to be very early, specifically that it did not make use of *Hallfreðar saga*, *Bjarnar saga*, and *Egils saga*, but rather served as a source for these texts. Furthermore, the romantic inflections are not borrowed from foreign narratives but replicate native romance as it was known in Iceland in the early thirteenth century.

Gunnlaugs saga and *Hallfreðar saga*

We may begin with *Hallfreðar saga* because it has the most obvious link to *Gunnlaugs saga*. In chapter 10, about two thirds of the way through the text, *Gunnlaugs saga* relates Gunnlaugr's visits to several northern courts. He travels from the court of King Olaf of Sweden to England, where he is well received by King Ethelred II but is eager to return to Iceland to honor his betrothal to Helga the Fair. King Ethelred detains him for a time because of an impending invasion by the Danes. Once released, he goes to the court of Eiríkr jarl Hákonarson in Norway hoping to find passage to Iceland. At first it appears that all the ships bound for Iceland have departed, but then it emerges that the ship belonging to the skald Hallfreðr "vandræðaskáld" Óttarsson is not yet on the high seas. Jarl Eiríkr therefore arranges for Gunnlaugr to reach his ship, and Hallfreðr gives him a warm welcome.

During the passage Hallfreðr reveals that Gunnlaugr's rival Hrafn has asked for the hand of Helga the Fair. When Gunnlaugr belittles Hrafn in a dismissive stanza, Hallfreðr wishes him better luck with Hrafn than he himself has had. He then tells the story of how he withheld payment from one of Hrafn's workers and how Hrafn cut his ship's cable and stranded his ship, thus extracting self-judgment from him. The same story is told in substantially abbreviated form in the last chapter of *Hallfreðar saga*. In adjacent columns the texts run as follows:

Gunnlaugs saga (ÍF 3.84–85)
Eiríkr jarl lét þá flytja Gunnlaug út til Hallfreðar, ok tók hann við honum með fagnaði, ok gaf þegar byr undan landi, ok váru vel kátir. Þat var síð sumars. Hallfreðr mælti til Gunnlaugs: "Hefir þú frétt bónorðit Hrafns Ǫnundarsonar við Helgu ina fǫgru?" Gunnlaugr kvezk frétt hafa ok þó ógǫrla. Hallfreðr segir honum slíkt sem hann vissi af ok þat með at margir menn mæltu þat, at Hrafn væri eigi órǫskvari en Gunnlaugr Gunnlaugr kvað þá vísu:

Rœkik lítt, þótt leiki,
létt veðr es nú, þéttan

Hallfreðar saga (ÍF 8.196)
Ok at sumri fór Hallfreðr út til Íslands ok kom skipi sínu í Leiruvág fyrir sunnan land [Fl. neðan heiði]. Þá bjó Ǫnundr at Mosfelli. Hallfreðr átti at [gjalda] hálfa mǫrk silfrs húskarli Ǫnundar ok svaraði heldr harðliga. Kom húskarlinn heim ok sagði sín vandræði. Hrafn kvað slíks ván, at hann myndi lægra hlut bera í þeira skiptum. Ok um morgunin eptir reið Hrafn til skips ok ætlaði at hǫggva strengina ok stǫðva brottferð þeira Hallfreðar. Síðan áttu menn hlut í at sætta þá, ok var goldit hálfu meira en húskarl átti, ok skilðu at því.
Annat sumar eptir áttu

The Native Romance of Gunnlaugr and Helga the Fair

austanvindr at ǫndri
andness viku þessa;
meir séumk hitt, en hæru
hoddstríðandi bíðit,
orð, at eigi verðak
jafnrǫskr talðir Hrafni.

þeir Hallfreðr ok Gunnlaugr
ormstunga ferð saman ok kómu
á Melrakkasléttu; þá hafði
Hrafn fengit Helgu. Hallfreðr
sagði Gunnlaugi, hversu honum
hafði vegnat við Hrafn.

Hallfreðr mælti þá: "Þess þyrfti, félagi, at þér veitti betr [en] mér málin við Hrafn. Ek kom skipi mínu í Leiruvág fyrir neðan Heiði fyrir fám vetrum, ok átta ek at gjalda hálfa mǫrk silfrs húskarli Hrafns, ok helt ek því fyrir honum; en Hrafn reið til vár með sex tigu manna ok hjó strengina, ok rak skipit upp á leirur, ok búit við skipbroti. Varð ek at selja Hrafni sjálfdœmi, ok galt ek mǫrk, ok eru slíkar mínar at segja frá honum."

(Jarl Eiríkr had Gunnlaugr conveyed out to Hallfreðr's ship, and he welcomed him gladly. There was a prompt offshore breeze, and they were in good spirits. It was late in the summer. Hallfreðr addressed Gunnlaugr: "Have you learned of Hrafn Ǫnundarson's wooing of Helga the Fair?" Gunnlaugr said he had heard something but not in detail. Hallfreðr told him what he knew about it and added that lots of people were saying that Hrafn was no less a man than Gunnlaugr. Gunnlaugr recited a stanza: "I care little whether the east wind

(In the summer Hallfreðr sailed out to Iceland and brought his ship into Leiruvágr in the south [Fl. below the heath]. At that time Ǫnundr lived at Mosfell. Hallfreðr owed one of Ǫnundr's men half a mark of silver and gave him a rather hard answer. The man returned home and told of his problem. Hrafn said that he could expect to come out second best in their dealings. The next morning Hrafn rode to the ship thinking that he would cut the cable and prevent the departure of Hallfreðr and his men. Then others intervened to make peace between

blows stiffly at the snowshoe of the promontory [ship] during this week—there is clear weather now; I fear the report more that I am not considered as Hrafn's equal in courage—a treasure breaker [outstanding man] does not await (expect) old age." Then Hallfreðr said: "Companion, you would need to come out better against Hrafn that I did. I sailed my ship into Leiruvágr [Mud Bay] south of the Heath a few years ago and I owed a half mark in silver to one of Hrafn's men. I withheld it from him. But Hrafn rode at us with sixty (or seventy-two) men and severed the cable so that the ship pitched up on the mud and it almost came to a shipwreck. I had to give Hrafn self-judgment and pay a mark, and that is my experience with him.")

them and twice as much as was owed to the man was paid up. With that they parted. The next summer Hallfreðr and Gunnlaugr Serpent Tongue traveled together to Melrakkaslétta [Fox Field]. At that time Hrafn had married Helga. Hallfreðr told Gunnlaugr how he had fared with Hrafn.)

That the two passages are interdependent is suggested not only by motival and verbal similarities but by other factors as well. Both passages are bipartite; they tell on the one hand of the poets' shared voyage to Iceland and on the other hand of Hallfreðr's run-in with Hrafn on a previous occasion. It seems unlikely that this particular collocation would recur twice independently and more likely that one text is reproducing the other. That the joint voyage and the encounter between Hallfreðr and Hrafn are connected is explained by the fact that Hallfreðr reports the incident to Gunnlaugr in a conversation during the voyage. *Gunnlaugs saga* provides a fuller account, while the report in *Hallfreðar saga* appears more in the light of a summary.[1]

---

1. See W. Van Eeden, *De overlevering van de Hallfreðar saga*, Verhandelingen der Koninklijke Akademie van Wetenschappen te Amsterdam, afdeeling letterkunde (Amsterdam: Johannes Müller, 1919), nieuwe reeks, vol. 19, no. 5: "[U]it den excerptachtigen stijl waait ons een pergamentlucht tegemoet ..." (p. 95).

That the incident is more at home in *Gunnlaugs saga* is also suggested by the appearance of Hrafn, a co-protagonist in *Gunnlaugs saga* but only a momentary extra in *Hallfreðar saga*. The conversation in *Gunnlaugs saga* is about Hrafn's personal distinction. That has no place in *Hallfreðar saga* and is accordingly suppressed. Indeed, the incident is tacked on at the last moment in *Hallfreðar saga* and seems to be an oddment that the author picked up as an afterthought.

That the author of *Hallfreðar saga* is referring not just to the incident but knows *Gunnlaugs saga* as a whole, is indicated by the information to which he appears to have access but does not himself convey. *Gunnlaugs saga* explains Gunnlaugr's delay in detail and relates specifically that Gunnlaugr in effect caught the last ship to Iceland. The author of *Hallfreðar saga* accounts for none of this detail, but it clearly underlies his story because he adds at the last moment that "Hrafn had already married Helga." That presupposes the chronology of *Gunnlaugs saga*.

We can observe further that there is a particular drift in *Hallfreðar saga*'s revision of the incident as it is told in *Gunnlaugs saga*. The author of *Hallfreðar saga* is clearly intent on improving the image of his protagonist.[2] In *Gunnlaugs saga* Hallfreðr explicitly withholds payment from his creditor ("helt ek því fyrir honum"), but the author of *Hallfreðar saga* shrinks from making him a debt defaulter and refers more generally to hard words ("Hallfreðr átti at [gjalda] hálfa mǫrk silfrs húskarli Ǫnundar ok svaraði heldr harðliga"). In *Gunnlaugs saga* Hrafn cuts Hallfreðr's ship's cable and strands his ship, but in *Hallfreðar saga* he merely intends to do so ("ætlaði at hǫggva strengina"). That modification reduces the seriousness of the damage done to his protagonist. Finally, in *Gunnlaugs saga* Hallfreðr is forced to surrender self-judgment ("Varð ek þá at selja Hrafni sjálfdœmi"), but in *Hallfreðar saga* he saves face because others intervene to settle the matter ("Síðan áttu menn hlut í at sætta þá."). It makes sense to suppose that the author of *Hallfreðar saga* intervenes on his hero's behalf, but much less sense to believe that the author of *Gunnlaugs saga* revised *Hallfreðar saga* in such a way as to derogate a figure who is quite peripheral in his story.

---

2. See Björn Magnússon Ólsen, *Om Gunnlaugs saga ormstungu. En kritisk undersøgelse*, Det Kongelige Danske Videnskabernes Selskabs Skrifter, historisk og filosofisk afdeling (Copenhagen: Høst, 1911), 7. række, vol. II, no. 1, p. 39. Hereafter abbreviated as B. M. Ólsen.

All critics seem to agree that this episode is more original as it stands in *Gunnlaugs saga* and is secondary in *Hallfreðar saga*.[3] At the same time, this recognition has posed a considerable problem for critics like Björn M. Ólsen, who considered *Gunnlaugs saga* to be a much later composition than *Hallfreðar saga*. The only escape from this impasse was to view the shared episode as a later interpolation in *Hallfreðar saga*, and B. M. Ólsen tries to reinforce this supposition by interpreting two other verbal correspondences as loans from an original *Hallfreðar saga* into *Gunnlaugs saga*.[4] In a certain sense, we may accept the idea of an interpolation; the episode involving Hallfreðr and Hrafn is tacked onto the end of *Hallfreðar saga* in a rather mechanical way and looks superimposed. On the other hand, the interpolation seems to be more the work of the saga author, with an overview of *Gunnlaugs saga* and a definite partisanship on behalf of his protagonist Hallfreðr, rather than the work of a later interpolator making a small mechanical addition.

The invocation of an interpolator is often a desperate remedy and prompts skepticism. The alternative in this case is that *Gunnlaugs saga* is older than *Hallfreðar saga* and that the author of the latter drew on the former. That possibility runs counter to the thesis advanced by B. M. Ólsen, who argued for a late date for *Gunnlaugs saga*, at least in the middle of the thirteenth century and, allowing for the possibility of a loan from *Njáls saga*, perhaps as late as 1300.[5] B. M. Ólsen's argument seems to have convinced almost all later critics,[6] and there is no doubt that his monograph is an extraordinarily thorough investigation, remarkable for an unmatched familiarity with all the sources. It should

---

3. See B. M. Ólsen, p. 39; Van Eeden, *De overlevering*, p. 95; Sigurður Nordal in *Íslenzk fornrit* 3 (Reykjavík: Hið íslenzka fornritafélag, 1938), p. L. Hereafter *Íslenzk fornrit* will be abbreviated ÍF with volume and page numbers.

4. See B. M. Ólsen, pp. 40–41. For the dating of *Hallfreðar saga*, see Russell Poole, "The Relation between Verses and Prose in *Hallfreðar saga* and *Gunnlaugs saga*" in *Skaldsagas: Text, Vocation, and Desire in the Icelandic Sagas of Poets* (Berlin and New York: de Gruyter, 2001), p. 137. Hereafter: *Skaldsagas*.

5. See B. M. Ólsen, pp. 53–54.

6. Finnur Jónsson, in his edition of *Gunnlaugs saga ormstungu*, Samfund til Udgivelse af Gammel Nordisk Litteratur 42 (Copenhagen: S. L. Møller, 1916), p. XXVI, maintained a dating around 1200. Margaret Clunies Ross, "The Skald Sagas as a Genre: Definitions and Typical Features" in *Skaldsagas*, ed. Russell Poole, p. 40, leaves latitude for both an early and a late date. More typical is Jónas Kristjánsson's assumption of a late date in *Eddas and Sagas: Iceland's Medieval Literature* (Reykjavík: Hið íslenska bókmenntafélag, 1988), p. 284.

nonetheless be reviewed in some detail on the chance that *Gunnlaugs saga* might after all be dated earlier.

Gunnlaugs saga and *Egils saga*

According to B. M. Ólsen's analysis, easily the most important source for *Gunnlaugs saga* is the neighboring *Egils saga*; indeed, he considers *Gunnlaugs saga* to be a sort of continuation of *Egils saga* (p. 30). This hypothesis rests to a large extent on the supposition that *Gunnlaugs saga* borrows genealogical material from *Egils saga* (pp. 14–19). By now the fallacy in this thinking has become rather clearer than it was a century ago. B. M. Ólsen and many of his successors in Iceland approached the sagas with the idea that genealogies were derived from written rather than oral sources, notably from *Landnámabók*. B. M. Ólsen's long series of papers on *Landnámabók* and various sagas is predicated on this supposition, and the monograph on *Gunnlaugs saga* carries the argument one step further.[7]

Where *Egils saga* fails as a genealogical source, direct loans from *Landnámabók* do service instead (pp. 13–19). Only where both *Egils saga* and *Landnámabók* fail does B. M. Ólsen allow for the possibility of oral transmission (as in the case of Hrafn's two brothers) or authorial invention (as in the case of two cousins). Helga's second husband, Þorkell Hallkelsson, is also not to be found in written sources and is therefore given the benefit of oral transmission (p. 19). The difficulty in this system is that when oral transmission can be invoked to explain the presence of minor characters, it seems strained to invoke only written sources for the major characters. B. M. Ólsen is inclined to argue that one loan from *Landnámabók* justifies the assumption of other loans by analogy (e.g., p. 15), but we could just as well argue that the loan of two brothers, two cousins, and Helga's second husband from oral tradition also justifies other loans from oral tradition.

B. M. Ólsen posits literary as well as genealogical loans from *Egils saga*. Thus he argues that the description of Helga's father, Þorsteinn Egilsson, in *Gunnlaugs saga* (chap. 1; ÍF 3.51) is borrowed directly from *Egils saga* (chaps. 79–84; ÍF 2.274–93).

---

7. I list these papers in *The Growth of the Medieval Icelandic Sagas (1180–1280)* (Ithaca: Cornell University Press, 2006), p. 222.

Egils saga	*Gunnlaugs saga*
Þorsteinn, sonr Egils, þá er hann óx upp, var allra manna fríðastr sýnum, hvítr á hár ok bjartr álitum; hann var mikill ok sterkr, ok þó ekki eptir því sem faðir hans. Þorsteinn var vitr maðr ok kyrrlátr, hógværr, stilltr manna bezt.	Þorsteinn hét maðr; hann var Egilsson, Skalla-Gríms sonar, Kveld-Úlfs sonar hersis ór Nóregi; en Ásgerðr hét móðir Þorsteins ok var Bjarnardóttir. Þorsteinn bjó at Borg í Borgarfirði; hann var auðigr at fé ok hǫfðingi mikill, vitr maðr ok hógværr ok hófsmaðr um alla hluti. Engi var hann
Þorsteinn var maðr órefjusamr ok réttlátr ok óaleitinn við menn, en helt hlut sínum, ef aðrir menn leituðu á hann, enda veitti þat heldr þungt flestum, at etja kappi við hann.	afreksmaðr um vǫxt eða afl sem Egill faðir hans, en þó var hann it mesta afarmenni ok vinsæll af allri alþýðu. Þorsteinn var vænn maðr, hvítr á hár ok eygr manna bezt.
(Egill's son Þorsteinn was a very handsome man when he grew up, with blond hair and a bright countenance. He was tall and strong, though not to the same degree as his father. Þorsteinn was a wise and peaceable man, gentle and very calm. Þorsteinn was an unbelligerent man, just and unaggressive toward others, but he could hold his own if others challenged him. And indeed, anyone who took issue with him was likely to suffer the consequences.)	(There was a man named Þorsteinn, the son of Egill, who was the son of Skalla-Grímr, who was in turn the son of Kveld-Úlfr, a chieftain in Norway. Ásgerðr was the name of Þorsteinn's mother, and her father was named Bjǫrn. Þorsteinn lived at Borg in Borgarfjǫrðr. He was a wealthy man and a great chieftain, gentle and moderate in all respects. He was no superman in stature or strength, like his father Egill, but nonetheless he was an outstanding man and popular with everybody. Þorsteinn was a handsome man, blond and with a fine look in his eyes.)

One could argue that important saga characters are described consistently throughout the corpus; thus Snorri goði is recognizably the same personality whatever saga he appears in. The characterizations of Þorsteinn above are, however, somewhat more than consistent.

It is particularly the phrasing, "vitr maðr ok kyrrlátr, hógværr, stilltr manna bezt" or "vitr maðr ok hógværr ok hófsmaðr um alla hluti" and the feature that Þorsteinn is big and strong but not to the same degree as his father that suggests more than a general similarity. But if one passage echoes the other, is *Egils saga* necessarily the lender and *Gunnlaugs saga* the borrower? The other direction for this borrowing would in fact be easier because the author of *Egils saga* had only to look at the first page of *Gunnlaugs saga* to draw his portrait. It is slightly more cumbersome to imagine that the author of *Gunnlaugs saga* pieced his opening paragraph together from late chapters in *Egils saga*. But we may leave the question in abeyance for the moment.

Another close parallel between *Gunnlaugs saga* and *Egils saga* is found in the well-known remark that there were two contrary strains in the family of the Mýramenn, one notably handsome and the other no less ill-favored. This observation is formulated as follows (*Gunnlaugs saga* [Stockholm 18 4to], chap. 1: ÍF 3.51; *Egils saga*, chap. 87: ÍF 2.299–300):

Svá segja fróðir menn, at margir í ætt Mýramanna, þeir sem frá Agli eru komnir, hafi verit menn vænstir, en þat sé þó mjǫk sundrgreiniligt, því at sumir í þeira ætt er kallat, at ljótastir menn hafa verit. Í þeiri ætt hafa ok verit margir atgǫrvismenn um marga hluti, sem var Kjartan Óláfsson pá ok Víga-Barði ok Skúli Þorsteinsson. Sumir váru ok skáldmenn miklir í þeiri ætt: Bjǫrn Hítdœlakappi, Einarr prestr Skúlason, Snorri Sturluson ok margir aðrir.

Frá Þorsteini er mikil ætt komin ok mart stórmenni ok skáld mǫrg, ok er þat Mýramannakyn, ok svá allt þat er komit er frá Skalla-Grími. Lengi helzk þat í ætt þeiri, at menn váru sterkir ok vígamenn miklir, en sumir spakir at viti. Þat var sundrleitt mjǫk, því at í þeiri ætt hafa fœzk þeir menn, er fríðastir hafa verit á Íslandi, sem var Þorsteinn Egilsson ok Kjartan Óláfsson, systursonr Þorsteins, ok Hallr Guðmundarson, svá ok Helga in fagra, dóttir Þorsteins, er þeir deildu um Gunnlaugr ormstunga ok Skáld-Hrafn; en fleiri váru Mýramenn manna ljótastir.

(Wise men relate that many men in the family of the Mýramenn, descended from Egill, were

(Þorsteinn had many descendants, many important men and many poets. They make up the family

very handsome, although there were major differences, because some men in this family are said to have been very ugly. In this family there were also outstanding men in many respects, for example Kjartan Óláfsson Peacock and Warrior-Barði and Skúli Þorsteinsson. Some in the family were also great skalds: Bjǫrn Hítdœlakappi, Einarr Skúlason the priest, Snorri Sturluson, and many others.)

of the Mýramenn and they are all descended from Skalla-Grímr. It was a long tradition in that family that the men were strong and great warriors, and some were wise. But there were major differences because into the family were born some who were the handsomest in Iceland, for example Þorsteinn Egilsson and Kjartan Óláfsson, Þorsteinn's nephew, and Hallr Guðmundarson, and Helga the Fair as well, Þorsteinn's daughter, over whom Gunnlaugr and Skáld-Hrafn quarreled. But many of the Mýramenn were very ugly.)

There can be little doubt that these passages are copied one from the other, but there are special considerations that complicate the question of priority. The passage is found only in one of the two manuscripts of *Gunnlaugs saga*. B. M. Ólsen thought that it was part of the original saga, but the editors of the Íslenzk fornrit edition, Sigurður Nordal and Guðni Jónsson, thought that it was an interpolation in Stockholm 18 4to and printed it as a footnote.[8] If it is an interpolation, it is certainly easier to believe that it was interpolated from *Egils saga*, where it is conspicuously located at the very end of the saga.

On the other hand, the passage is very logically placed in *Gunnlaugs saga*. The previous sentence states (ÍF 3.51): "Þorsteinn var vænn maðr, hvítr á hár ok eygr manna bezt" (Þorsteinn was a handsome man, blond and with a fine look in his eyes). The topic is therefore good looks, and it would make perfect sense for the author to continue in the same vein by generalizing about the history of good and ill-favored

---

8. See B. M. Ólsen, p. 21, and ÍF 3:51. See also Bjarni Einarsson, *Skáldasögur. Um uppruna og eðli ástaskáldsagnanna fornu* (Reykjavík: Bókaútgáfa Menningarsjóðs, 1961), pp. 268–69.

looks in the family as a whole. It would make particularly good sense if we believe that the author of *Egils saga* knew chapter 1 of *Gunnlaugs saga* and had already made use of the preceding sentences. We would not expect him to include the generalizing comment in his earlier description of Þorsteinn because he is not yet writing about the family as a whole and over time. He therefore reserves the generalization for the final summation.

It is of course perfectly possible that the author of *Gunnlaugs saga* fashioned his first chapter from scattered passages toward the end of *Egils saga*, but there are some indications that *Gunnlaugs saga* provides the original text. In the first place, *Gunnlaugs saga* is centrally about Þorsteinn and his beautiful daughter; Þorsteinn in *Egils saga* is a marginal and even slightly effete character. The real source on his life is *Gunnlaugs saga* and it is that source to which a writer on his ancestry might turn. As B. M. Ólsen points out (p. 21), the theme of personal beauty is also at the core of *Gunnlaugs saga* and is memorably embodied in Helga. The theme of beauty and idealized appearance is therefore more at home in *Gunnlaugs saga* than in *Egils saga* and is more likely to have originated in the former. Last but not least, the author of *Egils saga* concludes the passage by reminding the reader of the quarrel between Gunnlaugr and Hrafn over Helga, as he has already done once before in chapter 79 (ÍF 2.276). In effect he is referring to *Gunnlaugs saga*, and it might very well be the written *Gunnlaugs saga* we know since he echoes the text so closely.

If *Egils saga* is indeed referring to the written *Gunnlaugs saga*, and the chances that this is the case seem to me rather better than even, that does not help greatly with the absolute date of *Gunnlaugs saga*. Even if *Egils saga* was written by Snorri Sturluson, it could still be as late as 1240, and *Gunnlaugs saga* only slightly earlier, but a date around 1235 is not substantially different from B. M. Ólsen's earlier alternative of ca. 1250. We must therefore explore other literary relationships.

Gunnlaugs saga and Bjarnar saga Hítdœlakappa

Among the distinguished poets in the Mýramenn clan mentioned at the beginning of *Gunnlaugs saga* (in Stockholm 18 4to) is Bjǫrn Hítdœlakappi. According to B. M. Ólsen (p. 23), this mention suggests that the author of *Gunnlaugs saga* was familiar with *Bjarnar saga*

Hítdœlakappa. Without argument, he goes on to express certainty that *Bjarnar saga* is the older of the two (p. 32), and he proceeds to trace the influences in *Gunnlaugs saga*. He notes first of all that Skúli Þorsteinsson is assigned the same role in both sagas. In *Bjarnar saga* Skúli is Bjǫrn's host and patron at Borg: "He grew up with Skúli at Borg" (ÍF 3.112). Skúli outfits him for a voyage abroad, seconds his wooing of Oddný Þorkelsdóttir, and, when he is ready to sail, Skúli gives him a gold token as an introduction to his "friend" Eiríkr jarl Hákonarson. Accordingly, Bjǫrn is made welcome at Eiríkr's court.

In *Gunnlaugs saga,* Skúli becomes Gunnlaugr's protector at the court of the same Eiríkr when Gunnlaugr delivers his famous rejoinder to the effect that Eiríkr should make no dire predictions at his expense but rather wish for a better death than his father had (ÍF 3.69). Only Skúli's intervention saves Gunnlaugr's life. Aside from the fact that Skúli is located at his father's farm in Iceland in one case and at Eiríkr's court in Norway in the other case, and that he functions as a reference in one case but as a rescuer in the other, the motif of intervention by a friend or relative on behalf of a man who has incurred a monarch's wrath is commonplace in the sagas. The parallel is not close enough to suggest borrowing.

In both sagas, the rival skalds and ultimately wooers, Gunnlaugr and Hrafn in *Gunnlaugs saga* and Bjǫrn and Þórðr in *Bjarnar saga,* meet at a foreign court. Here, too, B. M. Ólsen (p. 34) believes that one meeting has influenced the other but once again there are significant differences. In *Gunnlaugs saga,* the two skalds meet at the court of King Olaf of Sweden and compete with their panegyrics in a lively scene that aligns their poetry with their characters. In *Bjarnar saga* the skalds Bjǫrn and Þórðr meet at the court of Jarl Eiríkr of Norway and manage to live on companionable terms despite earlier frictions; there is no rival presentation of praise poetry. As we know from the *Legendary Saga of Saint Óláfr,* simultaneous visits to royal courts by more than one skald were not unusual and such double visits in the skald sagas may not be striking enough to suggest a literary connection.

B. M. Ólsen (p. 35) also saw a significant similarity between Bjǫrn Hítdœlakappi's gift of a cloak presented to him by King Óláfr Haraldsson (ÍF 3.134) to Oddný (ÍF 3.150) and the cloak given to Gunnlaugr by King Ethelred in England (ÍF 3.71) and later presented to Helga (ÍF 3.90). The Íslenzk fornrit editors, Sigurður Nordal and

Guðni Jónsson, have pointed out, however, that the cloak given by King Óláfr to Bjǫrn is not the same as the one he gives to Oddný.[9] Quite apart from that discrepancy, the parallel is not close enough to carry conviction. It is an inconspicuous moment in *Bjarnar saga* but a highly significant moment in *Gunnlaugs saga* because Helga's dying gesture is to unfold the cloak and gaze at it (ÍF 3.107). It does not therefore appear that B. M. Ólsen was able to make loans from *Bjarnar saga* into *Gunnlaugs saga* plausible.

If we reverse the procedure, however, and explore the possibility that *Bjarnar saga* made use of *Gunnlaugs saga*, the result is a little more promising.[10] Both Gunnlaugr and Bjǫrn go abroad with the understanding that the betrothed woman will wait for three years. The stipulation is more clearly spelled out in *Bjarnar saga* (ÍF 3.114):

> Fóru þá þegar festar fram, ok skyldi hon sitja í festum þrjá vetr, ok þó at Bjǫrn sé samlendr fjórða vetrinn ok megi eigi til komask at vitja þessa ráðs, þá skal hon þó hans bíða, en ef hann kemr eigi til á þriggja vetra fresti af Nóregi, þá skyldi Þorkell gipta hana ef hann vildi. Bjǫrn skyldi ok senda menn út at vitja þessa ráðs ef hann mætti eigi sjálfr til koma.

(The engagement was contracted, and [it was stipulated] that she would remain engaged for three years. Even if Bjǫrn was in the country [Iceland] in the fourth year but unable to revisit his engagement, she should still wait for him. But if he did not arrive from Norway within the three-year period, Þorkell would be free to marry her off if he wished. [It was also stipulated] that Bjǫrn

---

9. See ÍF 3:150n1.
10. This possibility has already been explored in detail by Bjarni Guðnason in "Aldur ok einkenni Bjarnar sögu Hítdœlakappa" in *Sagnaþing helgað Jónasi Kristjánssyni sjötugum 10. Apríl 1994*, 2 vols. (Reykjavík: Hið íslenska bókmenntafélag, 1994), vol. 1, pp. 69–85. He took the view that *Bjarnar saga* implicitly measures its protagonist against such saga heroes as Gunnlaugr ormstunga, Bjǫrn Breiðvíkingakappi, and Kjartan Óláfsson (p. 76). Despite earlier views assigning priority to *Bjarnar saga* (see p. 78, notes 28–29), Bjarni argued that *Gunnlaugs saga* served as a model. In particular, he suggested Gunnlaugr's combat with Þórormr in England as the prototype for Bjǫrn's single combat with Kaldimarr in Russia (p. 78). He did not, however, use this evidence to date *Gunnlaugs saga* early; instead he argued that *Bjarnar saga* drew on ten different sagas, including *Njáls saga*, and was not written until 1300 or a little later. I persist in believing that *Bjarnar saga* is early, but *Gunnlaugs saga* even earlier.

should dispatch men out [to Iceland] to revisit the engagement if he could not make the trip himself.)

The provisions seem a trifle over-specific, as if there were in fact some expectation that Bjǫrn will not appear at the appointed time. If he returns in three years but cannot make a personal appearance, Oddný must wait a fourth year. If he does not return in three years, Þorkell is free to marry his daughter to someone else, unless Bjǫrn sends delegates to confirm the arrangement.

These provisions recapitulate in a nutshell the circumstances in *Gunnlaugs saga*, although the stipulations are not nearly so precise in the latter case. Under pressure from Gunnlaugr's father Illugi, Helga's father Þorsteinn agrees to an informal marriage commitment for three years but not to a formal betrothal (ÍF 3.67–68): "Þá skal Helga vera heitkona Gunnlaugs, en eigi festarkona, ok bíða þrjá vetr; ... en ek skal lauss allra mála, ef hann kemr eigi svá út...." (Helga should be committed to Gunnlaugr, but not be his fiancée, and should wait three years; ... but I will be released from all commitments if he does not come out [to Iceland] ...). These general terms are then more precisely articulated when Gunnlaugr is delayed and Hrafn makes his bid for Helga's hand (ÍF 3.81–82):

> Þorsteinn svarar: "Hon er áðr heitkona Gunnlaugs, ok vil ek halda ǫll mál við hann, þau sem mælt váru." Skapti [the lawspeaker Skapti Þóroddsson, who is acting on Þóroddr's behalf] mælti: "Eru nú eigi liðnir þrír vetr, er til váru nefndir með yðr?" "Já," sagði Þorsteinn, "en eigi er sumarit liðit, ok má hann enn til koma í sumar." Skapti svarar: "En ef hann kemr eigi til sumarlangt, hverja ván skulu vér þá eiga þessa máls?" Þorsteinn svarar: "Hér munu vér koma annat sumar, ok má þá sjá, hvat ráðligast þykkir, en ekki tjár nú at tala lengr at sinni."

> (Þorsteinn replied: "She was committed to Gunnlaugr before, and I wish to maintain all the commitments that were stipulated with him." Skapti said: "Have the three years not passed that were agreed on by you?" "Yes," said Þorsteinn, "but the summer has not passed, and he could still make it here during the summer." Skapti answered: "But if he does not arrive during the summer, what is to

be our expectation in this matter?" Þorsteinn answered: "We will come here next summer and look into what seems most advisable, but there is no point in talking further for the time being.")

The theme here, as in *Bjarnar saga*, is the matter of extensions; Gunnlaugr has not returned, but may still do so. Even if he does not, Þorsteinn wants to hold the agreement open for a fourth year. In both cases there are two back-up positions to prevent foreclosing the agreement prematurely. The difference is that the author of *Bjarnar saga* anticipates all the contingencies at once, perhaps a less realistic alternative. It looks as though *Gunnlaugs saga* has provided him with an overview of the possible contingencies and the author of *Bjarnar saga* has availed himself of the blueprint.

B. M. Ólsen thought that a significant shared feature in the two sagas was the intermediary role of Skúli Þorsteinsson at Jarl Eiríkr's court, but perhaps a greater similarity can be found in the way the skalds are introduced at court. Gunnlaugr introduces himself, but the jarl immediately turns to Skúli to ask about him (ÍF 3:69):

"Herra," segir hann, "takið honum vel; hann er ins bezta manns sonr á Íslandi, Illuga svarta af Gilsbakka, ok fóstbróðir minn."

("Sir," he said, "give him a good welcome; he is the son of an excellent man in Iceland, Illugi the Black from Gilsbakki, and he is my foster brother.")

In *Bjarnar saga* he turns to Bjǫrn to get information on the newly arrived Þórðr (ÍF 3.116):

Jarl spurði Bjǫrn, ef honum væri kunnleiki á Þórði. Bjǫrn kvazk gǫrla kenna Þórð ok kvað hann vera skáld gott,—"ok mun þat kvæði rausnarsamligt, er hann flytr." Jarl mælti: "Þykki þér þat ráð, Bjǫrn, at ek hlýð kvæðinu?" "Þykki mér víst," segir Bjǫrn, "því at þat mun báðum ykkr til sœmðar."

(The jarl asked Bjǫrn if he knew Þórðr. Bjǫrn said that he knew Þórðr very well and said that he was a good poet—"and any poem that he presents will be splendid." The jarl asked: "Do you think that it would be advisable for me to listen to the poem?" "I do indeed," said Bjǫrn, "for it will be a source of honor for both of you.")

In both cases the acceptance of the guest is by recommendation, though in *Bjarnar saga* there is an ironic undertone, voluntary or involuntary, because the referee and the beneficiary of the reference become bitter rivals and deadly enemies.

After Bjǫrn and Þórðr have spent a sociable winter at Jarl Eiríkr's court, Bjǫrn resolves to go harrying, but Þórðr advises against it in the following terms (ÍF 3.118):

Þat sýnisk mér óráðligt, fengit nú áðr góða sœmð ok virðing, en hætta sér nú svá, ok far þú miklu heldr með mér í sumar út til Íslands, til frænda þinna gǫfugra, ok vitja ráðahags þíns.

(It seems to me inadvisable, now that you have gotten honor and respect, to take such a risk. [You should] much rather travel with me out to Iceland this summer to your distinguished kinsmen, in order to revisit your engagement.)

This advice is either illogical or deeply hypocritical because Þórðr presumably already has it in mind to make off with Bjǫrn's betrothed. That option becomes more plausible the longer Bjǫrn stays away from Iceland, and the advice to return home therefore contradicts Þórðr's intention. The delayed return is also a prominent feature in *Gunnlaugs saga* and is formulated one final time in the following terms (ÍF 3.82):

Þorsteinn gekk þá til Skapta, ok keyptu þeir svá, at brúðlaup skyldi vera at vetrnáttum at Borg, ef Gunnlaugr kœmi eigi út á því sumri, en Þorsteinn lauss allra mála við Hrafn, ef Gunnlaugr kœmi til ok vitjaði ráðsins.

(Þorsteinn then went to Skapti, and they arranged that the wedding should take place at the beginning of winter at Borg if Gunnlaugr did not come out [to Iceland] that summer, but that Þorsteinn should be free of all commitments to Hrafn if Gunnlaugr arrived and revisited his engagement.)

The phrase "vitja ráðs" (or "ráðahags") is a very slight echo, but it is precisely what both suitors fail to do. Both betrothal stories are centered on the failure of the grooms to appear at the appointed time, but the author of *Gunnlaugs saga* handles the theme more logically. There may, therefore, be a suspicion that the author of *Bjarnar saga* took it over mechanically and failed to make the necessary logical adjustments.

The final impediment to prompt arrival is that it is late in the summer and all the ships have already sailed from Norway to Iceland. Jarl Eiríkr informs Gunnlaugr in the following words (ÍF 3.84): "Nú eru ǫll skip í brottu, þau er til Íslands bjuggusk" (now all the ships that were readied for Iceland have sailed). But the bad news turns out to be premature, and Jarl Eiríkr is able to get passage for Gunnlaugr with Hallfreðr (ibid.):

Eiríkr jarl lét þá flytja Gunnlaug út til Hallfreðar, ok tók hann við honum með fagnaði, ok gaf þegar byr undan landi, ok váru vel kátir. Þat var síð sumars.

(Jarl Eiríkr had Gunnlaugr conveyed out to Hallfreðr's ship, and he welcomed him gladly. There was a prompt offshore breeze and they were in good spirits. It was late in the summer.)

The departure of all the ships to Iceland and the lateness of the season are duplicated when Bjǫrn returns to Norway from Kiev (ÍF 3.122): "Ok er hann kom þar, váru ǫll skip gengin til Íslands, ok var þat síð sumars" (and when he got there, all the ships had sailed to Iceland, and it was late in the summer).

One final similarity occurs at the end of *Bjarnar saga*, when Þórðr overcomes Bjǫrn in a notably one-sided combat and must bring his wife Oddný the news, along with a torque belonging to Bjǫrn (ÍF 3.205). At the sight of it, Oddný falls back unconscious and lapses into an illness that leads to her death. Her fate is not a little reminiscent of Helga's final moments as she unfolds and gazes at the cloak given her by Gunnlaugr. In both scenes the woman is described as gazing at the treasure and collapsing (ÍF 3.107: "hné hon aptr"; ÍF 3.205: "hneig hon aptr").

The echoes in these texts are not unambiguous; it can still be argued that both authors are working from literary commonplaces. Even if we believe that the echoes are textual, there is not much to suggest which text has the priority. I would nonetheless argue that *Gunnlaugs saga* is more likely to have set the tone. It is more thoroughly constructed on and pervaded by the theme of the procrastinating groom. In *Bjarnar saga*, on the other hand, this theme is confined to the first four short chapters and the death of Oddný at the end. The body of the saga, which is about twice as long as *Gunnlaugs saga*, has no reminiscences of this theme and is focused single-mindedly on the exchange of stanzas and the hostilities between Bjǫrn and Þórðr. Here the author seems entirely dependent on the stanzas and whatever tradition may have accompanied them. My own sense of the composition as a whole is that the author was intent on telling the story of the feud between Bjǫrn and Þórðr but prefaced and concluded that core story with a romantic frame inspired by *Gunnlaugs saga*.

Further textual correpondences

Other echoes detected by B. M. Ólsen are slight in comparison. I mention only two cases because they were accepted by Sigurður Nordal.[11] Chapter 1 of *Gunnlaugs saga* notes the marriage of Þorsteinn to Jófríðr, daughter of Gunnarr Hlífarson. The Stockholm manuscript provides a comment on Gunnarr not found in the other manuscript (ÍF 3.52):

> Gunnarr hefir bezt vígr verit ok mestr fimleikamaðr verit á Íslandi af búandmǫnnum, annarr Gunnarr at Hlíðarenda, þriði Steinþórr á Eyri.

> (Of all the farmers in Iceland Gunnarr was the most stalwart and agile next after Gunnarr of Hlíðarendi, and Steinþórr at Eyrr was the third.)

B. M. Ólsen (p. 26) saw no reason to consider the passage to be an interpolation and viewed it as a combination of a passage in *Hœnsa-Þóris saga* and another in *Eyrbyggja saga*. *Hœnsa-Þóris saga* comments as follows (ÍF 3.44):

---

11. See ÍF 3:XLIX, LII–V.

"Já," sagði Gunnarr, "svá er þat," ok gengr heim til bœjarins ok tók boga, því at hann skaut allra manna bezt af honum, ok er þar helzt til jafnat, er var Gunnarr at Hlíðarenda.

("Yes," said Gunnarr, "that is so." He went back to the house and took his bow, because he was the best of shots, and Gunnarr of Hlíðarendi is the best comparison.)

The passages are not close enough to suggest first-hand borrowing; one is about general athleticism, the other specifically about bowmanship. It is easy to believe that there were general traditions about comparative prowess, as there may have been about Barði Guðmundarson and Grettir Ásmundarson.[12] The following passage from *Eyrbyggja saga* illustrates the same point (ÍF 4.212–2):

Steinþórr var framast barna Þorláks; hann var mikill maðr ok sterkr ok manna vápnfimastr ok inn mesti atgørvismaðr; hógværr var hann hversdagliga. Steinþórr var til þess tekinn, at inn þriði maðr hafi bezt verit vígr á Íslandi með þeim Helga Droplaugarsyni ok Vémundi kǫgur.

(Steinþórr was foremost among Þorlákr's children. He was a tall man, strong and most accomplished with weapons, a man of prowess, though he was gentle on a daily basis. Steinþórr was considered to have been the third greatest warrior in Iceland along with Helgi Droplaugarson and Vémundr kǫgurr.)

Steinþórr recurs in this passage but is compared to entirely different men. Once again the echo is too thin to carry conviction.

A few pages later B. M. Ólsen (p. 29) identifies another loan from *Eyrbyggja saga*. When Gunnlaugr asks Þorsteinn for the hand of his daughter and is turned down, he responds in his characteristically undiplomatic fashion by telling his potential father-in-law that he is a lesser man than his own father Illugi. As a case in point he refers to Illugi's triumph over Þorgrímr Kjallaksson at the Þórsnessþing (ÍF 3.66):

---

12. See ÍF 7:106–7.

Eða hvat hefir þú í móti því, er hann deildi kapp við Þorgrím goða Kjallaksson á Þórsnessþingi ok við sonu hans ok hafði einn þat, er við lá?

(Or what can you compare to his having contested against the chieftain Þorgrímr Kjallaksson and his sons at the Þórsnes Assembly, with the result that he won the whole stake?)

The exchange develops into a little flyting, but Þorsteinn soon appreciates that it is foolish and disengages.

The dispute between Illugi and Þorgrímr Kjallaksson is narrated in a little greater detail in *Eyrbyggja saga* (ÍF 4.31–33). We learn that the dispute was over the marriage portion of Illugi's wife Ingibjǫrg Ásbjarnardóttir. It came close to armed conflict, but the money was finally paid out on Illugi's terms. It is quite unlikely that the author of *Gunnlaugs saga* needed to refer to *Eyrbyggja saga* for this information, especially because the event was commemorated in a praise poem by a certain Oddr and titled "Illugadrápa." Two stanzas are quoted in the retelling of *Eyrbyggja saga*, and the author of *Gunnlaugs saga* could just as well have taken the reference from the poem. The author in fact treats it as general knowledge that any reader could be expected to have.

B. M. Ólsen (p. 36) nonetheless argues for the influence of *Eyrbyggja saga* in yet a third passage. In *Gunnlaugs saga* Illugi visits Þorsteinn at Borg to support Gunnlaugr's wooing of Helga. Þorsteinn suggests that they walk up to the overhanging hill (*borg*) in order to talk (ÍF 3.67): "Gǫngum upp á borgina ok tǫlum þar" (let us climb the hill and talk there). This scene reminds B. M. Ólsen of a scene in *Eyrbyggja saga* in which Víga-Styrr (Arngrímr Þorgrímsson) visits Snorri goði at Helgafell to ask for advice on his troublesome berserks. Snorri suggests that they climb up Helgafell to discuss the matter (ÍF 4.71–72):

Snorri spurði, ef hann hefði nǫkkur vandamál at tala. "Svá þykki mér," segir Styrr. Snorri svarar: "Þá skulu vit ganga upp á Helgafell; þau ráð hafa sízt at engu orðit, er þar hafa ráðin verit."

(Snorri asked if he had any problems to discuss. "I think I do," said Styrr. Snorri replied: "Then we should climb Helgafell; the plans forged there have been least likely to come to nothing.")

During the consultation on Helgafell Snorri hatches a plan that will enable Styrr to kill off the two berserks. Part of the secret deal is that Snorri will then get the hand of Styrr's daughter in marriage. Thus the situation in both sagas revolves around a marriage negotiation. B. M. Ólsen acknowledges that there is no mention of the idea that Borg, like Helgafell, is auspicious for consultations, but he believes that the idea is implied, even though the betrothal of Gunnlaugr and Helga is anything but auspicious. This parallel too seems less than compelling, and I can find no strong evidence that *Gunnlaugs saga* echoes *Eyrbyggja saga*.

Far more interesting is the case to be made for our author's having known *Laxdæla saga*. He cites that saga explicitly in chapter 5 (ÍF 3.64):

Reið Illugi þá heiman skjótt ok keypti skip hálft til handa Gunnlaugi, er uppi stóð í Gufuárósi, at Auðuni festargram. Þessi Auðunn vildi eigi útan flytja sonu Ósvífrs ins spaka eptir víg Kjartans Óláfssonar, sem segir í Laxdæla sǫgu, ok varð þat þó síðar en þetta.

(Illugi rode off from home quickly and purchased half a ship in Gufuáróss from Auðunn festargramr. This Auðunn did not want to give passage to the sons of Ósvífr the Wise after the killing of Kjartan Óláfsson, as it is told in *Laxdæla saga*, but that happened after this [i.e., after what is told here].)

There would seem to be no good reason to believe that this is not a reference to the written *Laxdæla saga* and no good reason to believe that the reference in *Gunnlaugs saga* is interpolated (ÍF 3.64n1). B. M. Ólsen was in no doubt that the author of *Gunnlaugs saga* made use of *Laxdæla saga*, although the reference above is not precise.[13] *Laxdæla saga* (ÍF 5.158–59) does not state that Auðunn refused passage to the sons of Ósvífr, only that he made a dire prediction about their survival. The remark in *Gunnlaugs saga* that "the latter [the passage of Ósvífr's sons abroad] was later than this [Gunnlaugr's voyage abroad]" is also peculiar. Looking at the reconstructed chronologies in the *Íslenzk fornrit* editions, we can observe that modern scholars estimate that

---

13. See B. M. Ólsen, pp. 23, 27, 30–32, 50.

Gunnlaugr went abroad in 1002 and Ósvífr's sons probably in the summer of 1003.[14] That medieval authors or scribes would have made such a narrow calculation is indeed surprising and difficult to explain. It is more likely that the sequence is based on a vague tradition than on a written source.

Apart from this passage, the evidence that the author of *Gunnlaugs saga* made use of *Laxdœla saga* is again very thin. B. M. Ólsen (p. 23) believed that the reference to Kjartan Óláfsson in the first chapter of *Gunnlaugs saga* presupposes a knowledge of *Laxdœla saga*, but surely a reference to one of the most famous heroes of the Saga Age does not equate to the knowledge of a particular text. B. M. Ólsen (p. 27) also supposed that the mention of the spouses Óláfr pá and Þorgerðr Egilsdóttir in chapter 3 rested either on *Egils saga* or on *Laxdœla saga*, probably the latter. Again, the mention of these Saga Age notables hardly requires a written source. In addition, B. M. Ólsen urges a verbal echo in the introduction of Óláfr pá (ÍF 3.57):

> Ok þá reið Þorsteinn til heimboðs vestr í Hjarðarholt, til Óláfs pá, mágs síns, Hǫskuldarsonar, er þá þótti vera með mestri virðingu allra hǫfðingja vestr þar.
>
> (Then Þorsteinn rode to a feast west in Hjarðarholt, at the residence of his kinsman Óláfr Peacock Hǫskuldarson, who at that time was reputed to be the worthiest of all the chieftains there in the west.)

It is theorized that we can find the source for this description in chapter 24 of *Laxdœla saga*, where there are remarks such as "gerðisk hann hǫfðingi mikill" (he became a great chieftain) (ÍF 5.66) and "óxu nú mjǫk metorð Óláfs" (Óláfr's reputation was now greatly increased) (ÍF 5.68). Once more, the similarity is too approximate and the sentiment too general to allow for such a conclusion.

On p. 32 B. M. Ólsen associates Þorsteinn's memorable dream forecasting his daughter's marriages with Guðrún Ósvífrsdóttir's fourfold dream visions of her marriages in *Laxdœla saga*, but we will see below that there is a considerably closer parallel in the Eddic material. Since the plot of *Gunnlaugs saga* can be documented for a prior tradition

---

14. See ÍF 3:LIX and ÍF 5:LIX.

because of various references to it, B. M. Ólsen (pp. 31–32) does not subscribe to the view that the author invented the romantic plot under the influence of *Laxdœla saga*. Indeed, it seems more likely that both authors owe their romantic impulses to the Eddic antecedents, but B. M. Ólsen (p. 46) mentions only two Eddic echoes from *Helgakviða Hundingsbana II* and *Atlamál*. We will see that the Eddic substratum can be construed to yield a good deal more.

In summary, B. M. Ólsen was convinced that the author of *Gunnlaugs saga* was palpably influenced by *Hallfreðar saga*, *Egils saga*, *Bjarnar saga Hítdœlakappa*, *Eyrbyggja saga*, and *Laxdœla saga*. In the first three cases I believe that the influence ran not to *Gunnlaugs saga* but from it. In the case of *Eyrbyggja saga* and *Laxdœla saga*, I find the evidence inadequate, although the direct reference to the latter poses a real puzzle. B. M. Ólsen also believed in influences from *Heiðarvíga saga*, *Hœnsa-Þóris saga*, and *Njáls saga*, but Sigurður Nordal considered that the case had not been made and I will not pursue it further.[15]

The romantic undertone

Readers of Björn M. Ólsen's treatise, after a few years' time, are more likely to remember his general assessment of the romantic flavor in *Gunnlaugs saga* than the details on the possible influences from other sagas, even though his treatment of the romantic streak is very brief (pp. 10–11). He speaks of the "chivalric-romantic undertone that pervades the saga from beginning to end," although he qualifies that description by suggesting that the tone is downplayed to accord with normal saga style. He detects the romantic tone in Þorsteinn's conferral of the name "Helga the Fair" and in her golden tresses, but also in the chivalric sensibilities of the male protagonists. It emerges most emphatically in the motif of unquenchable love until death and the sentimental conclusion. B. M. Ólsen sums up the evidence by labeling *Gunnlaugs saga* a "chivalric romance against a Norse backdrop" and the male protagonists "knightly figures in disguise." In particular he judges the description of Helga's golden hair ("fagrt sem barit gull") to have undergone the influence of chivalric romance.

---

15. See B. M. Ólsen, pp. 23, 26, 36–37, and Sigurður Nordal in ÍF 3:XLIX.

One need not resort to foreign romance to find models for beautiful, lovelorn, and grief-stricken women, and we will locate more immediate models presently. Generally speaking, however, it appears in retrospect that B. M. Ólsen's emphasis on chivalric romance was considerably exaggerated. This criticism was voiced most forthrightly by Vésteinn Ólason:[16]

> It has often been maintained that the Saga of Gunnlaug bears the marks of the influence of a fashionable literary genre of the twelfth and thirteenth centuries, the French chansons de geste and romances of chivalry that were being translated into Norse and enjoyed considerable popularity in the later part of the thirteenth century at least among the upper classes. In fact this influence was quite limited and not very profound.

Vésteinn tries, for example, to moderate the glorification of Helga's beauty and align it with other sagas. The most memorable detail is probably the comparison of Helga's hair to "barit gull" (beaten gold). B. M. Ólsen (p. 11) takes the phrase to reflect chivalric style, but his two examples are not from chivalric texts; one is from *Þiðreks saga* and the other is from a curious little text in *Flateyjarbók* titled *Hauks þáttr hábrókar*. These instances are the only ones recorded in the dictionaries and are a thin basis for arguing chivalric style.[17]

Whether *Gunnlaugs saga* is chivalric and inspired by foreign models or not, most critics can agree that in some sense it is a love story. The less it is judged to partake of foreign influence, the more it constitutes

---

16. See *The Saga of Gunnlaug Snake-Tongue together with the Tale of Scald-Helgi*, trans. Alan Boucher, with an Introduction by Vésteinn Ólason (Reykjavík: Iceland Review, 1983), p. 16. See also Else Mundal's "Foreword" in *Gunnlaugs saga ormstungu* (Oslo, etc.: Universitetsforlaget, 1980), pp. 11 and 16, and Alison Finlay, "Skald Sagas in Their Literary Context 2: Possible European Contexts" in *Skaldsagas*, ed. Russell Poole, p. 237.

17. Susanne Kramarz-Bein's recent and compendious book *Die Þiðreks saga im Kontext der altnorwegischen Literatur* (Tübingen and Basel: A. Francke Verlag, 2002), especially pp. 207–63, associates *Þiðreks saga* with chivalric romance, but I continue to believe that it was translated from a Low German text composed in Soest ca. 1180 at a time when chivalric romance had hardly begun in Germany. The phrase "barit gull" could reflect an original Low German or High German "gehemertes golt" or the like. The *Hauks þáttr hábrókar* to which the dictionaries refer, not to be confused with the *Hauks þáttr hábrókar* in *Óláfs saga Tryggvasonar en mesta*, ed. Ólafur Halldórsson, Editiones Arnamagnæanæ, Ser. A, vol. 3 (Copenhagen: C.A. Reitzel, 2000), pp. 104–5, is found only in *Flateyjarbók*. It is printed in *Fornmanna sögur*, 12 vols. (Copenhagen: S. L. Møller, 1825–1837), vol. 10,

evidence for a native tradition of love stories. That such a tradition existed is borne out by the existence of love stanzas and a variety of love anecdotes pertaining to both kings and commoners, not least of all skalds such as Þormóðr Bersason and Kormákr Ǫgmundarson.[18] The chief guarantee of a native romantic tradition is the legend of Brynhild and Sigurd, with a blighted love story at its core. Romantic blight seems in fact to be the preferred mode in the native tradition, in which a happy outcome is quite unknown. The wrong match is the rule; the passionate swains never get the beloved, and the objects of their affection, passionate in action in the poetry but passionate only in grief in the sagas, become so many *mal mariées*.

Both the women and the men differ greatly in verse and prose. The men of heroic poetry are decisive, Sigurd in his wooing and the Burgundian brothers in their action against Sigurd. The men in the sagas, on the other hand, are curiously irresolute; it is as if they had all partaken of Grimhild's potion of forgetfulness and lost track of their commitments.[19] The women of heroic poetry waver even less than the men; Brynhild contrives the death of Sigurd, and Gudrun avenges him with unexampled ferocity. The women in the sagas by contrast wither away in melancholy.

And yet there are similarities that suggest a continuity. The common theme is the thwarted marriage with tragic consequences. The sagas rarely attain the high passion of the Eddic poems, although *Gísla saga* and *Laxdœla saga* come close and *Gunnlaugs saga* has high moments in the encounter between Gunnlaugr and Hrafn and the death of

---

pp. 198–208, and later editions. In her recent *The Development of Flateyjarbók: Iceland and the Norwegian Dynastic Crisis of 1389* (N.p.: University Press of Southern Denmark, 2005), p. 100, Elizabeth Ashman Rowe reminds us that Finnur Jónsson believed that the run of text including *Hauks þáttr* could have been authored by Jón Þórðarson himself. Jón or a contemporary could very well have modeled his description of King Haraldr's hair as "fagrt sem silki eðr barit gull" (p. 206) on *Gunnlaugs saga*. On the *þáttr* in general see also Stefanie Würth, *Elemente des Erzählens. Die þættir der Flateyjarbók*, Beiträge zur nordischen Philologie 20 (Basel and Frankfurt am Main: Helbing & Lichtenhahn, 1991), p. 110.

18. For a survey of these stanzas see Bjarni Einarsson's *Skáldasögur* (note 8), pp. 11–39. See also Alison Finlay, "Skalds, Troubadours and Saga," *Saga-Book* 24 (1995), pp. 105–53, and "Skald Sagas in Their Literary Context 2: Possible European Contexts" in *Skaldsagas*, ed. Russell Poole, pp. 232–71.

19. See Robert G. Cook, "The Character of Gunnlaug Serpent-Tongue," *Scandinavian Studies* 43 (1971), p. 12.

Helga. Without rivaling the poems, the sagas do have certain devices, gestures, and phrasings that are reminiscent of them.

Both the heroic legend (most likely in the largely lost *Sigurðarkviða in meiri* now preserved only in the prose of *Vǫlsunga saga*) and *Gunnlaugs saga* begin with elaborate premonitory dreams.[20] In the legend, Gudrun dreams of holding a hawk with golden feathers, which she values above all things.[21] When she seeks counsel from Brynhild, she recounts another dream (Finch, p. 46) in which she sees a stag with a golden coat, also valued most highly, but which Brynhild strikes down at her feet. No less explicitly predictive is Þorsteinn's dream about two eagles succumbing in a fight over a beautiful swan in *Gunnlaugs saga*. The prophetic eagles are in fact matched in one of the premonitory dreams that warn Kostbera of the fate that awaits the Burgundian brothers if they travel to Hunland (Finch, p. 67). She dreams of an eagle flying through the hall splattering blood. For a chivalric parallel we can of course resort to the *Nibelungenlied*, but the Norse parallels are closer to hand.[22]

Saga readers remember Helga as the quintessential, almost proverbial, beauty. The theme of beauty has also put critics in mind of chivalric models; the figure of Enid in the romances of Chrétien and Hartmann might illustrate this tradition. It is true that feminine beauty is not much dwelt on in the sagas, but here again the heroic legend fills the gap. When Sigurd first sees Brynhild in her remote tower, he is captivated by her beauty (Finch, p. 42): "Þá sér hann eina fagra konu ok kennir at þar er Brynhildr. Honum þykkir um vert allt saman, fegrð hennar ok þat er hon gerir" (then he sees a fair woman and realizes that it is Brynhild. He is altogether struck by her beauty and by what [the work] she is doing). He reports the vision to his companion

---

20. In "Die Lieder der Lücke im Codex Regius der Edda," *Germanistische Abhandlungen, Hermann Paul dargebracht* (Strassburg: Trübner, 1902), pp. 1–98; rpt. in his *Kleine Schriften*, ed. Stefan Sonderegger (Berlin: de Gruyter, 1969), vol. 2, pp. 223–91 (esp. pp. 249–56) Andreas Heusler posited a separate "Traumlied" to account for the premonitory dream. In "The Lays of the Lacuna in Codex Regius," *Speculum Norroenum: Studies in Memory of Gabriel Turville-Petre*, ed. Ursula Dronke et al. (Odense: Odense University Press, 1981), pp. 6–26, I suggested that the dream could well have been part of "Meiri."

21. *The Saga of the Volsungs*, ed. and trans. R. G. Finch (London and Edinburgh: Nelson, 1965), p. 44. Hereafter cited as: Finch.

22. See *Das Nibelungenlied*, ed. Helmut de Boor, rev. Roswitha Wisniewski (Wiesbaden: Brockhaus, 1979), p. 6.

Alsviðr; then, when he makes his first visit, he kisses Brynhild and praises her unique beauty (Finch, p. 43): "Enga kona hefir þér fegri fœzk" (no woman more beautiful than you has been born).

The chief symptom of love in both legend and saga is melancholy. Sigurd's first view of Brynhild depresses his spirits and prompts a sympathetic inquiry from Alsviðr (Finch, p. 42):

> "Hví eru þér svá fálátir? Þessi skipan þín harmar oss ok þína vini. Eða hví máttu eigi gleði halda? Haukar þínir hnípa ok svá hestrinn Grani, ok þessa fám vér seint bót."

> ("Why are you so taciturn? This change of heart grieves us and your friends. Why can you not keep your spirits up? Your hawks are downcast and your horse Grani too, and it will take a time for us to recover.")

When Brynhild learns what has happened, her lovesickness takes on more epic dimensions (Finch, p. 51): "Brynhildr fór heim ok mælti ekki orð um kveldit" (Brynhild returned home and said not a word in the evening). What follows is a long sequence of efforts to rouse her from her catatonic state. Her condition is described as illness (Finch, p. 53): "Brynhildr er sjúk" (Brynhild is ill). A series of interviews remains without effect on her, other than providing an opportunity for Brynhild to vent her indignation and grief, a venting with analogues in *Guðrúnarkviða fyrsta* and *Guðrúnarkviða ǫnnur*.

In Brynhild's case there is no question of consolation, although Gudrun entertains the vain idea that returning to the hall and taking up her needlework might cheer her. She instructs one of her companions accordingly (Finch, p. 54): "Vek Brynhildi, gǫngum til borða ok verum kátar" (awaken Brynhild and let us go to our embroidery and be of good cheer). In the case of Guðrún this strategy actually succeeds. She takes refuge with King Hálfr in Denmark after Sigurd's death and stays there for seven years, during which time Þóra Hákonardóttir distracts her with embroidery (Finch, p. 62):

> [H]on sló borða fyrir henni ok skrifaði þar á mǫrg ok stór verk ok fagra leika er tíðir váru í þann tíma, sverð ok brynjur ok allan konungs búnað, skip Sigmundar konungs er skriðu fyrir land fram.

Ok þat byrðu þær er þeir bǫrðusk Sigarr ok Siggeirr á Fjóni suðr. Slíkt var þeira gaman ok huggaðisk Guðrún nú nǫkkut harms síns.

(She embroidered and pictured many a great deed and fair pursuits that were customary at that time, swords and byrnies and all the royal accouterments, King Sigmund's ships that sailed along the coast. And they embroidered Sigarr and Siggeirr south on Fyn. This was their amusement and Gudrun was somewhat consoled in her grief.)

This passage is guaranteed for the poetic record by stanzas 14–17 of *Guðrúnarkviða ǫnnur*.[23] Perhaps the consolation afforded by needlework echoes in Helga's death scene in *Gunnlaugs saga* where the point is made that Helga's only consolation was to unfold and gaze at the cloak given her by Gunnlaugr.

It will be recalled that it is precisely at one of these moments that she falls back and dies (ÍF 3.107):

Ok er skikkjan kom til hennar, þá settisk hon upp ok rakði skikkjuna fyrir sér ok horfði á um stund. Ok síðan hné hon aptr í fang bónda sínum ok var þá ørend.

(And when the cloak was given her, she sat up and unfolded the cloak before her and gazed at it for a time. And then she collapsed back into her husband's arms and expired.)

The falling back also echoes Eddic passages. As Brynhild commits suicide, she too falls back against the cushions (Finch, p. 60)—"hneig upp við dýnur." Guðrún duplicates this posture when she sees her slain husband in *Guðrúnarkviða fyrsta* (st. 15):

Þá hné Guðrún   hǫll við bólstri;
Haddr losnaði,   hlýr roðnaði,
Enn regns dropi   rann niðr um kné.

---

23. See *Edda. Die Lieder des Codex Regius nebst verwandten Denkmälern*, ed. Gustav Neckel, rev. Hans Kuhn (Heidelberg: Winter, 1962), pp. 226–27.

(Then Gudrun collapsed   athwart the cushions;
Her hair was loosened,   her cheek was reddened,
And liquid drops   ran down her lap.)

We do not need to have recourse to chivalric models to explain the romantic inflections in *Gunnlaugs saga*. Most of them are anticipated in the heroic and elegiac poems of the *Edda*. The elegies are particularly revealing, although they do not shed any light on the dating. If they are late, as Heusler thought, they could have been part of a new literary wave at the time *Gunnlaugs saga* was written, let us say 1210 to 1220. If they are part of an earlier heritage, as Daniel Sävborg has argued, they could have been available at almost any time before that period, a feature of the general tradition rather than the current literary scene.[24]

Conclusion

We do not need to take recourse to the flowery meadows of medieval chivalry to account for *Gunnlaugs saga*. The passion and melancholy of the native poetic tradition are more apposite. Consequently there is no need to posit a late date for the saga. Bjarni Einarsson in particular was convinced that there must have been an early *Gunnlaugs saga* available to the author of *Egils saga*.[25] That led him to posit one version early in the century and one version considerably later, but there is not much evidence that sagas were rewritten for the sake of different styles. Nothing stands in the way of supposing that there was only one *Gunnlaugs saga* and that it was written early.

The most likely progression of saga writing in Borgarfjörður appears to me to be first *Gunnlaugs saga*, then *Bjarnar saga Hítdælakappa*, and finally *Egils saga*. The tone of *Gunnlaugs saga*, the premonitory dream, the misdirected marriage, and the lovesickness are all drafts on the heroic elegies of the *Edda*, which were probably being committed to parchment in the same period. The author of *Bjarnar saga Hítdælakappa* borrowed these effects, not without awkwardness, from *Gunnlaugs saga* and cast them as a frame for the rivalry between

---

24. Daniel Sävborg, *Sorg och elegi i Eddans hjältediktning* (Stockholm: Almqvist & Wiksell, 1997).
25. See Bjarni Einarsson, *Skáldasögur* (as in note 8), pp. 267–70.

Bjǫrn Arngeirsson and Þórðr Kolbeinsson. Both sagas are anchored at Borg and both are skald biographies, perhaps elaborations of the skald anecdotes included in the *Oldest Saga of Saint Óláfr*. *Egils saga* stands in the same tradition but greatly expands every aspect by adding a great deal more verse, creating a far fuller biography, and enlarging the historical context.

This little slice of literary history from Borgarfjörður may serve to demystify ever so slightly the miracle of *Egils saga*. If it really was composed as early as the 1220s, it is a prodigy of the first order that such a fully formed and perfected composition could have come into being at the dawn of saga writing.[26] If we consider it as an incomparably more ambitious elaboration of the skald saga form as the author found it in *Gunnlaugs saga* and *Bjarnar saga*, there is at least the semblance of a historical progression, although the mystery of narrative genius can never be satisfactorily dispelled.

Bibliography

Andersson, Theodore M. *The Growth of the Medieval Icelandic Sagas (1180–1280)*. Ithaca: Cornell University Press, 2006.

———. "The Lays of the Lacuna in Codex Regius." *Speculum Norroenum: Studies in Memory of Gabriel Turville-Petre*. Ed. Ursula Dronke et al. Odense: Odense University Press, 1981. Pp. 6–26.

Bjarni Einarsson. *Skáldasögur. Um uppruna og eðli ástaskáldsagnanna fornu*. Reykjavík: Bókaútgáfa Menningarsjóðs, 1961.

Bjarni Guðnason. "Aldur og einkenni Bjarnar sögu Hítdœlakappa." *Sagnaþing helgað Jónasi Kristjánssyni sjötugum 10. apríl 1994*. 2 vols. Reykjavík: Hið íslenska bókmenntafélag, 1994. Vol. 1, pp. 69–85.

Björn Magnússon Ólsen. *Om Gunnlaugs saga ormstungu. En kritisk undersøgelse*. Det Kongelige Danske Videnskabernes Selskabs Skrifter, historisk og filosofisk afdeling. Copenhagen: Høst, 1911. 7. række, vol. II, no. 1.

Clunies Ross, Margaret. "The Skald Sagas as a Genre: Definitions and Typical Features" in *Skaldsagas: Text, Vocation, and Desire in the Icelandic Sagas of Poets*. Ed. Russell Poole. Berlin: de Gruyter, 2001. Pp. 25–49.

Cook, Robert G. "The Character of Gunnlaug Serpent-Tongue." *Scandinavian Studies* 43 (1971): 1–21.

Edda. Die Lieder des Codex Regius nebst verwandten Denkmälern. Ed. Gustav Neckel. Rev. Hans Kuhn. Heidelberg: Winter, 1962.

Finlay, Alison. "Skald Sagas in Their Literary Context 2: Possible European Contexts." In *Skaldsagas: Text, Vocation, and Desire in the Icelandic Sagas of Poets*. Ed. Russell Poole. Berlin: de Gruyter, 2001. Pp. 232–71.

———. "Skalds, Troubadours and Saga." *Saga-Book* 24 (1995), 105–53.

---

26. On this puzzle see Anne Holtsmark, "Det nye syn på sagaene," *Nordisk tidskrift för vetenskap, konst och industri* 35 (1959), p. 521.

Fornmanna sǫgur. 12 vols. Kaupmannahöfn: H.F. Popp, 1825–1837.
Gunnlaugs saga ormstungu. Ed. Finnur Jónsson. Samfund til Udgivelse af Gammel Nordisk Litteratur 42. Copenhagen: S. L. Møller, 1916.
Heusler, Andreas. "Die Lieder der Lücke im Codex Regius der Edda." *Germanistische Abhandlungen, Hermann Paul dargebracht*. Strassburg: Trübner, 1902. Pp. 1–98.
———. *Kleine Schriften*. 2 vols. Ed. Stefan Sonderegger. Berlin: de Gruyter, 1969.
Holtsmark, Anne. "Det nye syn på sagaene." *Nordisk tidskrift för vetenskap, konst och industri* 35 (1959): 511–23.
Jónas Kristjánsson. *Eddas and Sagas: Iceland's Medieval Literature*. Reykjavík: Hið íslenska bókmenntafélag, 1988.
Kramarz-Bein, Susanne. *Die Þiðreks saga im Kontext der altnorwegischen Literatur*. Tübingen and Basel: A. Francke Verlag, 2002.
Mundal, Else. "Foreword" in *Gunnlaugs saga ormstungu*. Oslo, etc.: Universitetsforlaget, 1980.
Das Nibelungenlied. Ed. Helmut de Boor, rev. Roswitha Wisniewski. Wiesbaden: Brockhaus, 1979.
Óláfs saga Tryggvasonar en mesta. Ed. Ólafur Halldórsson. Editiones Arnamagnæanæ, Ser. A, vol. 3. Copenhagen: C.A. Reitzel, 2000.
Poole, Russell. "The Relation between Verses and Prose in *Hallfreðar saga* and *Gunnlaugs saga*." In *Skaldsagas: Text, Vocation, and Desire in the Icelandic Sagas of Poets*. Ed. Russell Poole. Berlin: de Gruyter, 2001. Pp. 125–71.
Rowe, Elizabeth Ashman. *The Development of Flateyjarbók: Iceland and the Norwegian Dynastic Crisis of 1389*. N.p.: University Press of Southern Denmark, 2005.
The Saga of Gunnlaug Snake-Tongue together with the Tale of Scald-Helgi. Trans. Alan Boucher, with an Introduction by Vésteinn Ólason. Reykjavík: Iceland Review, 1983.
The Saga of the Volsungs. Ed. and trans. R. G. Finch. London and Edinburgh: Nelson, 1965.
Sävborg, Daniel. *Sorg och elegi i Eddans hjältediktning*. Stockholm: Almqvist & Wiksell, 1997.
Sigurður Nordal and Guðni Jónsson. *Borgfirðinga sǫgur. Hœnsa-Þóris saga, Gunnlaugs saga ormstungu, Bjarnar saga Hítdœlakappa, Heiðarvíga saga, Gísls þáttr Illugasonar*. Íslenzk fornrit 3. Reykjavík: Hið íslenzka fornritafélag, 1938.
Van Eeden, W. *De overlevering van de Hallfreðar saga*. Verhandelingen der Koninklijke Akademie van Wetenschappen te Amsterdam, afdeeling letterkunde. Amsterdam: Johannes Müller, 1919. Nieuwe reeks, vol. 19, no. 5.
Würth, Stefanie. *Elemente des Erzählens. Die þættir der Flateyjarbók*. Beiträge zur nordischen Philologie 20. Basel and Frankfurt am Main: Helbing & Lichtenhahn, 1991.

Romance, Marriage, and Social Class in the Saga World

JENNY JOCHENS

It is hard to imagine a more romantic scene than the one portrayed in two Icelandic sagas, *Vatnsdœla saga*, and *Hallfreðar saga*, involving Ingólfr and Valgerðr.[1] During a ball game in Northern Iceland one of the players, the young Ingólfr, happens to roll a ball in the direction of Valgerðr, one of the spectators. Coyly hiding the ball under her cloak, she declares that the person who has thrown it shall fetch it. Ingólfr forsakes the game and talks with her for the rest of the day, finding her "remarkably beautiful." Thus starts one of the most famous love affairs in the saga literature. The love was mutual and lasted a lifetime. The story is interesting not only because it is mentioned in two sagas, but also because it has a pendant in the same two sagas involving another couple, Hallfreðr and Kolfinna. Furthermore, Valgerðr and Hallfreðr were siblings. At some point the couples undoubtedly consummated their relationship. Eventually the four were married but not to their first love. Clearly something went wrong in these

---

1. This is a reworked and enlarged version of an article entitled "Extramarital Sex and Social Class in the Saga World" originally written in 1997 for a Festschrift to honor Professor Aaron Gurevich on his 75th birthday. I presented it as a paper at the 1998 meetings of the Society for the Advancement of Scandinavian Study. The Gurevich Festschrift was published in Russian by the Russian Academy of Sciences and appeared in Moscow in the year 2000. This reworking has been done with the permission of one of the editors, Dr. Maria Paramonova. While my essay has been under its Russian wrap Torfi Tulinius has published an essay in which he arrives at some of the same conclusions as in my original essay; see Torfi H.Tulinius, "The Prosimetrum Form 2: Verses as an Influence in Saga Composition and Interpretation," in *Skaldsagas: Text, Vocation, and Desire in the Icelandic Sagas of Poets*, ed. Russell Poole (Berlin: de Gruyter, 2000), pp. 199–205.

romances. The purpose of this article is to illuminate the problems the two couples encountered in their romantic and married lives.

The mutual interest of two young people will invariably raise the specter of extramarital sex for parents or guardian of the young woman. Nonetheless, it is obvious that sexual activities outside marriage were ubiquitous in medieval Iceland according to all literary genres as well as other sources. The phenomenon is particularly obvious in the contemporary sagas, such as *Sturlunga saga*, where most men are depicted as having concubines. The problem even caught the attention of the papacy,[2] but it also appears in the Sagas of Icelanders in the form of occasional mistresses and, more clearly, in the common topos of the illicit love visit.[3] Such visits occurred when an unmarried man took a fancy to a young girl and came to see her regularly with the purpose, not of marriage but of seduction. The family would have allowed marriage at any moment if the suitor would follow proper procedures, but such visits dishonored the family and devalued the woman in future marriage negotiations. Asked to stay away, the man might comply for a while, but eventually his continued attention to the woman would initiate a series of murderous actions that often dominated the rest of the narrative and brought death to the suitor in the end.

Neither violence nor social disapproval, however, presented sufficient deterrents for high-ranking young men in such matters. The two related episodes referred to above, both depicted in *Vatnsdæla saga* and *Hallfreðar saga*, illustrate the different treatment of two young men who engaged in illicit love visits but who belonged to different social classes.[4] Ingólfr and Hallfreðr each visited and seduced a young

---

2. The Icelandic problem was brought to the attention of Innocent 3; see Jenny Jochens, "The Church and sexuality in medieval Iceland," *Journal of Medieval History* 6 (1980), p. 386.

3. See Jenny Jochens, "The Illicit Love Visit: An Archaeology of Old Norse Sexuality," *Journal of the History of Sexuality* 1 (1991), pp. 357–92.

4. *Vatnsdæla saga* will be cited from Einar Ól. Sveinsson, ed. *Vatnsdæla saga*, Íslenzk fornrit 8 (Reykjavík, Hið íslenzka fornritafélag, 1949), pp. 1–131. (*Vtn* followed by page number). *Hallfreðr saga* exists in a shorter version (from *Möðruvallabók*) also published in Íslenzk fornrit 8 (pp. 134–200) and in a longer inserted in sections into *Óláfs saga Tryggvasonar en mesta*; a third version found in *Flateyjarbók* seems to conflate these two. Since the differences in the manuscripts are important, *Hallfreðar saga* will be cited from Bjarni Einarsson, ed. *Hallfreðar saga* (Reykjavík: Stofnun Árna Magnússonar, 1977) that includes all versions, indicating manuscript (*M*, 61 and 62 (for *Óláfs saga*) and *F* respectively) and page number.

woman, Valgerðr and Kolfinna respectively. Both cases produced violence, but Ingólfr, the son of a chieftain, got away with this behavior throughout his life, whereas Hallfreðr, the son of a farmer, was forced to leave the country. The stories are particularly interesting because Hallfreðr and Valgerðr were siblings. Their father Óttarr therefore faced the double problem of successfully curtailing the sexual aggression of his own son while at the same time suffering humiliation from not being able to prevent the continued visits to his daughter from another young man. Eventually, Óttarr was forced to leave the region thus removing his daughter.

The action takes place in Vatnsdalur in Northern Iceland in the late tenth century. The chieftain in the area was Þorsteinn at Hof. He had two sons, Ingólfr and Guðbrandr, of whom the older became chieftain in due course. Further to the south, at Grímstungur, lived Óttarr. Born in Norway, he had sailed to Iceland with his foster brother Ávaldi in their own ship after successful Viking expeditions to England and Orkney. Óttarr obtained land in exchange for the ship and Ávaldi stayed with him the first winter, supposedly working for him. The following spring Ávaldi bought land at Knjúkur further north in the valley beyond Hof and near the lake Þórdísarlækur. He married a certain Hildr and the couple had a daughter, Kolfinna, and a son, Brandr.[5] Meanwhile Óttarr had become acquainted with his neighbor Óláfr at Haukagil north of Grímstungur. Óláfr was rich, and when Óttarr married his daughter Ásdís she brought a large dowry. The couple had three children, the sons Hallfreðr and Galti and the daughter Valgerðr.[6] Hallfreðr, who became a famous poet, was fostered by his grandfather Óláfr.[7] The children at Grímstungur and Knjúkur were about the same age, with the boys at Hof probably a little older.

---

5. He is called Hermundr in *Vtn* p. 123.
6. The boys were named after Óttarr's maternal relatives.
7. Marianne Kalinke provides a Freudian interpretation of *Hallfreðar saga*, arguing that the hostility between Hallfreðr and his father explains the young man's attachment to King Óláfr; see Marianne Kalinke, "*Stæri ek brag*: Protest and Subordination in *Hallfreðar saga*," *Skáldskaparmál* 4 (1997), pp. 50–68. She probably overemphasizes the hostility. Fostering was a common phenomenon in the North; Óttarr himself had been sent out for fostering as a child. Hallfreðr stayed with his grandfather until he left for Norway. In turn he sent his own two sons out to be fostered. His departure for Norway does not entail a complete break with his father and grandfather, as Kalinke suggests. Regarding his yearly returns to Iceland all manuscripts state that he landed in the south, an area to where his father has been forced to move with the purpose of preventing Ingólfr from visiting Valgerðr,

At the age of twenty, Hallfreðr fell in love with Kolfinna Ávaldadóttir. Her father was not pleased. He declared that he would not tolerate that Hallfreðr seduced his daughter (61, 62:18), although he was willing to let him marry her, but Hallfreðr was not interested. When Hallfreðr's father Óttarr was faced with Ingólfr's visit to his daughter Valgerðr, he also took the step of offering her in marriage. When Ingólfr refused, Óttarr complained to the young man's father. It may seem strange that in this case Ávaldi did not appeal to Óttarr, Hallfreðr's father,[8] especially since the two older men had been foster brothers.[9] They had grown up together in Norway and had spent their youths on Viking expeditions. From childhood and throughout their youths, however, a clear social distinction can be perceived between them. It is, of course, not surprising that Galti, Óttarr's uncle, states that he considers his nephew the leader of the two, but throughout their youths Ávaldi always deferred to Óttarr. The start capital for their Viking expeditions was acquired when Galti sold "their lands." Supposedly, they also had equal share in the ship that brought them to Iceland. Nonetheless, only Óttarr obtained land in return for the ship, whereas Ávaldi had to work for a year for Óttarr before he was able to settle. While not as pronounced as between Valgerðr and Ingólfr, the social difference between them is still noticeable. Once settled in Iceland, they seem to have avoided each other. Furthermore, it appears that the social difference between the fathers was transferred to their children. Ávaldi may have understood the lesson at an early stage that Óttarr learned only with difficulty, that it was impossible to stop a higher-ranking male from intruding on the sexual integrity of a woman from a lower class.[10]

---

as mentioned. One text (61:37) specifically mentions that he stayed with his father. The purpose of the statement is to make clear that he didn't see Kolfinna. On the importance of Christianity in this text, see also John Lindow, "Akkerisfrakki. Traditions Concerning Óláfr Tryggvason and Hallfreðr Óttarsson vandræðaskáld and the Problem of Conversion," in *Sagas and the Norwegian Experience: 10th International Saga Conference, Trondheim, 3.-9. August 1997* (Trondheim: NTNU, 1997), pp. 409–18.

8. Despite Kalinke, "Stæri ek brag," p. 55.
9. The difference in status between Óttarr's and Ávaldi's families in Norway is indicated by the fact that Óttarr was fostered by Ávaldi's father. When their fathers were killed, the boys sought refuge with Galti, Óttarr's maternal uncle, who undoubtedly had more resources.
10. Bjarni Einarsson, *To skjaldesagaer: En analyse af Kormáks saga og Hallfreðar saga* (Oslo: Universitetsforlaget, 1976), p. 136, thinks that Ingólfr behaved in a manner normal

Instead of going to Óttarr then, Ávaldi explained his predicament to his friend Már who lived on the other side of the lake. This was a good choice since Már was the cousin of Þorsteinn, Ingólfr's father and thus related to the mighty Vatnsdœlir clan.[11] Only a suitor willing to marry Kolfinna immediately could erase the damage done to her and the family. Normally, however, a father was supposed to wait for a suitor to arrive and could not actively promote his daughter on the marriage market.[12] Már understood this and immediately proposed his friend Gríss Sæmingsson who lived at Geitaskarð in Langadalur, the next valley to the east. He recommended Gríss by saying that he was wealthy, well liked, and had traveled widely, serving the Byzantine emperor with honor. Ávaldi accepted Gríss' candidature and returned home. Már sent a message to Gríss, asking him to come.

When Gríss arrives Már proposes the marriage to Kolfinna, explaining that she is a good party, that there is no lack of money in the family, but adds that he has heard that Hallfreðr Óttarsson often comes to talk with her (M: 25).[13] Assembling a party of seven, Gríss and Már set out immediately to make the formal proposal to Ávaldi. Gríss' assets and liabilities become apparent immediately: he is carrying a gold-inlaid spear symbolic of his wealth, but he demonstrates poor eyesight, suggesting he is no longer young. Már presents the case and Ávaldi receives it well, replying that Már shall decide.[14] As the formal engagement is being concluded, Hallfreðr arrives and understands immediately what is happening. Kolfinna tells him curtly to let those decide on her engagement who have the right to do so. She nonetheless

---

for the son of a chieftain toward the daughter of a farmer, whereas he does not see a social distinction in Hallfreðr's case.

11. Már had been against Þorsteinn and his brothers in the so-called Hjallaland dispute (*Vtn* pp. 75–81), but Þorsteinn had settled the issue to everybody's satisfaction, and in the last problems Þorsteinn encountered before his death Már was firmly on his side (*Vtn* pp. 92, 95). In other words, by relying on help from his neighbor Már, Ávaldi, the lowest male on the social scale in this story, perhaps unwittingly, bypassed the middle layer, represented by his former foster brother Óttarr, and was able to rely on help from the highest layer in society, the class of chieftains. Már became a faithful supporter of Ávaldi and his family during the length of the dispute. Twenty-five years later it is still Már who encounters Hallfreðr with twenty men to take revenge on behalf of Gríss (*Hallfreðar saga* p.. 93).

12. See Jenny Jochens, *Women in Old Norse Society* (Ithaca, NY: Cornell University Press, 1995), pp. 24–9.

13. 61:19 adds that she is beautiful, stated earlier in *M*: 16.

14. 61:20 suggests a slight hint of female consent by letting Ávaldi express the hope that his daughter will agree with him.

lets Hallfreðr place her on his lap outside the house. The couple is thus visible when the engagement party leaves, at which moment Hallfreðr "pulled her toward him and it came to a few kisses" (M: 27). Poor eyesight forces Gríss to ask who this intimate couple might be. When Ávaldi identifies them as Hallfreðr and his daughter Kolfinna, Gríss asks if they often behave in this manner. Ávaldi confirms it but adds that it now is Gríss's problem since Kolfinna is his fiancée. Before leaving, Hallfreðr assures Gríss that he will become his enemy if he goes ahead with the marriage. When Már responds that Ávaldi has the right to marry his daughter to whom he wants, Hallfreðr delivers two stanzas and leaves angry, returning to Haukagil, his grandfather's residence.

Gríss, Már, and their party (that did not include Ávaldi) pursued Hallfreðr and his companion who were overpowered and tied down.[15] Gríss's victory was short-lived, however, because Óláfr, Hallfreðr's grandfather, had summoned help from Óttarr, his son, and Hallfreðr's father. The two men encountered Gríss with a large force. Informing Óttarr that his son was "tied down but not killed,"[16] Gríss granted the father sole judgment in the case. When Óttarr had released Hallfreðr from his restraints the son implored him not to allow Gríss to marry Kolfinna. Óttarr responded that Gríss should indeed have the woman[17] and he, Hallfreðr, go abroad. Hallfreðr received the offer with a threat to challenge his rival to a duel.

Óttarr returned home and Hallfreðr finally reached his grandfather's house. Óláfr sensed that Hallfreðr would not keep the agreement and sent a message to his son-in-law, warning him that trouble might be ahead. He may even have advised that the marriage agreement between Gríss and Kolfinna be broken.[18] Perhaps inspired by Gríss' unique remedy of temporarily incapacitating Hallfreðr by binding him, Óttarr responded with a remarkable ruse. He sent a message to Hallfreðr that he was gravely ill and asked him to come immediately. It was merely a subterfuge, however, because when Hallfreðr arrived,

---

15. *F: XXXII* adds the detail that the peaceful Gríss suggests they throw clothes on the two men's weapons.
16. *F: XXXIII* adds that the latter "would have been more deserved."
17. *F: 34* adds that Kolfinna shall be engaged for three years. This is a common feature but it does not fit this case since it would imply that she would be waiting for Hallfreðr.
18. See *Hallfreðar saga*, pp. 27 and 34.

Óttarr placed him in chains and offered him the choice of remaining there or letting him, Óttarr, decide. Reluctantly, Hallfreðr opted for the latter. Accepting money from his grandfather but refusing a share of Óttarr's settlement with Gríss, he went abroad, while Már celebrated Gríss's and Kolfinna's marriage.

Trying to avoid the violence, which invariably resulted from young men's unbridled sexual aggression, Óttarr's behavior was exemplary. When his son had been flirting in an unseemly manner with a young neighborhood girl without being willing to marry her he sent him abroad, thus cutting short the relationship, and he supported the marriage arranged for the dishonored girl. No wonder that Óttarr expected the same behavior from the father of a young man who at the same time was bothering his own daughter. But, before I turn to the story of Valgerðr and Ingólfr, I shall follow the sequel to the relationship within the triangle composed of Kolfinna, Gríss, and Hallfreðr.

In Norway, Hallfreðr became acquainted with Earl Eiríkr and later formed a close personal relationship with King Óláfr Tryggvason, who persuaded him to become a Christian. He returned to Iceland several times, landing in the south where his father was now living. One text states specifically that he stayed with him for the winter, but all three manuscripts stress that he never came to the north to make it clear that he did not see Kolfinna.[19]

A quarter of century later, however—after marriage, children, and widowhood in Sweden—Hallfreðr did land in northern Iceland. He headed straight for the summer pastures and shieling belonging to Gríss where he assumed Kolfinna would be without her husband.[20] Despite Kolfinna's obvious reluctance to receive him, he spent the night with her in the hut and recited insulting poetry about Gríss that he attributed to her.[21] During the night the shepherd had summoned Gríss from the main farm. Arriving a short time after Hallfreðr's departure, Gríss found his wife depressed *(skapþúng,* p. 91), a condition clearly not

---

[19]. See *Hallfreðar saga*, p. 37.

[20]. 61:83 indicates that Hallfreðr's return took place during the Spring after King Óláfr had sent Leifr Eiríksson to Greenland and 61:94 places it in connection with the battle at Svǫldr.

[21]. For further analysis of this scene, see Jenny Jochens, "Representations of Skalds in the Sagas 2: Gender Relations," in *Skaldsagas: Text, Vocation, and Desire in the Icelandic Sagas of Poets*, ed. R. Poole (Berlin: de Gruyter, 2001), pp. 309–32.

the result of Hallfreðr leaving, but of the forced intercourse. As often happened in times of stress to men not otherwise known as poets, Gríss composed a stanza in which he expressed outrage and described the sad looks of his wife (91: st. 25).

Accompanied by his relative Einarr Þórisson,[22] Gríss set out after Hallfreðr and caught up with him as he was crossing the river. Gríss threw a spear against Hallfreðr who caught it in mid-air and returned it, killing Einarr. Gríss did not pursue Hallfreðr who spent the winter at Óttarsstaðir, the parental farm managed since Óttarr's death by the younger son Galti. During this time, Hallfreðr composed insulting verses about Gríss.[23] At this point Hallfreðr had thus committed three crimes against Gríss: the rape of his wife Kolfinna, the killing of his kinsman Einarr, and the insulting verses. The poetic insult finally spurred Gríss into action. With Einarr killed, he could still count on his friend Már and his brother-in-law Brandr, Kolfinna's brother. Additionally he now sought support and advice from Húnrøðr whose *þingmaðr* he was. Húnrøðr lived at Móberg in Langadalur to the south of Gríss's own farm. On Hallfreðrss side was his brother Galti and he requested support from his relative Þorkell krafla, the current chieftain of the district. Married to a sister of Hallfreðr's mother, Þorkell was the son of a cousin of Ingólfr whom he had replaced at Hof. Þorkell was willing to arbitrate if Hallfreðr would offer concession to Gríss. Admitting that he had gone too far in his dealings with Gríss, Hallfreðr agreed. According to the text in *Möðruvallabók*, Húnrøðr urged Gríss to prosecute but did not specify the charges; on his own Gríss selected only one, the killing of Einarr (96). In the two other versions (61 and F) Húnrøðr recommended prosecution of the killing and of the verses, but he suggested that the Kolfinna case be kept quiet, because, as he said, "it is more ugly" (F, 61: 96), indicating the common disapproval of Hallfreðr's behavior.

During the negotiations at the *þing*, Brandr, Gríss's brother-in-law, killed Galti, Hallfreðr's brother. Hallfreðr and Þorkell demanded that Gríss deliver the murderer, but thanks to a ruse of Þorkell—by which he paid back an old debt to Brandr's mother—the young man escaped

---

22. 61:91 makes him Gríss' *systrungr*, but he is not known elsewhere.
23. 61:95 and F: 93 identify these verses as *hálfníð*. Kari Ellen Gade is undoubtedly correct when in an unpublished lecture she suggested that these stanzas are the ones Hallfreðr recited to Kolfinna in bed.

in female disguise.[24] Hallfreðr was furious and challenged Gríss to a duel. The denouement to this tense situation came through the indirect intervention of King Óláfr, recently deceased. Appearing in a dream to Hallfreðr, he encouraged him to abandon the duel and accept settlement, because Gríss "has prayed to God for victory for the one who has the better case" (*M*: 99). Hallfreðr accepted the advice unmindful of his companions' teasing that he now was afraid of "the hog" (a play on Gríss's name). Þorkell settled the case in such a way that the killings of Einarr and Galti compensated each other in view of the fact that the difference between the two dead men (social difference combined with their degree of kinship to the protagonists) was considered to make up for the *heimsókn* of Kolfinna. Normally used about theft and attack, the word *heimsókn* suggests the seriousness with which Hallfreðr's visit was considered. To pay for the insulting poetry, Hallfreðr must give Gríss a treasure of Hallfreðr's own choosing (to avoid parting with gifts from the king requested earlier by Gríss). Reluctantly, Hallfreðr complied. Deeply affected by the news of the king's death, Hallfreðr decided to return to Norway and placed his sister Valgerðr in charge of Óttarsstaðir.[25]

This decision provides a good transition to examine Valgerðr's life. At the time when Hallfreðr began his flirtation with Kolfinna, Valgerðr became acquainted with Ingólfr, oldest son of the chieftain at Hof and known as the best looking man in the north.[26] The relationship started during a ball game arranged at Grímstungur, Óttarr's farm. The men played and the women watched. Ingólfr threw the ball in Valgerðr's direction and she hid it under her cloak, saying that the person who had thrown it should fetch it.[27] Ingólfr forsook the game and talked with her for the rest of the day, finding her, as we saw, "remarkably beautiful" *(Vtn*: 99).[28]

---

24. A fuller version of this part of the story is found in *Vtn* pp. 115–24.

25. Daniel Sävborg provides an interesting comparison between the love theme in *Hallfreðar saga* and *Kormáks saga*; see his *Saga om kärleken: Erotik, känslor och berättarkonst i norrön litteratur*, Acta Universitatis Upsaliensis, Historia Litterarum 27 (Uppsala: Uppsala Universitet, 2007), pp. 396–439.

26. Both sagas include a stanza that describes the infatuation of women, from the youngest to the oldest, with the handsome man. He was undoubtedly known as a womanizer, and he was humorously aware of his good looks. Near death he asked to be buried, not in the mound used by his kinsmen but closer to the road to enable the girls from the Vatnsdalur region to remember him better (*Vtn* p. 109).

27. This is a rare occasion of a woman taking the initiative to a sexual relationship.

28. The two fullest accounts are in *Vtn* and in the *M* version of *Hallfreðar saga*. (The

Ingólfr's regular visits to Valgerðr from then on displeased Óttarr. Speaking to the young man and asking him to refrain, he added that he would not tolerate his provocations, but would rather give him his daughter to marry with honor than see her seduced with shame. Ingólfr answered that he intended to come and go as he pleased and that no dishonor accrued to Óttarr *(Vtn:* 99). With a direct reference to his father's prominent position he made it clear (in *M:* 21 and 61:31), that considering the situation in the valley he was not going to take orders from anyone.[29] Thus rebuffed by Ingólfr, Óttarr went to his father Þorsteinn and asked him to rein in his son because he, Óttarr, considered Þorsteinn "a wise man with good intentions" (*M:* 23). Þorsteinn assured Óttarr that Ingólfr was acting against his will but he promised to speak with him. Upbraiding his son in a speech reminiscent of one his own grandfather, also named Þorsteinn, had received from his father Ketill back in Norway,[30] Þorsteinn made Ingólfr stop his visit for a while. Unfortunately, his feelings for Valgerðr were so strong and his frustration over their separation so intense that, although not known as a poet before, he composed and recited a love poem in the forbidden genre of *mansöngsvísur,* thereby merely increasing Óttarr's anger.

Óttarr again went to Þorsteinn and asked permission to prosecute his son at the *þing.* According to the main version of the story in *Hallfreðar saga,* the father would not prohibit it, but, knowing the temperament of his relatives—a reference to his brother Jökull who was present—neither could he recommend it (*M:* 23). Instead, having obtained Óttarr's permission, Þorsteinn settled the case himself. With the case fresh in his mind concerning his own son, Óttarr was undoubtedly not prepared for Þorsteinn's decision. Like Þorsteinn at this moment, Óttarr earlier had asked Gríss for permission to settle his case against Hallfreðr. He acted admirably, as we saw, giving Gríss complete satisfaction by sending his own son abroad and guaranteeing Gríss's engagement to Kolfinna. In contrast, Þorsteinn offered only a minor concession to Óttarr, granting him the fine of half a hundred of silver, but ordering him to sell his land and leave the district.

F version is almost identical to the latter). Shorter versions are found in 62:20–21 and 61:30–35.

29. The clan's prestige, in particular in marriage alliances, is stated most clearly in connection with the marriage of Þorsteinn, Ingólfr's father (*Vtn* pp. 71–2).

30. Cf. *M:* 22 and *Vtn* 99 with *Vtn* pp. 4–5.

In *Vatnsdœla saga*, the high-handedness of the chieftain and his family is even more pronounced. When Óttarr complained about Ingólfr's verse-making, Þorsteinn excused himself by saying that he had spoken to his son but without effect. Óttarr retorted that Þorsteinn should either pay fines for his son or allow Óttarr to prosecute him. When Þorsteinn offered no objections, Óttarr initiated a court case. Jökull, however, became furious at the possibility that Þorsteinn and his family might be outlawed from their own lands. Claiming that his brother was getting old, he was ready to settle the case with violence since he was not well trained in law. During the winter, Ingólfr asked his father for advice about the proceedings in the upcoming case at the Húnavatnsþing, warning him that otherwise he would sink an ax in Óttarr's head. Apparently sensing his growing weakness, Þorsteinn asked Ingólfr to assume the position as chieftain from now on. When Óttarr presented his case at the court, Ingólfr and his uncle broke up the proceedings and prevented the case from being heard. Later Óttarr told Óláfr, his father-in-law, that he would not remain in the area but planned to sell his land and move away. He bought land in Norðrárdalur in the Borgarfjörður region, calling his new place Óttarsstaðir.

In other words, Óttarr who had forced his son to leave the country to prevent him from causing sexual harassment to a neighboring family was himself forced to leave the region, in which he had spent his adult life, in order to remove his daughter and thereby prevent another young man from provoking similar trouble. Whether Þorsteinn ordered Óttarr to leave or whether the latter left of his own free will because Ingólfr's behavior prevented him from a hearing at court, both fathers may have assumed that although they had not been able to stop Ingólfr's visits to Grímstungur, the removal of Valgerðr to the more distant Óttarsstaðir might eliminate the problem. In this hope, however, they were profoundly disappointed. We recall that the epilogue to the Kolfinna-Hallfreðr story did not occur for several decades, but no break intervened in the Valgerðr-Ingólfr romance. When Þorsteinn died a short time later, Ingólfr married, but this didn't prevent him from continuing his relationship with Valgerðr.[31] Although she was no longer

---

31. Like Óttarr, Ingólfr married a daughter of Óláfr at Haukagil. The author of *Vtn* specifies that she was younger than her sister, the mother of Valgerðr (38:100). A third daughter married Þorkell krafla from the following generation (61:95).

nearby, her new domicile was conveniently located on Ingólfr's route to and from the *þing* meetings. Óttarr's displeasure was undoubtedly augmented by Valgerðr's complicity: she made fashionable clothing for her lover. In the semiotics of saga narrative the sewing of shirts or other clothing was a sure sign of love.

Deciding on revenge for both Ingólfr's behavior toward his daughter and his own humiliation at the Húnavatnsþing, Óttarr took two actions.[32] In the first, he sent a certain Þórir to the north with the mission of killing either Ingólfr or his brother Guðbrandr. Þórir did not succeed but was himself killed. Perfectly aware of the instigator behind this attack, the brothers headed straight for Óttarsstaðir. Since Óttarr had secured reinforcements, the brothers were forced to a settlement whereby Óttarr agreed to a fine of a hundred silver for his scheme but nothing was paid for Þórir. Furthermore, Óttarr managed to insert into the agreement the condition that Ingólfr could be slain unprotected by the law if he came to visit Valgerðr again without being in the company of Guðbrandr. Since the relationship clearly had been continuing, Óttarr did not expect it to cease. He merely tried to cloak it with respectability by making Ingólfr's brother his chaperone. That he expected, and perhaps hoped, that Ingólfr would not obey this rule is indicated by the proviso that would allow him to kill Ingólfr with impunity. At the end of the meeting, Ingólfr warned Óttarr against sending further hostile expeditions his way, assuring him that the next time he would not escape with a fine.

Óttarr nonetheless tried again. The second time, he hired a certain Svartr to cut off Ingólfr's hand or foot or kill Guðbrandr. He succeeded in the latter but died in the process. Despite his previous threat to Óttarr, Ingólfr was forced to accept a compromise worked out by friends of the two men, because he had not kept his agreement with Óttarr concerning Valgerðr. Óttarr paid three hundred pieces of silver for the killing of Guðbrandr. In return Ingólfr obtained acknowledgment that his breach of the agreement over Valgerðr would be disregarded. In other words, Ingólfr continued his visits and Guðbrandr's death now eliminated the chaperone.

Ingólfr did eventually die, but his death was not caused by Óttarr

---

32. This part of the story is found only in *Vtn*, see pp. 39–40:101–9.

but by thieves ranging throughout the country.[33] Wounded in battle against them, Ingólfr died of his wounds the following summer. It is easy to imagine Óttarr's glee and Valgerðr's grief at the news. With Ingólfr out of the way, Óttarr was able to arrange Valgerðr's marriage to a local man from Stafaholt nearby.[34] By then she was probably in her early forties and she may not have had children. She was therefore free to obey Hallfreðr's summons fifteen years later to take care of Óttarsstaðir, the parental farm, while he returned to Norway. After Hallfreðr's death, his son by the same name lived at Óttarstaðir with his family, and we may assume that Valgerðr returned to Stafaholt.

As in other stories involving the topos of the illicit love visit, the two interrelated romances of Hallfreðr's and Ingólfr's involvement with Kolfinna and Valgerðr produced violence both initially and over time. A clear distinction involving social class, however, is perceptible in the two cases.[35] Ingólfr, a young man from the class of chieftains, was able to establish a relationship with Valgerðr despite both hers and his own father's opposition. Even after she moved away and he married another woman, he kept up the relationship until his death. In contrast, when Hallfreðr, a man from the class of free farmers, sought to establish a similar relationship with Kolfinna, a woman only slightly below his own rank, the opposition of their fathers effectively barred him and he was sent abroad. Although he did not forget Kolfinna, his brief relationship with her years later was pursued less out of love for her than of spite for her husband.

Turning to the two women, there seems to be no doubt about Valgerðr's initial attraction to the handsome Ingólfr; furthermore, as

---

33. One of the targets was Óláfr at Haukagil. As long as Óttarr had lived at Gríms-tungur Óláfr had been closely allied with this son-in-law, as we have seen. When Óttarr was forced to move to the south, it became more convenient for Óláfr, now getting on in years, to rely on Ingólfr, another son-in-law who lived close by at Hof. Appealing to him for help against the thieves, Óláfr admonished him to be careful, assuring him that his safe return was more important than to discover the whereabouts of the stolen goods.

34. This information is found only in *Vtn* (p. 109).

35. I have stressed the importance of social class in this analysis. Naturally the role of personality and character is also important. It is worth noticing, however, that the ideal social behavoir was that of moderation, *hóf*, which entailed a certain amount of aggression, but not too much. This characteristic is found primarily among successful chieftains thus adding to the social distinction. On this isssue see Jesse Byock, *Viking Age Iceland* (London: Penguin, 2001), chs. 10 and 12.

time went by she seemed to develop a genuine love for him, marrying another man only after Ingólfr's death. The feelings of Kolfinna for Hallfreðr are more difficult to interpret. The only sign she might have loved him is the authorial comment that there was no great love between her and Gríss at the beginning of their marriage. Later, however, during Hallfreðr's unexpected visit she professed that she and her husband got along well, as was expected in any marriage, and that she was not happy to see her old suitor. It is worth noticing the reproductive careers of the four protagonists. It may be no coincidence that although Ingólfr and Hallfreðr each fathered two sons with their legal wives, children are not reported for Valgerðr and for Kolfinna. This may reflect authorial attitudes toward the topos of illicit love visit, or, if biographically correct, that Kolfinna's husband was old and Valgerðr was married relatively late, undoubtedly also to an older man; for both couples conception may have been excluded. These two stories suggest that illicit love visits generally led to violence and only occasionally provided romantic and sexual satisfaction, primarily for men, while preventing women from their reproductive function.

Bibliography

Bjarni Einarsson. *To skjaldesagaer: En analyse af Kormáks saga og Hallfreðar saga*. Oslo: Universitetsforlaget, 1976.
Byock, Jesse. *Viking Age Iceland*. London: Penguin, 2001.
Hallfreðar saga. Ed. Bjarni Einarsson. Reykjavík: Stofnun Árna Magnússonar, 1977.
Jochens, Jenny. "The Church and Sexuality in Medieval Iceland." *Journal of Medieval History* 6 (1980): 377–92.
———. "The Illicit Love Visit: An Archaeology of Old Norse Sexuality." *Journal of the History of Sexuality* 1 (1991): 357–92.
———. *Women in Old Norse Society*. Ithaca, NY: Cornell University Press, 1995.
———. "Extramarital Sex and Social Class in the Saga World." The 88th Annual Meeting of the Society for the Advancement of Scandinavian Study. Tempe, Arizona, 1998.
———. "Representations of Skalds in the Sagas 2: Gender Relations." In *Skaldsagas: Text, Vocation, and Desire in the Icelandic Sagas of Poets*. Ed. Russell Poole. Berlin: de Gruyter, 2001. Pp. 309–32.
Kalinke, Marianne. "*Stæri ek brag*: Protest and Subordination in *Hallfreðar saga*." *Skáldskaparmál* 4 (1997): 50–68.
Lindow, John. "*Akkerisfrakki*. Traditions Concerning Óláfr Tryggvason and Hallfreðr Óttarsson vandræðaskáld and the Problem of Conversion." In *Sagas and the Norwegian Experience. 10th International Saga Conference, Trondheim, 3.–9. August 1997*. Trondheim: NTNU, 1997. Pp. 409–18.

Sävborg, Daniel. *Saga om kärleken: Erotik, känslor och berätterkonst i norrön litteratur.* Acta Universitatis Upsaliensis. Historia Litterarum 27. Uppsala: Uppsala Universitet, 2007.

Tulinius, Torfi H. "The Prosimetrum Form 2: Verses as an Influence in Saga Composition and Interpretation." In *Skaldsagas: Text, Vocation, and Desire in the Icelandic Sagas of Poets.* Ed. Russell Poole. Berlin: de Gruyter, 2000. Pp. 191–217.

Vatnsdœla saga. Ed. Einar Ól. Sveinsson. Íslenzk fornrit 8. Reykjavík, Hið íslenzka fornritafélag, 1949. 1–131.

The Anomalous Pursuit of Love in *Kormaks saga*

MARGRÉT EGGERTSDÓTTIR

Kormaks saga[1] belongs to a subdivision of the Sagas of Icelanders called skald sagas, all of which deal in some way with romantic matters.[2] *Kormaks saga*, which is thought to have been written around 1200, is one of the oldest Sagas of Icelanders, but differs from them in a number of ways. The narrative is not centered on one dramatic event; there is, in fact, no climax. No important character is killed, and no one exacts a heavy duty of revenge. Honor and prestige are key concepts in the Sagas of Icelanders and the society in which they were created, but the protagonist of *Kormaks saga*, the skald Kormakr, behaves in a way that runs counter to ideals of honor. Moreover, sorcery and supernatural powers have a considerable influence on the course of events in *Kormaks saga*, and women very often play a key role in this connection. The saga's main plot concerns the love affair between Kormakr and Steingerðr, and the clarity with which the saga depicts the position of women in society and their point of view

---

1. Einar Ól. Sveinsson has argued that Kormakur is the authentic version of the protagonist's name, and in accordance with this view the saga is here called *Kormaks saga*, not *Kormáks saga* (see Einar Ól. Sveinsson, "Kormakur skáld og vísur hans," *Skírnir* 1966, p. 164).

2. When I wrote this article, I had not yet seen Daniel Sävborg's *Sagan om kärleken. Erotik, känslor och berättarkonst i norrön litteratur*, which appeared in 2007. I wish to express my gratitude to Sävborg for his comments and the interesting discussion we have had on the subject. I also owe several colleagues thanks for reading the article and giving useful comments. Many years ago, I attended a course at the University of Iceland on the Icelandic family sagas, where I chose *Kormaks saga* as a project. I am grateful to my teachers, Vésteinn Ólason and Jónas Kristjánsson, for their guidance.

is unusual. *Kormaks saga* is in almost every respect an anomaly. In this paper, I consider the saga's presentation of honor, love, women's views, and society's attitude toward those men who let their feelings control their actions and do not concern themselves with ideals of honor and prestige. I also attempt to determine if the saga is intended as a tragedy or a comedy.

Kormaks saga

Kormaks saga, which is rather short, may be divided into five parts. A brief introduction describes Kormakr's grandfather and namesake in Norway, and how it happened that Kormakr's father went to Iceland and settled there. It is not specified where in Norway Kormakr's grandfather lived, only that he was "powerful and of prominent family."[3] Kormakr and his brother are then introduced, and Kormakr is described. The introduction concludes in the third chapter, when Steingerðr appears on the scene. The plot commences when she and Kormakr fall in love, at which time their problems begin. It is the events and activities of this section that have the most influence on the saga's course of events (in short that Kormakr asks for Steingerðr's hand, but when the wedding is to be held, he does not attend). The third part begins when Bersi is introduced and then becomes both Steingerðr's husband and Kormakr's adversary. The disputes and quarrels between Bersi and Kormakr are described, but little by little the saga's focus shifts almost exclusively to Bersi. The fourth part of the saga begins when Steingerðr leaves Bersi and is married to Þorvaldur Tinteinn, who becomes the greatest thorn in Kormakr's side. Many different conflicts occur between Kormakr and Þorvaldr, and especially between Kormakr and Þorvaldr's supporters, his brothers and friends. In the fifth part of the saga, Steingerðr, Kormakr, and Þorvaldr Tinteinn continue to form the classic love triangle, but the saga's stage is expanded beyond the borders of Iceland, mainly to Norway. The saga concludes overseas, with the death of Kormakr in Scotland.

---

3. "Kormáks Saga" in *Sagas of Warrior-Poets*, ed. Örnólfur Thorsson and Bernard Scudder, trans. Rory McTurk with introduction and notes by Diana Whaley (London: Penguin, 2002), p. 5. Here and in the following, references are to this translation.

Dating the saga

Kormaks saga, once considered among the youngest Sagas of Icelanders, is now thought to be among the oldest. The primary evidence for its dating is found in the saga itself, since no other sources mention it.[4] Most scholars of the nineteenth century considered the saga "post-classical," that is, written after the peak period of Icelandic saga-writing. They based their dating on the fact that the saga's many verses overshadow the prose narrative, that it is replete with references to magic, and that its beginning differs from what is found in typical Sagas of Icelanders. The conclusions of these scholars were shaped to a great extent by their shared opinion that the oldest sagas were the best ones, as well as by their rationalism and antipathy toward "superstition." Björn M. Ólsen later argued in support of an older date for the saga but drew different conclusions from the evidence given by earlier scholars for the saga's young age, and believing that the roots of Icelandic saga-writing could be traced to an earlier period:

> ... sem má kalla kveðskaparöldina, þegar alt var lagt á minnið og kvæði skáldanna voru hinn besti stuðningur til að muna sagnirnar. Firsta sporið í þá átt að skrifa samanhangandi sögur mun hafa verið fólgið í því, að söguritarinn safnaði í eitt vísum um viðburðina og tengdi þær saman með frásögnum í sundurlausu máli, sem vísunum filgdu.[5]

(... that may be called the age of poetry, when everything was dedicated to memory and the skalds' poems were the best means for keeping the sagas fresh in memory. The first step toward writing comprehensive sagas would have involved the saga-writer's gathering together of verses about events and connecting them with snatches of narrative that accompanied the verses.)

---

4. The saga is preserved in *Möðruvallabók* (AM 132 fol.) from the middle of the fourteenth century. A very short fragment of the saga is found in AM 162 f fol. from the late fourteenth century.

5. Björn M. Ólsen, "Um Íslendingasögur. Kaflar úr háskólafyrirlestrum," in *Safn til sögu Íslands og íslenzkra bókmennta að fornu og nýju* 6.3 (1937–1939), p. 226.

In Ólsen's view, the large number of verses, the anecdotes involving magic spells, sorcery, and supernatural phenomena, and odd words that appear in it and almost nowhere else, testified to an earlier dating. He claimed that he could find nothing in the saga's diction indicative of it being young and placed it at the end of the twelfth century, ca. 1180.

In his preface to the edition of the saga in the *Íslenzk fornrit* series, Einar Ól. Sveinsson shared Ólsen's view, claiming that the saga writer had been "samvizkusamur, en ekki fimur að skrifa, lítill fræðimaður og ekki rýninn."[6] He admitted that this in itself gives no indication of the saga's age, but agreed that it was old. Although Bjarni Einarsson had different ideas about the origin and creation of *Kormaks saga*, he was in agreement with Björn M. Ólsen and Einar Ól. Sveinsson about its age.

The verses and their relationship to the saga's prose narrative

Kormaks saga preserves more verses than any of the other Sagas of Icelanders. Of its 85 total verses, 65 are attributed to Kormakr, and approximately half of the ones recited by him are love poems. Most are concerned exclusively with love, passionate feelings, and amorous glances, although the first verse in the saga has a more melancholy tone; here love is blended with pain, and sorrow and mourning are the result of deep, uncontrollable love. Some of the verses are poems in praise of women, in which feminine charm is admired in an almost fanatical way. The other verses recited by Kormakr are unlike the love poems in both content and style. They are comprised of rebukes, threats, and insults on the one hand, and on the other descriptions of battles, swords, and the like. Some of the poems in the saga are occasional verses tied to specific events; they include verses about Þórdís the prophetess, her witchcraft, and her sacrifice of geese. The second half of the saga contains several verses, in which Kormakr describes a battle and laments the woman he still loves. These verses, which express hopelessness, are different in tone from the first love poems and characterized by strong, passionate feeling.

---

6. Einar Ól. Sveinsson, ed., *Vatnsdæla saga*, Íslenzk fornrit 8 (Reykjavík: Hið íslenzka fornritafélag, 1939): "conscientious, but not an agile writer, not much of a historian, and not scrutinous" (p. cvi).

Like Björn M. Ólsen, Einar Ól. Sveinsson was convinced that the verses were old. Both he and the *Íslenzk fornrit* series are known as the chief representatives of the so-called Icelandic school, whose main critical focus is on "such matters as the individual saga's literary sources (its *rittengsl* or literary connections), use of skaldic stanzas, manuscript transmission, dating, authorship, and provenance . . . [rather than] its oral background, its social and political biases, or its narrative art."[7] Bjarni Einarsson thus took a different approach when he proposed that the verses were of the same age as the saga and in fact were composed by its writer.[8] Einar Ól. Sveinsson objected to his idea on prosodic, linguistic, and in some way contextual grounds, and Theodore M. Andersson also disputed his theories.[9] Bjarni Einarsson did not give up, however, and later reasserted his theories more convincingly than before.[10]

Recently, scholars have been for the most part in agreement in viewing the verses in *Kormaks saga* as one of many sources used by the narrator or writer in the composition of the saga, that is, that the verses and the saga's narrative were brought together in oral tradition before the saga was written down. Heather O'Donoghue, for example, states: "There are some verses which allude in such detail to the specific circumstances of their recitation that it is hard to imagine how the verse could ever have survived transmission without accompanying explanatory prose, indeed, without the very prose context which at present frames them in the saga narrative."[11]

---

7. Carol J. Clover, "Icelandic Family Sagas (*Íslendingasögur*)," in *Old Norse-Icelandic Literature. A Critical Guide*, ed. Carol J. Clover and John Lindow, Islandica 45 (Ithaca and London: Cornell University Press, 1985), p. 241.

8. Bjarni Einarsson, *Skáldasögur. Um uppruna og eðli ástaskáldasagnanna fornu* (Reykjavík: Menningarsjóður, 1961).

9. Einar Ól. Sveinsson, "Kormakur skáld," pp. 163–201; Theodore M. Andersson, "Skalds and Troubadours," *Mediaeval Scandinavia* 2 (1969), pp. 7–41.

10. Bjarni Einarsson, *To skjaldesagaer. En analyse af Kormáks saga og Hallfreðar saga* (Bergen: Universitetsforlaget, 1976).

11. Heather O'Donoghue, *The Genesis of a Saga Narrative. Verse and Prose in Kormaks saga* (Oxford: Clarendon Press, 1991), p. 174; cf. Russell Poole, "Introduction," *Skaldsagas. Text, Vocation, and Desire in the Icelandic Sagas of Poets*, ed. Russell Poole, Ergänzungsbände zum Reallexikon der Germanischen Altertumskunde 27 (Berlin and New York: Gruyter, 2001), p. 2, and Daniel Sävborg, "*Kormáks saga*—en norrön kärlekssaga på vers och prosa," *Scripta Islandica* 56 (2005), p. 70.

Bjarni Einarsson's views reevaluated

Various scholars have long considered it likely that both older and younger Sagas of Icelanders display the influence of the story of Tristan and Iseult (Tristram and Ísönd), which supposedly reached Iceland not only through the Anglo-Norman poet Thomas' poetic romance that was translated by Brother Robert into Norse in 1226, but in other ways as well. Bjarni Einarsson believed that various narratives or versions of the saga of Tristram and Ísönd had been known in Iceland at an early stage. He suggested the idea—which is still debated—that this influence is seen both in *Kormaks saga* and in its verses. He pointed out that (1) *Kormaks saga* is about love that is prevented by magic from coming to fruition, while *Tristrams saga* is about love that is incurable because of magic; (2) *Kormaks saga* contains an episode involving a duel that is similar to the duel episode in *Tristrams saga*; (3) both Kormakr and Tristram go to meet their loved ones but wind up in a trap laid for them by their enemies; (4) both sagas have love triangles and show sympathy for the lovers at the expense of the husband.

For many years, the artistic composition of the saga received little attention, and most scholars thought that it was poorly written and clumsy. For a long time, Bjarni Einarsson was the only one to draw attention to the ingenious narrative that the writer seemed to have completely under his control, yet his theory that the writer composed both the narrative and the verses met with a great deal of opposition and is still not widely accepted. In recent years, however, the opinion has gained some ground that although Bjarni's theory about the young age of the verses may not hold up, his reading of the saga, his approach and viewpoint, are quite valid. Daniel Sävborg reads the saga as a unified narrative and criticizes the opinions of Roberta Frank and Heather O'Donoghue, who place most emphasis on the discrepancies between the saga and the verses.[12] Like Bjarni Einarsson, Sävborg prefers to interpret the saga first and foremost as a love story: "Trots att stroferna säkerligen är äldre än prosan utgör de til sammans—som Kormáks saga—en analyserbar enhet . . . Vers och prosa samverkar till en helhet, vars kärleksskildring alls inte är torftig eller oroman-

---

12. Roberta Frank, "*Kormáks Saga*," in *Dictionary of the Middle Ages* 7 (New York, 1986), p. 299; O'Donoghue, *The Genesis of a Saga Narrative*, p. viii.

tisk."[13] He points out that Bjarni Einarsson has been alone in his interpretation of *Kormaks saga*, since most scholars have considered the saga "oromantisk, torftig och rå berättelse utan kärleksuttryck eller kärleksdialog, där kärlek överlag underordnas strid och konflikter män emellan. Det märkliga är givetvis at dessa påståenden möter om just en saga som mer än någon annan islänningasaga är uppbyggd kring en mans kärlek till en kvinna."[14]

I agree with Sävborg's interpretation of *Kormaks saga* as primarily a love story. He correctly notes that in *Kormaks saga*, more so than in any of the other Sagas of Icelanders, the protagonist expresses his love directly and openly.[15] Nevertheless, it is a fact that *Kormaks saga* has more than one thematic thread and two different voices. One is the voice that always speaks the language of lovers; the other is the voice that examines matters from the viewpoint of society. This double voice makes the saga provocative and entertaining, but it also gives rise to ambiguity.

One of the Sagas of Icelanders, a skald saga, or a saga under the influence of romance?

Kormaks saga is grouped with the Sagas of Icelanders despite its lack of various features that are considered typical for such sagas. Marianne Kalinke has delineated the key features that are thought to distinguish the Sagas of Icelanders from the romances: "The standard against which Old Norse-Icelandic romance has been measured has been the family saga with its objectivity, realism, and lucid style."[16]

---

13. Sävborg, "*Kormáks saga*," pp. 71 and 76: "Although the verses are certainly older than the prose, together—as *Kormáks Saga*—they form a unit that is possible to analyze . . . Verse and prose work together to form a single work whose depiction of love is not at all plain or unromantic."

14. Sävborg, "*Kormáks saga*," p. 67: ". . . an unromantic, plain and raw story without expressions of love or conversations between lovers, where love on the whole is subordinated to the fights and conflicts between men. The strange thing is of course to read such statements about a saga that more than any other *Íslendingasaga* is based on a man's love for a woman." See also Einar Ól. Sveinsson,"Kormakur skáld," pp. 163–201, and Theodore M. Andersson, *The Icelandic Family Saga. An Analytic Reading* (Cambridge: Harvard University Press, 1967), p. 233.

15. Sävborg, p. 68.

16. Marianne Kalinke, "Norse Romance (*Riddarasögur*)," in *Old Norse-Icelandic Literature. A Critical Guide*, ed. Carol J. Clover and John Lindow, Islandica 45 (Ithaca and London: Cornell University Press, 1985), p. 317.

Neither objectivity nor realism are, in my opinion, terms that can be used to describe *Kormaks saga*, but its style is certainly closer to that of the Sagas of Icelanders than the very different style of the romances, such as *Tristrams saga*.

A key feature of the Sagas of Icelanders is that they tell of events having to do with disputes or with the development of events and actions considered to be of great consequence since they are often tragic in some way. Events comprising the climaxes of the narratives are followed by descriptions of what happens in their wake, what consequences these events have. A comparison of *Kormaks saga* with other Sagas of Icelanders shows how different it is. The narrative of *Kormaks saga* is not focused on one dramatic event, and no one bears the heavy burden of exacting revenge. The saga describes many fights, often in the form of duels, but there are few killings, due mostly to the fact that the quarreling parties are often protected by magic spells.

Kormaks saga is a skald saga, and it has often been noted that the skald sagas are unlike other Sagas of Icelanders: "Tellingly, one of the most salient characteristics of the skald saga is the negative one of its not being a family saga [. . .] instead, its emphasis falls upon individuals at the margin of the Icelandic social order, who do not succeed in perpetuating their family line."[17] Skald sagas are considered to have their own particular characteristics, but as Poole points out, the distinctions and demarcations do not work precisely: "Formally, a notable aspect of the skald sagas is their characteristic blending of prose and verse, a format that would seem a natural corollary of encapsulating the life-story of a poet. But this is no conclusive genre marker either, since many sagas of Icelanders, whether they are centrally concerned with poets or not, contain an essentially similar blend."[18] The skald sagas share with the romances the fact that love is a central theme, which overshadows other events in the life of the characters.

It is important to consider how the Tristan material could have influenced Old Norse-Icelandic literature without it having been a direct literary model. Bjarni Einarsson believed that the French chivalric romances were brought orally to Iceland and influenced

---

17. Poole, "Introduction," p. 5.
18. Poole, "Introduction," p. 5.

the oral stories that existed there, among them the story of the skald Kormakr and his love affair, and the view that *Kormaks saga* is a "romance" must be considered. Love affairs are certainly important in many of the *Íslendingasögur*, but *Kormaks saga* differs from such well-known Sagas of Icelanders as *Njáls saga* and *Laxdœla saga* in that Kormakr's feelings for the female character are clear to the audience. Moreover, in other sagas, different issues are intertwined with the love affairs, whereas in *Kormaks saga* the love affair stands alone as the central thread. Finally, the narrator of *Kormaks saga* seems strangely detached from the events described; duels, trips abroad, and activities at the king's court are all described as if the narrator is not familiar with actual circumstances.

The narrative method of *Kormaks saga*

In *Kormaks saga*, Kormakr becomes the focal point of the narrative after a very short introduction that describes his family and upbringing, and the saga ends with his death. One may define the saga as the biography of a skald, but it is clear that the saga's main theme (and the narrator's primary interest) is the love affair between Kormakr and Steingerðr. Kormakr's achievements and exploits in foreign countries are told in just a few sentences. On the whole, the narrative focus is maintained, but it is interrupted by the introduction of material about Bersi after his separation from Steingerðr. It is possible that the writer of the saga knew oral tales about Bersi that he considered natural to include, but Bjarni Einarsson drew attention to the fact that the chapters about Bersi are incorporated into the saga when the saga's suspense is at its peak: Steingerðr has left Bersi, and the reader/listener must wait in suspense to find out whether her path will again cross Kormakr's.[19] Concerning the Bersi material, O'Donoghue correctly states that "all of the events in Bersi's life are carefully linked together in a causal chain, and as a result each episode can be traced back ultimately to the story of Kormakr and Steingerðr."[20] Although the Bersi episode is long-winded, its conclusion is nevertheless important for the development of Kormakr's and Steingerðr's love story; as the

---

19. Bjarni Einarsson, *To skjaldesagaer*, p. 81.
20. O'Donoghue, *The Genesis of a Saga Narrative*, p. 89.

narrator points out: "As a result of these events Steingerd conceived a dislike for Bersi and wished to divorce him" (p. 36). The statement awakens the reader's/listener's curiosity: is there any hope that the lovers will be reunited?

The saga's narrative pace is noticeably rapid in the chapters that take place outside of Iceland (the introduction and all of the final chapters). On the other hand, the pace decelerates a great deal in the chapters that take place in Iceland, which describe the time that the lovers spend together; the description of Kormakr's and Steingerðr's final meeting in Miðfjörður after their long separation, where they sit down in the grass together and idle the day away, is an example. On the whole, the narrative of *Kormaks saga* is more concerned with domesticity and the realm of women than with what happens on the broader social stage of men. This is clear at the very start of the saga, in the conversation between Steingerðr and the maidservant.[21]

In recent years, several studies on the social position of skalds in Old Norse-Icelandic society have appeared, examining men's expression of love, the arrangements of married life, and the consequences of not following established rules, as well as the importance of women's consent to marriage plans, the nature and influence of magic, and love as a central theme in the sagas. Here an attempt will be made to use the findings of this research to show how different viewpoints in *Kormaks saga* make it a provocative and classic work of art: (1) the viewpoint of lovers whose love justifies their actions; (2) the viewpoint of a society that condemns anything that causes imbalance; (3) the comic viewpoint; (4) and the tragic viewpoint.

Bjørn Bandlien suggests that it is possible to explain Kormakr's reluctance to marry Steingerðr because of her unworthiness for him; or, to put it better, by continuing to court her without asking for her hand in marriage, Kormakr is sending the message to society that he does not consider her worthy of him and that her family is so unimportant that he need not show it any overt concern. Þorkell, Steingerðr's father, reacts as one might expect; his behavior reveals his concern for his dignity and family honor: "Þorkell shows his power

---

21. Another minor example is when Kormákr comes to find Steingerðr after she is wed to Þorvaldr Tinteinn: he meets "a woman there on the farm" (p. 53), they start speaking, and Kormakr recites a verse to better explain his errand.

to decide on his daughter's marriage after all; he chooses a strategy where he manages to retain much of the honour he was in danger of losing if he had settled for Kormákr's reluctance to become his son-in-law."[22] *Kormaks saga* and other sagas containing the same motif (a man courts a woman but will not marry her) show the importance of the person called *giptingarmaðr*, a parent or guardian who is responsible for bringing a particular person into a marriage. Courtship visits or love affairs that do not end in marriage bring disgrace to the *giptingarmaðr* and threaten the balance of society, for a suitor who courts a woman continuously prevents the possibility of her being betrothed to another man. Although it can be argued that Þorkell in Tunga reacts as he should when he decides not to accept Kormakr's behavior, the saga-writer is not "behind him," as evident from the description of Þorkell's collaborators, Oddr and Guðmundr; they are "a boisterous pair" (p. 13), and Narfi, who helps him most, is "an impetuous and foolish man, and given to beasting, for all the pettiness of his character" (p. 12).

As is well known, the *mansöngur* (love song) was prohibited by law in the Free State period. Jenny Jochens claims that it has deep historical roots and may originally have been addressed to slave women. She believes that the *mansöngur* consisted primarily of an insult directed either at a woman's *giptingarmaðr* or her husband.[23] Bandlien considers it likely that the *mansöngur*, like other poetry, was powerful and influenced the position of the woman it described, turning her mind toward the man who least deserved it.[24] *Kormaks saga* shows that it was also possible to falsify a *mansöngur*, by composing an obscene poem and lying about the identity of the writer: when Steingerðr marries a second time, Þorvarðr and Narfi hire a tramp to recite an obscene verse to her and attribute it to Kormakr, thus damaging his reputation and infuriating Steingerðr, since, as she says, this news has "now been spread around the whole district" (p. 52).

---

22. Bjørn Bandlien, *Strategies of Passion. Love and Marriage in Old Norse Society*, trans. Betsy van der Hoek, Medieval texts and cultures of northern Europe 6 (Turnhout: Brepols, 2005), p. 68.
23. Jenny Jochens, "From Libel to Lament: Male Manifestations of Love in Old Norse" in *From Sagas to Society: Comparative Approaches to Early Iceland*, ed. Gísli Pálsson (Enfield Lock: Hisarlik, 1992), pp. 247–64.
24. Bandlien, *Strategies of Passion*, p. 75.

Honor and the attitude of society

Luck, fate, and honor are key concepts in the Sagas of Icelanders. Preben Meulengracht Sørensen, William Ian Miller, Jesse Byock, and others have pointed out that the course of events in the sagas is determined especially by the characters' responses to the demands upon them to protect their honor and, in particular, to increase it. In *Kormaks saga*, the honor of all the characters involved is important, and their actions are judged in terms of whether they serve to increase or decrease honor. Kormakr, however, holds a unique position in that all of his actions are more or less dubious with regard to the concept of prestige or honor.[25]

The position and prestige held by women in the thirteenth century was determined by the positions of their fathers and husbands, as well as by considerations of how good a match they were. Nevertheless, women had their "own" prestige;[26] although an affair between a woman and a man could put the reputation of a *giptingarmaðr* and his family in danger, the woman was often considered a decent match no matter what might have happened earlier; as Bandlien says: "Despite the multitude of stories about unwanted suitors in the early Icelandic sagas, there are few signs that women suffered from a lack of regard because of the situation."[27]

In *Kormaks saga*, the reader's attention is often drawn to the fact that Kormakr makes decisions that are unlikely to increase his honor. Examples include "Thorgils [. . .] thought the situation would bring them little honour" (p. 23) and "Bersi said he would come, declaring that Kormak was choosing the less honourable option" (p. 29). Kormakr almost always does things that conflict with the rules of

---

25. Yet, as Poole, "Introduction," p. 3, points out, skalds usually enjoyed the respect of society: "Many of them [the skalds] enjoyed prestige and prosperity both at home and abroad, not least because of their verse-making skills" (p. 3).

26. Sólborg Una Pálsdóttir, "Hlutu konur enga virðingu?" in *Sæmdarmenn. Um heiður á þjóðveldisöld*, ed. Helgi Þorláksson (Reykjavík: Hugvísindastofnun Háskóla Íslands, 2001), pp. 41–55. See also Guðrún Ingólfsdóttir, "'En mér þykir illt að láta risnu mína'—Um virðingu kvenna og stöðu á heimili í Fljótsdæla sögu," in *Sagnaþing helgað Jónasi Kristjánssyni sjötugum 10. apríl 1994*, ed. Sigurgeir Steingrímsson, 2 vols. (Reykjavík: Bókmenntafélagið, 1994), vol. 1, pp. 257–268; Bandlien, *Strategies of Passion*, p. 88.

27. Bandlien, *Strategies of Passion*, p. 87.

society, and good advice always comes to nothing in his hands. Among other things, he kills the sons of Þórveig, refuses to pay compensation to her, and drives her away from the fjord. This is unjust, and Þórveig does the only thing she can to take revenge, declaring, "This is how I'll pay you back for it: you will never enjoy Steingerd's love" (p. 16). Kormakr's behavior is therefore one of the saga's explanations for the problems that it recounts. All of the interaction between the lovers is colored by the fact that their relationship is problematic. Kormakr blames Steingerðr, telling her "he felt that she had let him down in wishing to marry another man" (p. 24). But Steingerðr goes right to the heart of the matter, when she says: "You were the cause of things going wrong before, Kormak [. . .]" (p. 24).

Kormakr uses every opportunity he can to express his contempt or distrust for sorcerers and their powers, as when he ironically says: "What will you sorcerers think of next?" (p. 25). In fact, it seems that this attitude is a main cause of his misfortune. The only time that Kormakr follows a prophetess' advice is when he rejects Helga, Bersi's sister, and it is noteworthy that Kormakr is here associated with his mother. The prophetess names his mother, when she warns Kormakr about marrying Bersi's sister, but when his mother learns that he has rejected the match she takes it very badly. Like the prophetess, she uses the word fate (*forlög*) and says: "Not much luck will come to us from the way your fate's turning out, since you've refused the best of matches there" (p. 24). In this instance, Kormakr chooses to challenge Bersi to a duel, and his mother helps him prepare for the fight. She asks what sword he intends to use and advises him to visit Miðfjarðar-Skeggi and borrow the sword Sköfnungur. Kormakr shows Skeggi little respect and again does not do as he is told. This and other incidents reveal that in the saga-writer's view Kormakr almost always makes wrong decisions.

When Steingerðr is married to Þorvaldr Tinteinn, Kormakr tests the patience of the men with whom Steingerðr is associated. Actually, Steingerðr's husband is such a milksop that it seems he will make no attempt to end Kormakr's continued courtship of his wife. In fact, it is his brother, Þorvarðr, as well as Narfi, who view the courtship as dishonorable, although their immediate reaction is ignoble in that they falsify the *mansöngur* and attribute it to Kormakr.

Everything goes well for the brothers at the court of Hákon Aðalsteinsfóstri in Norway, and later the brothers become friends of Hákon's successor, Haraldr Grey-Cloak, "who was sympathetic to their interests" (p. 46). However, the chapters that describe the travels of Kormakr and his brother in foreign countries give very few details. One chapter states briefly that the brothers were held in high honor at the court in Norway and that in the summer they went on Viking raids, performed valorous deeds, and earned a great deal of fame. Nevertheless, it is obvious that what matters most in the narrative is the fact that Kormakr cannot stop thinking about Steingerðr. The verses play a key role here, because in these Kormakr expresses his incurable love. It is Þorgils, Kormakr's brother, who expresses what must be on the readers'/listeners' minds when he says: "You're always mentioning her, but you wouldn't marry her when the opportunities were there." To this Kormakr replies: "That had more to do with the spell-casting of evil spirits than with my fickleness" (pp. 45–6). The reply suggests that even Kormakr recognizes the role that his capriciousness may have played in the non-marriage, even though he lays the blame on the evil spell of Þórveig.

Due to Kormakr's insomnia and malaise because of his longing for Steingerðr, he decides to go to Iceland. Kormakr's physical sufferings certainly indicates that he is "lovesick," cf. the medieval disease "lovesickness" described by, for instance, Gerard of Berry and Andreas Capellanus (d. after 1191) in *De Amore* (ca. 1181–86).[28] His brothers' and the king's responses to this decision represent the voice of society and reveal how unwise Kormakr's decision is. His brother says: "I don't know at this stage how things will turn out," but the king said "he was acting unwisely and tried to dissuade him from the journey" (pp. 47–8). The episode demonstrates how Kormakr's feelings, especially his incurable love for Steingerðr, work steadily against his gaining social prestige both in Iceland and Norway. These dramatic prophecies, which in other Sagas of Icelanders would lead to damaging events, do not have real consequences in *Kormaks saga*, but instead give the saga a melodramatic or comic character. Various things occur on the way home, such as miserable weather and rough seas, but no

---

28. Cf. Mary F. Wack, *Lovesickness in the Middle Ages: The Viaticum and Its Commentaries* (Philadelphia: University of Pennsylvania Press, 1990), p. 51).

sooner has Kormakr cast anchor in Miðfjörður than he sees a woman riding by on shore, and it is none other than Steingerðr!

The feminine point of view in Kormaks saga

Carol Clover maintains that "[m]odern feminism has had less impact on saga studies than on other medieval literatures, perhaps because saga women, prominent as they are, were discovered long ago as scholarly subjects and their literary role remarked by generations of critics." She points out that "Kellogg has made the intriguing literary-historical suggestion that the peculiar persistence of the vernacular in Iceland may indirectly testify to the participation of women, for whom the study of Latin was seldom feasible, in the production of literature."[29]

The first scene in *Kormaks saga* describes the very first meeting between Kormakr and Steingerðr when they fall in love. The description, which is precise, vibrant, and beautiful, is given from the point of view of both parties. Later in the narrative, it is the women, Steingerðr and her servant, who consider the man and ponder his qualities:

In the evening Steingerd left her room, and with her was a slave-woman. They could hear the voices of the strangers in the hall.

The slave-woman said, 'Steingerd dear, let's take a look at the visitors.'

Steingerd said there was no need for that, but nevertheless she went to the door, stepped up on to the threshold, and looked over the wood stacked by the door; there was a space between the bottom of the door and the threshold, and her feet showed.

Kormak saw that [. . .].

Steingerd now sensed that she was being observed [. . .] The light now shone on to her face [. . .].

Tosti said, 'She's starting to stare at you.' (pp. 7–8)

---

29. Clover, "Icelandic Family Sagas (*Íslendingasögur*)," pp. 256–7. Cf. Robert Kellogg, "Sex and the Vernacular in Medieval Iceland" in *Proceedings of the First International Saga Conference, University of Edinburgh 1971* (London: Viking Society for Northern Research, 1973), pp. 244–58.

Helga Kress argues that in *Kormaks saga* the gender roles are in fact reversed: "Það tilheyrir gamanseminni að hér er það kona sem bendir annarri konu á spennandi karla. Það eru *þeir* sem eru í sjónmáli, sem þannig er afhjúpað og haft til sýnis. Hlutverkum er snúið við."[30] Helga makes no attempt to determine why this is the case in *Kormaks saga* as opposed to all the other Sagas of Icelanders from which she derives examples; she views the role-reversal first and foremost as comedy or a humorous exposition. Poole, on the other hand, argues that "Kormákr, for one, describes his male gaze as contested, if not anticipated, by a gaze from Steingerðr. That, along with the experience of falling in love at first sight, appears to unnerve him."[31]

In his *Fragments d'un discours amoureux*, Roland Barthes maintains that "every lover who falls in love at first sight has something of a Sabine Woman (or of some other celebrated victim of ravishment)"; the person in question ceases to be a *subject* and is transformed into an *object*: ". . . the object of capture becomes the subject of love; and the subject of the conquest moves into the class of loved object."[32] Barthes suggests that the language of love is feminine by nature, and that a man in love can therefore be considered feminine, since his feelings have taken control of him. For this reason, he runs counter to the rules of society, and the language of love is a kind of babel, the language of poetry. In the quest for love, the goal always remains distant: it exists elsewhere and can never be reached. For this reason, a man in love is restless, lonely, and depressed; to be in love is a condition that is in direct opposition to society and that always tries to fight against

---

30. Helga Kress, "'Gægur er þér í augum'. Konur í sjónmáli Íslendingasagna" in *Fyrir dyrum fóstru. Greinar um konur og kynferði í íslenskum fornbókmenntum* (Reykjavík: Rannsóknastofa í kvennafræðum, 1996), p. 148: "It is comical that here it is a woman who directs the attention of another woman to interesting men. It is the *men* who are being viewed, and thus are uncovered and put on display. The roles are reversed."
31. Poole, "Introduction," p. 22.
32. Roland Barthes, *Fragments d'un discours amoureux* (Paris: Éditions du Seuil, 1977); *A lover's discourse. Fragments*, trans. Richard Howard (Harmondsworth: Penguin, 1990), p. 188. In this connection, it is interesting that not only does Steingerðr watch Kormakr; she and the maid also openly discuss his looks: "Kormak heard them talking about his looks. The slave-woman declared him dark and ugly. Steingerd declared him good-looking and as fine as he could be in every respect, but added: 'There is just one fault—that the hair is curled on his forehead'" (p. 9). When Kormakr's appearance is described, it is specified that he looks like his mother:"Kormak had dark curly hair and a fair complexion and was rather like his mother" (pp. 6–7). Some medieval physicians and writers regarded love as a disease, and one of the symptoms was that it feminized the male lover (cf. Wack, *Lovesickness*, p. 65).

society in a subconscious, silent way. A man in love cannot express his feelings except through the language of poetry and madness.[33]

In Norse-Icelandic sources from the early Middle Ages, men who let themselves be controlled by love are viewed negatively: "Excessive love-longing positioned the man as submissive both socially and by gender and could also effect a questioning of the social identity of his entire household or social group."[34] For this reason, scholars, including Bjarni Einarsson, have argued that *Kormaks saga* could never have been written without influence from the French Tristan material. However, Bandlien maintains that there is much evidence that Norse males could express their love without resorting to forms imported from the continent, even if such expression was in fact bound formally; it was, for example, natural to express one's feelings in *dróttkvætt*. Bandlien says: "There are in my opinion good reasons to believe that skalds could express their passionate love in the early Middle Ages, and further that their poems could find a public that preserved them until they were written down centuries later."[35] He further argues that *dróttkvætt* provided men with "a legitimate language for their love."[36] In his view, Norse men sought out both the love of women and the recognition from them that served to increase the respect in which they were held. He claims that Egill Skallagrímsson, Kormakr Ögmundarson and Hallfreðr vandræðaskáld gained respect because of women's love for them: "[A]ll win honour by winning women's love."[37] What is interesting about *Kormaks saga* is that although the social respect granted Kormakr is extremely limited because of his behavior, he enjoys the sympathy of the narrator and probably the audience as well.

The role of women in conflicts

Although *Kormaks saga* describes conflicts between men, the prominent role that women play in these conflicts is clear. At the beginning of the saga it is told that "Helga, the daughter of Earl Frodi, had a

---

33. Cf. Julia Kristeva, *Histoires d'amour* (Paris: Denoel, 1983); *Tales of Love*, trans. Leon S Roudiez (New York: Columbia University Press, 1987).
34. Bandlien, *Strategies of Passion*, p. 93.
35. Bandlien, *Strategies of Passion*, p. 93.
36. Bandlien, *Strategies of Passion*, p. 108.
37. Bandlien, *Strategies of Passion*, p. 129.

foster-mother who could foretell the future [. . .]. [She] used to feel men with her hand before they went into battle; she did this to Ogmund before he left home, and declared that at no point would he be severely harmed [. . .]. The viking presented his side, but nothing could pierce him" (p. 6).[38] When Þorvarðr, the brother of Þorvaldr Tinteinn, plans his attack against Kormakr, he goes first to the prophetess Þórdís and asks her for help. Kormakr goes for the same reason and "[tells] his mother his intention" (p. 54). Dillmann maintains that in the Sagas of Icelanders and *Landnámabók*, the number of women and men practicing magic arts is about equal, with the number of women being slightly higher. Of the twenty-six sorcerous women mentioned in the Sagas of Icelanders, half of them are married women or widows,[39] and the prophetess Þórdís in *Kormaks saga* is married.

One of the distinguishing external traits of individuals who in the sagas practice magic is the look of their eyes, as seen, for example, in Þórdís and Þórveig in *Kormaks saga*.[40] Dillmann claims that in the scene in which Kormakr meets Þórveig in the guise of a "hrosshvalr," no particular walrus or whale is meant, but rather a strange creature characterized first and foremost by its huge eyes; in other words, the creature displays the main distinguishing trait of people involved in sorcery.[41]

The description of Bersi, Kormakr's adversary and foil

Bersi is in many ways Kormakr's adversary in that he makes the right decisions with respect to the rules of society. Indeed, he is introduced as "góðr drengr" (a decent person, p. 17). One way in which Bersi gains the advantage over Kormakr is that he respects Þórveig, "who was very skilled in magic" (p. 17) and follows her advice. When Bersi is offered the opportunity to marry Steingerðr, he considers her a good match, but with a "drawback" (p. 18). This "drawback"

---

38. Cf. Francois-Xavier Dillmann, *Les magiciens dans l'Islande ancienne. Études sur la représentation de la magie islandaise et de ses agents dans les sources littéraires norroises*, Acta Academiae Regiae Gustavi Adolphi 92 (Uppsala: Kungl. Gustav Adolfs Akademien för svensk folkkultur, 2006), pp. 61–2.
39. Dillmann, *Les magiciens dans l'Islande ancienne*, pp. 423–5.
40. Dillmann, *Les magiciens dans l'Islande ancienne*, pp. 186–7.
41. "People thought they recognized Thorveig's eyes when they saw it [i.e., the animal]" (p. 45). Dillmann, *Les magiciens dans l'Islande ancienne*, pp. 249–258.

obviously refers to Steingerðr's relationship with Kormakr. Bersi is told that he need not fear Kormakr because Kormakr has "made a point of dissociating himself from this affair" (p. 18). The fact that the match is made "very much against Steingerd's wishes" (p. 19) is important, as is the fact that steps are taken to prevent news of the wedding plans from being spread around the district. It is typical of *Kormaks saga*, however, for a woman to try to take matters into her own hands, and here Steingerðr asks Narfi to tell Kormakr about the plan. Narfi is not exactly a trustworthy messenger (he is described as impetuous, foolish, boastful, and petty), and attempts are made to delay his journey. He therefore arrives too late to inform Kormakr of the wedding plans. The description of how he brings Kormakr the news is spirited, comical, and has a certain crescendo, displaying admirably the narrative abilities of the composer of the saga. For Kormakr, it is important to know if Steingerðr was in agreement, and when he asks if Steingerðr knew about this in advance, Narfi replies: "Not until the very same evening, when people had arrived at the feast" (p. 20). This information becomes important for events later in the saga. Bersi is valorous and comports himself well in most things, but when Steingerðr decides to divorce him, her being forced into the marriage against her will seems to be a sufficient reason.

The role of women in *Bersa þáttr*

The segment focusing on Bersi is, in the opinion of various scholars, a digression from the saga's main plot. There are, nevertheless, various elements that connect it with the saga's primary theme, the love shared by Kormakr and Steingerðr; in this segment, too, events are to a great extent determined by the will and opinions of women. Chapter 12, for example, relates that the sons of Þórðr Arndísarson and Ásmundr, Bersi's son, participate in a ball game that ends badly:

> [. . .] the sons of Thord often came home blue and bloody. This displeased Thordis, their mother, who asked Thord to raise the matter with Bersi [. . .].
>
> [. . .] Bersi now felt sure that Thordis had been behind the claim that Thord put to him. (p. 31)

Here the reaction of a mother's discontentment with the treatment of her sons sets events in motion. The men are of a different opinion and consider her demands for compensation out of the question. As a consequence, Bersi is insulted, and the friendship between him and Þórðr suffers a setback. At the Alþingi, Bersi fights with both Steinarr, Kormakr's uncle, who demands compensation from him on behalf of Kormakr, and Þórðr, a former friend. Bersi receives bad wounds that will not heal, and to add insult to injury, Steingerðr turns her back on him: "As a result of these events Steingerd conceived a dislike for Bersi and wished to divorce him" (p. 36). She parts from him with words of contempt. Steingerðr appears coarse and heartless, but her reaction is probably due ultimately to her having married Bersi against her will. Her father is supportive of her when she makes the decision, which may be proof that a woman's consent was important for a successful marriage.

Steingerðr's abandonment of Bersi is followed by the story of two new women in his life, Steinvör, his mistress, and Þórdís, his wife. The audience is told that "Steinvor stayed with Bersi, which displeased Thordis [. . .] Bersi brought Halldor home with him and gave him to Steinvor to foster. This displeased Thordis" (p. 41). As pointed out by O'Donoghue, the jealousy displayed by Bersi's wife's indicates that he is more interested in Steinvör.[42] The love triangle formed by his taking two women into his home leads Bersi to plan a conspiracy against Þórdís, which provides him with an opportunity to kill her brother Váli. Bersi, a representative of social values, now behaves ignobly and, like Kormakr, lets his feelings control his actions. In the light of this narrative, Steingerðr's decision to abandon Bersi receives a certain amount of support. Yet at the same time it is possible that the writer used the situation to display the consequences of a marriage built on economics, rather than on love and passion.

Steingerðr has scarcely left her husband before a suitor shows up: "Thorvald Tintein asked for Steingerd's hand in marriage, and she was granted to him with the consent of her kinsmen and with no protest from her" (p. 27). When Kormakr learns of the marriage, he keeps his

---

42. O'Donoghue, *The Genesis of a Saga Narrative*, p. 98: "Her jealousy suggests an attachment between Bersi and Steinvǫr which the saga narrative discreetly fails to mention."

knowledge of it hidden. Evidently, he has also decided to change course in life, because he is on his way overseas. However, he goes first to visit Steingerðr and asks her to make a shirt for him. As readers of the Sagas of Icelanders know, such a request has a specific and unambiguous meaning, and Steingerðr takes his request extremely badly.

The influence of women on the saga's course of events

Despite the fact that the social position of women in the Free State period in Iceland put limitations on the influence that they could exercize, *Kormaks saga* gives many examples of women affecting the course of events.[43] Steingerðr, for instance, often resorts to her own devices, the most telling example being when she tells Kormakr to ask for her hand in marriage.[44] Indeed, as Poole points out, women are more active in the skald sagas than in other Sagas of Icelanders: "In general the skald saga women are shown as no mere passive vessels but as acting deliberately, whether to thwart or to support their lovers' schemes."[45]

Another unusual feature of *Kormaks saga* is that a love verse is spoken by a woman.[46] Kormakr recites a half-verse in which he asks Steingerður whom she would choose for a husband. She completes the verse by replying that she would choose him, even if he were blind, for then the gods and the fates would treat her well ("Brœðr mynda ek blindum, / bauglestir, mik festa, / yrði goð sem gerðisk / góð mér ok skǫp, Fróða").[47]

As Poole observes: "While there may be some mentions of women skalds and even sporadic attributions of love verses to women, notably Steingerðr in *Kormáks saga*, we do not hear a great deal about love relationships from the women's point of view [. . .]."[48] Steingerðr is

---

43. Bandlien, *Strategies of Passion*, p. 90: "Women's opportunities for direct influence in the economic and public spheres were limited. As a rule, women did not take the initiative."
44. "Steingerd now asked Kormak to cultivate her father's friendship and obtain the promise of her hand in marriage, and for Steingerd's sake Kormak gave Thorkel gifts" (p. 17).
45. Poole, "Introduction," p. 22.
46. See, however, Guðrún Nordal's discussion in "Tilbrigði um *Njálu*," *Ritið* 3 (2005), p. 67, of the verses spoken by Unnur in *Njáls saga*.
47. *Kormáks saga*, ed. Einar Ól. Sveinsson in *Vatnsdæla saga*, p. 223.
48. Poole, "Introduction," p. 22.

an extremely active participant in events throughout the saga. When her brother-in-law fights a duel with Kormakr, "Steingerd said she wished to go to the duel, and that was what happened" (p. 56). She then reveals her independent spirit and decision-making abilities when Kormakr gains the upper hand in the fight. He wipes his sweat triumphantly on her mantle and asks her "to leave with him," but she snubs him, saying that "she would be the one to decide who accompanied her" (p. 57). Clearly, she is now the one in charge, not her fickle and poetic lover.[49] After Kormakr has returned to Norway, Steingerðr asks Þorvaldr Tinteinn to go abroad with her, evidently so that she might follow Kormakr; Þorvaldr's reply—"He said that that was not advisable, but nevertheless could not refuse her" (p. 60)—shows it is she who ultimately decides. Again, when Steingerðr decides to follow Kormakr to Norway, her own initiative in doing so is clear, although the saga, as Sävborg rightly points out, never makes her motivation explicit:

> Steingerðrs önskan att fara utomlands motiveras aldrig. Med hänsyn till att närmast föregående episod skildrat Kormákrs avfärd till Norge samt till hur ovanligt det är i *Íslendingasögur* att kvinnor alls tar initiativ till utlandsfärder synes det likväl rimligt att tolka hennes önskan som en längtan efter att återse Kormákr, och det handlar därmed om ett underförstått kärleksuttryck.[50]

The episode is certainly unusual and not in accord with *Laxdæla saga*'s account of Guðrún's wish to go abroad with Kjartan.[51] It appears that the author of *Kormaks saga* had other ideas about women's wishes to journey abroad as well as decisions by women in general.

---

49. It appears, however, that from this point on their relationship blossoms, because shortly afterward the saga states that "Kormak was now always meeting Steingerd" (p. 57).

50. Sävborg, "*Kormáks* saga," p. 94: "Steingerðr's motives for going abroad are never fully explained. Considering the fact that the previous episode describes Kormákr's departure for Norway and how unusual it is in the Sagas of Icelanders for women to take the initiative regarding journeys abroad, it seems all the same reasonable to interpret her wish as a longing to see Kormákr again, and consequently as an implicit expression of love."

51. As Helga Kress, "'Mjök mun þér samstaft þykkja': Um sagnahefð og kvenlega reynslu í Laxdælu sögu," in *Konur skrifa til heiðurs Önnu Sigurðardóttir* (Reykjavík: Sögufélag, 1980), p. 104, has pointed out, there are several examples in *Laxdæla saga* of women who are supposed to stay at home, and do so, while their husbands/lovers travel abroad.

Kormaks saga as a comedy

Kormaks saga contains descriptions so comical that it seems likely that the saga was intended primarily as entertainment. One of the traits of a comic narrative is that people from low social levels play key roles; either they themselves are funny or they act as foils for comic characters or situations. In *Kormaks saga*, the maidservant plays an important role in that she helps bring the lovers together, among other things by putting into words what they themselves are not prepared to say plainly:

> The slave-woman said to Steingerd, 'That good-looking man's coming now, Steingerd.'
> 'He's certainly a brave-looking man,' Steingerd said. She was combing her hair.
> Kormak said, 'Will you lend me the comb?'
> Steingerd handed it to him; she was the finest-haired of women.
> The slavewoman said, 'You would have to pay a high price for a wife with such hair as Steingerd has, or such eyes.'
> Kormak spoke a verse [. . .].
> The slavewoman said, 'So you two have taken a liking to each other.' (p. 10).

In the account of the fight between Kormakr and the sons of Þórveig, it is the situation itself that is comical. Narfi "sneaked about on the fringes of the fighting" (p. 15), and when Steingerðr's father tries to join in, Steingerðr grabs his hands and prevents him from doing so:[52]

> At that moment Steingerd came out and saw what her father was about; she seized him in her arms and he got nowhere near to supporting the brothers. (p. 15)

Other amusing episodes concern Þórveig, who controls the fate of the men and rewards those who do her bidding (Bersi), but punishes those who don't (Kormakr). When Þórveig causes Kormakr's boat to

---

52. Cf. Poole, "Introduction," p. 22: "Steingerðr, in *Kormáks saga*, grabs on to her father in order to prevent him adding his strength to an attack on Kormákr."

fill with water under him, she says that "it was just a little trick" (p. 22). Kormakr simply cannot restrain himself and follow the rules; his curiosity is overwhelming, and when seeking help from Þórdís he manages to ruin everything she tries to do for him. Despite all of the humor, the conclusion is shameful: "'It's going to prove all too true, Kormak, that helping you will be far from easy. It was my intention now to avert the evil destinies that Thorveig had cast upon you and Steingerd; the two of you might have enjoyed each other's love if I had slaughtered the third goose without anyone knowing about it.' Kormak said, 'I don't believe in such things'" (p. 55).

Who told the saga and what was its audience?

In order to gain a proper understanding of ancient texts, one must consider their contents. What do these narratives reveal? The answer may lead to evidence about the context in which a text was created, who participated in its creation, and/or who partook in hearing or reading it. Poole points out that many of the Sagas of Icelanders are concerned with journeys and the complicated relationships between kings and Icelanders, but that in *Kormaks saga* these elements are passed over quickly, even though the saga's subject matter seems to direct the audience toward such material:

> *Kormáks saga* ... does little more than skirt past these topics, even though, to judge from other sources, the potential for a full realization of the pattern must have existed in the wider community's repository of knowledge about Kormákr.[53]

One may consequently ask why the saga's composer seems uninterested in material that is prominent in other comparable narratives.

Oral tradition and the saga audience are necessarily intertwined. Those who told sagas and those who listened were connected by unbreakable bonds, but were they men, women, or both? Most current scholars emphasize the fact that the Sagas of Icelanders developed from oral tradition.[54] If the sagas were recited orally, their contents were, as Poole argues, almost certainly changed at each recitation: "There

---

53. Poole, "Introduction," p. 17.
54. See, e.g., Clover, "Icelandic Family Sagas (*Íslendingasögur*)," p. 293.

is increasing evidence that the skald sagas, like many other sagas, as we see them now, represent just one selection and arrangement of story materials that would have varied in substance and sequence from performance to performance."[55] Recently, Gísli Sigurðsson has reiterated the importance of working from the central assumption that oral legends lie behind the sagas. He claims that in order to explain the interaction between oral tradition and written literature one has to have a working hypothesis, and that, therefore, there is "much to recommend the revised version of the '*þáttr* theory' proposed by Carol Clover (1986), which appears to be broad enough and to rest on solid enough foundations to bring scholarship some way forward toward a valid reassessment of our attitudes toward the sagas."[56]

I consider it important to approach *Kormaks saga* from the premises described by Gísli Sigurðsson: "Instead of squabbling about whether particular works come from oral tradition or are purely written literature, we now speak of works being grounded in oral tradition; and instead of bickering about whether formulas and formulaic narrative themes are evidence of oral origins or stylistic tics on the part of the writers, we now attempt to assess their aesthetic value . . . ."[57] Scholars agree that the sagas were built on oral tradition, but who preserved them and told them? Is it possible that the sagas reflect different narrative environments (for example, stories preserved and told by men versus stories told and preserved by women)? Is it possible that a saga's point of view may provide evidence of its having been preserved and told by women, as is perhaps the case with *Kormaks saga*? The Sagas of Icelanders appear to be directed at both readers and listeners, and almost everything indicates that the audience was mixed socially, that is, composed of people from different segments of society.[58] The manner in which both women and magic, or, in particular, sorceresses and prophetesses, influence events is a noticeable feature of *Kormaks saga* and likely reflects the fact that women were no less engaged in sorcerous activities than men.

---

55. Poole, "Introduction," p. 12.
56. Gísli Sigurðsson, *The Medieval Icelandic Saga and Oral Tradition. A Discourse on Method*, Publications of the Milman Parry Collection of Oral Literature 2 (Cambridge, Massachusetts: Harvard University Press, 2004), pp. 330–31.
57. Gísli Sigurðsson, *The Medieval Icelandic Saga*, p. 44.
58. Cf. Carol J. Clover, *The Medieval Saga* (Ithaca: Cornell University Press, 1982), pp. 188–204.

Historical facts

Kormakr is named in *Landnámabók*, and *Skáldatal* states that he recited poems about Earl Sigurðr Hákonarson (d. 963) and Haraldr Greycloak (d. 970). *Heimskringla* makes reference to a verse from *Sigurðardrápa* by Kormakr, and Snorri's *Edda* attributes six half-verses, which are clearly from this *drápa*, to Kormakr. Kormakr is mentioned in *Egils Saga*, and in Haukr Valdísarson's *Íslendingadrápa* three characters from *Kormaks saga* are named: Kormakr, Bersi, and Miðfjarðar-Skeggi. Finally, in the *Third Grammatical Treatise* a half-verse is attributed to Kormakr. All of the evidence suggests that a skald named Kormakr existed in Iceland during the Saga Age. But it is peculiar that there seems to be no connection between these sources and the saga about Kormakr. *Landnámabók* speaks of the Skíðungar, the family of Þorvaldr Tinteinn, as a great and important family. The composer of *Kormaks saga* traces Þorvaldr's family nowhere near as precisely as *Landnámabók*, misnaming Þorvaldr's brothers and claiming that the family enjoyed little favor. It is also unusual that the saga places Kormakr at the court of Haraldr Greycloak but does not mention that he composed verses about the king. Here it seems appropriate to bear in mind the views of Gísli Sigurðsson and others who stress the importance of oral sources: "If we take the view that the sagas were grounded in an oral tradition, we have to assume that their audiences already possessed a certain amount of knowledge about the people who turn up in them. Each saga then becomes a link in the unrecorded, 'immanent' tradition as a whole. . . ."[59] The disinterest of the composer of *Kormaks saga* in historical sources indicates that in his opinion and perhaps in the opinion of the audience other events concerning Kormakr were more important and more interesting.

Conclusion and overview

As noted above, scholars now generally agree that *Kormaks saga* is among the oldest Sagas of Icelanders, and that it is based on oral sources, among them verses that are a part of the material from which the saga was created. The fact that women play a key role in the saga's

---

59. Gísli Sigurðsson, *The Medieval Icelandic Saga*, p. 330.

events and that some of these are told from a woman's viewpoint, may indicate that in origin (that is, while the sagas were still being orally recited and before they were committed to writing) the role of women in the creation of the sagas was more active than it was later, and that scholars have generally considered it to be. I am reluctant to take a position as to whether the Tristan material directly influenced the saga, but I believe it is likely that ideas about incurable love made their way into the society in which *Kormaks saga* was created.[60]

Kormaks saga is, in my opinion, a well-written narrative with lively, precise descriptions, many-sided characters, and a gripping plot. The fact that the saga is comical and tragic at the same—the comical having to do with Steingerðr's ambition and Kormakr's disobedience, and the tragic having to do with the fact that the lovers have no way out—suggests that the narrator's primary concern was to entertain the audience and rouse it to laughter at the same time that he appealed to its sympathy.

What makes *Kormaks saga* both difficult to understand and yet fascinating is that it is told from two points of view. One is the viewpoint of love, which justifies lovers' actions. The other is the viewpoint of society, which prioritizes prestige and honor. These two key concepts in the Sagas of Icelanders are in *Kormaks saga* treated in an unusual way, because the protagonist behaves in ways that are contrary to the ideals of honor. Kormakr is a poet who lets his feelings control his deeds, and social ideals are constantly being stretched to the limit because love is regarded as an unconquerable force. The saga testifies to a great respect for sorcerers, among whom women have a great deal of spiritual power. Only one person, Kormakr, scorns this power—and pays dearly for it—suggesting that *Kormaks saga* is in many ways a moral marker set up to protect against the behavior displayed by its protagonist.

TRANSLATED BY PHILIP ROUGHTON

---

60. In the light of the prominent role played by women in the saga, it may be interpreted as a way of showing the consequences of a relationship between a beautiful woman and a man, who does not adhere to the moral guidelines of society, displays no social responsibility, lets his feelings control his actions, and pays little heed to his own honor and prestige. On the other hand, it is clear that the saga gives some weight to the notion that love is an overpowering emotion causing people (in this case both Kormákr and Steingerðr) to lose control of their actions. It is difficult to determine whether such a view had any resonance in Icelandic society in the Middle Ages, but influence from French chivalric romances brought to the north can be detected.

Bibliography

Andersson, Theodore M. *The Icelandic Family Saga. An Analytic Reading*. Cambridge: Harvard University Press, 1967.
———. "Skald Sagas in their Literary Context 3: The Love Triangle Theme." In *Skaldsagas. Text, Vocation, and Desire in the Icelandic Sagas of Poets*. Ed. Russell Poole. Ergänzungsbände zum Reallexikon der Germanischen Altertumskunde 27. Berlin: de Gruyter, 2001. Pp. 272–284.
Bandlien, Bjørn. *Å finne den rette. Kjærlighet, indvid og samfunn i norrøn middelalder*. [Oslo]: Den Historiske Forening, 2001.
———. *Strategies of Passion. Love and Marriage in Old Norse Society*. Trans. Betsy van der Hoek. Medieval texts and cultures of northern Europe 6. Turnhout: Brepols, 2005.
Barthes, Roland. *Fragments d'un discours amoureux*. Paris: Éditions du Seuil, 1977.
———. *A lover's discourse. Fragments*. Trans. Richard Howard. Harmondsworth: Penguin, 1990.
Bjarni Einarsson. *Skáldasögur. Um uppruna og eðli ástaskáldasagnanna fornu*. Reykjavík: Menningarsjóður, 1961.
———. "The lovesick scald: a reply to Theodore M. Andersson." *Mediaeval Scandinavia* (1971): 21–41.
———. *To skjaldesagaer. En analyse af Kormákur's Saga og Hallfreðar saga*. Oslo: Universitetsforlaget, 1976.
Björn M. Ólsen. "Um Íslendingasögur. Kaflar úr háskólafyrirlestrum." In *Safn til sögu Íslands og íslenzkra bókmennta að fornu og nýju* 6.3 (1937–9).
Clover, Carol J. *The Medieval Saga*. Ithaca: Cornell University Press, 1982.
———. "Icelandic Family Sagas (*Íslendingasögur*)." In *Old Norse-Icelandic Literature. A Critical Guide*. Ed. Carol J. Clover and John Lindow. Islandica 45. Ithaca: Cornell University Press, 1985. Pp. 239–315.
———. "*Kormáks Saga*." In *Medieval Scandinavia: An Encyclopedia*. Ed. Phillip Pulsiano et al. New York: Garland Publishing, 1993. P. 368.
Dillmann, François-Xavier. *Les magiciens dans l'Islande ancienne. Études sur la représentation de la magie islandaise et de ses agents dans les sources littéraires norroises*. Acta Academiae Regiae Gustavi Adolphi 92. Uppsala: Kungl. Gustav Adolfs Akademien för svensk folkkultur, 2006.
Einar Ól. Sveinsson. "Kormakur skáld og vísur hans." *Skírnir* 140 (1966): 163–201.
Frank, Roberta. "*Kormáks Saga*." In *Dictionary of the Middle Ages* 7. New York: Charles Scribner's Sons, 1986. Pp. 299–300.
Gísli Sigurðsson. *The Medieval Icelandic Saga and Oral Tradition. A Discourse on Method*. Trans. Nicholas Jones. Publications of the Milman Parry Collection of Oral Literature Cambridge, Massachusetts: Harvard University Press, 2004.
Guðrún Ingólfsdóttir. "'En mér þykir illt að láta risnu mina'—Um virðingu kvenna og stöðu á heimili í Fljótsdæla sögu." In *Sagnaþing helgað Jónasi Kristjánssyni sjötugum 10. apríl 1994*. 2 vols. Ed. Sigurgeir Steingrímsson et al. Reykjavík: Hið íslenska bókmenntafélag, 1994. Vol. 1, pp. 257–68.
Guðrún Nordal. "Tilbrigði um *Njálu*." *Ritið* 3 (2005): 57–76.
Jochens, Jenny. "From Libel to Lament: Male Manifestations of Love in Old Norse." In *From Sagas to Society: Comparative Approaches to Early Iceland*. Ed. Gísli Pálsson. Enfield Lock: Hisarlik, 1992. Pp. 247–64.
Kalinke, Marianne. "Norse Romance (*Riddarasögur*)." In *Old Norse-Icelandic*

Literature. A Critical Guide. Ed. Carol J. Clover and John Lindow. Islandica 45. Ithaca: Cornell University Press, 1985. Pp. 316–63.
Kormáks saga. In *Vatnsdœla saga.* Ed. Einar Ól. Sveinsson. *Íslenzk fornrit* 8. Reykjavík: Hið íslenzka fornritafélag, 1939.
"Kormak's Saga." In *Sagas of Warrior-Poets.* Trans. Rory McTurk. Introduction and Notes by Diana Whaley. Ed. Örnólfur Thorsson and Bernard Scudder. London: Penguin, 2002.
Kellogg, Robert. "Sex and the Vernacular in Medieval Iceland." In *Proceedings of the First International Saga Conference, University of Edinburgh 1971.* London: Viking Society for Northern Research, 1973. Pp. 244–58.
Kress, Helga. "'Mjök mun þér samstarft þykkja': Um sagnahefð og kvenlega reynslu í Laxdælu sögu." In *Konur skrifa til heiðurs Önnu Sigurðardóttur.* Reykjavík: Sögufélag, 1980. Pp. 97–109.
———. "'Gægur er þér í augum': Konur í sjónmáli Íslendingasagna." In *Fyrir dyrum fóstru. Greinar um konur og kynferði í íslenskum fornbókmenntum.* Reykjavík: Rannsóknastofa í kvennafræðum, 1996. Pp. 135–56.
Kristeva, Julia. 1983. *Histoires d'amour.* Paris: Denoel, 1983.
———. *Tales of Love.* Trans. Leon S Roudiez. New York: Columbia University Press, 1987.
Lange, Gudrun. "Andleg ást. Arabísk-platónsk áhrif og 'integumentum' í íslenskum fornbókmenntum?" *Skírnir* 166 (1992): 85–110.
O'Donoghue, Heather. *The Genesis of a Saga Narrative. Verse and Prose in Kormaks saga.* Oxford: Clarendon Press, 1991.
Poole, Russell. "Introduction." In *Skaldsagas. Text, Vocation, and Desire in the Icelandic Sagas of Poets.* Ed. Russell Poole. Ergänzungsbände zum Reallexikon der Germanischen Altertumskunde 27. Berlin: de Gruyter, 2001. Pp. 1–24.
Sävborg, Daniel. "*Kormáks saga*—en norrön kärlekssaga på vers och prosa." *Scripta Islandica* 56 (2005): 65–99.
Sólborg Una Pálsdóttir. "Hlutu konur enga virðingu?" In *Sæmdarmenn. Um heiður á þjóðveldisöld.* Ed. Helgi Þorláksson. Reykjavík: Hugvísindastofnun Háskóla Íslands, 2001. Pp. 41–55.
Wack, Mary F. *Lovesickness in the Middle Ages. The Viaticum and Its Commentaries.* Philadelphia: University of Pennsylvania Press, 1990.

Sturla Þórðarson on Love

ÚLFAR BRAGASON

Sturlu þáttr states that Sturla Þórðarson the historian (1214–1284) narrated *Huldar saga* better and more wisely than anyone on the ship of King Magnús the Law-Amender of Norway had ever heard (2, pp. 231–34).[1] A narrative scenario such as this, in which a storyteller transmits tales orally to an audience, represents a model for how the Icelandic sagas were told. In such a scenario, just as important as the existence of the storyteller is the idea of his story not being seen as his own fabrication, that is, that the audience listening to the story take it as true.[2] *Sturlu þáttr* is only preserved in one of the two main manuscripts versions of the *Sturlunga*, the compilation of so-called contemporary sagas, that is, sagas about events in Iceland in the twelfth and thirteenth centuries, believed to have been collected around 1300. The *þáttr* is thought not to have been included in the original version, and in its preserved form was most likely written in the fourteenth century.[3]

---

1. Jón Jóhannesson, Magnús Finnbogason, and Kristján Eldjárn, ed. *Sturlunga saga*, 2 vols. (Reykjavík: Sturlunguútgáfan, 1946). Here in the following, the references are to this edition. For quoted translation, see Julia H. McGraw and R. George Thomas, trans., *Sturlunga saga*, 2 vols. (New York: Twaine, 1970–74). Some amendments have, however, been made in the passages quoted from the translation, and the spelling of proper names changed in accordance with the main text.

2. M.C. van den Toorn, "Erzählsituation und Perspektive in der Saga," *Arkiv för nordisk filologi* 77 (1962), pp. 68–83.

3. See Jón Jóhannesson, Magnús Finnbogason, and Kristján Eldjárn, ed. *Sturlunga saga*, vol. 1, pp. xlviii–xlix.

In *Sturlu þáttr* it is Queen Ingilborg who passes judgment on Sturla's narrative, and through her enthusiasm and high opinion Sturla gains an audience with the king and his favor. Subsequently Sturla becomes the king's faithful retainer. This leads to Sturla's later writing of both the saga of King Hákon, the father of Magnús, and the saga of Magnús himself. Although the *þáttr* follows traditional narrative convention in its description of how Sturla gains the king's favor,[4] it also suggests strongly that he is favored by the queen, a lovable and knowledgable person who uses her charm to influence the king's decision regarding Sturla's future at the court. The *þáttr* also suggests the possibility that Sturla's saga-writing had, at least in some ways, roots traceable to women's knowledge of groups of stories and their estimation of storytelling, even though King Magnús had little regard for the queen's opinion of the material. This might indicate, in fact, that the king got the point of the story of the troll-wife told by Sturla, but that the queen, who was Danish, did not. *Huldar saga*'s state of preservation does not allow us to know the story's contents. Preben Meulengrach Sørensen suggested that *Huldar saga* was concerned with the sorceress Huld mentioned in *Ynglinga saga*, whose curse on the Norwegian king was "at ættvíg skyldi ávallt vera í ætt þeira (*Heimskringla*, vol. 1, p. 31; that there would always be a murderer of his own kin in their lineage).[5] Thus the *þáttr* points to the bloodfeud and struggle for power within the Norwegian royal family, as well as to the dangers that could emanate from women's knowledge. It presents an ambiguous view of women in the Middle Ages as being lovable, helpful, charming, and insightful, as well as capricious and dangerous bearers of death. According to this view, men had to take particular care to control both them and their passion for them.[6]

My intention in this article is to study the emotional and intellectual relationship of the historian Sturla with those closest to him, especially the women in his life, as this is presented in *Íslendinga*

---

4. See Úlfar Bragason, "Um hvað fjallaði Huldar saga?" *Tímarit Máls og menningar* 54.4 (1990), pp. 76–81.

5. Preben Meulengrach Sørensen, *Saga og samfund: En indføring i oldislandsk litteratur* (Copenhagen: Berlinske, 1977), p. 163. Bjarni Aðalbjarnarson, ed., *Heimskringla*, vol. 1, Íslenzk fornrit 26 (Reykjavík: Hið íslenzka fornritafélag, 1974).

6. Cf. George Duby, *Love and Marriage in the Middle Ages*, trans. Jane Dunnett (Chicago: University of Chicago Press, 1994), p. 96–7.

saga, of which Sturla was not only the author, but also the narrator and a main character. It must be borne in mind, however, that the saga's main topics and choice of material are influenced by literary traditions in Iceland in the thirteenth century. The saga thus provides a very limited view of its characters, even though it pretends to tell of events in an objective manner. The narrative actually says more about the saga-writer's own point of view toward the men and women that he describes, and possibly about the public's opinion of them, than it does about how they might have seen themselves and their positions. It must also not be forgotten that the saga-writer was a child of his times, shaped by its ideals. His work thus needs to be viewed in the light of other contemporary witnesses to events, in both Icelandic and foreign sources. In this regard, it would do well to quote the French historian Georges Duby: "We must give up the positivist dream of attaining past reality. We shall always be separated from it."[7]

Íslendinga saga is the nucleus of *Sturlunga saga*. The saga has not, however, survived independently, and it is likely that it was originally conceived as part of a larger work.[8] Scholars have debated how comprehensive the saga was originally, but most likely it told of events that took place or were supposed to have taken place during the years 1183–1264.[9] Scholars have had different opinions concerning the age of the saga, but it seems now that most consider it to have been written around 1280, that is, in the last years of Sturla Þórðarson's life.[10]

Íslendinga saga tells of the struggle for power between chieftains and families. The saga brings together many different stories and biographies, covering several generations, into its genealogical frame. One of the principal families in *Íslendinga saga* is that of the Sturlungs, and hence the compilation has generally been known by that name. Sturla Þórðarson is considered to be the author of the saga, according to a statement made in the so-called prologue to *Sturlunga saga*. The compiler says:

---

7. Duby, *Love and Marriage*, pp. 100–1.
8. See Jón Jóhannesson, "Um Sturlunga sögu," p. xxxviii.
9. See Jón Jóhannesson, "Um Sturlunga sögu," p. xxxiv–xxxviii.
10. See Jón Jóhannesson, "Um Sturlunga sögu," pp. xxxviii–xxxix. Cf. Helgi Þorláksson, "Sturla Þórðarson, minni og vald," 2. *íslenska söguþingið. Proceedings*, 2 vols. (Reykjavík: Sagnfræðistofnun, 2002), vol. 2, pp. 320–21.

[...] en þær sögur, er síðan hafa gerzt, váru lítt ritaðar, áðr Sturla skáld Þórðarson sagði fyrir Íslendinga sögur, ok hafði hann þar til vísandi af fróðum mönnum, þeim er váru á öndverðum dögum hans, en sumt eftir bréfum þeim, er þeir rituðu, er þeim váru samtíða, er sögurnar eru frá. Marga hluti mátti hann sjálfr sjá ok heyra, þá er á hans dögum gerðust til stórtíðinda. Ok treystum vér honum bæði vel til vits ok einurðar at segja frá, því at hann vissa ek alvitrastan ok hófsamastan. Láti guð honum nú raun lofi betri. (1, p. 115)

([...] but those stories concerning events that took place later were little written before the skald Sturla Þórðarson dictated the sagas of the Icelanders. For this he drew on both the knowledge of wise men who lived during his early years and also on some documents written by those who lived at the same time as the events that the sagas relate. He himself saw and heard many of the most important events of his time. And we may trust well both to his understanding and his judgment of what to tell, for I know him to be a very wise and a most temperate man. May God allow his experience to prove better for him than praise.)

The *Sturlunga* compiler is generally believed to have been expressing his own familiarity with Sturla the historian and knowledge of his historical writings, although the prologue is probably based to some extent on Sturla's own foreword to *Íslendinga saga*, especially regarding the sources of his saga.[11]

For many years, scholars have drawn attention to the epic-dramatic form of the sagas and their objective narrative method. The English literary critic W. P. Ker clarified the position of the saga narrator, the sagas' dramatic point of view and their impartial narrative, taking Sturla Þórðarson's *Íslendinga saga* as an example.[12] Ker stated:

---

11. See Björn M. Ólsen, *Om den saakaldte Sturlunga-prolog og dens formodede vidnesbyrd om de islandske slægtsagaers alder*, Christiania videnskabs-selskabs forhandlinger 6 (Oslo: s.n., 1910); Sverrir Tómasson, *Formálar íslenzkra sagnaritara á miðöldum: Rannsókn bókmenntahefðar*, Rit Stofnunar Árna Magnússonar á Íslandi 33 (Reykjavík: Stofnun Árna Magnússonar, 1988), pp. 384–5.

12. W. P. Ker, *Epic and Romance: Essays on Medieval Literature* (1897; rev. ed. 1908, rpt. New York: Dover, 1957).

[...] the Icelandic narrators give the succession of events, either as they might appear to an impartial spectator, or (on occasion) as they are viewed by someone in the story, but never as they merely affect the writer himself, though he may be as important a personage as Sturla [Þórðarson] was in the events of which he wrote the Chronicle.[13]

This narrative method naturally makes it difficult for the critic to pin down the views that the saga presents. Nevertheless, *Íslendinga saga* is shaped by its writer's point of view and the opinions that he had toward its characters and events.[14]

At about the same time as Ker, the Icelandic philologist Björn M. Ólsen pointed out that the contemporary sagas conformed to the same narrative conventions as the Sagas of Icelanders. In his essay *Um Sturlungu*, Ólsen used the narrator's knowledge, the literal perspective, and the point of view of the narrative to distinguish between the individual sagas of the compilation and to theorize on the identity of the saga's authors. For instance, he used these particular elements to distinguish what parts of the compilation belonged to *Íslendinga saga*.[15]

Sturla Þórðarson plays a major role in the events of *Íslendinga saga* after he establishes himself in it. He is also, as mentioned above, the saga's narrator. Naturally, as the narrator he is impersonal, following the general rule for the Sagas of Icelanders, but there are three notable exceptions to this. Twice he expresses himself in the first person (1, pp. 325 and 334). In the third instance the first person is used both for the narrator and his source, Sturla Þórðarson, when he points out the limitations to the validity of Sturla's witness to the course of events (1, p. 470). The identity of the narrator also becomes more prominent due to the fact that his knowledge and that of the source/the character Sturla are often the same.[16] Sturla, however, is always described in the

---

13. Ker, *Epic and Romance*, p. 273.
14. See Úlfar Bragason, "Sturla Þórðarson og Íslendinga saga: Höfundur, sögumaður, sögupersóna," in *Líf undir leiðarstjörnu*, ed., Haraldur Bessason, Rit Háskólans á Akureyri 3 (Akureyri: Háskólinn á Akureyri, 1994), pp. 139–52.
15. Björn M. Ólsen, *Um Sturlungu*, Safn til sögu Íslands og íslenzkrabókmennta 3 (Copenhagen: Hið íslenzka bókmenntafélag, 1902), pp. 193–510.
16. Björn M. Ólsen, *Um Sturlungu*, pp. 394–415.

same way as the other characters, in the third person. The story of his life is only one of many that are twisted together in the narrative of *Íslendinga saga*.

Sources of information are usually not mentioned in *Íslendinga saga*. Björn M. Ólsen made it clear that Sturla was a direct eyewitness only to portions of the saga, particularly those following his childhood. Ólsen was of the opinion that the best source for events occurring in the saga before the days of Sturla and during his youth was Sturla's father, the chieftain Þórðr Sturluson, and that all of the other likely sources relied upon by Sturla had been men.[17] This idea certainly gains support from the statement in the prologue to *Sturlunga saga* that the narrative is based in a certain way on the knowledge of wise men, as well as from the saga's limited choice of material—men's struggles for power and position. The Icelandic philologist Pétur Sigurðsson employed similar methods as Ólsen to distinguish the sagas in the compilation and their sources. However, he suggested that the account in *Íslendinga saga* of the Flugumýrr burning in 1253 was to some extent based on the memory of Ingibjörg Sturludóttir, the daughter of Sturla the historian, who survived the event.[18] It is thus not out of the question that the saga's narrative could have been based on stories told by women of events that occurred during their day, or to which they had been direct or indirect witnesses.

The American literary scholar Marlene Ciclamini argues that *Íslendinga saga* displays the affection and respect of Sturla the historian for Þórðr Sturluson, his father: "What he did value was his father's affection and teachings."[19] For Sturla, Þórðr had become a model that he was obligated to imitate. Cathy Jorgensen Itnyre has come to similar conclusions about the relationship between fathers and sons in the Sagas of Icelanders and the contemporary sagas, but has pointed out that "fathers demand obedience and are angry when it is not forthcoming; sons above all demand tangible proof (property and advantageous marriage) that they are their heirs, and often their impatience for both is palpable and a source of discontent with the

---

17. Björn M. Ólsen, *Um Sturlungu*, pp. 415–30.
18. Pétur Sigurðsson, *Um Íslendinga sögu Sturlu Þórðarsonar*, Safn til sögu Íslands og íslenzka bókmennta 6 (Reykjavík: Hið íslenzka bókmenntafélag, 1933–5), pp. 111–2.
19. Marlene Ciclamini, "Biographical Reflections in *Íslendinga saga*: A Mirror of Personal Values," *Scandinavian Studies* 55 (1983), p. 208.

elder generation."[20] Since Sturla the historian was illegitimate, he was favored with neither power nor wealth, even though his father was a chieftain. *Íslendinga saga* clearly indicates that Sturla was very aware that he was not truly noble by birth. His close relationship to his father was particularly important to him, since his future depended on his father's supporting him financially and promoting him in other ways. Þórðr also placed his faith in Sturla by granting him an inheritance and sanctioning him on the day of his death, thereby both according him recognition and laying a more stable foundation for his future advancement (1, p. 401).

Sturla's relationship with the saga-writer Snorri Sturluson, his uncle, is no less important, and Snorri appears in the saga as Sturla's substitute father. *Íslendinga saga* witnesses to the fact that in his childhood and teenage years Sturla spent a great deal of time with Snorri, most likely to study various subjects under him and other learned men at Reykjaholt: poetry, law, history, and saga-writing.[21] It was at Reykjaholt that the major works attributed to Snorri were composed: *Snorra Edda* and *Heimskringla*. Sturla was in Snorri's service (1, p. 362), and Snorri finds himself obliged to give Sturla a fatherly warning when Sturla makes legal claims that put the two of them at odds (1, p. 450). However, Snorri also trusts Sturla better than his own son for taking over the hereditary chieftaincy (1, p. 447). Despite the fact that *Íslendinga saga* condemns Snorri for fickleness in romantic matters and for having neglected his relationship with his children and foster sons due to his frugality, Sturla feels that it is his duty to avenge Snorri after his murder in 1241, even though this means attacking Klængr, Snorri's foster son (1, pp. 456–7). Klængr is called Sturla's foster brother in the saga (1, p. 413), and they stayed together at Reykjaholt. Klængr offered Sturla quarter after the Battle of Örlygsstaðir, in which numerous other members of the Sturlung clan were killed (1, p. 437).

---

20. Cathy Jorgensen Itnyre, "The Emotional Universe of Medieval Icelandic Fathers and Sons," in *Medieval Family Roles: A Book of Essays*, ed. Cathy Jorgensen Itnyre (New York and London: Garland, 1996), p. 191.
21. See Guðrún Ása Grímsdóttir, "Sturla Þórðarson," in *Sturlustefna: Ráðstefna haldin á sjö alda ártíð Sturlu Þórðarsonar sagnaritara 1984*, ed. Guðrún Ása Grímsdóttir and Jónas Kristjánsson, Rit Stofnunar Árna Magnússonar á Íslandi 32 (Reykjavík: Stofnun Árna Magnússonar, 1988), pp. 11–2.

Georges Duby states that "[t]he Middle Ages were resolutely male."[22] This can truly be said of the image that *Íslendinga saga* gives of Iceland in the thirteenth century. The saga is male-centric, dominated by men's dealings with each other, their relationships, disagreements, and factional disputes. Nevertheless, women play a part in *Íslendinga saga*, as they did in the life story of Sturla Þórðarson himself, although they function in the saga, as in most Sagas of Icelanders, primarily as accessories to the stories of men. The preparation leading up to the wedding of Ingibjörg Sturludóttir, which took place at Flugumýrr in 1253, supports the idea that to the heads of houses the female body had a generic, one might almost say, genealogical function.[23] It is Sturla who decides to marry Ingibjörg to Hallr Gizurarson, in order to ensure the peace between himself and Hallr's father, Gizurr Þorvaldsson, one of the most powerful chieftains in the country. Sturla seems not to have had any interest in seeking her consent and was obviously thinking mainly of increasing his own power and influence under the pretext of strengthening bonds of peace in society.[24] Otherwise, *Íslendinga saga* witnesses to the fact that men not only desired women but also feared the social disorder that could arise from casual associations with them, their goading and long memories.[25] All of Sturla's actions suggest that he supported propriety in matters of love and maintained an aristocratic view of marriage; a marriage would be most fortunate if it were entered into prudently, the couple would be an equal match, and their children would be a blessing.[26] On the other hand, it must not be forgotten that *Íslendinga saga* provides only a miniscule view of the life of most men and women of that time,[27] and

---

22. Duby, *Love and Marriage*, p. vii.
23. See Duby, *Love and Marriage*, p. 54.
24. See Björn Bandlien, *Strategies of Passion: Love and Marriage in Medieval Iceland and Norway*, trans. Betsy van der Hoek (Turnhout: Brepols, 1902), p. 277; Jenny Jochens, *Women in Old Norse Society* (Ithaca, NY: Cornell University Press, 1995), pp. 52–4.
25. Cf. Carol Clover, "Hildigunnr's lament," in *Structure and Meaning in Old Norse Literature: New Approaches to Textual Analysis and Literary Criticism*, ed. John Lindow, Lars Lönnroth, and Gerd Wolfgang Weber (Odense: Odense University Press, 1986); Jenny Jochens, "Old Norse Motherhood," in *Medieval Mothering*, ed John Carmi Parsons and Bonnie Wheeler (New York and London: Garland, 1996), p. 214; Duby, *Love and Marriage*, pp. 97–8.
26. Úlfar Bragason, "'Hart er í heimi, hórdómr mikill': Lesið í Sturlungu," *Skírnir* 163 (1989), p. 62 and 68.
27. See Jón Jóhannesson, "Um Sturlunga sögu," p. xii.

can thus only be taken as a limited source for knowledge of women's roles, their independence, and power. Marriage was the foundation of medieval society. But just as relationships could increase men's power, a woman's social position was stronger the more power and influence her husand had; as George Duby words it: "The comparable nature of the conditon of men and women stems from the fact that the foundation of social organization during the period with which we are concerned was the family, and more precisely, the house, or *domus*."[28] A woman's position was based on her marriage, her control of the household, and her rearing of children, especially sons. She could benefit immensely from having her sons support her, not least after she became a widow.[29]

Since *Íslendinga saga* takes place in the political arena and not within the household, most women appear in it as names in genealogical lists. Björn M. Ólsen was of the opinion that the genealogical section in the *Sturlunga* compilation had roots traceable to Sturla Þórðarson, although the compiler obviously dealt with it rather freely. *Íslendinga saga* was "svo efnismikil og víðtæk að allar þær ættir, sem taldar eru í ættartölubálkinum, snerta hana, sumar meira, aðrar minna" (so rich in material and comprehensive that all of the families that are counted in the genealogical section touch it, some more, some less).[30] Duby states: "There is no need to emphasize the importance of kinship bonds in the society we call 'feudal'. They are its inner framework." He continues: "Kinship plays a great part also in the unfolding life of politics, in the game of alliance and opposition, and the advancement of careers."[31] Knowledge of one's family and heritage was crucial in the Middle Ages, among other things because of hereditary rights and land claims, not least after the church began to restrict marriages between relatives, even to the fifth degree.[32] Genealogy also lies at the heart of *Íslendinga saga*, and its narratives recount the histories of the chief families of the country, not least the Sturlungs, to the third or fourth generation.

---

28. Duby, *Love and Marriage*, pp. 95–6.
29. Duby, *Love and Marriage*, p. 98. See also Jenny Jochens, *Women in Old Norse Society*, pp. 61–4.
30. Björn M. Ólsen, *Um Sturlungu*, p. 385.
31. Duby, *Love and Marriage*, p. 105.
32. Úlfar Bragason, "'Hart er í heimi, hórdómr mikill'," pp. 54–71.

In the genealogical section of the *Sturlunga* compilation, the Sturlung family is counted as being among Iceland's predominent clans. The lineage of Sturla Þórðarson, the grandfather of Sturla the historian, is traced through the female line to Snorri the Chieftain at Helgafell and Guðmundr the Powerful at Möðruvellir, both prominent figures in the Sagas of Icelanders. The genealogies state that the paternal grandmother of Guðný, the grandmother of Sturla the historian, was the daughter of Markús Skeggjason, who was the lawspeaker in the period 1084–1107 (1, p. 52). One might expect that such information about the maternal side of the family had best been preserved in the female line, since more emphasis is clearly laid in the genealogical section on tracing the male line, except when attempts are made to trace the female line to renowned individuals. A distinguished lineage made women more attractive. The Oddaverjar clan was very proud of having Þóra, the illegitimate daughter of King Magnús Barefoot of Norway, among its foremothers (1, p. 51 and 60).

According to *Þorláks saga helga* (ca. 1200), Bishop Þorlákr had at a young age spent a great deal of time "at bóknámi, en at riti optliga, á bœnum þess í millum, en nam þá er eigi dvaldi annat þat er móðir hans kunni kenna honum, ættvísi ok mannfrœði" (at booklearning, and often at writing, and at his prayers in between, and when he had no other tasks he learned what his mother could teach him, genealogy and tales of great men).[33] The Icelandic literary critic Helga Kress argues that "það hafi einkum verið konur sem í upphafi stunduðu munnlega frásagnarlist og stóðu fyrir munnlegri hefð skáldskaparins" (it was particularly women who originally engaged in the oral transmission of sagas and were responsible for the oral storytelling and poetic traditions in Iceland).[34] It must not be forgotten that during the Middle Ages, "we are for the most part dealing with societies which functioned orally."[35] It is therefore most likely that both men and women played important parts in preserving both genealogical lists

---

33. Ásdís Egilsdóttir, ed. *Þorláks saga byskups in elzta*, Biskupa sögur 2, Íslenzk fornrit 16 (Reykjavík: Hið íslenzka fornritafélag, 2002), pp. 50–1.

34. Helga Kress, *Máttugar meyjar: Íslensk fornbókmenntasaga* (Reykjavík: Háskólaútgáfan, 1993), p. 13.

35. Marcus Bull, *Thinking Medieval: An Introduction to the Study of the Middle Ages* (Houndmills: Palgrave Macmillan, 2005), p. 77. See also Jacques Le Goff, *History and Memory*, trans. Steven Rendall and Elizabeth Claman (New York: Columbia University Press, 1992), p. 74.

and oral tales based on them. On the other hand, it might be right, as Helga Kress suggests, that written culture was primarily in the hands of men, and that when this culture became dominant it muted the female oral tradition.[36]

In *Íslendingabók* (ca. 1130), Ari Þorgilsson the Wise names a woman, Þuríðr, who is a descendant of Snorri goði just like the Sturlungs, and "es bæði vas margspǫk ok óljúgfróð" (who was both knowledgeable in many things and a truthful narrator of the past),[37] as a source for information on the settlement of Iceland. This information is repeated in the preface to *Heimskringla* (ca. 1230), where it is said that "Ari nam ok marga frœði af Þuríði, dóttur Snorra goða. Hon var spǫk at viti. Hon mundi Snorra, fǫður sinn, en hann var þá nær háffertøgr, er kristni kom á Ísland, en andaðisk einum vetri eptir fall Óláfs konungs ins helga" (p. 7; Ari also gained much information from Þuríðr, the daughter of Snorri the Chieftain. She was a wise woman. She remembered her father Snorri, who was almost thirty-five years old when Christianity came to Iceland, and who died one year after the fall of King Óláfr the Saint). This and other sources clearly indicate that women in medieval Iceland participated in the transmission of knowledge about genealogy and important people and events.[38] Therefore, women in Sturla's family might have kindled his love for history, and he might have gotten some of his information on the past from female informants.

The genealogical section of the *Sturlunga* compilation tells of the parents of Sturla the historian and their children: "Þórðr [Sturluson] átti frillu, er Þóra hét,—þeira börn Óláfr, Sturla, Guttormr, Þórðr, Valgerðr, Guðrún (1, p. 52; Þórðr [Sturluson] had a concubine called Þóra—their children were Óláfr, Sturla, Guttormr, Þórðr, Valgerðr, Guðrún). Concerning the genealogy of Þóra, the mother of Sturla, nothing more is known. *Íslendinga saga* does not mention that she was Sturla's mother, but tells of her death in 1224, when he was ten years old, in the following words: "Þetta vár, er nú var frá sagt, andaðist Þóra, frilla Þórðar Sturlusonar, en hann tók til sín Valgerði, dóttur Árna

---

36. See Helga Kress, *Máttugar meyjar*, pp. 13-4.
37. Jakob Benediktsson, ed. *Íslendingabók*, Íslenzk fornrit 1 (Reykjavík: Hið íslenzka fornritafélag, 1985), p. 4.
38. Cf. Elizabeth van Houts, *Memory and Gender in Medieval Europe 900-1200* (Toronto: University of Toronto Press, 1999), pp. 65-92.

ór Tjaldanesi, ok gerði brúðlaup til hennar um sumarit" (1, p. 303; In the spring just mentioned, Þóra, the mistress of Þórðr Sturluson, died, and he took in Valgerðr, the daughter of Árni from Tjaldanes, and married her in the summer). Either Þóra had been of such poor lineage that her son did not consider mentioning her family, or else there had been some sort of violation of canon law in this parents' relationship that prevented him from going into more detail.[39] It has been argued that in medieval times it was the mother who nurtured the small child and that "[t]he woman who taught children to speak also transmitted the oral tradition through songs and taught them their first prayers."[40] Most likely, however, Sturla did not spend much time with his mother in his youth, probably because she had all her six children with Þórðr in about ten years. In addition, the rearing of sons was the father's responsibility once they reached the age of seven.[41] Sturla was, therefore, not as emotionally attached to his mother as his father, and later gave neither of his daughters her name. Finally, it remains unknown if he could have learned from her information about genealogy and tales of important men, as St. Þorlákr had done from his mother.

Íslendinga saga calls Sturla Þorðarson the foster son of Guðný, his grandmother. The saga says that she had overseen the homesteads of her son Þórðr at Staðr or in Eyrr, but that in 1218 she had gone to dwell in Reykjaholt when Snorri Sturluson, her son, went to Norway (1, p. 271). There she died in 1221, when Sturla was only seven years old. Sturla had most likely been under her care in his childhood and

---

39. See Ciclamini, "Biographical Reflections in *Íslendinga saga*," p. 208. See also Rolf Heller, "Þóra, frilla Þórðar Sturlusonar," *Arkiv för nordisk filologi* 81 (1966), pp. 39–56, who suggests that Þóra was the daughter of Bishop Páll Jónsson of Skálaholt (1195–1211), and thus a third cousin to Þórðr Sturluson's second wife. Others have suggested that she was Þóra Jónsdóttir, the niece of the aforementioned Þóra Pálsdóttir of the Hítardalr family (which could explain the friendship between Ketill Þorláksson, lawspeaker and member of the Hítardalr family, d. 1273), and Sturla (see also Stefán Karlsson, "Alfræði Sturlu Þórðarsonar," in *Sturlustefna: Ráðstefna haldin á sjö alda ártíð Sturlu Þórðarsonar sagnaritara 1984*, ed. Guðrún Ása Grímsdóttir and Jónas Kristjánsson, Rit Stofnunar Árna Magnússonar á Íslandi 32 [Reykjavík: Stofnun Árna Magnússonar, 1988], p. 51). The compiler of *Sturlunga* explains his relationship to Helga, Sturla's wife, in *Geirmundar þáttr heljarskinns* (1, p. 10). It is unlikely that he would not have detailed, in any of the compilation's genealogical lists, his familial relationship to Sturla, if Sturla, like himself, had been a member of the Hítardalr family, even though Sturla might have preferred to keep his mother's side of the family as private information.

40. Sulamith Shahar, *Childhood in the Middle Ages*, trans. Chaya Galai (London and New York: Routledge, 1990; rpt. 1992), p. 114.

41. Duby, *Love and Marriage*, p. 97.

been dear to her, because she bequeathed to him all of her wealth after her death: "ok var þat mikit fé" (1, p. 303; and that was a great deal of money), says the saga. He was also fond of her memory, as evident from the fact that he named one of his daughters Guðný. Although Sturla was a child when Guðný died, it is not unlikely that she inspired in him interest in genealogy and tales of important men,[42] although his historical understanding was doubtless better nurtured while he lived during his teenage years at Reykjaholt with Snorri Sturluson. Guðný is also cited as a source in *Eyrbygga saga* for the story of the transferral of the bones of Snorri the Chieftain and other descendants of the Sturlung clan to the churchyard of the new church in Sælingsdalstunga (1, pp. 183–4), the farm where Sturla's mother-in-law later lived.

It can be determined from this that Guðný had known stories of past times.[43] Nevertheless, Björn M. Ólsen did not count Guðný among Sturla's sources for *Íslendinga saga*. The saga, however, says that after Guðný became a widow she had an affair with the chieftain Ari Þorgilsson the Strong of Staðr, a descendant of the historian Ari the Wise. She went with Ari to Norway, after he gave his only daughter and heir in marriage to Þórðr Sturluson, Guðný's son, but Ari died on the trip (1, pp. 229–31). The story of this love affair could just as well have come from Guðný as from her son Þórðr. It is certain, however, that she herself must have told of her dream at the birth of Sturla Sighvatsson, her grandson, in the year 1199. The saga says:

> Guðný Böðvarsdóttir bjó í Hvammi ok leiddi mjök fréttum um mátt Halldóru [Tumadóttur]. Ok eina nótt dreymði hana, at maðr kæmi ór Hjarðarholti, ok þóttist hon spyrja at mætti Halldóru. Hann kvað hana hafa barn fætt ok kvað vera sveinbarn. Guðný spurði, hvat héti. "Hann heitir Vígsterkr," segir hann. En um morgininn eftir kom maðr ór Hjarðarholti ok segir, at Halldóra var léttari. Guðný spurði, hvárt væri. Hann kvað vera svein ok heita Sturlu. (1, pp. 236–7)

(Guðný Böðvarsdóttir lived in Hvammr and was very concerned about the health of Halldóra [Tumadóttir, her daughter-in-law]. And

---

42. See Ciclamini, "Biographical Reflections in *Íslendinga saga*," p. 209.
43. See Guðrún Ása Grímsdóttir, "Sturla Þórðarson," p. 11.

one night she dreamed that a man came from Hjarðarholt, and it seemed that she asked him about Halldóra's health. He said that she had given birth to a child and that it was a boy. Guðný asked what the boy was named. "He is named Vígsterkr," he said. And on the next morning a man came from Hjarðarholt and said that Halldóra had given birth. Guðný asked whether it was a boy or girl. He said that it was a boy and was named Sturla.)

Íslendinga saga contains many dream-narratives, and it appears that the narrator accepted their prophetic validity. One might presume that the saga-writer would have put more stock in this particular dream-narrative if he had heard it himself from the mouth of his grandmother and foster mother.[44] Þórðr, Sturla's father, doubtless had no less faith in his mother's sagacity than he; she was in charge of the household, and he sent Sturla to her for fosterage. It may almost certainly be attributable to her as to Þórðr concerning how much emphasis the saga-writer places on the saga's genealogical lists and faith in a "social order [...], since the existing order was considered both good and proper."[45] She herself came from a line of aristocrats, and had both been married to one dashing chieftain and had an affair with another. Her three sons were also extremely ambitious, and she doubtless played a part in inspiring that ambition.[46]

As mentioned above, Sturla was most likely supported by his grandmother in Reykjaholt, where she managed the estate of her son Snorri and lived until the end of her life. Several years after her death Snorri became a half-share partner with Hallveig Ormsdóttir, whose grandfather, Jón Loftsson of Oddi, had fostered Snorri as a child. Hallveig had by then become a widow and the wealthiest woman in Iceland. Although Snorri had thought "hennar ferð heldr hæðilig ok brosti at" (1, p. 299; her appearance somewhat ludicrous and smiled at it) when he met her on the road soon after she became a widow, and Þórðr, his brother, had made an unfavorable prophecy about their relationship

---

44. Gunnar Benediktsson, *Sagnameistarinn Sturla* (Reykjavík: Menningarsjóður, 1961), pp. 15–6, 177–8.
45. Shahar, *Childhood in the Middle Ages*, p. 167; cf. Gunnar Karlsson, "Siðamat Íslendingasögu," in *Sturlustefna: Ráðstefna haldin á sjö alda ártíð Sturlu Þórðarsonar sagnaritara 1984*, ed. Guðrún Ása Grímsdóttir and Jónas Kristjánsson, Rit Stofnunar Árna Magnússonar á Íslandi 32 (Reykjavík: Stofnun Árna Magnússonar, 1988), pp. 204–21.
46. Cf. Jochens, *Women in Old Norse Society*, pp. 7–16.

(1, p. 304), they lived together in Reykjaholt until she died in the summer of 1241. Hallveig was thus in charge of Snorri's estate during the years when he was at the height of his power, which was based among other things on her wealth. By that time Sturla Þórðarson had been in Reykjaholt for many years. Hallveig could thus have been a substitute mother-figure for him, even an object of desire similar to the young knight who desires the lady in the castle in chivalric romances.[47] A statement made in *Sturlu þáttr* might even apply mutatis mutandis to Sturla's stay in Reykjaholt: "Konungr tók þá Sturlu vel ok tærði honum vel ok sæmiliga. Drottning var til hans forkunnar vel, ok svá gerðu aðrir eftir" (2, p. 234; The king then warmly received Sturla into his court and entertained him well and graciously. The queen showed him great friendliness and so did the others thereafter). The narrator of *Íslendinga saga* also conveys Snorri's sorrow when he tells of the death of Hallveig: "[...] þótti Snorra þat allmikill skaði, sem honum var" (1, p. 452; This seemed to Snorri a great loss, and so it was for him). Sturla also takes it badly that Klængr, the son of Hallveig, participated in the attack on Snorri that same fall, and that he needs to take vengeance on him (1, p. 457). It is thus entirely uncertain that the saga-writer had been in agreement with his father concerning Snorri's domestic arrangement. On the other hand, the saga's wavering attitudes toward Snorri could have been colored as much by Sturla's feeling for Hallveig and her stories of her life—Snorri had conflicted with Björn Þorvaldsson, Hallveig's previous husband, and was even responsible for his death (1, p. 280)—as by the fact that Þórðr and Snorri did not always see eye-to-eye.

Although Sturla seems not to have been emotionally attached to his mother, he certainly was to his grandmother, and even to Hallveig Ormsdóttir, two eminent women who gained power at the same time as they became widowed. The third strong widow in Sturla's life was his mother-in-law. The Sturlusons, Þórðr, Sighvatr and Snorri, argued over who was to take charge of their hereditary chieftaincy in the Dalir. Into this dispute was blended the so-called Jóreiðr case, which came about when Ingimundr Jónsson, a supporter of the chieftain Sturla Sighvatsson and a first-cousin of both him and Sturla the historian, proposed to the widow Jóreiðr Hallsdóttir of Sælingsdalstunga, although, as the saga

---

47. Shahar, *Childhood in the Middle Ages*, p. 218.

tells us, "hon vildi eigi giftast, því at hon vildi eigi ráða fé undan dóttur sinni" (1, p. 309; she did not want to get married, because she did not want to deprive her daughter of her property). In the winter of 1225–6, Ingimundr and Sturla brought her without her consent from her home to Sauðafell, where Sturla was living, and Sturla tried to persuade her to marry Ingimundr; she, however, refused both this plan and food, leaving them no choice but to release her. Later, Magnús Gizurarson, the bishop of Skálaholt, made them pay her twenty hundreds for this degradation, which was no small amount of money (1, p. 311). Björn M. Ólsen says that the saga-writer learned at least part of this story from Þórðr Sturluson, who was a party to the dispute.[48] However, when it is considered that Jóreðr Hallsdóttir later became the mother-in-law of Sturla the historian, and that his wife Helga was her only daughter, it appears most likely that he learned the story directly from Jóreiðr. It seems that she herself oversaw her household as a widow for a long time, and the saga mentions chieftains going to visit her, which suggests that she must have been considered a prominent person (1, p. 321 and 392). At the very least, her son-in-law portrayed her favorably and with great respect in his saga. Further, her kinsmen and in-laws were among the most loyal supporters of Sturla's chieftaincy.

It is not certain when Sturla married Helga Þórðardóttir, but it was prior to 1240, because their daughter Ingibjörg was most likely born in that year.[49] Helga is only once mentioned directly in *Íslendinga saga*, when she goes with her husband to the wedding of Ingibjörg Sturladóttir at Flugumýrr in 1253. This is why we do not know about Sturla's love for his wife, or whether his saga gains anything from her storytelling. The French historian Philippe Ariés mentions that in the Middle Ages "men preferred not to speak of the love they found in marriage [...]. Such silence may indicate indifference or ignorance, a sense or propriety or a desire for secrecy."[50] Most likely, Helga was an obedient wife who gained her husband's respect. This respect may perhaps be seen in a chapter, probably written by Sturla, which is included in one of the two main manuscripts of *Sturlunga saga*, since Helga is called a matron in it ("húsfreyja"; 2, p. 288). The saga says

---

48. Björn M. Ólsen, *Um Sturlungu*, pp. 413–4, 420.
49. See Guðrún Ása Grímsdóttir, "Sturla Þórðarson," pp. 12–3.
50. Philippe Ariés, "Love in Married Life," in *Western Sexuality: Practice and Perception in Past and Present Times*, ed. Phillippe Ariés and André Béjin, trans. Anthony Foster (Oxford: Oxford University Press, 1985, rpt. 1986), p. 135.

nothing of Sturla's love affairs (*amor*) or children outside of marriage; instead he appears to have a respectful marriage (*dilectio*), with respect (*reverencia*) for his wife, and he has four children with her.[51] The conclusion may be derived from *Íslendinga saga* that Sturla, who was born out of wedlock, was a staunch supporter of matrimonial propriety, and he used his marriage to strengthen his position, wealth, and influence.

Sturla lived off his wife's wealth, and her kinsmen held the title to the great estate of Staðarhóll, where they made their home for the longest time. Sturla's first cousin, Órækja Snorrason, wanted to take possession of Staðarhóll and claimed to have greater rights to it than Sturla (1, p. 448–51). The cousins ended up in a dispute over this, and Sturla came out better with the support of his wife's family and kinsmen, although this required digging up old family ties and old hereditary rights.[52] This information could perhaps have come from Sturla's wife and mother-in-law, although the saga names Páll Hallsson, Helga's uncle, in this regard.

Sturla and Helga had two daughters, Ingibjörg and Guðný. Guðný plays little part in the saga, and it is doubtful that she had been its source, although her husband and his family might have been.[53] Ingibjörg was named after Helga's maternal grandmother and would have spent some time with Jóreiðr, her grandmother, at Sælingsdalstunga. There she was betrothed, at the age of thirteen, to Hallr, the son of Gizurr Þorvaldsson—obedient daughter as she truly was. Jóreiðr donated a considerable part of her dowry (1, p. 480). That same autumn, the wedding was celebrated at Flugumýrr in Skagafjörðr, and was a well-attended and prestigious event. After the wedding, however, the former comrade-in-arms of Sturla Þórðarson made an attack on Gizurr in his home. The saga tells of Ingibjörg and her mother-in-law, Gróa Álfsdóttir, after the attackers set fire to the houses at Flugumýrr:

Þá kom þar til Gróu í anddyrit Ingibjörg Sturludóttir ok var í náttserk einum ok berfætt. Hon var þá þrettán vetra gömul ok var bæði mikil vexti ok sköruleg at sjá. Silfrbelti hafði vafizt um fætr henni,

---

51. Úlfar Bragason, "'Hart er í heimi, hórdómr mikill'," p. 62; cf. Duby, *Love and Marriage*, pp. 97–8.
52. Sveinbjörn Rafnsson. "Um Staðarhólsmál Sturlu Þórðarsonar: Nokkrar athuganir á valdsmennsku um hans daga," *Skírnir* 159 (1985), pp. 143–59.
53. Pétur Sigurðsson, *Um Íslendinga sögu Sturlu Þórðarsonar*, p. 20.

er hon komst ór hvílunni fram, var þar á pungr ok þar í gull hennar mörg, hafði hon þat þar með sér. Gróa varð fegin henni mjök ok segir, at eitt skyldi yfir þær ganga báðar. [...]

Þær Gróa ok Ingibjörg gengu nú út at durunum. Gróa bað Ingibjörgu útgöngu. Þat heyrði Kolbeinn grön, frændi hennar, ok bað hana út gang til sín. Hon kvaðsk eigi þat vilja, nema hon köri mann með sér. Kolbeinn kvað eigi þat mundu. Gróa bað hana út gang,—"en ek verð at leita sveinsins Þorláks, systursonar míns," segir hon. [...]

Þat er sumra manna sögn, at Þorsteinn genja hryndi Gróu inn í eldinn, ok þar fannst hon í anddyrinu.

Kolbeinn grön hljóp inn í eldinn eftir Ingibjörgu ok bar hana út til kirkju. Tóku þá húsin mjök at loga. (1, pp. 490–1)

(Then Ingibjörg, Sturla's daughter, came up to Gróa there at the front door; she was wearing only her nightdress and was barefoot. She was then thirteen years old, but was both tall and stately in appearance. Her silver belt had wrapped itself around her feet when she had come from her bed; on it were a purse and the many gold rings that she had with her on that occasion. Gróa was very happy to see her and said that now one fate should prevail for them both. [...]

Gróa and Ingibjörg meanwhile went out to the door. Gróa asked that Ingibjörg be allowed to go out. Kolbeinn grön, her kinsman, heard this and asked her to come out to him. She said that she would not come out unless she might choose one person to accompany her. Kolbeinn refused. Gróa then bade Ingibjörg to go out:—"but I must look to the boy Þorlákr, my nephew," she said. [...]

Some men say that Þorsteinn genja shoved Gróa into the fire; she was later found there at the front door.

Kolbeinn grön ran into the fire after Ingibjörg and carried her out to the church. Then the flames on the house blazed up even higher.)

As mentioned above, Ingibjörg appears to have been one of her father's sources for information about this horrific and unforgivable event, which forms the second climax of his *Íslendinga saga*. Many people died in the attack from wounds or burns, among them Gizurr's wife and their sons, although Gizurr himself was saved. The burning of Flugumýrr thus represents Ingibjörg's baptismal fire, as events are described in *Íslendinga saga*. The innocence of her youth ends with her marriage, and death is just as quickly revealed to her. The horrible truth of her life crashes down upon her, like the protagonists in a Greek tragedy: as she stands on the porch of Flugumýrr, tall and stately, hardly out of childhood, clad in a nightdress, barefoot, a silver belt wrapped about her feet and a sea of fire all around her, she commands the audience's sympathy completely. The sympathy that the narrative creates for Ingibjörg Sturludóttir causes the audience of the saga to understand in an instant that this age of terror had to come to an end.

Shortly after the description of the burning at Flugumýrr, *Íslendinga saga* says: "Ingibjörgu bauð til sín eftir brennuna Halldóra, dóttir Snorra Bárðarsonar, frændkona hennar, er þá bjó í Odda. Fór hon þangat ok förunautar hennar með henni. Var hon þrekuð, barn at aldri" (1, 494; Halldóra, the daughter of Snorri Bárðarson, who was living then at Oddi, invited her kinswoman Ingibjörg to stay with her after the burning. Ingibjörg went to Oddi with her companions. Still a child in years, she was quite worn out). The pathos of these words emphasizes the cruelty of the times, as well as the way that the father, the narrator of the story, shares the pain of his daughter, whom he himself has placed in peril.[54] Her innocence is powerless against the works of men without scruples. The saga chorus, in the meantime, judges the burners at Flugumýrr harshly, while the narrator asks for God's mercy on them: "Þessi tíðindi spurðust brátt, ok þótti öllum vitrum mönnum þessi tíðindi einhver mest hafa orðit hér á Íslandi, sem guð fyrirgefi þeim, er gerðu, með sinni mikilli miskunn ok mildi" (1, 493; The news now spread quickly, and it seemed to all the wiser men of the land that this was perhaps the most significant event that had ever occurred here in Iceland—may God in His great mercy and mildness forgive them). The objectivity of the narrative is clearly broken, and its emotional perspective revealed. W. P. Ker emphasized the tragic undertone of *Íslendinga saga*: "[T]he Icelandic tragedy had no reconciliation at the end, and there was no national strength underneath the disorder, fit to be called out by a peacemaker

---

54. See Pétur Sigurðsson, *Um Íslendinga sögu Sturlu Þórðarsonar*, p. 111.

or a 'saviour of society'."⁵⁵ This view is most clearly expressed at the climactic points of *Íslendinga saga*, especially in the description of the Flugumýrr burning. One may even ask whether it is Ingibjörg Sturludóttir's cruel experience and knowledge, and in her father's empathy with her, that the saga has its emotional origin.⁵⁶ Thus the plainness (*bersögli*) of *Huldar saga* is connected to the "truth" of *Íslendinga saga*; the love of Sturla for Ingibjörg, his daughter, and his anquish over the suffering that he caused her as a child, is tied to Queen Ingilborg's appreciation of the sagacity of the saga-master.

After the burning of Flugumýrr, the saga says that the following occurred:

> Þá var borinn út á skildi Ísleifr Gizurarson, ok var hans ekki eftir nema búkrinn steiktr innan í brynjunni. Þá fundust ok brjóstin af Gróu, ok var þat borit út á skildi at Gizuri.
>
> Þá mælti Gizurr: "Páll [Kolbeinsson] frændi, "segir hann," hér máttu nú sjá Ísleif, son minn, ok Gróu konu mína."
>
> Ok fann Páll, at hann leit frá, ok stökk ór andlitinu sem haglkorn væri. (1, 494)

> (Then borne out on a shield was Ísleifr Gizurarson, and nothing was left of him but his torso, fried inside his armor. Gróa's breast was also found, and it was born out on a shield to Gizurr.
>
> Gizurr said: "Páll [Kolbeinsson], my kinsman, here you can now see Ísleifr, my son, and Gróa, my wife."
>
> And Páll saw that Gizurr turned away, and tears poured from his eyes like hailstones.)

The description shows that Sturla the historian understood a husband's love for his wife and children. It displays the sympathy that the saga writer has for Gizurr in his sorrow, the shame that comes with the burnings, the indiscriminate violence against women, and Gizurr's right and responsibility for taking revenge. Gróa's breast becomes a symbol of the power of life that can do little against the destructive urges of men. This symbol takes on even deeper meaning when one

---

55. Ker, *Epic and Romance*, p. 257.
56. Cf. Gunnar Karlsson, "Siðamat Íslendingasögu," p. 220.

considers that it is the motherless child, Sturla Þórðarson, who tells the story; it might even also indicate his "nostalgia for the maternal breast" from which he had been removed,[57] an experience that could have colored his position toward women all his life.

It therefore seems almost pathetic when the narrator continues by saying, after having counted all the losses in the fire, that "[þ]ar brunnu ok margir gripir, er átti Ingibjörg Sturludóttir" (1, p. 494; Many of the treasures that Sturla's daughter Ingibjörg owned also burned up in the fire). In the context of the disaster, the loss of a part of Ingibjörg's dowry was a mere trifle. As Björn M. Ólsen has indicated, however, *Íslendinga saga* deals with "ýmislegt, sem snertir fjárhag Sturlu [Þórðarsonar] beinlínis eða óbeinlínis" (various things that touch on the financial situation of Sturla [Þórðarson], directly or indirectly).[58] Among other things, it deals with the disputes over Sturla's inheritance from Guðný, his grandmother, the Jóreiðr case, and the Staðarhóll case. In all of these events, women in Sturla's life play important roles. They were the source of both his wealth and power, and subsequently supported his aristocratic position.

In spite of the objectivity of the saga, Sturla the historian was capable of communicating his concern and love for his daughter Ingibjörg in *Íslendinga saga*. However, she is taken care of after the burning by her third cousin, not her father or grandmother (although this might have been seen as appropriate, since she had been married off). But it might also indicate her father's fear of her memory of the burning, and serve as a reminder that he might be obliged to support Gizurr in his revenge.[59] After all, the Flugumýrr burning was incited by a woman, who slandered her husband's courage in suggesting that her father had not been avenged well enough (1, pp. 480–1). Illegitimate child as this woman is, she is portrayed in the saga as both a devourer and bearer of death, which like all weak creatures uses it serpent-tongue as a weapon.[60]

Íslendinga saga is a masculine saga. Nevertheless, it is possible to contend that the saga has its roots in the paternal love—and fear—of the saga-writer. The cruelty that his daughter suffered as a child might

---

57. Duby, *Love and Marriage*, p. 97.
58. Björn M. Ólsen, *Um Sturlungu*, p. 413.
59. Cf. Clover, "Hildigunnr's lament."
60. Cf. Duby, *Love and Marriage*, p. 97.

have opened her father's eyes to the fear that feuding in Icelandic society would have no end. Sturla's love and respect for the women in his life shine through his storytelling. But women played little part in the disputes of the Sturlung Age, which the saga described; their domain was the home, even though they might have kindled disputes. Overall, they had little to do with the material of *Íslendinga saga*. What ties together the narratives dealing with women in the life of Sturla is the fact that nearly all of them concern his financial affairs. The women in his life could have been, in some instances, his source for genealogical knowledge and story-events, and they most likely kindled his love of storytelling. But it is a cold, hard fact that Sturla Þórðarson the historian was much more occupied in his *Íslendinga saga* with the property rights that he obtained from women than with his love for them and what he might have learned from them. According to the saga, it seems that his domain was built much more on the wealth of the women in his life than their knowledge and his love for them.

TRANSLATED BY PHILIP ROUGHTON.

Bibliography

Ariés, Philippe. "Love in Married Life." In *Western Sexuality: Practice and Percept in Past and Present Times*. Ed. Philippe Ariés and André Béjin. Trans. Anthony Foster. Oxford: Oxford University Press, 1985, rpt. 1986. Pp. 130–9.

Bandlien, Björn. *Strategies of Passion: Love and Marriage in Medieval Iceland and Norway*. Trans. Betsy van der Hoek. Turnhout: Brepols, 2005.

Björn M. Ólsen. Um Sturlungu. Safn til sögu Íslands og íslenzkra bókmennta 3. Copenhagen: Hið íslenzka bókmenntafélag, 1902. Pp. 193–510.

———. *Om den saakaldte Sturlunga-prolog og dens formodede vidnesbyrd om de islandske slægtsagaers alder*. Christiania videnskabs-selskabs forhandlinger 6 (Oslo: s.n., 1910)

Bull, Marcus. *Thinking Medieval: An Introduction to the Study of the Middle Ages*. Houndmills: Palgrave Macmillan, 2005.

Ciklamini, Marlene. "Biographical Reflections in *Íslendinga saga*: A Mirror of Personal Values." *Scandianvian Studies* 55 (1983): 205–21.

Clover, Carol. "Hildigunnr's lament." In *Structure and Meaning in Old Norse Literature: New Approaches to Textual Analysis and Literary Criticism*. Ed. John Lindow, Lars Lönnroth, and Gerd Wolfgang Weber. Odense: Odense University Press, 1986. Pp. 141–83.

Duby, Georges. *Love and Marriage in the Middle Ages*. Trans. Jane Dunnett. Chicago: University of Chicago Press, 1994.

Eyrbyggja saga. Ed. Einar Ól. Sveinsson. Íslenzk fornrit 4. Reykjavík: Hið íslenzka fornritafélag, 1935. Pp. 1–186.

Gunnar Karlsson. "Siðamat Íslendingasögu." In *Sturlustefna: Ráðstefna haldin á sjö alda ártíð Sturlu Þórðarsonar sagnaritara 1984*. Ed. Guðrún Ása Grímsdóttir and Jónas Kristjánsson. Rit Stofnunar Árna Magnússonar á Íslandi 32. Reykjavík: Stofnun Árna Magnússonar, 1988. Pp. 204–21.
Guðrún Ása Grímsdóttir. "Sturla Þórðarson." In *Sturlustefna: Ráðstefna haldin á sjö alda ártíð Sturlu Þórðarsonar sagnaritata 1984*. Ed. Guðrún Ása Grímsdóttir and Jónas Kristjánsson. Rit Stofnunar Árna Magnússonar á Íslandi 32. Reykjavík: Stofnun Árna Magnússonar, 1988. Pp. 9–36.
Gunnar Benediktsson. *Sagnameistarinn Sturla*. Reykjavík: Menningarsjóður, 1961.
Heimskringla. Ed. Bjarni Aðalbjarnarson. Vol. 1. Íslenzk fornrit 26. Reykjavík: Hið íslenzka fornritafélag, 1974.
Helga Kress. *Máttugar meyjar: Íslensk fornbókmenntasaga*. Reykjavík: Háskólaútgáfan, 1993.
Helgi Þorláksson. "Sturla Þórðarson, minni og vald." 2. *íslenska söguþingið. Proceedings*. 2 vols. Reykjavík: Sagnfræðistofnun, 2002. vol. 1, pp. 319–41.
Heller, Rolf. "Þóra, frilla Þórðar Sturlusonar." *Arkiv för nordisk filologi* 81 (1966): 39–56.
Houts, Elizabeth van. *Memory and Gender in Medieval Europe 900–1200*. Toronto: University of Toronto Press, 1999.
Íslendingabók. Ed. Jakob Benediktsson. Íslenzk fornrit 1. Reykjavík: Hið íslenzka fornritafélag, 1985. Pp. 1–28.
Itnyre, Cathy Jorgensen. "The Emotional Universe of Medieval Icelandic Fathers and Sons." *Medieval Family Roles: A Book of Essays*. Ed. Cathy Jorgensen Intyre. New York and London: Garland, 1996. Pp. 173–96.
Jochens, Jenny. *Women in Old Norse Society*. Ithaca, NY: Cornell University Press, 1995.
———. "Old Norse Motherhood." In *Medieval Mothering*. Ed. John Carmi Parsons and Bonnie Wheeler. New York and London: Garland, 1996. Pp. 201–22.
Jón Jóhannesson. "Um Sturlunga sögu." In *Sturlunga saga*. Ed. Jón Jóhannesson, Magnús Finnbogason, and Kristján Eldjárn. Vol. 2. Reykjavík: Sturlunguútgáfan, 1946. Pp. vii–lvi.
Ker, W. P. *Epic and Romance: Essays on Medieval Literature*. 1897. Rev. ed. 1908; rpt. New York: Dover, 1957.
Le Goff, Jacques. *History and Memory*. Trans. Steven Rendall and Elizabeth Claman. New York: Columbia University Press, 1992.
Pétur Sigurðsson. *Um Íslendinga sögu Sturlu Þórðarsonar*. Safn til sögu Íslands og íslenzkra bókmennta 6. Reykjavík: Hið íslenzka bókmenntafélag, 1933–5.
Shahar, Sulamith. *Childhood in the Middle Ages*. Trans. Chaya Galai. London and New York: Routledge, 1990, rpt. 1992.
Stefán Karlsson. "Alfræði Sturlu Þórðarsonar." *Sturlustefna: Ráðstefna haldin á sjö alda alda ártíð Sturlu Þórðarsonar sagnaritara 1984*. Ed. Guðrún Ása Grímsdóttir and Jónas Kristjánsson. Rit Stofnunar Árna Magnússonar á Íslandi 32. Reykjavík: Stofnun Árna Magnússonar, 1988. Pp. 37–60.
Sturlunga saga. Ed. Jón Jóhannesson, Magnús Finnbogason, and Kristján Eldjárn. 2 vols. Reykjavík: Sturlunguútgáfan, 1946.
Sturlunga saga. Trans. Julia H. McGrew and R. George Thomas. 2 vols. The Library of Scandinavian Literature 9–10. New York: Twayne, 1970–4.
Sveinbjörn Rafnsson. "Um Staðarhólsmál Sturlu Þórðarsonar: Nokkrar athuganir á valdsmennsku um hans daga." *Skírnir* 159 (1985): 143–59.

Sverrir Tómasson. *Formálar íslenzkra sagnaritara á miðöldum: Rannsókn bókmenntahefðar.* Rit Stofnunar Árna Magnússonar á Íslandi 33. Reykjavík: Stofnun Árna Magnússonar, 1988.

Sørensen, Preben Meulengracht. *Saga og samfund: En indføring i oldislandsk litteratur.* Copenhagen: Berlingske, 1977.

Toorn, M. C. van den. "Erzählsituation und Perspektive in der Saga." *Arkiv för nordisk filologi* 77 (1962): 68–83.

Úlfar Bragason. "'Hart er í heimi, hórdómr mikill': Lesið í Sturlungu." *Skírnir* 163 (1989): 54–71.

———. "Um hvað fjallaði Huldar saga?" *Tímarit Máls og menningar* 51.4 (1990): 76–81.

———. "Sturla Þórðarson og Íslendinga saga: Höfundur, sögumaður, sögupersóna." *Líf undir leiðarstjörnu.* Ed. Haraldur Bessason. Rit Háskólans á Akureyri 3. Akureyri: Háskólinn á Akureyri, 1994. Pp. 139–52.

Þorláks saga byskups in elzta. Ed. Ásdís Egilsdóttir. Biskupa sögur 2. Íslenzk fornrit 16. Reykjavík: Hið íslenzka fornritafélag, 2002. Pp. 45–99.

Klári saga as an Indigenous Romance

SHAUN F. D. HUGHES

Klári saga (also known as *Clári* or *Clarus saga*) survives incomplete in two vellum manuscripts from the late fourteenth century (AM 657b, 4to and Stock. Perg. 4to no. 6) and in a fifteenth-century vellum, AM 589d 4to, as well as in numerous later manuscripts.[1] The saga was edited by Gustav Cederschiöld first diplomatically in 1879 and then in a normalized version which appeared in 1907.[2] Despite being long accessible, the saga has not excited much critical attention.[3] Because

---

1. In addition to *Klári* saga, AM 657a–b 4to contains a considerable collection of *exempla*. Also the earliest version of the *Sögupáttur af Jóni biskupi*, originally catalogued as AM 764b 4to, has been restored to AM 657 4to of which it was originally a part (Kristian Kålund, *Katalog over den Arnamagnæanske håndskriftsamling*, 2 vols. [Copenhagen: Gyldendal, 1888–94], vol. 2, pp. 68–70, 184–5). AM 589d 4to, on the other hand, is a saga manuscript (Kålund, *Katalog*, vol. 1, p. 755). See Marianne Kalinke and P. M. Mitchell, *Bibliography of Old Norse-Icelandic Romances*, Islandica 44 (Ithaca: Cornell University Press, 1985), pp. 72–5 for the complete list of the surviving manuscripts of *Klári saga*, plus editions, translations, and scholarship. To the translations should be added: Dennis Ferrell Kearney, "Clárus saga: An Edition and Translation" (Ph.D. Dissertation, University of Mississippi, 1990).

2. Quotations from *Klári* saga will be taken from the slightly modernized version printed in Bjarni Vilhjálmsson, ed. *Riddarasögur*, 6 vols. (Akureyri: Íslendingasagnaútgáfan, 1952–4), vol. 5, pp. 1–61 based on Cederschiöld's 1907 edition. All translations are my own.

3. The sole monograph on the saga is Alfred Jakobsen, *Studier i Clarus saga: til spørsmålet om sagaens norske proveniens*, Årbok for Universitetet i Bergen, Humanistisk serie 1963.2 (Bergen: Universitetsforlaget, 1964), which attempts to claim that the saga was translated from Latin into medieval Norwegian subsequently making its way to Iceland, a position which has garnered little support. See also Marianne Kalinke, "Klári saga," in *Dictionary of the Middle Ages* 7 (New York: Charles Scribner's Sons, 1986), pp. 274–5 and "Table Decorum and the Quest for a Bride in

the prologue to the saga states that it is based on a Latin poem which the author encountered in France, it has been classified as belonging to that group of romances translated from continental models, largely French, and as a consequence of little interest.[4] Marianne Kalinke in her *Bridal-Quest Romance in Medieval Iceland* finds *Klári saga* particularly important for her purposes, as it appears to be the vehicle whereby the literary motif of the bridal quest entered Icelandic literature where it was to flourish like nowhere else.[5] Because the bridal quest romance in Iceland is so closely linked with *Klári saga* and because neither the saga's putative continental original nor anything closely approximating it has ever materialized, the time has come to once again take a closer look at the saga. The following examination argues that *Klári saga* is not translated from a continental original, but is an indigenous Icelandic composition, in its present form from the second quarter of the fourteenth century. To support this hypothesis, some of the striking features of the saga's language will be considered followed by an examination of its narrative content.

Language

Klári saga is written in idiomatic Icelandic, which among other features demonstrates a penchant for metaphors and expressions from Icelandic legal language. The syntax is often markedly influenced by Latin, and while the vocabulary of the saga is sprinkled with elements which are identified as Norwegianisms, there is a much more striking influx in the narrative of words from Middle Low German. The clue to this linguistic mixture can be found in the person who is identified as author in the opening sentence:

Clári saga" in *At the Table: Metaphorical and Material Cultures of Food in Medieval and Early Modern Europe*, eds. Timothy J. Tomasik and Juliann M. Vitello, Arizona Studies in the Middle Ages and Renaissance 18 (Turnhout: Brepols, 2007), pp. 51–72.

4. Because *Klári saga* is considered a "translated saga," it is unfortunately not considered where it belongs in Jurg Glauser, *Isländische Märchensagas: Studien zur Prosaliteratur im spätmittelalterlichen Island*, Beiträge zur nordischen Philologie 12 (Basel: Helbing und Lichtenhahn, 1983).

5. Marianne Kalinke, *Bridal-Quest Romance in Medieval Iceland*, Islandica 46 (Ithaca: Cornell University Press, 1990), pp. 98–107.

Þar byrjum vér upp þessa frásögn, sem sagði virðulegur herra Jón Halldórsson, ágætrar minningar,—en hann fann hana skrifaða með latínu í Franz í það form, er þeir kalla *rithmos*,[6] en vér köllum hendingum[7] ...

(There we begin this story which the worthy reverend Bishop Jón Halldórsson of blessed memory told—and he found it in France written in Latin in that form which they call *ritmos* but which we call "versification.")

It is generally assumed that Jón Halldórsson (†1339), thirteenth Bishop of Skálholt, 1322–1339, was Norwegian in origin, because he entered the Dominican monastery in Bergen as a youth and from there went to study at the Dominican run universities in Paris and Bologna.[8] However, the claim to regard Jón as a Norwegian rests on shaky grounds. *Flateyjarannáll* begins the entry for 1323 with: "kom vt Jonn byskup Freygerdarson" (Bishop Jón, the son of Freygerðr, arrived in Iceland").[9] The woman's name "Freygerðr" is quite rare, being found, apart from here, only in *Landnámabók* and *Vápnfirðinga saga*, but it is distinctly Icelandic and not Norwegian.[10] On the other

---

6. Medieval Latin *rhythmus*, "poem" (see J. F. Niermeyer, *Mediae latinitatis lexicon minus*, 2nd ed., 2 vols, [Leiden: Brill, 2002], p. 1202.)
7. Used here in the sense of "poetry," "verse," rather than in reference to a specific verse style or meter. Cf. "Mælti hann [Óðinn] allt hendingum svo sem nú er það kveðið er skáldskapur heitir" (And he [Óðinn] spoke everything in verse just as that is now recited which is called poetry). *Ynglinga saga*, chap. 6 in Snorri Sturluson, *Heimskringla*, ed. Bergljót Kristjánsdóttir *et al.*, 3 vols. (Reykjavík: Mál og menning, 1991), vol. 1, p. 10. *Riddarasögur*, vol. 5, p. 3.
8. See *Biskupa sögur*, ed. Guðrún Ása Grímsdóttir *et al.*, 3 vols., Íslensk fornrit 15–17 (Reykjavík: Hið íslenzka fornritafélag, 1998–2000), vol. 1, pp. cii-iv, and Gunnar Kristjánsson, *Saga biskupstólanna* (Reykjavík: Bókaútgáfan Hólar, 2006), pp. 36–37. Scholars have also assumed that Jón was Norwegian, because since the middle of the previous century the Norwegian Metropolitan had shown a preference for Norwegians as bishops in Skálholt and Hólar as part of a policy of strengthening Norwegian control over the Icelandic church. Archbishop Eilífur Árnason must have been aware of Jón Halldórsson's linguistic and scholarly abilities honed during his studies on the continent, and what better candidate for the post at Skálholt than one educated in Norway and overseas and, in addition, having a thorough knowledge of Icelandic.
9. Gustav Storm, ed., *Islandske Annaler indtil 1578* (Christiania [Oslo]: Grøndahl and Søn, 1888), p. 395.
10. E. H. Lind, *Norsk-Isländska Dopnamn och fingerade Namn från Medeltiden.* 3 vols. (Uppsala: Lundequistska Bokhandeln, 1905–31), vol. 1, p. 283.

hand, Halldór, Jón's father, could have been either Norwegian or Icelandic. The fact that *Flateyjarannáll* identifies Jón by his mother's name suggests that his father had died early. Jón also had a brother, Finnur, who like him was a priest in Bergen.[11] While *Klári saga* may be stylistically influenced by Latin, it is still also written in highly idiomatic Icelandic. This permits the following scenario. One or possibly both of Jón's parents are Icelandic. They travel to the bustling Hansa port of Bergen. There both parents die and their children are received in religious order as oblates.[12]

In their search for Norwegian and Latin elements in *Klári saga*, scholars have tended to overlook how *rammíslensk* (strictly Icelandic) the saga is—and this apart from the fact that the long hundred is used and the text is sprinkled with collocations such as *makt og manér* (honor and conduct), *kukl og klókskapur* (sorcery and cunning), *með heilu ok holdnu* (with body and soul in one piece), *fúss og feginn*[13] (ready and fain), *volk og vandræði*[14] (turmoils and tribulations)[15] and that it also uses proverbs such as *hinn ríkari verður ráð að segja*[16] (the powerful are the ones to give counsel) and *eigi ver einn eiður*

---

11. See the discussion in Hugo Gering, ed. *Íslendzk æventýri: Isländische Legenden Novellen und Märchen*, 2 vols. (Halle: Buchhandlungen des Waisenhauses, 1882–83), vol. 2, pp. vi-vii. Jakobsen, *Studier i Clarus saga*, p. 18, admits the possibility that he may be Icelandic on his mother's side, but even so insists on his being Norwegian.

12. On the practice of abandoned or orphaned children being taken in by monastic orders, see John Boswell, *Kindness of Strangers: The Abandomnent of Children in Western Europe from Late Antiquity to the Renaissance* (New York: Pantheon, 1988). Chapter 5 of the *Söguþáttur af Jóni biskupi* notes that Bishop Jón became fatally ill in Bergen (in 1339) while spending the winter "at predikaraklaustri er hann hafði first inn genget þegar í barndómi" (in the Dominican Monastery where he had first enetered while still a child") (*Biskupa sögur*, vol. 1., p. 454).

13. This collocation is found in *Tristrams saga ok Ísondar*, chap. 19 ("En þegar þeir, fúsir og fegnir, undu sitt segl upp ... " [And then they, ready and fain, raised their sail ...]) (*Riddarasögur*, vol. 1, p. 36), and in the *exemplum*: "Af einum sjúkum manni ok Kristi," *Íslendzk æventýri* #35, line 35 (vol. 1, p. 123): "'Ek vil þá fúss ok feginn gjarna miskunnar biðja ...'" ("'I wish then, ready and fain, willingly to pray for mercy ...'").

14. This is a fairly common collocation found, for example, in *Alexanders saga*, book 7: "... eftir þau mörgu volk og vandræði ... " (... after those many turnoils and tribulations ...), Galterus de Castellione, *Alexandreis: það er Alexanders saga á íslensku*, ed. Gunnlaugur Ingólfsson (Reykjavík: Steinholt, 2002), p. 123. The form *volk* is the modern form of an earlier *valk* with the same meaning.

15. *Riddarasögur* vol. 5, pp. 6–7, 8, 20, 55, 58.

16. *Riddarasögur* vol. 5, p. 38. There is a version of this proverb in the thirteenth-century poem, *Málsháttarkvæði* 32.1: "Jafnan segir hin ríkri ráð" (The powerful always give counsel), *Carmina Scaldica*, ed. Finnur Jónsson, 2nd ed. (Copenhagen: Gad, 1929).

alla[17] (one oath does not cover all oaths). Another striking example of Icelandic cultural influence occurs when the princess Serena wakes up after having spent the night in the arms of Klárus disguised as Eskelvarð, son of the king of Bláland. She discovers that she is no longer in her palace, and in fact everything familiar to her has vanished. Instead of the elegant bed with embroidered linen sheets in which she went to sleep, she is now lying on the ground covered in a "skarpur skinnstakkur" (coarse leather smock).[18] No longer gazing out over the magnificent griffin-pavilion, she sees instead that:

Raftar eru þar niður lagðir á sléttum velli og við bundnir staurar með skörpum álum, sem féhirðar eru vanir að búast um.

(Long cross-pieces are laid down on the level field and bound to posts with coarse leather straps such as shepherds are accustomed to set up.)

This is nothing more nor less than the humble *færikví*, or portable sheep pen, which was a ubiquitous sight in the Icelandic countryside from the Middle Ages until well into the nineteenth century.[19] And while such devices may also have existed in Norway and on the European mainland, Bishop Jón was a scholar, not a farmer, and seems to have spent his time in urban centers, not the countryside. Besides, when the sheep were at home from October to May, he could hardly have stepped out from the cathedral church at Skálholt without one or more of these structures impinging themselves upon his sight. The man sleeping beside Serena is also described in ways that share similarities with depictions in subsequent centuries of Icelandic farm laborers, especially by writers who wish to distance themselves socially and intellectually from the working poor.

Another specifically Icelandic feature of the saga is the metaphorical

---

17. *Riddarasögur* vol. 5, p. 35. This proverb is quite widespread being found in addition to other places in *Bjarnar saga Hítdælakappa* chap. 11 (*Íslendinga sögur og þættir*, ed. Bragi Halldórsson *et al.*, 3rd ed., 3 vols [Reykjavík: Mál og menning, 1998], vol. 1, p. 88) and *Njáls saga*, chap. 13 (*Íslendinga sögur*, vol. 1, p. 142).

18. This garment is used both as a bed-covering and as her husband's wearing apparel.

19. *Riddarasögur*, vol. 5, p. 43. See the drawing in Jónas Jónasson, *Íslenzkir þjóðhættir*, ed. Einar Ól. Sveinsson, 3rd. ed. (Reykjavík: Ísafold, 1961), p. 174.

use of language that is drawn from the specialized idiom of Icelandic legal vocabulary. Bishop Jón had studied in Bologna, which was famous for its legal school. And while he was bishop of Skálholt, he was clearly involved in legal issues at the Alþingi. In 1326 he was responsible for having the *Bannsakabréf* (a document listing the causes for excommunication, 24 in all) added to the law. And from 1326–1328 he was involved in the so-called "Möðruvallamál," the struggle he had with Lárentíus Kálfsson (1267–1330), Bishop of Hólar, in an effort to enforce the Archbishop's edict that the monastery at Möðruvellir be re-established against the wishes of Bishop Lárentíus, who had confiscated the lands and income of the monastery after the drunken monks had burned the coister to the ground in 1316.[20] At the Alþingi the legal debates were conducted in Icelandic and Bishop Jón would have had plenty of opportunity to absorb the specialized vocabulary subsequently found reflected in the saga.

The first example to be encountered of this legal idiom is the description of Tecla, daughter of the king of Scots, and maiden-in-waiting to Princess Serena:

Bæði var hún listug og fögur með heiðurlegri málsnilld og myndi þykja hið kurteisasta konungsbarn, ef eigi hefði þvílíkur gimsteinn legið í annað skaut sem var Serena konungsdóttir.[21]

(She was both refined and beautiful with noble elequence and would have seemed the most courteous king's child if such a jewel had not lain in another lap of a garment, namely Serena the king's daughter.)

The term *að leggja í skaut* is a legal term referring to the casting lots which were marked and placed in the lap or fold (*skaut*) of a garment from which they would be drawn by some third person as is explained in *Grágás*: "Hver maður skal merkja hlut sinn og bera alla saman í skaut" (Each man must mark his piece [in the drawing

---

20. On the "Möðruvallamál" (1326–1328), see Torfi K. Stefánsson Hjaltalín, *Eldur á Möðruvöllum: Saga Möðruvalla í Hörgárdal frá öndverða til okkar tíma*, 2 vols. (Reykjavík: Flateyjarútgáfan, 2001), vol. 1, pp. 31–5, 47–8.
21. *Riddarasögur*, vol. 5, p. 10.

of lots] and bring all together in the lap of a garment).[22] The term is used here metaphorically to indicate that it was not to fall to Tecla's lot to be drawn for the honor of being considered the most elegant and accomplished young woman in the realm, that being reserved for the Princess Serena. Later on in the same chapter Serena listens to the "framburður" of Tecla to treat Klárus respectfully.[23] Here the word can only be used in its legal sense of "a plea presented in a law court" as in *Grágás*: "Ef maður hefir þá sök að sækja er vottorð fylgir og á hann að beiða réttingar að og framburðar" (If a man has a case to prosecute which requires sworn evidence, also he has to request the proper wording and the plea-making).[24] When Serena scolds Klárus for spilling soft-boiled egg on his tunic, she does so, in the phrasing of the narrator, "með svo föllnum orðum" (with the words as follows). The use of *fallinn* in this sense had developed also as a legal idiom in the fourteenth century.[25] *Fallinn* is used in the same sense later in the saga when Tecla reports Serena's message to Eskelvarð: "er það svo fallið" (and it is as follows).[26] When Serena promises the hideous creature she believes is her husband, that she will love him with all her strength and see to it that he becomes king of Frakkland, she introduces her pledge by saying: "og eg vil borga þér upp á mína trú" (and I shall pledge on my troth). The verb she uses, *að borga*, is used in the legal sense "to go bail for."[27] Finally there is the use of collocations with legal overtones such as *land og lög* (land and sea) (twice) and *að*

---

22. *Grágás: Lagasafn íslenska þjóðveldisins*, ed. Gunnar Karlsson et al. (Reykjavík: Mál og menning, 2001), p. 383 (see also p. 401); "þá leggja þeir hluti í skaut" (then they placed their lots in the lap of a garment), *Vatnsdœla saga*, chap. 42 (*Íslendinga sögur*, vol. 3, p. 1896. While this latter example does not take place in a legal setting, the action is equally formal and binding. Furthermore, even though a new law code (*Jónsbók*) had been adopted in 1281, that does not mean traditional legal vocabulary and expressions disappeared overnight, especially since the text of *Jónsbók* was subject of various amendments (*réttarbœtur*) and not stabilized until the middle of the fourteenth century. See *Jónsbók. Lögbók Íslendinga hver samþykkt var á alþingi árið 1281 . . .*, ed. Már Jónsson (Reykjavík: Háskólaútgáfan, 2002), pp. 16–24.
23. *Riddarasögur*, vol. 5, p. 13.
24. *Grágás*, p. 385.
25. *Riddarasögur*, vol. 5, p. 18. See the *Máldagi* of Vilkin Hinriksson, Bishop of Skálholt (1391–1405): *svo fallinn vitnesburð* (the testimony as follows), *Diplomatarium Islandicum*, vol. 1, p. 47.
26. *Riddarasögur*, vol. 5, p. 29.
27. *Riddarasögur*, vol. 5, p. 45. The phrase is not common in early Icelandic, but frequently encountered in Old Norwegian and may be best regarded here as a Norwegianism.

hlýða boði og banni (to heed command and prohibition).[28] The first is a legal formula found in *Grágás* (p. 283) and while the second is something of a commonplace, it too is legal in origin.[29]

While it must remain a matter of speculation whether or not Bishop Jón's first language may have been Icelandic, there is less ambiguity concerning his knowledge of Latin. In the summer of 1327, Bishop Jón visited Hólar in pursuit of a settlement of the "Möðruvallamál" already mentioned. The southerners had brought with them many books of canon law and Bishop Jón began the proceedings in Latin. When his turn to reply came, Bishop Lárentíus did so in the vernacular (*á norrænu*): "Vita menn þat, herra Jón, at yðr er svo mjúkt latínu at tala sem móður-tungu yðra, en þó skilir þat ekki alþýða." (People know that, reverend Jón, that Latin is as easy for you to speak as your mother tongue, but on the other hand the ordinary people do not understand it).[30]

That the syntax of *Klári saga* is indeed influenced by Latin is hardly a revelation as this aspect of the saga was studied in detail by Alfred Jakobsen in his *Studier i Clarus saga*.[31] These Latinisms manifest themselves, for example, in the form of participial phrases ("styrkjandi hans ráð og ríki með öllum mætti og megni" [strengthening his rule and realm with all might and main]), tags such as "og hvað meira" (and what more [to say]) reflecting Latin "quis multa"; ablative absolute constructions ("og að skipunum búnum og öllum hlutum vel til fengnum" [And the ships being ready and matters well taken care of]); and puns ("og betur má hún nú kallast Severa en Serena" [and it would be better to call her 'Stern' rather than 'Serene']).[32] Furthermore, Latinate names are inflected after prepositions and in oblique cases

---

28. *Riddarasögur*, vol. 5, pp. 5, 45, 22.
29. "Konongr skal raða bode og banne" (the king must control commands and prohibitions) (*Gulathings-lov*, #295, *Norges Gamle Love*, vol. 1, p. 96; *Frostathings-Lov*, VII.1, *Norges Gamle Love*, vol. 1, p. 198); cf. "helldr hlyddv allir þeirra boði og banni" (rather all of them heeded the commands and prohibitions [of Joshua]), *Stjorn: Gammelnorsk Bibelhistorie*, ed. C. R. Unger (Christiania [Oslo]: Feilberg and Landmark, 1862), p. 375; also *Egils saga*, chapter 66 (*Íslendinga sögur*, vol. 1, p. 470) and *Vatnsdœla saga*, chapter 7 (*Íslendinga sögur*, vol. 3, p. 1851).
30. *Biskupa sögur*, vol. 1, pp. 405–6 (*Lárentíus saga biskups*, chapter 55). *Lárentíus saga* also remarks that Bishops Jón and Lárentíus were considered the two most skilled practitioners of Latin in the country (*Biskupa sögur*, vol. 1, p. 383).
31. See also *Clári saga*, pp. xx-xxiv.
32. *Riddarasögur*, vol. 5, pp. 3, 5 (and *passim*), pp. 9, 18.

after verbs, but in accordance with Latin, not Icelandic grammar ("til Teclam," [to Tecla] rather than "til Teclae" reflecting the Latin "ad Teclam") (see also "með ráðum Teclae" [with the advice of Tecla]). Latin vocabulary is also inserted into the text: "er þeir kalla *rithmos* (< Latin *rhythmus* "poem"); "í *Paradisum*"; "hann velur ... *bissum* ... *og cicladem* (he chooses fine linen [< *bissus*] and rich gold-embroidered fabric (< *cyclas, -dis*); "af þeim *carbunculo*" (< *carbunculus*, a bright red stone such as a ruby or red garnet); "þar til sem honum gerist *signum*" (until is given to him a *signum* [hand signal]); "upp í það *solarium*" (up in the upper room < *solarium*); and "og í durum þess tjalds setur hann ein *limitem*; það köllum vér þresköld" (and in the doorway of this tent he places a *limes*; we call that a threshold).[33] This latter presents a small problem because *limitem* is the accusative singular of *limes* "a boundary," not of *limen* "a threshold" whose accusative singular is *liminem*. Since *limitem* is the *lectio dificilior*, there is a strong argument that it is the original reading and not a later corruption, and that the Latin word is used here to indicate that Pérús places a marker at the door of the tent to distinguish the boundary between the space where Tecla walks freely from the space where she will be constrained to reveal the truth. At some subsequent point in the text's transmission, however, it was felt necessary to gloss *limitem* and because the text says shortly afterwards that Tecla "kemur inn um þresköldinn" (crosses over the threshold), a redactor with a less than adequate memory of his Latin grammar, makes an elementary mistake, because it is not possible to believe that Bishop Jón, even on a bad day, would be capable of such a schoolboy's blunder.

The pervasive influence of Latin on the text is furthermore not *a priori* evidence that the saga was translated from Latin, for these Latinisms are just as likely to have been second nature to someone as well versed in Latin as Bishop Jón. In addition, these Latinisms are no more than a reflection of what Mattias Tveitane has identified as aspects of a learned style which he discusses in terms of translated prose,[34] but which again is likely to have been equally a feature of the prose style

---

33. *Riddarasögur*, vol. 5, pp. 28 (37), 3, 16, 24 (and 18), 24, 27, 32, 37.
34. Mattias Tveitane, *Den lærde stil: oversetterprosa i den norrøne versjonen av Vitæ Patrum*, Årbok for Universitetet i Bergen, Humanistisk serie; 1967.2 (Bergen, Norwegian Universities Press, 1967).

of a man like Bishop Jón whose skill in Latin was remarkable enough for his contemporaries to comment upon it.

But if this is not sufficient to argue against a supposed Latin original as being the source text for *Klári saga*, then there is the third notable linguistic feature of the saga which can be called "the German connection." Whereas the Latinity of the saga is no more than might be expected given who its author is, what is striking about the text is the large amount of vocabulary derived from Middle Low German. This is not the place to investigate this evidence in detail, so it will suffice just to list some of these words used in the text:[35] *alþingis* (absolutely < MLG *aldinc*); *angst* (misery); *espinger* (ship's boat); *fordrifast* (to exclude); *frygð* (sensuousness); *fyrirstanda* (to understand); *heimullig* (private); *hóf* (banquet) *junkeri* (young man); (?) *klódrep* (blow with the hand)[36]; *klókskapur* (cunningness); *krankur* (sick); *kukl* (sorcery, a Scandinavian back-formation from Middle Low German *kokeler* [*kökeler*], juggler, trickster); *kvitta* (to acquit); *kyndugskapur* (wiliness); *lista* (a streak, i.e., interpreting the smear from the soft-boiled egg as yet another decoration on Klárus' richly ormnamented garment < MLG *listen*, a strip of material forming a border); *lykt* (smell); *pláz* (place); *mekt* (pomp); *skari* (company); *skerfur* (penny); *spázéra* (to walk); *spegill* (mirror)[37]; *spíza* (to provide); *stolz* (proud); *tyftunarmeistari* (task-master, cf. Modern German *Zuchtmeister*); *æra* (privilege); and *ævintýr* (matter, i.e., something written or reported < MLG *eventūr* < OFr *avanture* [adventure]).[38] Some of these words were already

---

35. While Otto Höfler, *Altnordische Lehnwortstudien* (Lund: Håkon Ohlsson, 1931) has some information on Old Norse loans from Middle Low German, a great deal more is found in Christian Westergård-Nielsen, *Låneordene i det 16. århundredes trykte islandske litteratur*, Bibliotheca Arnamagnæana 6 (Copenhagen: Munksgaard, 1946), although his corpus is restricted to Post-Reformation printed texts, and Veturliði Óskarsson, *Middelnedertyske låneord i islandsk diplomsprog frem til år 1500*, Bibliotheca Arnamagnæana 43 (Copenhagen: C.A. Reitzel, 2002).

36. This word occurs only in *Klári saga* and in the *exemplum*: "Af rómverska dáranum," *Íslendzk æventýri* #83 line 51 (vol. 1, p. 241), a text attributed to Bishop Jón Jakobsen, *Studier i Clarus saga*, p. 98, considers it possible that Jón himself made up the word, but it is just as likely to be based on a slang form otherwise unrecorded.

37. The late fourteenth-century AM 657b 4to uses the indigenous word *gler* (a glass) instead of *spegill* (*Clári saga* [1907], p. 34).

38. At one point in the saga *ævintýr* it is used in the sense "chance," a usage also found in Low German, see: Pekka Katara, *Das französische Lehngut in mittelniederdeutschen Denkmälern von 1300 bis 1500*, Mémoires de la Société Néophilologique de Helsinki 30 (Helsinki: Société Néophilologique, 1966), pp. 24–5 under "aventür(e)." Old French *aventure* is frequently encountered in this meaning.

established in the Icelandic and the Norwegian of the time. Others are used here for the first and only time.[39] There also seems to be a significant overlap between the Low German derived vocabulary of *Klári saga* and that found in *Stjórn I* but the significance of this has been long disputed.[40] But if it can be agreed that the surviving version of *Stjórn I* was composed at Skálholt in the first half of the fourteenth century, then it would be possible to conclude that the Low German colored vocabulary of *Stjórn I* and *Klári saga* represent the fashionable Icelandic of the elite circles in the bishopric during this period which took as its model the Icelandic spoken by the Bishop.

As was mentioned earlier, Bishop Jón grew up in a Dominican monastery in Bergen and lived there for approximately two decades after his return from his studies in Paris and Bologna.[41] This is sufficient to explain why his Icelandic is so colored with Middle Low German vocabulary since Bergen was a Hansa port and the Low German of the Hansa merchants a prestige language.[42] Furthermore, in the case of Bishop Jón, since the possibility has been raised that he was bilingual in Icelandic and Norwegian before he came to Iceland, the Low German vocabulary he used was available for utilization in both languages, and so the question of whether or not they were borrowed first into

---

39. In the *Sagan af Klarusi keisarasyni*, ed. Bjarni Bjarnason (Reykjavík: Ísafold, 1884), a version of *Klári saga* taken from a later paper manuscript, much of this vocabulary has vanished or been replaced with more familiar Icelandic words.

40. The main points of view are summarized in Reidar Astås, *An Old Norse Biblical Compilation: Studies in* Stjórn, American University studies 7: Theology and Religion 109 (New York: Peter Lang, 1991), pp. 9–11. Jakobsen, for example, proposed in *Studier i Clarus saga*, pp. 109–111, that Bishop Jón Halldórsson was the compiler of *Stjórn I*, a position rejected by Tveitane, *Den lærde stil*, pp. 26–34.

41. There are five documents dated between 1310–1320 from Bergen in which he is mentioned (*Íslendzk æventýri*, vol. 2, p. viii).

42. See Olav Brattegard, *Die mittelniederdeutsche Geschäftssprache des hansischen Kaufmanns zu Bergen*, 2 vols., Skrifter fra norges Handelshøyskole i rekken språklige avhandlinger 2–3 (Bergen: John Grieg, 1945–46). The first volume gives a description of this language based on written materials from 1365–1535. Even though Hansa merchants had first legally established themselves in Bergen in 1186 and increased their presence in the following century (vol. 1, pp. 12–3), there are no documents in German surviving from this early period, but: "Bergen war im 14. und 15. Jahrhundert der Stapelplatz für den grössten Teil der norwegischen Westküste und für die Zinsländer Island, Shetland, Færøyane und Orknøyane" (vol. 1, p. 105). For a recent study which stresses the sociolinguistic aspects of the language contact (stressing also that Low German was itself a mix of dialects), see Agnete Nesse, *Språkkontakt mellom norsk og tysk i hansatidens Bergen*, Det Norske Videnskaps-Akademi II: Hist.-Filos. Klasse Skrifter og avhandlinger 2 (Oslo: Det Norske Videnskaps-Akademi, 2002).

Norwegian and then into Icelandic becomes moot—especially if he also had in addition a working knowledge of Hansa German. As Veturliði Óskarsson has demonstrated in *Middelnedertyske låneord i islandsk diplomsprog*, Low German vocabulary entered Icelandic much earlier and in much greater quantities than has generally been considered the case. While one such venue for this vocabulary was certainly through Norwegian language contact or from Norwegian speakers living in Iceland, more recognition needs to be given to the existence through the centuries of a not inconsiderable number of Icelanders who were fluent in Low German in their own right, and who adopted vocabulary directly from the manuscripts in Low German which circulated in Iceland as well as from books which entered the country after the beginning of printing in that language.[43]

But Bishop Jón absorbed more than linguistic influences from Icelandic, Latin and Low German; he also absorbed from all three language traditions narrative elements, which he proceeded to reword in the striking and original way they appear in *Klári saga*.

Narrative structure

The redactor of *Klári saga* states that Bishop Jón "found [the story] in France written in Latin" verse. Finnur Jónsson says with respect to this:

> Denne oplysning er vistnok rigtig. Her siges der intet om, at Jon selv skulde have nedskrevet den. Det er med den som med æventyrene; han har fortalt den, andre har så nedskrevet den.[44]

---

[43] Marianne Kalinke, *The Book of Reykjahólar: The Last of the Great Medieval Legendaries* (Toronto: University of Toronto Press, 1996) has shown how numerous of the saints' lives in the early sixteenth-century *Reykjahólarbók* have Middle Low German sources printed and otherwise. In MS Icel. 15 in the Houghton Library, Harvard University, written in the winter of 1822, Ólafur Sveinsson á Purkey (c. 1762–1845) writes that he had access to "þá gòmlu Lybsku grasa bók" (150r), a Low German version of the "Smaller" or "German Ortus" attributed to Johannes de Cuba (fl. 1484–1503), *Dit is de genochlike garde der suntheit to latine Ortulus sanitatis, edder herbarius genömet: dar me ynne vindet alle arth, nature vð eghenschop & frudere, vnde der eddelen sten* ... (Lübeck: Steffen Arndes, 1520). This copy used by Ólafur had been brought to Iceland by Magnús *prúði* Jónsson (c. 1525–91) when he returned to Iceland after his studies in Germany in the middle of the sixteenth century.

[44] Finnur Jónsson, *Den oldnorske og oldislandske litteraturs historie*, 2nd ed., 3 vols. (Copenhagen: Gad, 1920–24), pp. 96–7.

(This information is certainly correct. It does not say here that Jón himself is said to have written it down. It is the same with fairy-tales; he has narrated the story, but someone else has written it down.)

Most scholars appear to agree with this position. But Jan de Vries is having none of it. He rejects the saga's claim that it originated with Jón Halldórsson: "'Die Bemerkung der Saga über die Autorschaft des Jón Halldórsson betrachte ich als reine Erfindung; nachdem er die Ævintýri nach Island gebracht hatte, konnte er ja leicht auch als Importeur anderer abenteuerlicher Geschichten ausgegeben werden." And further: "Es ist reine Phantasie, wenn Cedersciöld annimmt daß dieser Norweger in Paris das lateinische Gedicht übersetzt habe, und wenn er darauf eine Datierung um 1290 gründet."[45] Torfi H. Tulinius in the new Icelandic literary history straddles the fence by reporting the saga's opening sentence and speculating that the lost poem may have been one like Galterus de Castellione's *Alexandreis*, but then adding with respect to authorship: "en þó kann vera að þessi klausa sé einvörðungu ritklif, að sögumaðurinn vitni til frægra manna til að frásögn hans fái aukið vægi" (but on the other hand it may be that this clause is merely a topos, that the author makes reference to a famous person so that his narrative should gain by it increased importance.)[46]

There seems no particular reason to doubt the claim that Jón Halldórsson is the author of *Klári saga*. But on the other hand there is no reason to believe that he based the story on a Latin poem found in France. France after all was the country which produced the best romances, a number of which had already been translated into Old Norse with great success. It is easy, for example, to find passages in which an author makes the claim that the work being presented is translated from French when all the available evidence suggests otherwise. The Middle High German *Ogier von Dänemark* is clearly translated from a Middle Dutch original.[47] Yet the text is replete with

---

45. Jan de Vries, *Altnordische Literaturgeschichte*, 2nd ed., 2 vols. (Berlin: de Gruyter, 1964-67), p. 535.
46. Torfi H. Tulinius, "Kynjasögur úr fortíð og framandi löndum," *Íslensk bókmenntasaga*, vol. 2, ed. Vésteinn Ólason (Reykjavík: Mál og menning, 1992), pp. 165-245 at p. 196.
47. Only fragments of the Dutch original survive. They have been edited by H. van Dijk, "Ogier van Denemarken: Diplomatische uitgave van de Middelnederlandse fragmenten ...," *De Nieuwe taalgids* 67 (1974), pp. 177-202, and H. van Dijk and H. Kienhorst, "Ogier

phrases such as: "Uß dem welsche von wort zů wort" (From the French word for word) (line 19) and "Das ich uß welscher sprache / Dis bůch wolte in tútsch machen" (That I from the French language wished to translate this book into German) (lines 4215–16).[48] An even clearer set of examples is found in the Middle Dutch *Roman van Heinric en Margriete van Limborch*.[49] There is general agreement that the work is an original Dutch composition,[50] yet the poet insists in Book I, line 2542, and on numerous other occasions: "Dat Welsche sade, dar icht en las" (The French in which I read this said).[51] Therefore Jón Halldórsson had every reason to claim that the story he was presenting originated in France. That the supposed poem from which the narrative was translated should be in Latin was also in keeping with his reputation as a Latin scholar. In fact elements of the story may have had their inspiration in Latin texts, but they were texts in prose, not in verse.

The opening chapter of the *Söguþáttur af Jóni biskupi* states: "En hverr man greina mega hverr hans góðvili var at gleðja næverandis menn við fáheyrðum dæmisögum er hann hafði tekit í útlöndum, bæði með letrum ok eigin raun" (And everyone is able to determine what

---

van Denemarken, Nieuwe fragmenten," *Wat Duikers vent is dit! Opstellen voor W. M. H. Hummelen* ed. G. R. W. Dibbets et al. (Wijhe: Quarto, 1989), pp. 3–24. The poem is dated to the fourteenth century (van Dijk, p. 180). For an edition of the Middle High German version which includes the Middle Dutch fragments, see: *Ogier von Dänemark nach der Heidelberger Handschrift CPG 363*, ed. Hilkert Weddige with Theo J. A. Broers and Hans van Dijk, Deutsche Texte des Mittelalters 83 (Berlin: Akademie, 2002). The colophon on the manuscript CPG 363 dates it 1479.

48. See similar sentiments in lines 1132, 4162–63, 6038, 6745, 9764, 9869–70, 11941, 12037, 12181, 12309, 13860–61, 13267, 14687, 17196, 19635, and 20095.

49. Examples are taken from the edition of MS Brussels, Koninklijke bibliotheek, No. 18231, dated first half of the fifteenth century, *Roman van Heinric en Margriete van Limborch: Uitgeven volgens het Brusselse Handschrift*, ed. Robertus Meesters, Two parts (Amsterdam: Stichting "Onze Oude Letteren," 1951), pp. lvi-lvii. Meesters states "we moeten wel aannemen dat het werk ± 1300 geschreven is" (we can easily accept that the work is written around 1300") (p. xvi). It is sometimes attributed to Hein van Aken, the translator into Middle Dutch of the *Roman de la rose*, pp. xli-xlii.

50. "Alle kenners ... houden de *Limborch* voor oorspronkelijk, in die zin, dat ze de roman niet zien als de vertaling van een kant en klaar Frans voorbeeld en ook niet als de vrije bewerking van een Frans origineel" ("All scholars ... consider the *Limborch* to be original in the sense that the romance is not seen as the translation of a ready-made French model, and also not as the free adaptation of a French original") (*Roman van Heinric en Margriete van Limborch*, p. xli). This is based on the lack of a French *exemplum* and the fact that the subject matter is one that would neither interest nor benefit a French poet.

51. See also I: 1909, 2798; III: 1163; IV: 1461–62; V: 1706, 2014, 2166; VI: 266, 1435, 2085, 2589; VII: 1677; VIII: 1161, 1211.

kind his benevolence was to entertain people within hearing with rarely heard *exempla*[52] which he had picked up in foreign countries both in written form and as the result of his own experience).[53] Numerous large collections of *exempla* were compiled in the Middle Ages both for entertainment and as aids for the clergy when composing their sermons, the *Disciplina clericis* of Petrus Alfonsi (1062–1110) and the *Gesta Romanorum* (c. 1300) being among the best known. A number of the *exempla* attributed to Bishop Jón have been preserved and edited in *Íslendzk æventýri*, several of them being translations of stories from the *Disciplina clericis*,[54] but exactly what role Jón Halldórsson may have had in the narratives collected in *Íslendzk æventýri* remains a matter of contention and the issues will not be rehearsed here. Bishop Jón was a Dominican and one of the largest collections of *exempla* was that collected by the Dominican Stephen of Bourbon (Stephanus de Borbone) (c. 1180–1261)[55] under the title *Tractatus de*

---

52. Medieval Latin *exemplum* means a moral anecdote. It was originally translated into Old Norse as *dæmisaga*, "fable," "parable," "a tale with a moral." The loan-word *æventýr / æventýri* meant "tale," "adventure" and later "(international-) fairy tale." The fifteenth-century manuscripts containing the Icelandic *exempla* confuses the matter by only occasionally referring to them as *dæmisögur*, preferring instead *ævintýri*, a usage followed by modern scholars. On the other hand, in the cophon to *Klári saga*, the narrator, presumably Bishop Jón, states that the saga has served as a "ljós dæmi" (clear examle) of how women should behave (*Riddarasögur*, vol. 5, p. 61).

53. *Biskupa sögur*, vol. 1, p. 445. The sentence continues: "ok til vitnis þar um harðla smátt ok lítit man setjaz í þenna bækling af því stóra efni, því at sumir menn á Íslandi samsettu hans frásagnir sér til gleði ok öðrum" (and as an example of this, some small and insignificant examples will be placed in this little treatise from that large body of material, because some people in Iceland gathered his narratives together both for their own entertainment and that of others).

54. In addition to the exempla collected in *Íslendzk æventýri* see those edited by Jonna Louis-Jensen, "Nogle Æventýri," *Opuscula* 5, Bibliotheca Arnamagnæana 31 (Copenhagen: Munksgaard, 1975), pp. 263–77, Peter A. Jorgensen, "Four Æventýri," *Opuscula* 5 (1975), pp. 295–328, and Ólafur Halldórsson, "AM 240. fol. XV, tvinn úr handriti með ævintýrum," *Gripla* 18 (2007): 23–46. *Exempla* translated from English into Icelandic are edited by Jorgensen, "Ten Icelandic Exempla and their Middle English Source," *Opuscula* 4, Bibliotheca Arnamagnæana 30 (Copenhagen: Munksgaard, 1970), pp. 177–207, and by Einar G. Pétursson, *Miðaldaævintýri þýdd úr ensku* (Reykjavík: Stofnun Árna Magnússonar á Íslandi, 1976). They are discussed by Jorgensen in "The Icelandic Translations from Middle English," *Studies for Einar Haugen*, ed. Evelyn Scherabon Firchow *et al.* (The Hague: Mouton, 1972), pp. 305–20. A longer narrative from an English translation of the *Gesta Romanorum* is edited by Jorgensen as *The Story of Jonatas in Iceland* (Reykjavík: Stofnun Árna Magnússonar á Íslandi, 1997).

55. Stephen is the inquisitor featured in Jean-Claude Schmitt, *The Holy Greyhound: Guinefort, Healer of Children since the Thirteen Century*, trans. Martin Thom, Cambridge Studies in Oral and Literate Culture 6 (Cambridge: Cambridge University Press, 1983).

diversis materiis predicabilibus, designed as a compilation illustrating the seven gifts of the Holy Spirit. Only the sections on Fear, Piety, Knowledge, Fortitude and the beginning of Counsel were completed before Stephen died.[56] The *Tractatus* is a text that Bishop Jón could have encountered in Paris in particular, and at least one of the narratives in *Íslendzk æventýri* is translated from this work (although it is not identified in the manuscript as one of the *exempla* by Bishop Jón),[57] and perhaps additional examples will come to light when the complete edition is available. Bishop Jón's demonstrated fondness for *exempla* is important because *Klári saga* can be seen as the combination of *exempla* grafted on to an older narrative structure.

As is mentioned above, *Klári saga* is the earliest surviving bridal quest romance in Icelandic. There is no reason to suppose that it had any predecessors and a case can be made that the popularity of the genre in the subsequent Icelandic literary scene may owe a not inconsiderable debt to the authority that *Klári saga* gave to it. Claudia Bornholdt has demonstrated that the medieval bridal quest narrative is a specifically German phenomenon with its roots in Merovingian historical accounts,[58] and Bishop Jón was probably exposed to such stories during his time in Bergen. Even so, *Klári saga* is not a typical bridal-quest romance as it lacks many of the narrative elements characteristic of the genre. Its closest analogue is found in a passage in the Old English poem *Beowulf*. In determining the appropriateness of her own behavior, Hygd, the wife of Hygelac, "Mōd Þrȳðo wæg ... firen' ondrysne" (weighed the pride of Þrȳð ... the terrible wickedness).[59]

---

56. The first complete edition of the work is underway: Stephan de Borbone, *Tractatus de diversis materiis predicabilibus*, gen. ed. Jacques Berlioz, Corpus Christianorum: Continuatio Mediaevalis 124 (Turnout: Brepols, 2002-). So far volumes 1 and 3 have appeared.

57. "Af tveimr munkum," *Íslendzk æventýri* #44 (1: 147–49).

58. Claudia Bornholdt, *Engaging Moments: The Origins of the Medieval Bridal-Quest Narrative*, Ergänzungsbände zum Reallexikon der Germanischen Altertumskunde 46 (Berlin: de Gruyter, 2005).

59. Beowulf: *An Edition with Relevant Shorter Texts*, ed. Bruce Mitchell and Fred C. Robinson, rev. ed. (Malden, MA: Blackwell, 2006), lines 1931–2. The entire episode runs lines 1931–62. Much about this passage is disputed. Some editors deny *Þrȳð* is a proper noun, reading instead *mōdþrȳð*, a compound meaning "arrogance," while others interpret the name of the queen as *Mōdþrȳð*. However, various traditions associated with the "cruel queens" in the family of the fourth-century king of the continental Angles, Offa, are relevant here. The founder of Offa's line was married to a woman called Herminthruth who had the habit of killing her suitors, while in later narratives, Offa's descendant, the eighth-century Offa of Mercia, was said to be married to a cruel woman called Drida. See R. W. Chambers, *Beowulf: An Introduction to the Study of the Poem*, 3rd ed. (Cambridge: Cambridge

Like Serena in *Klári saga*, Þrýð is not a *meykóngur* or maiden queen,[60] but a princess who lets no one look at her except her "sinfrea" (greatlord)[61] on pain of death. The poet continues with sentiments that are also applicable to Serena:

> Ne bið swylc cwēlīc þēaw
> idese tō efanne, þēah ðe hīo ǣnlīcu sȳ,
> þætte freoðuwebbe fēores onsǣce
> æfter ligetorne lēofne mannan.[62]

(Nor is suchlike a queenly custom for a woman to carry out even though she may be peerless, that a peace-weaver should deprive a dear man of life for an imagined insult.)

However, for reasons unexplained, Þrýð is given in marriage on her father's counsel ("be fæder lāre," line 1950) to Offa, king of the Continental Angles. After this happens, people begin to tell quite different stories about her. She now becomes a model queen, to her own credit and the greater glory of her husband. While only the

---

University Press, 1959), pp. 31–40. The connection of this episode with Tale Type 900, "King Thrushbeard," was noted by Ernst Philippson, *Der Märchentypus von König Drosselbart*, FF Communications 50 (Greifswald: Suomalainen Tiedeakatemia, 1923), pp. 93–4, but not linked specifically to *Klári saga*, while Frederick Amory, "Things Greek and the Riddarasögur," *Les Sagas de Chevaliers (Riddarasögur)*, ed. Régis Boyer, Civilizations 10 (Paris: Presses de l'Université Paris-Sorbonne, 1985), pp. 417–30 at p. 422, and *Speculum* 59 (1984), pp. 509–23, at p. 517, links the story of Þrýð to the concept of the *meykóngur* in general (the form *meykonungur* is sometimes found in normalized texts but "this form is nonexistent in medieval or modern Icelandic" (Amory, "Things Greek," *Speculum* 59 [1984], p. 517). See also Kalinke, *Bridal-Quest Romance*, pp. 36, 103.

60. While not a *meykóngur*, Serena has all the features of the type. See Shaun F. D. Hughes, "The Ideal of Kingship in the *Riddarasögur*," *Michigan Academician* 10 (1978), pp. 321–36 at pp. 230–2; Marianne Kalinke, "The Misogamous Maiden Kings," *Bridal-Quest*, pp. 66–108 (on *Klári saga*, pp. 66–8 and *passim*); Eric Wahlgren, *The Maiden King in Iceland* (Chicago: University of Chicago Libraries, 1938); and Harald Müller, "Kampf der Geschlechter? Der Mädchenkönig im isländischen Märchensaga," *Mann und Frau im Märchen*, ed. Harlinda Lox et al. (Kreutzlingen: Heinrich Hugendubel [Diederichs], 2002), pp. 62–79. Amory, "Things Greek and the *Riddarasögur*," p. 422 and *Speculum* 59 (1984), p. 517, suggests the concept of the *meykóngur* may have its origins in the figure of "the Byzantine female autocrat."

61. *Beowulf*, line 1934. While some editors interpret *sinfrea* to mean "husband," it seems more appropriate that at this stage in the narrative it refer to Þrýð's father.

62. *Beowulf*, lines 1940–3.

broad outlines of the story are sketched out in *Beowulf*, this is exactly the same plot structure that Bishop Jón uses for his saga. To flesh out the details he used narratives that have long been familiar to folklorists and are classified by Antti Aarne and Stigh Thompson as Tale Types 900 "King Thrushbeard" (corresponding to *Klári saga*, chapters 1–15) and 901 "Taming of the Shrew" under the heading "The Shrewish wife is Reformed" (now "The Obstinate Wife Learns to Obey")[63] (corresponding to *Klári saga*, chapters 16–19), although the behavior of Serena in the second half of the saga in the face of the overweening cruelty of her husband is more reminiscent of Tale Type 887, "Griselda."[64]

Ernest Philippson in his study of Tale Type 900 identifies the Middle High German verse *Märe* ("folktale"), "Die halbe Birne," attributed to Konrad von Würzburg (d. 1287),[65] as the earliest surviving version of the story while the next in chronological order is *Klári saga*.[66] Marianne Kalinke has recently investigated the breaches of table decorum which allow the women in "Die halbe Birne" and *Klári saga* to reject their (subsequently successful) suitors and relates these episodes to a body of literature in Middle High German and Latin

---

63. Antti Aarne and Stith Thompson, *Types of the Folktale: A Classification and Bibliography*, FF Communications 184 (Helsinki: Suomalainen Tiedeakatemia, 1981), pp. 310–2. Now revised by Hans-Jörg Uther, *The Types of International Folktales: A Classification and Bibliography. Based on the System of Antti Aarne and Stith Thompson*, 3 vols., FF Communicatins 284–86 (Helsinki: Suomalainen Tiedeakatemia, 2004), vol. 1, pp. 523–7. Einar Ól. Sveinsson, *Verzeichnis Isländischer Märchenvarianten*, FF Communications 83 (Helsinki: Suomalainen Tiedeakatemia, 1929) classifies Icelandic folktales according to the Aarne-Thompson system.

64. Aarne-Thompson, *Types of the Folktale*, pp. 302–3; Uther, *The Types of International Folktales*, vol. 1, pp. 521–2.

65. Konrad von Würzburg (attrib.), "Die halbe Birne," *Novellistik des Mittelalters. Märendichtung*, ed. Klaus Grubmüller (Frankfurt am Main: Deutscher Klassiker Verlag, 1996), pp. 178–207, 1083–101. For a convenient summary of the story see Helmut Birkhan, Karin Lichtblau, Christa Tuczay et al. for the Austrian Academy of Sciences, ed., *Motif-Index of German Secular Narratives from the Beginning to 1400*, 7 vols. (Berlin: de Gruyter, 2005–06), vol. 4, p. 334.

66. Philippson, *Der Märchentypus von König Drosselbart*, pp. 3–5. See also *Klári saga*, pp. xvi–xvii; Johannes Bolte and Georg Polivka, *Anmerkungen zu den Kinder- und Hausmärchen der Brüder Grimm*, rev. ed., ed. Ernst Schade, 5 vols. in 4 (1913–32, rpt. Hildesheim: Olms-Weidmann, 1992–94), no. 52; König Drosselbart, vol. 1, pp. 443–9. Outside of *Klári saga*, the tale type is found in Icelandic only in the folktale "Meykóngurinn," collected from Guðríður Eyjólfsdóttir (c. 1811–78) from Ákvörn on Fljótshlíð, and written down in 1865 (Einar Ól. Sveinsson, *Verzeichnis Isländischer Märchenvarianten*, p. 136) and published in Jón Árnason, *Íslenzkar þjóðsögur og ævintýri*, new ed., ed. Árni Böðvarsson and Bjarni Vilhjálmsson, 6 vols. (Reykjavík: Bókaútgáfan Þjóðsaga, 1954–61), vol. 5, pp. 234–6.

which was concerned with improving the table manners of those in elite society.[67] Thus while Tale Type 900 is not found in the *exempla* collections analyzed by Frederic Tubach, a parallel may yet surface when a more thorough analysis of medieval *exempla* is completed, because the story has a sufficient moral dimension to have made it attractive to those who put such collections of stories together.[68] To the narrative of the princess who humiliates her suitors until she finds herself married, a narrative structure going back at least as far as *Beowulf*, as has already been suggested, Bishop Jón added elements that he is likely to have encountered in medieval German romances. For example, when Tiburcius, the emperor of Saxland, wants a tutor for his son Klárus, who had already mastered the seven liberal arts and was considered the most learned scholar in Europe, he learns of a superior *meistari* out in Arabia, named Pérús, and engages him to be the boy's tutor.[69] This figure of Pérús has much in common with the court magicians who are a feature of the medieval German romances.[70] Of particular interest is the magician Gansguoter in Heinrich von dem Türlin's *Diu Crône*, a sprawling Gawain-romance dated to the second quarter of the thirteenth century.[71] Gansguoter

---

67. Kalinke, "Table Decorum," pp. 60–5.
68. Frederic C. Tubach, *Index Exemplorum: A Handbook of Medieval Religious Tales*, FF Communications 204 (Helsinki: Suomalainen Tiedeakatemia, 1981). For the limitations of this ground-breaking analysis of 5400 *exempla*, see Jacques Berlioz and Marie Anne Polo de Beaulieu, ed., *Les* Exempla *médiévaux: Introduction á la recherché, suivie des tables critiques de l'*Index exemplorum *de Frederic C. Tubach* (Carcassonne: Garae / Hesiode, 1992), while their volume *Les* Exempla *médiévaux: Nouvelles perspectives* (Paris: Honoré Champion, 1998) reports on the progress of "Le Groupe de Récherce sur les *Exempla* Médiévaux" headquartered in Paris in providing a more complete analysis.
69. The origin of the name is obscure, but it may be a variant of Porus, the king of India, who was one of the main opponents of Alexander the Great (and it is perhaps not irrelevant that in *Klári saga* the king of the French is named Alexander). See Galterus de Castellione, *Alexandreis: það er Alexanders saga*, book 9, pp. 158–76. *Klári saga* states that there are many adventures (*ævintýr*) told involving Pérús and, indeed, three (rather unremarkable) stories about him survive, *Íslendzk æventýri* #81: "Af meistara Pero ok hans leikum" vol. 1, pp. 217–31. The third story is similar in outline to "De lo que conteşçió a un Deán de Santiago cor Don Illán, el grand Maestro de Toledo" (What happended to a Dean of Santiago with Don Illán, the grand master of Toledo), *El conde Lucanor*, pp. 84–91. See footnote 80 below. See also Tubach, *Index Exemplorum*, pp. 245–46, #3137.
70. On these magicians seem Stephan Maksymiuk, *The Court Magician in Medieval German Romance*, Mikrokosmos 44 (Frankfurt am Main: Peter Lang, 1996).
71. For a detailed summary of the story, see Helmut Birkhan *et al.*, ed. *Motif-Index of German Secular Narratives*, vol. 1, pp. 120–207, while Niel Thomas, *Diu Crône and the Medieval Arthuran Cycle*, Arthurian Studies 50 (Cambridge: Brewer, 2002) provides a useful introduction to the romance.

is very much an engineer, responsible for the design and construction of three remarkable castles which are full of mechanical tricks and wonders.[72] Pérús also turns out to be an engineer and uses the entire resources of Saxland to build three magnificent land-tents or pavilions, each of which is drawn to land by a splendid mechanical creature. The creature chosen for the first pavilion is a brown bear, a totemic animal in the northern regions, while the creature chosen for the second pavilion is a lion, a totemic animal in the southern regions. The creature chosen for the third pavilion is called a *gammur*, which has been translated as "vulture,"[73] although to have a vulture for the third and most magnificent pavilion is hardly appropriate. However, it has been pointed out that *gammur* can also refer to an entirely apposite creature, the griffin, with its head and wings of an eagle and body of a lion.[74] As an heraldic figure, the griffin here may be meant to signify the imperial rank of the disguised Klárus.[75] While these creatures Pérús has constructed are not strictly automata (in that they require human muscle-power to work them), the three animals have

---

72. Christine Zach, *Die Erzählmotive der* Crône *Heinrichs von dem Türlin und ihre altfranzösischen Quellen*, Passauer Schriften zu Sprache und Literatur 5 (Passau: Wissenschaftsverlag Richard Rothe, 1990), pp. 130–9, examines the sources for these mechanical devices and constructions, but there is nothing in *Diu Crône* at all like the mechanical marvels in *Klári saga*. Marianne Kalinke also draws attention to a mechanical ship in the early thirteenth-century *Moriz van Craon* (Helmut Birkhan *et al.*, ed., *Motif-Index of German Secular Narratives*, vol. 4, pp. 326–9), but that is built by the hero himself not by a court attendant ("Table Decorum," p. 69).

73. Einar Ól. Sveinsson, "Viktors saga ok Blávus: Sources and Characteristics," in *Viktors saga ok Blávus*, ed Jónas Kristjánsson, Riddarasögur 2 (Reykjavík: Handritastofnun, 1964), pp. cix-ccx at p. xciv.

74. John Bernström, "Gamar," *Kulturhistorisk Lexikon för nordisk medeltid*, vol. 5, cols. 169–70.

75. The three animals may also have Christian symbolism: the bear who licks its cubs into shape as the symbol of Christianity "which reforms and regenerates heathen peoples (George Ferguson, *Signs and Symbols in Christian Art* [1959, rpt. New York: Oxford University Press, 1966], p. 12); the lion is the symbol of the evangelist Mark who "proclaims with great emphasis the royal dignity of Christ" (Ferguson, *Signs and Symbols*, p. 21); the Griffin in its positive aspect represents Christ (Ferguson, *Signs and Symbols*, p. 20). Thus Klárus disguised as Eskelvarð, son of the king of Bláland (Ethiopia, or Africa in general) and ostensibly a pagan, thereby symbolically affirms his Christian faith. In Johannes von Würzburg's *Willhelm von Österreich* written in 1314, there is a sorceress, Parklise, who rides around on a griffin and who advises the hero Wilhlem how to deal with the wicked magician Merlin who has defended himself with two fire-spewing iron dragons. The romance also features other mechanical creatures as well as a magnificent pavilion which shares some superficial features with those constructed by Pérús (for a detailed summary see Helmut Birkhan *et al.*, ed. *Motif-Index of German Secular Narratives*, vol. 3, pp. 87–101).

much in common with the mechanical marvels that feature frequently in medieval romances.[76] Nevertheless, the creatures in *Klári saga* have no precise literary models, and it is possible that Bishop Jón may have got the idea for them from one of the elaborate festivals or processions with their mechanical figures whose movements were a source of delight to the crowds of onlookers that he might have encountered in Paris or Bologna.[77] It is also from these urban experiences that he would have been exposed to the world of elegant clothing and costly fabrics, something in which he must have taken an interest, as the saga is remarkable for the extensive and detailed vocabulary relating to this topic.

It has also been observed that *Klári saga* is a version of the "Taming of the Shrew" story.[78] This is apparently based on the latter part of the story where Serena and the ugly churl whom she believes to be her husband travel from Frakkland to Saxland and during which time Serena is bullied and humiliated, a situation bearing some very superficial resemblance to Act 4, scene 6 of Shakespeare's *Taming of the Shrew*. The play has no printed source and Jan Brunvand concludes that Shakespeare composed it out of folklore elements with which he was familiar.[79] The oldest surviving version of the story is found in the Spanish collection of *exempla*, *El Conde Lucanor* (Count Lucanor) compiled by Juan Manuel (1282–1348), regent of Castille 1321–1325, and founder of the Dominican convent at Peñafiel.[80] But there is little

---

76. For details see: Rosemary Ascherl, "The Technology of Chivalry in Reality and Romance," *The Study of Chivalry: Resources and Approaches*, ed. Howard Chickering and Thomas H. Seiler (Kalamazoo: Consortium for the Teaching of the Middle Ages and Medieval Institute Publications, 1988), pp. 263–311, and the articles in Klaus Grubmüller and Markus Stock, ed., *Automaten in Kunst und Literatur des Mittelalters und der Frühen Neuzeit*, Wolfenbütteler Mittelalter-Studien 17 (Wiesbaden: Harrassowitx, 2003).

77. Such processions at the height of their magnificence are described in Jacob Burckhardt, *The Civilization of the Renaissance in Italy*, trans. S. G. C. Middlemore, rev. and ed. Irene Gordon (New York: Mentor / New American Library, 1961), pp. 283–301.

78. See *Clári saga*, p. xvi.

79. Jan Harold Brunvand, "The Folktale Origin of *The Taming of the Shrew*," *Shakespeare Quarterly* 17 (1966), pp. 345–59 at p. 357. See also his extensive survey of Tale Type 901, "The Taming of the Shrew: A Comparative Study of Oral and Literary Versions" (Ph.D. Dissertation, Indiana University, 1961). In Iceland, Tale type 901 is only recorded in an uncollected tale from Vestur Skaftafellssýsla, "Þið hafið ekki borið söðulinn eins og ég" (You've not worn a saddle as I have), told by Vilborg Einarsdóttir, the mother of Einar Ól. Sveinsson (*Verzeichnis Isländischer Märchenvarianten*, p. 137).

80. "Se lo que conteçió a un mançebo que casó con una muger muy fuerte et muy brava" (What happened to a young man who married a fierce and truculent woman),

if any connection between Tale Type 901 and chapters 16–19 of *Klári saga*, because at this point in the saga Serena is no longer a "shrew." She is totally obedient and humble no matter what outrage the churl visits upon her, and there is no indication at all of her having to be "tamed" as in the other variants of the story. Rather, she has more in common with the extraordinarily patient wife found in Tale Type 887, "Griselda," a tale medieval in origin, being first recorded in Boccaccio's *Decameron* (1352), day 10, tale 10. While the narrative details of the "Griselda" tale (which is well known in Iceland, although all surviving versions belong to the early modern period)[81] differ from those in *Klári saga*, in both versions the patience of the wife remains constant and unwavering. Towards the end of the fourteenth century, Chaucer in the *Canterbury Tales*[82] put a version of the Griselda story in the mouth of the Clerk ("scholar") from Oxford. The episode is introduced with the host commenting on the Clerk's silence thus far during the pilgrimage as if he were studying a sophism, that is, a fallacious argument. He then asks the Clerk to tell a tale unadorned by the colors of rhetoric. The tale the Clerk tells may well be based on a sophism, namely the so-called fallacy "wives are patient," and this certainly appears to be the surface reading of the story to judge by the comments in the Clerk's envoi to his tale.[83] But it is also possible that the Clerk is denying the moral consequences of his own tale and this interpretation has proven attractive to modern audiences. However, there is no such interpretive leeway in *Klári saga*, as the epilogue to the saga makes abundantly clear.

Juan Manuel, *El Conde Lucanor: A Collection of Medieval Spanish Stories*, ed. and trans. John England (Warminster: Aris and Phillips, 1987), pp. 216–23. See also Tubach, *Index Exemplorum*, p. 333, #4354.

81. The principal texts have been studied in detail and published by Halldór Hermannsson in *The Story of Griselda in Iceland*, Islandica 7 (Ithaca: Cornell University Library, 1914).

82. See W. F. Bryan and Germaine Dempster, ed. *Sources and Analogues of* Chaucer's Canterbury Tales (1914, rpt. New York: Humanities Press, 1958), pp. 288–331, and Robert M. Correale and Mary Hamel, ed. *Sources and Analogues of the Canterbury Tales*, 2 vols. (Cambridge: Brewer, 2002–05), vol. 1, pp. 101–67, both of which contain the Latin text of Petrarch's version of the tale and its French translation which Chaucer drew on to write the "Clerk's Tale." See also Tubach, *Index Exemplorum*, p. 188, #2383, and Einar Ól. Sveinsson, *Verzeichnis Isländischer Märchenvarianten*, pp. 132–3.

83. "The Clerk's Tale" has proven distasteful to modern audiences, and scholars have long debated over how to read it. See the discussion in Helen Cooper, "The Clerk's Tale," *Oxford Guides to Chaucer: The Canterbury Tales*, 2nd ed. (Oxford: Oxford University Press, 1996), pp. 185–201 at pp. 193–200.

En hún [Serena] þoldi allan þenna tíma angist og armæðu fyrir ekki vætta utan fyrir sig sína einlega dyggð og einfaldleik ... Og þetta allt lagði hún að baki sér og þar með föður, frændur og vini og allan heimsins metnað, upp takandi viljanlegt fátækt með þessum hinum herfilegan stafkarli, gefandi svo á sér ljós dæmi hversu öðrum góðum konum byrjar að halda dyggð við sína eiginbændur eða unnasta. Fór það og eftir verðugu að síðustu, að hún fékk það, er hún var makleg fyrir sína fáheyrða staðfestu, að ... varð hún yfirdrottning alls Saxlands ...[84]

(But she [Serena] endured all the time the misery and distress for no other reason than her singular probity and simplicity ... And absolutely everything she put behind her, including father, kin and friends and all the world's honor, taking up poverty willingly with this miserable beggar, giving so by her behavior a clear example, how it befits other good women to maintain their probity with their husbands or betrothed ones. That also turned out in due course as it was deserved, that she received that which was fitting for her because of her unheard of steadfastness, that ... she became sovereign queen of all Saxland ...

It is clear from the epilogue to *Klári saga*, that Bishop Jón is using the romance genre as an elaborate *exemplum* to promote his uncompromising views on the responsible behaviors of wives towards their husbands.[85] Tale Type 887, however, is not one about which an audience remains neutral. Marianne Kalinke points out that although later authors quickly followed *Klári saga* with their own versions of bridal quest romances, they "chose to ignore a most important part of *Clári saga*, its exemplary character, residing in its Christian view of marriage."[86] A modern audience can "rescue" the "Clerk's Tale" by "reading it against the grain" to give it a meaning more in line

---

84. *Riddarasögur*, vol. 5, p. 61.
85. When the Jesuits came to New France in the early seventeenth century to convert the Native Americans, their comments in the "Jesuit Relations" reveal their attitudes to women and their place in society and marriage are very close to the views espoused by Bishop Jón at the conclusion of *Klári saga*. See Karen Anderson, *Chain Her by One Foot: The Subjugation of Native Women in Seventeeth-Century New France* (New York: Routledge, 1991), esp. pp. 67–100. It is possible that the missionaries were able to enforce a stricter morality among the Huron and Montagnais than they would have been allowed to get away with in France.
86. Kalinke, "Table Decorum," p. 71.

with contemporary sensibilities. Not having such an option available, imitators of *Klári saga* just omitted this aspect of their source while those who copied the saga down through the centuries appear also to have considered this aspect of the saga expendable.[87]

Conclusions

Klári saga was composed by Bishop Jón Halldórsson of Skálholt, who grew up in the Dominican house in Bergen and whose mother and possibly father were Icelandic. He studied in Dominican run universities on the continent, and there he became familiar with a rich *exempla* tradition, in the promoting and disseminating of which the Dominicans played a prominent role. Examples of this tradition he brought back with him to Norway and later on to Iceland. The opening statement of *Klári saga*, which claims that it is based on a Latin poem encountered in France, is a modesty topos: Latin is the prestige language, and France is the home of the romance. The idiomatic nature of the Icelandic suggests that it was composed after Bishop Jón had been some time in that country. After 1320 is as good a guess as any. The strong influence from Middle Low German in the language of the saga as well as numerous narrative elements that are indebted to medieval German romances reflect the time Bishop Jón lived in the Hansa port of Bergen.[88] Like Heinrich von dem Türlin's *Diu Crone*, *Klári saga* is a pastiche of romance and fairy tale, elements effectively woven together by a skilled story teller. There is no single source for the saga, rather the author has adapted *exempla* to a bridal quest narrative framework very similar to the one sketched out in the Þrýð episode in *Beowulf*.

If these conclusions are accepted, then the saga can no longer be considered as a translated romance, but should rightfully take its place among the Icelandic *riddarasögur* to whose development it has so significantly contributed.

---

87. In the nineteenth-century *Sagan af Klarusi keisarasyni*, the explanations and moralizing at the end of Bishop Jón's version of the text are reduced to: "Síðan er frú Seerína upp hafin í drottingar sæti, hafandi dýrð og heiður með Klarusi Keisarasyni" (Afterwards Lady Seerína is raised up to the queen's throne, having glory and honor with Klarus the Emperor's son) (28).

88. The role of Bergen and the Hansa in the dissemination of Medieval German literature in Scandinavia is the focus of the articles in Susanne Kramarz-Bein, *Hansische Literaturbeziehungen*, Ergänzungsbände zum Reallexikon der Germanischen Altertumskunde 14 (Berlin: de Gruyter, 1996).

Bibliography

Aarne, Antti, and Stith Thompson. *Types of the Folktale: A Classification and Bibliography.* FF Communications 184. Helsinki: Suomalainen Tiedeakatemia, 1981.
Anderson, Karen. *Chain Her by One Foot: The Subjugation of Native Women in Seventeenth-Century New France.* New York: Routledge, 1991.
Amory, Frederic. "Things Greek and the *Riddarasögur*," In *Les Sagas de Chevaliers (Riddarasögur).* Ed. Régis Boyer. Civilizations 10. Paris: Presses de l'Université Paris-Sorbonne, 1985. Pp. 417–430. *Speculum* 59 (1984): 509–23.
Ascherl, Rosemary. "The Technology of Chivalry in Reality and Romance." In *The Study of Chivalry: Resources and Approaches.* Ed. Howard Chickering and Thomas H. Seiler. Kalamazoo: Consortium for the Teaching of the Middle Ages and Medieval Institute Publications, 1988. Pp. 263–311.
Astås, Reidar. *An Old Norse Biblical Compilation: Studies in* Stjórn. American University studies 7: Theology and Religion 109. New York: Peter Lang, 1991.
Beowulf: *An Edition with Relevant Shorter Texts.* Ed. Bruce Mitchell and Fred C. Robinson. Rev. ed. Malden, MA: Blackwell, 2006.
Bernström, John. "Gamar." *Kulturhistoriskt Lexikon för nordisk medeltid från vikingatid till reformationstid.* 22 vols. Malmö: Allhems förlag, 1956–78. Vol. 5, cols. 169–70.
Birkhan, Helmut, Karin Lichtblau, Christa Tuczay *et al.* for the Austrian Academy of Sciences, ed. *Motif-Index of German Secular Narratives from the Beginning to 1400.* 7 vols. Berlin: de Gruyter, 2005–06.
Berlioz, Jacques, and Marie Anne Polo de Beaulieu, ed. *Les* Exempla médiévaux: *Introduction á la recherché, suivie des tables critiques de l'*Index exemplorum *de Frederic C. Tubach.* Carcassonne: Garae / Hesiode, 1992.
———, ed. *Les* Exempla médiévaux: *Nouvelles perspectives.* Paris: Honoré Champion, 1998.
Biskupa sögur. Ed. Guðrún Ása Grímsdóttir *et al.* 3 vols. Íslensk fornrit 15–17. Reykjavík: Hið íslenzka fornritafélag, 1998–2000.
Bjarni Vilhjálmsson, ed. *Riddarasögur.* 6 vols. [Akureyri]: Íslendingasagnaútgáfan, 1952–54. Rpt. 1961.
Bolte, Johannes, and Georg Polívka. *Anmerkungen zu den Kinder- und Hausmärchen der Brüder Grimm.* Rev. ed. Ed. Ernst Schade. 5 vols. in 4. *Werke.* Ed. Ludwig Erich Schmitt *et al.* Abt. 5, vols. 2–6. Hildesheim: Olms-Weidmann, 1992–94. [First published 1913–32.]
Bornholdt, Claudia. *Engaging Moments: The Origins of the Medieval Bridal-Quest Narrative.* Ergänzungsbände zum Reallexikon der Germanischen Altertumskunde 46. Berlin: de Gruyter, 2005.
Boswell, John. *Kindness of Strangers: The Abandonment of Children in Western Europe from Late Antiquity to the Renaissance.* New York: Pantheon, 1988.
Brattegard, Olav. *Die mittelniederdeutsche Geschäftssprache des hansischen Kaufmanns zu Bergen.* 2 vols. Skrifter fra Norges Handelshøyskole i rekken språklige avhandlinger 2–3. Bergen: John Grieg, 1945–46.
Brunvand, Jan Haro. "The Taming of the Shrew: A Comparative Study of Oral and Literary Versions." Ph.D. Dissertation, Indiana University, 1961.
———. "The Folktale Origin of *The Taming of the Shrew.*" *Shakespeare Quarterly* 17 (1966): 345–59.
Bryan, W. F., and Germaine Dempster, ed. *Sources and Analogues of Chaucer's Canterbury Tales.* New York: Humanities Press, 1958. [First published 1941.]

Burckhardt, Jacob. *The Civilization of the Renaissance in Italy*. Trans, S. G. C. Middlemore [from the second German edition of 1868]. Rev. and ed. Irene Gordon. New York: Mentor / New American Library, 1961.
Chambers, R. W. *Beowulf: An Introduction to the Study of the Poem*. 3rd ed. Suppl. by C. L. Wrenn. Cambridge: Cambridge University Press, 1959.
Clári saga. Ed. Gustaf Cederschiöld. Altnordische Saga-Bibliothek 12. Halle: Niemeyer, 1907. Text rpt. in: *Riddarasögur* vol. 5, pp. 1–61.
Clarus saga, Clari fabella. Ed. Gustaf Cederschiöld. Lat. trans. Samuel J. Cavallin. Lund. Gleerup, 1879.
Cooper, Helen. "The Clerk's Tale." In *Oxford Guides to Chaucer: The Canterbury Tales*. 2nd ed. Oxford: Oxford University Press, 1996. Pp. 185–201.
Correale, Robert M., and Mary Hamel, ed. *Sources and Analogues of the Canterbury Tales*. 2 vols. Cambridge: Brewer, 2002–05.
de Vries. Jan. *Altnordische Literaturgeschichte*. 2nd ed. 2 vols. Berlin: de Gruyter, 1964–67.
Diplomatarium Islandicum: Íslenzk fornbréfasafn. Ed. Jón Sigurðsson *et al*. 16 vols. Copenhagen and Reykjavík: S. L. Möller *et al.*, 1857–1972.
Einar G. Pétursson, ed. *Miðaldaævintýri þýdd úr ensku*. Rit 11. Reykavík: Stofnun Árna Magnússonar á Íslandi, 1976.
Einar Ól. Sveinsson, "Viktors saga ok Blávus. Sources and Characteristics." In *Viktors saga ok Blávus*. Ed. Jónas Kristjánsson. Riddarasögur 2. Reykjavík: Handritastofnun, 1964. Pp. cix–ccx.
———. *Verzeichnis Isländischer Märchenvarianten mit einer einleitenden Untersuchung*. FF Communications 83. Helsinki: Suomalainen Tiedeakatemia, 1929.
Ferguson, George. *Signs and Symbols in Christian Art*. New York: Oxford University Press, 1966. [First published 1959.]
Finnur Jónsson. *Den oldnorske og oldislandske litteraturs historie*. 2nd ed. 3 vols. Copenhagen: Gad, 1920–24.
———, ed. *Carmina Scaldica*. 2nd ed. Copenhagen: Gad, 1929.
Galterus de Castellione. *Alexandreis: það er Alexanders saga á íslensku*. Ed. Gunnlaugur Ingólfsson. Reykjavík: Steinholt, 2002.
Glauser, Jurg. *Isländische Märchensagas: Studien zur Prosaliteratur im spätmittelalterlichen Island*. Beiträge zur nordischen Philologie 12. Basel: Helbing und Lichtenhahn, 1983.
Grágás: Lagasafn íslenska þjóðveldisins. Ed. Gunnar Karlsson *et al*. Reykjavík: Mál og menning, 2001.
Grubmüller, Klaus, and Markus Stock, ed. *Automaten in Kunst und Literatur des Mittelalters und der Frühen Neuzeit*, Wolfenbütteler Mittelalter-Studien 17. Wiesbaden: Harrassowitz, 2003.
Gunnar Kristjánsson, gen. ed. *Saga biskupstólanna: Skálholt 950 ára–2006–Hólar 900 ára*. Reykjavík: Bókaútgáfan Hólar. 2006.
Halldór Hermansson. *The Story of Griselda in Iceland*. Islandica 7. Ithaca: Cornell University Library, 1914.
Hjaltalín, Torfi K. Stefánsson. *Eldur á Möðruvöllum: Saga Möðruvalla í Hörgárdal frá öndverða til okkar tíma*. 2 vols. Reykjavík: Flateyjarútgáfan, 2001
Höfler, Otto. *Altnordische Lehnwortstudien*. Sonderabdruck aus dem *Arkiv för nordisk filologi* XLVII [(1931): 248–97]-XLVIII [(1932): 1–30, 213–41]. Lund: Håkon Ohlsson, 1931.
Hughes, Shaun F. D. "The Ideal of Kingship in the *Riddarasögur*." *Michigan Academician* 10 (1978): 321–36.
Íslendinga sögur og þættir. Ed.Bragi Halldórsson *et al*. 3rd ed. 3 vols. Reykjavík: Mál og menning, 1998.

Íslendzk æventýri: Isländische Legenden Novellen und Märchen. Ed. Hugo Gering. 2 vols. Halle: Buchhandlungen des Waisenhauses, 1882–83.
Jakobsen, Alfred. Studier i Clarus saga; til spørsmålet om sagaens norske proveniens. Árbok for Universitetet i Bergen. Humanistisk serie; 1963, 2. Bergen, Universitetsforlaget, 1964.
Jón Árnason. Íslenzkar þjóðsögur og æventýri. New ed. Ed. Árni Böðvarsson and Bjarni Vilhjálmsson. 6 vols. Reykjavík: Bókaútgáfan Þjóðsaga, 1954–61.
Jónas Jónasson. Íslenzkir þjóðhættir. Ed. Einar Ól. Sveinsson. 3rd ed. Reykjavík: Ísafold, 1961.
Jónsbók. Lögbók Íslendinga hver samþykkt var á alþingi árið 1281... Ed. Már Jónsson. Sýnisbók íslenskrar alþýðumenningar 8. Reykjavík: Háskólaútgáfan, 2002.
Jorgensen, Peter A. "Ten Icelandic Exempla and their Middle English Source." Opuscula 4. Bibliotheca Arnamagnæana 30. Copenhagen: Munksgaard, 1970. Pp. 177–207.
———. "The Icelandic Translations from Middle English." Studies for Einar Haugen. Ed. Evelyn Scherabon Firchow et al. The Hague: Mouton, 1972. Pp. 305–20.
———. "Four Æventýri." Opuscula 5. Bibliotheca Arnamagnæana 31. Copenhagen: Munksgaard, 1975. Pp. 295–328.
———. The Story of Jonatas in Iceland. Rit 45. Reykavík: Stofnun Árna Magnússonar á Íslandi, 1997.
Kalinke, Marianne E. "Klári saga." Dictionary of the Middle Ages 7 (New York: Charles Scribner's Sons, 1986). Pp. 274–5.
———. Bridal-Quest Romance in Medieval Iceland. Islandica 46. Ithaca: Cornell University Press, 1990.
———. The Book of Reykjahólar: The Last of the Great Medieval Legendaries. Toronto: University of Toronto Press, 1996.
———. "Table Decorum and the Quest for a Bride in Klári saga." In At the Table: Metaphorical and Material Cultures of Food in Medieval and Early Modern Europe. Ed. Timothy J. Tomasik and Juliann M. Vitello. Arizona Studies in the Middle Ages and Renaissance 18. Turnhout: Brepols, 2007. Pp. 51–72.
Kalinke, Marianne E., and P. M. Mitchell. Bibliography of Old-Norse-Icelandic Romances. Islandica 44. Ithaca: Cornell University Press, 1985.
Katara, Pekka. Das französische Lehngut in mittelniederdeutschen Denkmälern von 1300 bis 1600. Mémoires de la Société Néophilologique de Helsinki 30. Helskinki: Société Néophilologique, 1966.
Kearney, Dennis Ferrell. "Clárús saga: An Edition and Translation." Ph.D. Dissertation, University of Mississippi, 1990.
Konrad von Würzburg (attrib.), "Die halbe Birne." Novellistik des Mittelalters. Märendichtung. Ed. Klaus Grubmüller. Bibliothek des Mittelalters 11. Frankfurt am Main: Deutscher Klassiker Verlag, 1996. Pp. 178–207, 1083–101.
Kramarz-Bein, Susanne, ed. Hansische Literaturbeziehungen. Ergänzungsbände zum Reallexikon der Germanischen Altertumskunde 14. Berlin: de Gruyter, 1996.
Lind, E. H. Norsk-Isländska Dopnamn och fingerade Namn från Medeltiden. 3 vols. Uppsala: Lundequistska Bokhandeln, 1905–31.
Louis-Jensen, Jonna. "Nogle Æventýri." Opuscula 5. Bibliotheca Arnamagnæana 31. Copenhagen: Munksgaard, 1975. 263–77.
Maksymiuk, Stephan. The Court Magician in Medieval German Romance. Mikrokosmos 44. Frankfurt am Main: Peter Lang, 1996.
Manuel, Juan. El Conde Lucanor: A Collection of Medieval Spanish Stories. Ed. and trans. John England. Warminster: Aris and Phillips, 1987.

Müller, Harald. "Kampf der Geschlechter? Der Mädchenkönig im isländischen Märchen und in der isländischen Märchensaga." *Mann und Frau im Märchen.* Ed. Harlinda Lox, Sigrid. Früh and Wolfgang Schultze. Kreutzlingen: Heinrich Hugendubel (Diederichs), 2002. Pp. 62–79.
Nesse. Agnete. *Språkkontakt mellom norsk og tysk i hansatidens Bergen.* Det Norske Videnskaps-Akademi II: Hist.-Filos. Klasse Skrifter og avhandlinger 2. Oslo: Det Norske Videnskaps-Akademi, 2002.
Niermeyer, J. F. *Mediae latinitatis lexicon minus.* 2nd rev. ed. 2 vols. Leiden: Brill, 2002.
Norges Gamle Love indtil 1387. Ed. R. Keyser and P. Munch. 5 vols. Christiania [Oslo]: Gröndahl, 1846–95.
Ogier von Dänemark nach der Heidelberger Handschrift CPG 363. Ed. Hilkert Weddige with Theo J. A. Broers and Hans van Dijk. Deutsche Texte des Mittelalters 83. Berlin: Akademie, 2002.
Ólafur Halldórsson. "AM 249 fol. XV, tvinn úr handriti með ævintýrum." *Gripla* 18 (2007): 23–46
Philippson, Ernst. *Der Märchentypus von König Drosselbart.* FF Communications 50. Greifswald: Suomalainen Tiedeakatemia, 1923.
Roman van Heinric en Margriete van Limborch: Uitgeven volgens het Brusselse Handschrift. Ed. Robertus Meesters. Two parts. Amsterdam: Stichting "Onze Oude Letteren," 1951.
Sagan af Klarusi keisarasyni. Ed. Bjarni Bjarnason. Reykjavík: Ísafold, 1884.
Schmitt, Jean-Claude. *The Holy Greyhound: Guinefort, Healer of children since the Thirteenth Century.* Trans. Martin Thom. Cambridge Studies in Oral and Literate Culture 6. Cambridge: Cambridge University Press, 1983. [First published in French 1979.]
Snorri Sturluson. *Heimskringla.* Ed. Bergljót Kristjánsdóttir *et al.* 3 vols. Reykjavík: Mál og menning, 1991.
Stephan de Borbone. *Tractatus de diversis materiis predicabilibus.* Gen. Ed. Jacques Berlioz. Corpus Christianorum: Continuatio Mediaevalis 124. Turnout: Brepols, 2002–.
Stjorn: Gammelnorsk Bibelhistorie. Ed. C. R. Unger. Christiania [Oslo]: Feilberg and Landmark, 1862.
Storm, Gustav, ed. *Islandske Annaler indtil 1578.* Christiania [Oslo]: Grøndahl and Søn, 1888; Rpt. Oslo: Norsk Historisk Kjeldeskrift-Institutt, 1977.
Thomas, Niel. *Diu Crône and the Medieval Arthurian Cycle.* Arthurian Studies 50. Cambridge: Brewer, 2002.
Torfi H. Tulinius, ""Kynjasögur úr fortíð og framandi löndum." *Íslensk bókmenntasaga.* Vol. 2. Ed. Vésteinn Ólason *et al.* Reykjavík: Mál og menning, 1992. 165–245.
Tubach, Frederic C. *Index Exemplorum: A Handbook of Medieval Religious Tales.* FF Communications 204. Helsinki: Suomalainen Tiedeakatemia, 1981.
Tveitane, Mattias. *Den lærde stil: oversetterprosa i den norrøne versjonen av Vitæ Patrum.* Årbok for Universitetet i Bergen. Humanistisk serie; 1967, 2. Bergen, Norwegian Universities Press, 1967.
Uther, Hans-Jörg. *The Types of International Folktales: A Classification and Bibliography. Based on the System of Antti Aarne and Stith Thompson.* 3 vols. FF Communications 284–86. Helsinki: Suomalainen Tiedeakatemia, 2004.
van Dijk, H. "Ogier van Denemarken: Diplomatische uitgave van de Middelnederlandse fragmenten ...," *De Nieuwe taalgids,* 67 (1974): 177–202.
———, and H. Kienhorst. "Ogier van Denemarken, Nieuwe fragmenten." *Wat*

Duikers vent is dit! Opstellen voor W. M. H. Hummelen. Ed. G. R. W. Dibbets et al. Wijhe: Quarto, 1989. 3–24.
Veturliði Óskarsson. *Middelnedertyske låneord i islandsk diplomsprog frem til år 1500.* Bibliotheca Armamagnæana 43. Copenhagen: C. A. Reitzel, 2002.
Wahlgren, Eric. *The Maiden King in Iceland.* Chicago: University of Chicago Libraries, 1938.
Westergård-Nielsen, Christian. *Låneordene i det 16. århundredes trykte islandske litteratur.* Bibliotheca Armamagnæana 6. Copenhagen: Munksgaard, 1946.
Ynglinga saga. Snorri Sturlson. *Heimskringla.* Ed. Bergljót S. Kristjánsdóttir *et al.* 3 vols. Reykjavík: Mál og Menning, 1991.
Zach, Christine. *Die Erzählmotive der* crône *Heinrichs von dem Türlin und ihre altfranzösischen Quellen.* Passauer Schriften zu Sprache und Literatur 5. Passau: Wissenschaftsverlag Richard Rothe, 1990.

When Skaði Chose Njǫrðr

JOHN LINDOW

In her presentation of *Bridal-Quest Romance* in the North, Marianne Kalinke noted that even if the motif occurs, "... the quest of a woman for a man was never the determinant of plot in any saga."[1] As far as I know, this statement holds for all sagas, not just the *riddarasögur* and *fornaldarsögur*. Within the topsy-turvy world of myth, however, we might term Skaði's marriage to Njǫrðr as indeed the result of the quest of a woman for a man, even if both actors belong to non-human mythological races and the quest is not at first portrayed as matrimonial in nature. Myth allows or even encourages the unexpected, to be sure, but it is always in the end plausible, if only in the way that dreams are plausible, and we must accept Skaði's quest for what it is, the quest of a Jǫtunn woman for a man from among the Æsir. This quest is indeed not portrayed as matrimonial in nature, but as Margaret Clunies Ross has pointed out, if Skaði carried rather than wore her armor, as the text suggests ("En Skaði, dóttir Þjaza jǫtuns, tók hjálm ok brynju ok ǫll hervápn ok ferr til Ásgarðs" [But Skadi, daughter of giant Thiassi, took helmet and mail-coat and all weapons of war and went to Asgard to avenge her father]),[2] she may have

---

1. Marianne E. Kalinke, *Bridal-Quest Romance in Medieval Iceland*, Islandica 46 (Ithaca and London: Cornell University Press, 1990), p. 22.
2. *Snorri Sturluson: Edda*, ed. Finnur Jónsson, ed., 2nd ed. (Copenhagen: Gad, 1926), p. 70; *Snorri Sturluson: Edda*, transl Anthony Faulkes (London: J. M. Dent & Sons, 1987), p. 61.

been seeking settlement rather than a move within the structures of bloodfeud.[3] What better settlement than a husband?

The story of Skaði's choice of Njǫrðr indeed subverts generic expectations in Old Icelandic literature, but it is not quite without parallels. In what follows, I will examine two important analogues to the myth that appear to offer suggestions on how it might be read. Both analogues are known; what I hope to do is use them to bring out some important and hitherto less discussed aspects of the myth.

We have the story of Skaði and Njǫrðr from only one source, the *Edda* of Snorri Sturluson (ca. 1220–30). It would be difficult to find a known medieval Icelandic author less interested in romance than Snorri seems to have been, despite his stay at the Norwegian court in 1218–20 and his continuing connection with king and court. The poem he composed on the occasion of his visit to the court of King Hákon Hákonarson and the regent Jarl Skúli Bárðarson was a *tour de force* in the old skaldic style, and it probably served as the basis for the composition of his entire *Edda*.[4] Skaldic poetry was clearly a sort of intellectual capital for Snorri,[5] and the romances that arrived at Hákon's court six years after Snorri's departure could not have been helpful to him.

The story that concerns us is part of the very first extended narrative in *Skáldskaparmál*. It is not elicited by a question put by Ægir to Bragi but rather is simply presented as the first of many things which Bragi told Ægir; that is, it is not part of the question-answer frame which Snorri attempted in the first part of *Skáldskaparmál*. This fact might suggest that the initial story bears special significance or in some way stands apart from the narratives that are elicited by a question Ægir puts to Bragi. That initial story is of course Loki's betrayal of Iðunn

---

3. Margaret Clunies Ross, *Prolonged Echoes: Old Norse Myths in Medieval Northern Society*, The Viking Collection 7 ([Odense:] Odense University Press, 1984), p. 122.

4. Elias Wessén, "Introduction," in *Codex Regius to the Younger Edda: MS n. 2367 4to in the Old Royal Collection in the Royal Library in Copenhagen*, Copus Codicorum Islandorum Medii Ævi 14 (Copenhagen: Munksgaard, 1940), pp. 1–30.

5. Kevin Wanner, *The Distinguished Norseman: Snorri Stuluson, The Edda, and the Conversion of Capital in Medieval Scandinavia*, Diss. (University of Chicago, 2003); cf. Torfi Tulinius, "Snorri og bræður hans: Framgangur og átök Sturlusona í félagslegu rými þjóðveldisins," *Ny saga* 12 (2000), Viðar Pálsson, "'Var engi höfðingi slíkr sem Snorri': Auður og virðing í valdabaráttu Snorra Sturlusonar," *Saga* 41 (2003), and Kevin J. Wanner, *Snorri Sturluson and the Edda: The Conversion of Cultural Capital in Medieval Scandinavia* (Toronto: University of Toronto Press, 2008).

and her apples to the giant Þjazi and his subsequent recovery of them. Þjazi dies in pursuit, and the marriage of Skaði to Njǫrðr is part of the compensation package the Æsir offer to Skaði when she arrives at Ásgarðr in helmet and byrnie with all her weapons.

En æsirnir buðu henni sætt ok yfirbœtr ok it fyrsta, at hon skal kjósa sér mann af ásum ok kjósa at fótum ok sjá ekki fleira af.
Þá sá hon eins manns fœtr forkunnarfagra ok mælti: 'Þenna kýs ek. Fátt mun ljótt á Baldri'—en þat var Njǫrðr ór Nóatúnum.[6]

(But the Æsir offered her atonement and compensation, the first item of which was that she was to choose herself a husband out of the Æsir and choose by the feet and see nothing else of them. Then she saw one person's feet that were exceptionally beautiful and said:
'I choose that one; there can be little that is ugly about Baldr.'
But it was Niord of Noatun.)[7]

Discussing this passage some years ago, I pointed out that the parallels with the Cinderella narrative that have long been in the literature[8] are not helpful (although parallels with other Märchen may be), and indeed that any choice of a spouse based on physical characteristics was a doomed venture.

To a medieval Icelandic audience, we can guess that such compensation was not worth a great deal. If marriage was essentially a political affair worked out for the interests of and approved (if not arranged) by the relevant fraternal interest group,[9] Skaði had little hope of bettering her position when she had to choose solely by the feet.[10] In that same

---

6. *Snorri Sturluson: Edda*, ed. Finnur Jónsson, p. 70; cf. *Edda Snorra Sturlusonar: Udgivet efter håndskrifterne*, ed. Finnur Jónsson (Copenhagen: Gyldendal/Nordisk forlag, 1931), p. 81.
7. *Snorri Sturluson: Edda*, trans. Faulkes, p. 61.
8. E.g. Friedrich von der Leyen, *Das Märchen in der Göttersagan der Edda* (Berlin: Reimer, 1899).
9. Theodore M. Andersson and William Ian Miller, *Law and Literature in Medieval Iceland: Ljósvetninga saga and Valla-Ljóts saga* (Stanford: Stanford University Press, 1989), pp. 18–19.
10. John Lindow, "Loki and Skaði," in *Snorrastefna: 25.-27. júlí 1990*, Ed. Úlfar Bragason, Rit Stofnunar Sigurðar Nordals 1 (Reykjavík: Stofnun Sigurðar Nordals, 1992), p. 132.

discussion, I also drew attention to some possible parallels within European medieval practices of punishments involving shame, such as making defeated warriors parade barefooted, bare-headed and beltless before their victors, a practice attested, for example, in the reconciliation of the archbishop and city council of Cologne in 1265:[11] "When a line of barefooted or barelegged æsir stands before Skaði, presumably with their faces covered, she plays the role of the triumphal figure of authority, always male, in such ritual contexts."[12]

My reading of the story, then, was that the Æsir engaged in a high medieval act of contrition and basically tricked Skaði out of more meaningful compensation. I concluded that the hand of Snorri is easily discerned in the story. I now feel that there is more to it, and I am no longer completely convinced that Skaði's choice was just a trick. I am led to these conclusions through a consideration of the two parallels, to which I now turn.

The first is from the mythic realm, and it involves Freyr and the giantess Gerðr, that is, another would-be marriage between one of the Vanir and a member of the giant race. This analogue has long been noted, and what I wish to do here is to focus on the aspects of the Freyr/Gerðr story that can help illuminate Skaði's choice of Njǫrðr. The most important of these for my purposes now is the mental state of Freyr. According to the prose header of *For Scírnis*, he suffered mental anguish ("hugsóttir miklar") as a result of his having seen Gerðr. If there is a parallel here too, then what happened to Freyr when he saw Gerðr's arms happened to Skaði when she beheld Njǫrðr's feet, and she made what we might term an irrational choice of her life partner. Perhaps this parallelism is what drew Skaði into the poem—or at least into the prose header, which makes her the speaker of the first stanza, addressed to Skírnir. In any case, her seemingly irrational choice of old Njǫrðr, because of his feet, may find a parallel in Freyr's situation: if not one of the Æsir or elves wishes Freyr and Gerðr to be joined (*For Scírnis*, st. 7), that would only underscore the irrationality of his choice. Make no mistake, the situation is dangerous. Snorri elaborates on the "hugsóttir miklar" which plague Freyr:

---

11. Lizzie Carlsson, "Pliktpallen i belysning av medeltida skamstraff," *Kyrkohistorisk årskrift* 57 (1957): 33–343; cf Lizzie Carlsson, "Staven: En maktens och ringhetens symbol," *Rig* 34 (1951): 6–8.

12. Lindow, "Loki and Skaði," p. 136.

Ok er hann kom heim, mælti hann ekki; ekki svaf hann, ekki drakk hann; engi þorði at krefja hann málsins.[13]

(And when he got home, he said nothing, he neither slept nor drank; no one dared to try to speak with him.)[14]

Freyr is rendered speechless and he withdraws from participation in the social life (drinking and talking) of the Æsir. The Jǫtnar have, in other words, incapacitated one of the gods. This withdrawal is especially serious if we consider the mythology from the Odinic point of view: wisdom is to be found in speech, and drinking makes at least a metaphoric nod to the mead of poetry, where wisdom is seated. The Odinic viewpoint suggests itself not least because according to Snorri (but not För Scírnis), Freyr's act of hubris ("mikillæti") in climbing up into Hliðskjálf caused the problem.

Drawing in Hliðskjálf suggests a contrast between Óðinn, who can handle the sight (and seduction) of female Jǫtnar, and Freyr, who apparently cannot. In either case, there is a crisis precipitated by contact between the mythological races, and involving the desire or need of the Æsir to move females from the realm of the Jǫtnar to their own.

For Snorri, the love-sickness that Freyr suffers seems to have been the equivalent to his giving up his sword to obtain Gerðr: that is, he was permanently unarmed, and thus made less than a man. Lest there be any doubt on this point, see Guðrún Nordal's comments on the implications of Sturla Sighvatsson's nickname "Dala-Freyr."[15] We must assume that Skaði too laid aside her weapons and armor when she got Njǫrðr in marriage. Thus the parallel between Freyr and Skaði shows a gender fault line, at least for Snorri. Their manic love (I take the term from Bjarni Einarsson[16]) unmans each of them, and that is bad for Freyr and good for Skaði. As Preben Meulengracht Sørensen

---

13. *Snorri Sturluson: Edda*, ed. Finnur Jónsson, p. 37; cf. *Edda Snorra Sturlusonar*, ed. Finnur Jónsson, p. 40.
14. *Snorri Sturluson: Edda*, trans. Faulkes, p. 31
15. Guðrún Nordal, *Ethics and Action in Thirteenth-Century Iceland*, The Viking Collection 11 ([Odense:] Odense University Press, 1998), p. 58 and esp. pp. 178–79.
16. Bjarni Einarsson, "The Lovesick Skald: A Response to Theodore M. Andersson," *Mediaeval Scandinavia* 4 (1971): 21–42.

pointed out, the armed woman is a positive figure in medieval Icelandic literature, but she needs to be overcome, to give up her weapons and her male role, and then to marry.[17]

I am tempted to regard *För Scírnis* 7, in which Freyr expands on his love for Gerðr, as highly exaggerated, not so much mythology but rather pathology.

> Mær er mér   tíðari enn manni hveim,
>   ungom, í árdaga;
> ása oc álfa   þar vill engi maðr,
>   at við sátt sém.[18]

(The maiden is dearer to me than to any young man,
in days of old;
of the Æsir and elves none wishes
that we be reconciled.) [My translation, as throughout unless otherwise noted]

Thus I do not take *í árdaga* as setting the narrative *in illo tempore*. Rather I propose to read the first half stanza as a lovestruck exaggeration: "no one even in days of yore ever fell in love as I have done." And the second helming, too, which scholars usually take literally, I propose to read as another lovestruck exaggeration: "no one wants us to marry." There is actually no external evidence to the effect that the Æsir (or elves) objected to this marriage, and no real reason why they should have done so, since the situation is one of acquisition of a desired commodity from giantland for the benefit of the gods.

Gerðr's reluctance to give herself to Freyr finds no parallel in the account of Skaði's choice of Njǫrðr. However, the marriage between Skaði and Njǫrðr fails. This part of the story, not how she chose or how Loki made her laugh, is the most widely attested from the Middle Ages. We have not only Snorri's quotation in *Gylfaginning* of two *ljóðaháttr* verses in which each complains about the noisy abode of the

---

17. Preben Meulengracht Sørensen, *The Unmanly Man: Concepts of Sexual Defamation in Early Nordic Society*, The Viking Series 1 ([Odense:] Odense University Press, 1983), pp. 22–24.

18. *För Scírnis* 6, *Edda: Die Lieder des Codex Regius nebst verwandten Denkmälern*, ed. Gustav Neckel, rev. Hans Kuhn (Heidelberg: Winter, 1962), p. 70.

other, thus suggesting a lost eddic dialogue poem, and his statement in *Ynglinga saga*, ch. 8, that they separated and Skaði remarried Óðinn, but also his quotation in *Skáldskaparmál* of a verse from the eleventh-century Icelandic skald Þórðr Særeksson alluding to their separate abodes. People knew that Skaði and Njǫrðr had separated after their marriage. I am among those who see the nine nights that Freyr must wait for Gerðr as a failed parallel to the failed vanic marriage of his father. Skaði and Njǫrðr separate after their wedding; Freyr and Gerðr remain, at the end of *For Scírnis*, in a state of separation. Freyr is not cured of his heartsickness; rather the poem ends with a lamentation over the time he must wait. Snorri, of course, marries them off, both in his *Edda* and in *Ynglinga saga*, just as he adds Skaði to the guest list of every banquet he mentions in his *Edda*, but the evidence of the Eddic poem is that both male Vanir are in a state of separation from their Jǫtunn wives.

I take these, then, as some implications of the Skaði/Njǫrðr Freyr/Gerðr parallel: Each made an irrational choice, which I have attributed to manic love. Skaði gets a stubborn old man who won't move away from home and with whom she is clearly incompatible, and Freyr gets sick; Skaði and Njǫrðr part ways, and Freyr and Gerðr come together only in our imaginations. The first marriage is an outright failure, the second a dangerous (Freyr is without his horse and sword) possible future event. Even if Freyr and Gerðr are married in the mythic present, may I be permitted to wonder about the success of a marriage in which one partner has a compulsive love for the other, who only agreed to the marriage under the compulsion of powerful mythological threats?

If Skaði's sexuality is ambiguous, so must be that of Njǫrðr. It is not just that he is the one chosen by a woman dressed as a man and that he can therefore symbolically be seen as dressed as a woman. An analogy from the homespun romance that is *Kormáks saga* underscores the fact that Njǫrðr is in a woman's role. I refer to the moment when the poet Kormákr first catches sight of Steingerðr, who has just been introduced, toward the beginning of the text.

> Þorkell hét maðr, er bjó í Tungu; hann var kvángaðr, ok áttu þau dóttur, er Steingerðr hét; hon var í Gnúpsdal at fóstri.
>
> Þat var eitt haust, at hvalr kom út á Vatnsnes, ok áttu þeir brœðr

Dǫllusynir. Þorgils bauð Kormáki, hvárt hann vildi heldr fara á fjall eða til hvals. Hann kaus at fara á fjall með húskǫrlum. Maðr hét Tósti; hann var verkstjóri ok skyldi skipa til um sauðaferðir, ok fóru þeir Kormákr báðir saman, þar til er þeir kómu í Gnúpsdal, ok váru þar um nóttina; þar var mikill skáli ok eldar gǫrvir fyrir mǫnnum. Um kveldit gekk Steingerðr frá dyngju sinni ok ambátt með henni. Þær heyrðu inn í skálann til ókunnra manna. Ambáttin mælti, "Steingerðr mín, sjám vit gestina." Hon kvað þess enga þǫrf ok gekk þó at hurðunni ok sté upp á þreskjǫldinn ok sá fyrir ofan hlaðann; rúm var milli hleðans ok þreskjaldarins; þar kómu fram fœtr hennar. Kormákr sá þat ok kvað vísu.[19]

> Nú varð mér í mínu
> menreið jǫtuns leiði
> réttumk risti snótar
> ramma-óst fyr skǫmmu;
> þeir munu fœtr at fári
> fall-Gerðar mér verða
> alls ekki veitk ella
> optarr an nú svarra.[20]

(It happened one fall that a whale washed up at Vatnsnes, and the Dallason brothers [Kormákr and Þorgils] had the rights to it. Þorgils asked Kormákr whether he wanted to go up into the mountains or to the whale. He chose to go into the mountains with the men. There was a man called Tósti. He was a supervisor and was to see to the sheepherding, and he and Kormákr went together until they came to Gnúpsdalr, and they spent the night there; there was a big hall, and fires had been made for the men. In the evening Steingerðr got up from her bed and her maid with her. They heard unknown men in the hall. The maid said: "Steingerðr, let's take a look at the guests." Steingerðr said there was no need of that, but still she went up to the door, stood on the threshold, and looked over the top of

---

19. Einar Ól. Sveinsson, ed. *Vatnsdœla saga. Hallfreðar saga. Kormáks saga. Hrómundar þáttr halta. Hrafns þáttr Guðrúnarsonar*, Íslenzk fornrit 8 (Reykjavík: Hið íslenzka fornritafélag, 1939), pp. 206–7.

20. Roberta Frank, "Onomastic Play in Kormakr's Verse: The Name Steingerðr," *Mediaeval Scandinavia* 3 (1970): 29.

the door; there was a space between the bottom of the door and the threshold; her feet stuck out there. Kormákr saw that and spoke a verse. [My translation.]

There has come a mighty love into my mind (fair wind of the woman of the giant); the necklace-bearer stretched out the instep of her foot to me just a little while ago; the feet of *fall-Gerðr* shall be fateful to me on other occasions. I know nothing else of the woman.)[21]

Here the sex roles are correct: a man spies a woman's physical charms and is smitten. When Kormákr gushes in later stanzas about Steingerðr's eyes, one may entertain arguments, however conflicting, of courtly or Troubador influence and of an "Orkney connection,"[22] but the feet are another matter.

Roberta Frank saw that the two sets of feet, those of Steingerðr and those of Njǫrðr, were parallel.[23] She also saw—this is the major argument of her 1970 analysis—that the structure of *Kormáks saga* may have followed the structure of the myth of Freyr and Gerðr, given the onomastic play she demonstrates so convincingly in Kormákr's verses about Steingerðr. She finds the curse that Þorveig placed on Kormákr's love for Steingerðr to be a clumsy attempt to follow the mythic structure of Freyr's delayed marriage to Gerðr; it would equally cover Skaði's failed marriage to Njǫrðr.

Kormákr's stanza is difficult. Frank would emend fall-Gerðr to fjall-Gerðr "'mountain-Gerðr' = Stein-Gerðr,"[24] and that seems a reasonable suggestion. The rest of the clause containing that kenning is, however, quite clear: the feet of the mountain-Gerðr (or of the fald-Gerðr "headdress-Gerðr," the emendation which Frank proposes to replace) will be dangerous to Kormákr on additional occasions.

---

21. Frank, "Onomastic Play," p. 29.
22. Bjarni Einarsson, *Skáldasögur: Um uppruna og eðli ástaskáldsagnanna fornu* (Reykjavík: Bókaútgáfa Menningarsjóðs, 1961); Bjarni Einarsson, "The Lovesick Skald," pp. 21–42; Bjarni Einarsson, *To skaldesagaer: En analyse af Kormáks saga og Hallfreðar saga* (Bergen: Universitetsforlaget, 1976); Theodore M. Andersson, "Skalds and Troubadors," *Mediaeval Scandinavia* 2 (1969): 7–41, Alison Finlay, "Skalds, Troubadors, and Sagas," *Saga-Book* 24 (1995): 105–53; Alison Finlay, "Skald Sagas in Their Literary Conext 2: Possible European Connections," in Russell Poole, ed., *Skaldsagas: Text, Vocation, and Desire in the Icelandic Sagas of Poets* (Berlin: de Gruyter, 2001), pp. 232–71.
23. Frank, "Onomastic Play, " p. 28, fn. 42.
24. Frank, "Onomastic Play," p. 29

The noun used here is *fœtr*, which was also used in the prose for what Kormákr saw, and is, of course, precisely the lexeme in Snorri's description of the moment when Skaði chose Njǫrðr. And just as these feet will prove harmful to Kormákr, so did the actual Gerðr's arms prove dangerous to Freyr, as I have shown above.

Another term is used in the first half of the stanza: *rist* ("instep of the foot"), which Kormákr says the woman stretched out toward him (*réttumk*). The form *risti* would be a unique accusative form,[25] but no one seems troubled by it. So, Kormákr saw first one instep, then both feet. The move from one to two constitutes a move toward the story of Skaði and Njǫrðr. The final clause makes the parallel certain. "I know nothing else of the woman," Kormákr declares, just as Skaði could have known nothing else of the potential spouses offered to her by the Æsir.

In *Skáldskaparmál*, Snorri quotes several stanzas of Kormákr's, although not of course this one. He does, however, twice quote this half-stanza:

Eykr með ennidúki
jarðhljótr día fjarðar
breyti, hún sás, beinan,
bindr. Seið Yggr til Rindar[26]

(The land-getter, who binds the mast-top straight, honours the provider of the deities' fjord [the mead of poetry, whose provider is the poet] with a head-band. Ygg [Odin] won Rind by spells.)[27]

The occasion for quoting the stanza is in the first instance to illustrate the kenning "wife of Odin" for earth; in the second, to illustrate the usage of the word *día* for gods. To the best of my knowledge, the word *día* is only attested here and in ch. 4 of *Ynglinga saga*.[28]

---

25. Einar Ól. Sveinsson, ed. *Vatnsdœla saga*, p. 208; cf. Finnur Jónsson, *Lexicon Poeticum Antiquae Linguae Septentrionalis: Ordbog over det gamle norsk-islandske skjaldesprog*, 2nd ed. (Copenhagen: Møller, 1931), p. 467, s.v. *rist*.
26. *Snorri Sturluson: Edda*, ed. Finnur Jónsson, pp. 76 and 128; *Edda Snorra Sturlusonar*, ed. Finnur Jónsson, pp. 90 and 166.
27. *Snorri Sturluson: Edda*, trans. Faulkes, pp. 68, 133.
28. Richard Cleasby and Gudmund Vigfússon, *An Icelandic-English Dictionary*, 2nd ed. (Oxford: Clarendon, 1957), p. 100, s.v. *día*.

Although the usage is not quite the same—with *díar* Snorri seems to mean "heathen priests" in *Ynglinga saga*—it seems not unlikely that Snorri got the word from Kormákr's verse. Certainly Snorri knew of and referred to Óðinn's siring Váli on Rindr, as he refers to it twice in *Gylfaginning*.[29] The second of these references immediately precedes his presentation of the story of Freyr and Gerðr.

Snorri cites none of the verses attributed to Kormákr that are found in *Kormáks saga*. Even so, we may perhaps imagine that he knew them, since he knew and cited so many others, and since they are rich in kennings with goddess names as base words; also, the kenning *stallr Hrungnis fóta* for shield (or perhaps sword[30]) echoes an important story Snorri told in *Skáldskaparmál*. Whether Snorri knew Kormákr's first *lausavísa* or not, anyone who did—that would include readers of *Möðruvallabók* and presumably those of AM 162 F fol., for the fragment in that manuscript starts midway in the scene in which Kormákr first encounters Steingerðr[31]—could have seen the parallel with the myth. In some sense, Kormákr's experience is the prototype, for as I have said, the gender roles are right. Why, then, would the myth (or Snorri's version of it) have the reversal, with the man's feet triggering the woman's affection?

Here I am not interested in Greek or Indic parallels,[32] Bronze Age rock carvings,[33] or notions of ritual imprints of divine footsteps,[34] but rather things that a medieval Icelandic audience might know or things that Snorri might have had in mind.

Let us return the story to the context of a woman (an *ásynja*) on

---

29. *Snorri Sturluson: Edda*, ed. Finnur Jónsson, pp. 31, 37; cf. *Edda Snorra Sturlusonar*, ed. Finnur Jónsson, pp. 33 and 40.

30. See John Lindow, "Thor's Duel with Hrungnir," *Alvíssmál: Forschungen zur mittelalterlichen Kultur Scandinaviens* 6 (1996), pp. 7–8.

31. Kr. Kålund, *Katalog over den arnamagnæanske håndskriftsamling*, 2 vols. (Copenhagen: Gyldendal, 1889–94), vol. 1, p. 124.

32. Jan de Vries, *Altgermanische Religionsgeschichte*, vol. 1: *Einleitung—Vorgeschichtliche Perioden—religiöse Grundlage des Lebens—Seelen- und Geisterglaube—Macht und Kraft—Das Heilige und die Kultformen*, vol. 2, *Die Götter—Vorstellungen über den Kosmos—Der Untergang des Heidentums*. 3rd ed. Grundriss der germanischen Philologie 12: 1–2 (Berlin: de Gruyter, 1970), vol. 1, p. 105, vol. 2, p. 336.

33. Régis Boyer, *Yggdrasil: La religion des anciens scandinaves*, Bibliothèque historique (Paris: Payot, 1981), p. 70.

34. Franz Rolf Schröder, "Njords nackte Füsse," *Beiträge zur Geschichte der deutschen Sprache und Literatur* 51 (1927): 31–32, and Franz Rolf Schröder, "Rituelle Barfüssigkeit," *Germanisch-Romanisch Monatsschrift* 16 (1928): 167–68.

a quest for a man (one of the Æsir), with whom she will mate. She is to choose her future sexual partner by his feet. Now, feet are not innocent body parts in this mythology, for the proto-giant—Skaði's direct ancestor, presumably—had feet that were active sexual partners. The result of this union was anything but good. The giant Vafþrúðnir put it this way:

> Undir hendi vaxa   qváðo hrímþursi
>   mey oc mǫg saman;
> fótr við fœti   gat ins fróða iotuns
>   sexhǫfðaðan son.[35]

(Under the arm of the frost giant they say
A maid and lad grew together;
One foot on the other begat
The six-headed son of the giant.)

Snorri paraphrased the verse in *Gylfaginning*. He added the details of sweat in the armpit and specified it as the left one—both additions typical of medieval thinking, and, like Thor with Starkarðr's arms, Snorri reduced to normal the number of heads of the offspring of the feet—typical of his objection to the truly fantastic. Snorri also made the monstrous procreator into Ymir, whom, he says, the frost giants called Aurgelmir—another Snorronic touch.

When Snorri wrote that Skaði was to choose on the basis of the feet and invited his readers or listeners to imagine a scene in which all the Æsir reveal their feet to her, then, Aurgelmir's or Ymir's monstrous, promiscuous, incestuous feet present themselves inevitably. The Æsir reminded Skaði of one of the many defects in her ancestry, and at the same time they showed that they had perfectly normal feet, without any sexual appetites whatever. To some extent, then, they would have mitigated the act of contrition I posited in my earlier piece on Skaði and would also have been mocking her.

Indeed, the metaphorical value of feet was generally quite positive. To be *á fótum* was and still is to be awake and conscious, not asleep, and a *fótheill* person is healthy, while one who is *fóthrumr* is decrepit.

---

35. *Vafþrúðnismál* 33; *Edda. Die Lieder*, ed. Neckel, p. 51.

In other words, the feet are sometimes metonyms for the entire body and metaphors for consciousness. Offering up their bare feet to Skaði certainly echoes an act of contrition, but it may also be a demonstration not only of the superiority of the ancestry of the Æsir, but also of their well-being as a whole, even when forced to compensate Skaði.

If the myths of Skaði-Njǫrðr and Freyr-Gerðr are indeed parallel, and there is anything to my drawing in the proto-giant's monstrous reproduction, then Gerðr's arms deserve attention. It is true that *For Scírnis* poses a problem of terminology: there it is Gerðr's upper arms (*armar*) that attract Freyr, whereas it is the lower arms (*hendr*) that made the children in *Vafþrúðnismál* 33.

Í Gymis gǫrðom   ec sá ganga
    mér tíða mey;
armar lýsto,   enn af þaðan
    alt lopt oc lǫgr.[36]

(In Gymir's holdings I saw walking
    a maiden dear to me;
her arms shone, and from them
    all the sky and sea.)

On the other hand, Snorri's paraphrase restores the parallelism.

[O]k er hon tók upp hǫndunum ok lauk hurð fyrir sér, þá lýsti af hǫndum hennar bæði í lopt ok á lǫg ok allir heimar birtusk af henni.[37]

(... and when she lifted her arms and opened the door for herself, light was shed from her arms over both sky and sea, and all worlds were made bright by her.)[38]

Since Snorri so clearly knew *For Scírnis* 6, the slight shift in body parts is interesting. Whatever Snorri did with sweat and armpits is

---

36. *For Scírnis* 6, *Edda. Die Lieder*, ed. Neckel, p. 70.
37. *Snorri Sturluson: Edda*, ed. Finnur Jónsson; cf *Edda Snorri Sturlusonar*, ed. Finnur Jónsson, p. 37.
38. *Snorri Sturluson: Edda*, trans. Faulkes, p. 31.

irrelevant to the fact that Skaði saw feet and according to Snorri, Freyr saw *hendr*; that is, each saw one of the paired peccant parts of Jǫtunn prehistory. If there is anything to this line of thinking, it would indicate a vital difference in the two situations. Skaði the giantess sees and is attracted to the feet, the unmediated extremities that in her ancestor reproduced, whereas Freyr, the god, sees either the *armar* (*For Scírnis*) or the gleaming upper part of the *hǫnd*, not the armpit that lies beneath it (Snorri). Perhaps the difference lies in the nature of Skaði's ambiguous sexuality at this point. As a woman playing a man's role, she perhaps invited thoughts of improper sexual activity and unnatural procreation. *Fátt mun ljótt um Baldri*: "There can be little that is ugly about Baldr." It is perhaps noteworthy that this line, catchy as it is, will not scan into the *ljóðaháttr* that Skaði and Njǫrðr speak about the other's dwelling according to Snorri in *Gylfaginning*. Was this line not part of the underlying poem that Snorri seems to be quoting?

Most observers think that Skaði made a mistake here, looking for attractive feet so that she might marry Baldr. Scholars have tried to rationalize this potential mistake; for example, Njǫrðr might be expected to have clean feet because they are so often wet, he being a god of the sea.[39] Margaret Clunies Ross is quite convinced that it was a deliberate trick,[40] and I have been on record saying the same. But what if Skaði's choice is neither a mistake nor the result of a trick? What if she has fallen for that pair of feet, feet that are exceedingly fair to her, and jubilantly wants to justify her choice: "I love those feet—they've the most beautiful feet I've ever seen; and so it's obvious they're Baldr's!" This would be manic, vanic love, just like that of Freyr and not unlike that of Kormákr in tenth-century Iceland.

In my reading, then, all three cases, not just the two from myth but also the third from the more recent and immediate past of early Iceland, are tales of compulsive, ambivalent, ambiguous, damaging, and ultimately self-destructive love. Despite his prowess, after succumbing to manic (vanic?) love, Kormákr fails to show up for his

---

39. Judith Jesch, *Women in the Viking Age* (Woodbridge: The Boydell Press, 1991), p. 138; Clunies Ross, *Prolonged Echoes*, p. 123; Jenny Jochens, *Old Norse Images of Women* (Philadelphia: University of Pennsylvania Press, 1996), p. 63.

40. Clunies Ross, *Prolonged Echoes*, pp. 122–27.

own marriage, fails to avert the marriage of Steingerðr to Bersi, never gains Steingerðr, and quietly accedes to her final refusal.

Is the theme of manic-vanic love played out in Kormákr's many duels? Before the first duel, against Bersi, Kormákr says first that he will oppose Bersi's sword Hvítingr with a great and sharp ax; does he not have a sword? Freyr does not, having given it to Skírnir in his manic-vanic attempt to win Gerðr. Kormákr must borrow a sword from Miðfjarðar-Skeggi, but he fails to follow the instructions for its proper usage and it malfunctions in the duel, causing him to lose by a technicality. In the two later duels against Þorvarðr, Kormákr uses a sword blunted by the witch Þórdís, and on both occasions he uses the blunted sword like a cudgel, or even, we might say, like the horn of a hart, which Freyr famously but mysteriously used to kill Beli. It is certainly true that Kormákr has and uses a sword in his final battle, against the *blótrisi* in Scotland, but it too fails him, in that he receives mortal wounds, and thoughts about the sword, and sword imagery, occupy his final three stanzas. It is almost as if he protests against the swordlessness, both real and symbolic, he shares with Freyr.

Romance is about getting to a marriage. The myth of Skaði's choice of Njǫrðr might therefore from a purely narrative point of view be taken as romance. Unlike romance, however, the myth goes on to the marriage itself, and it is an unhappy one. The two analogues taken up here also allow the relationship to continue, but without a marriage, either in the nine days of compressed mythic time in *Fǫr Scírnis* or the sad years that pass during the rest of Kormákr's life. In romance, a chance gaze can trigger a plot, and it does so in these three narratives as well, but when the eye falls on arms or feet, there are problems of mythic precedence and the abnormal procreation of the Other world. Vanic-manic love destroys. Kormákr may be a lovesick skald, but we should think more of pathology than of romance.

Bibliography

Andersson, Theodore M. "Skalds and Troubadors." *Mediaeval Scandinavia* 2 (1969): 7–41.
Andersson, Theodore M., and William Ian Miller. *Law and Literature in Medieval Iceland: Ljósvetninga saga and Valla-Ljóts saga.* Stanford: Stanford University Press, 1989.
Bjarni Einarsson. *Skáldasögur: Um uppruna og eðli ástaskáldsagnanna fornu.* Reykjavík: Bókaútgáfa Menningarsjóðs, 1961.

———. "The Lovesick Skald: A Response to Theodore M. Andersson." *Mediaeval Scandinavia* 4 (1971): 21–42.
———. *To skjaldesagaer: En analyse af Kormáks saga og Hallfreðar saga*. Bergen: Universitetsforlaget, 1976.
Boyer, Régis. *Yggdrasill: La religion des anciens scandinaves*. Bibliothéque historique. Paris: Payot, 1981.
Carlsson, Lizzie. "Staven: En maktens och ringhetens symbol." *Rig* 34 (1951): 1–8.
———. "Pliktpallen i belysning av medeltida skamstraff." *Kyrkohistorisk årskrift* 57 (1957): 25–38.
Cleasby, Richard, and Gudmund Vigfusson. *An Icelandic-English Dictionary*. 2nd ed. Oxford: Clarendon, 1957.
Clunies Ross, Margaret. *Prolonged Echoes: Old Norse Myths in Medieval Northern Society*. The Viking Collection 7. [Odense:] Odense University Press, 1994.
Edda. Die Lieder des Codex Regius nebst verwandten Denkmälern. Ed. Gustav Neckel. Rev. Hans Kuhn. Heidelberg: Winter, 1962.
Edda Snorra Sturlusonar: Udgivet efter håndskrifterne. Ed. Finnur Jónsson. Copenhagen: Gyldendal, 1931.
Einar Ól. Sveinsson, ed. *Vatnsdœla saga. Hallfreðar saga. Kormáks saga. Hrómundar þáttr halta. Hrafns þáttr Guðrúnarsonar*. Íslenzk fornrit 8. Reykjavík: Hið íslenzka fornritafélag, 1939.
Finlay, Alison. "Skalds, Troubadors, and Sagas." *Saga-Book* 24 (1995): 105–53.
———. "Skald Sagas in their Literary Context 2: Possible European Connections." In Russell Poole, ed., *Skaldsagas: Text, Vocation, and Desire in the Icelandic Sagas of Poets*. Berlin: de Gruyter, 2001. Pp. 232–71.
Finnur Jónsson. *Lexicon Poeticum Antiquae Linguae Septentrionalis:Ordbog over det gamle norsk-islandske skjaldesprog*. 2nd. ed. Copenhagen: Møller, 1931.
Frank, Roberta. "Onomastic Play in Kormakr's Verse: The Name Steingerðr." *Mediaeval Scandinavia* 3 (1970): 7–34.
Guðrún Nordal. *Ethics and Action in Thirteenth-Century Iceland*. The Viking Collection 11. [Odense:] Odense University Press, 1998.
Jesch, Judith. *Women in the Viking Age*. Woodbridge: The Boydell Press, 1991.
Jochens, Jenny. *Old Norse Images of Women*. Philadelphia: University of Pennsylvania Press, 1996.
Kalinke, Marianne E. *Bridal-Quest Romance in Medieval Iceland*. Islandica 46. Ithaca and London: Cornell University Press, 1990.
Kålund, Kr. *Katalog over den arnamagnæanske håndskriftsamling*. 2 vols. Copenhagen: Gyldendal, 1889–94.
Leyen, Friedrich von der. *Das Märchen in den Göttersagen der Edda*. Berlin: Reimer, 1899.
Lindow, John. "Loki and Skaði." In *Snorrastefna: 25.-27. júlí 1990*. Ed. Úlfar Bragason. Rit Stofnunar Sigurðar Nordals 1. Reykjavík: Stofnun Sigurðar Nordals, 1992. Pp. 130–42.
———. "Thor's Duel with Hrungnir." *Alvíssmál: Forschungen zur mittelalterlichen Kultur Scandinaviens* 6 (1996): 3–18.
Schröder, Franz Rolf. "Njords nackte Füsse." *Beiträge zur Geschichte der deutschen Sprache und Literatur* 51 (1927): 31–32.
———. "Rituelle Barfüssigkeit." *Germanisch-Romanisch Monatsschrift* 16 (1928): 167–68.
Snorri Sturluson: Edda. Ed. Finnur Jónsson. 2nd ed. Copenhagen: Gad, 1926.
Snorri Sturluson: Edda. Trans. Anthony Faulkes. London: J. M. Dent & Sons, 1987.

Sørensen, Preben Meulengracht. *The Unmanly Man: Concepts of Sexual Defamation in Early Nordic Society*. The Viking Series 1. [Odense:] Odense University Press, 1983.

Torfi Tulinius. "Snorri og bræður hans: Framgangur og átök Sturlusona í félagslegu rými þjóðveldisins." *Ný saga* 12 (2000): 49–60.

Viðar Pálsson. "'Var engi höfðingi slíkr sem Snorri': Auður og virðing í valdabaráttu Snorra Sturlusonar." *Saga* 41 (2003): 55–96.

Vries, Jan de. *Altgermanische Religionsgeschichte*. Vol. 1: *Einleitung—Vorgeschichtliche Perioden—religiöse Grundlage des Lebens—Seelen- un Geisterglaube—Macht und Kraft—Das Heilige und die Kultforman*, Vol. 2, *Die Götter—Vorstellungen über den Kosmos—Der Untergang des Heidentums*. 3rd ed. Grundriss der Germanischen Philologie 12: 1–2. Berlin: de Gruyter, 1970.

Wanner, Kevin. *Snorri Sturluson and the Edda: The Conversion of Cultural Capital in Medieval Scandinavia*. Toronto: University of Toronto Press, 2008.

Wessén, Elias. "Introduction." In *Codex Regius to the Younger Edda: MS n. 2367 4to in the Old Royal Collection in the Royal Library in Copenhagen*. Corpus Codicorum Islandorum Medii Ævi 14. Copenhagen: Munksgaard, 1940. Pp. 1–30.

Enabling Love:

Dwarfs in Old Norse-Icelandic Romances

ÁRMANN JAKOBSSON

For the last seventy years, most people in the Western hemisphere have known from early childhood that a good romance contains a beautiful, persecuted heroine, a handsome prince, an evil stepmother, and, of course, dwarfs, who by the graces of good fortune play a pivotal role in bringing the romance to its only acceptable conclusion: love, marriage, and retribution. Walt Disney's *Snow White and the Seven Dwarfs* familiarized the masses with romance dwarfs, though Disney neither invented the romance nor the dwarf. The film is ultimately a twentieth-century appropriation of the *Kinder- und Hausmärchen* of the brothers Grimm, which in turn hail from a long tradition, where love, adventure, and dwarfs are intertwined.[1] One branch of this tradition are the late mediaeval Icelandic romances, to which Marianne Kalinke's article in *Old-Norse Icelandic Literature: A Critical Guide* serves as an indispensable guide,[2] and which include a number of *fornaldarsögur* and *riddarasögur*.[3] Many of these romances deal not

---

1. As Paul Battles,"Dwarfs in Germanic Literature: Deutsche Mythologie or Grimm's Myths," in *The Shadow-Walkers. Jacob Grimm's Mythology of the Monstrous*, ed. Tom Shippey, pp. 29–82 (Tempe, Arizona: Arizona Center for Medieval and Renaissance Studies, 2005), puts it: "The continuity between medieval and modern depictions of dwarfs remains striking" (p. 69).
2. Marianne E. Kalinke, "Norse Romance (*Riddarasögur*)," in *Old Norse-Icelandic Literature: A Critical Guide*, ed. Carol J. Clover and John Lindow, Islandica 45 (Ithaca and London: Cornell University Press, 1985), pp. 316–63.
3. See Marianne E. Kalinke, *Bridal-Quest Romance in Medieval Iceland*, Islandica 46 (Ithaca and London: Cornell University Press, 1990), pp. 7–9.

merely with love and adventure but also with dwarfs. But how do dwarfs fit in with the romantic idealism of these narratives? What exactly is their function? And how does their presence in the romances reflect their previous tradition in Iceland as somewhat shadowy figures in Eddic poetry and the *Edda* of Snorri Sturluson?

In Old Norse-Icelandic literature, dwarfs may be classified into three categories:

1. Individual Eddic dwarfs. Very few dwarfs appear as characters or play an active part in an Eddic narrative (in the *Poetic* or the *Prose Edda*); those that do occur appear mostly in supporting roles.
2. Generic dwarfs. The *Edda*s provide generic information about dwarfs (including two different versions of their origins) as well as a large number of dwarf names.[4]
3. Later dwarfs. The dwarfs of romances and folktales.

This study is concerned with dwarfs of the third type. About the other two groups, it is at this point sufficient to mention the amusing coincidence that only seven dwarf characters appear in Eddic narratives: Alvíss in *Alvíssmál* and Andvari, Fjalarr, Galarr, Brokkr, Eitri and Litr in Snorri's *Edda*. In addition, there is the dwarf in *Ynglingatal*, who lures King Sveigðir into a stone, from which he never emerges. More curiously, the most prominent Eddic poem, *Vǫluspá*, dedicates eight whole verses (out of 59 or 63, depending on the manuscripts) to dwarf names. Since *Vǫluspá* is concerned with matters of great importance, such as the beginning and the end of the world, as well as its history and cosmology, the dwarf names may seem strangely superfluous, not least since dwarfs seem at first sight to occupy a limited role in Old Norse mythology.[5] As Lotte Motz puts it, they "are not drawn in the fullness of life, but in the narrowness of their employment."[6] Kevin Wanner notes the striking "uniformity which these figures exhibit across the range of Norse literary genres" and

---

4. See my article, "The Hole: Problems in Medieval Dwarfology" *Arv* 61 (2005): 53–76 and references there, esp. p. 4.
5. This is discussed in more detail in my article, "The Hole."
6. Lotte Motz, *The Wise One of the Mountain: Form, Function and Significance of the Subterranean Smith: A Study in Folklore* (Göppingen: Kümmerle, 1983), p. 92.

points out that their role as providers of precious objects to the gods is characterized by their inferiority.[7]

This may very well be the case, but when the dwarfs of romance are taken into consideration, the situation becomes much more complex. Dwarfs do not figure in the Sagas of the Icelanders and the contemporary sagas (*Sturlunga saga* and the sagas of bishops). Furthermore, as Einar Ólafur Sveinsson noted long ago, dwarfs are mostly absent from Icelandic folklore of the nineteenth century, which leads him to speculate that perhaps they did not survive the Christianization of Iceland,[8] though the *Kinder- und Hausmärchen* of the brothers Grimm bear witness to the fact that this is not the case when it comes to European folktales in general. Nevertheless, the lack of dwarfs in Old Norse-Icelandic myths and folktales of the modern period makes their prominence in the late mediaeval romances even more curious. It is tempting to explain their presence as a result of foreign influence, and, indeed, the dwarf of the Icelandic romances is in a way a replica of a type known from Celtic, German and French sources.[9] However, the fact that this type of narrative, along with its dwarfs, was so readily adopted by late medieval Icelandic romance writers and their audience also indicates that there pre-existed a notion of dwarfs with which the dwarfs of romance were compatible.

This article seeks to determine if a close reading of some of those Old Norse-Icelandic romances in which dwarfs have a prominent role leads to a better understanding of what the figure of the dwarf meant to a late medieval Icelandic audience. Rather than merely presenting examples, I have chosen to focus on the role of each dwarf within the narrative. Although the dwarfs of the romances are the primary object of scrutiny, I also use comparative material from other sources.

---

7. Kevin Wanner, "The Giant Who Wanted to be a Dwarf: The Transgression of Mythic Norms in Þórr's Fight with Geirrøðr," *Scandinavica* 40 (2001), pp. 204 and 213–14. See also Anatoly Liberman, "What Happened to Female Dwarfs?" in *Mythological Women: Studies in Memory of Lotte Motz (1922–1997)*, ed. Rudolf Simek and Wilhelm Heizmann, Studia Medievalia Septentrionalia 7 (Vienna: Fassbaender, 2003), who laconically suggests that this accounts for their diminutive size: "servants never grow up" (p. 260).

8. Einar Ólafur Sveinsson, *Um íslenskar þjóðsögur* (Reykjavík: Ísafold 1940), p. 140. See also Helmut de Boor, "Der Zwerg in Skandinavien," *Festschrift Eugen Mogk zum 70. Geburtstag 19. juli 1924*, ed. Elisabeth Karg-Gasterstädt (Halle an der Saale: Max Niemeyer, 1924), p. 545.

9. On mediaeval German dwarfs, see esp. Battles, "Dwarfs," pp. 50–67. On the dwarfs of the Celtic tradition and in romances, see Vernon Harward, *The Dwarfs of Arthurian Romance and Celtic Tradition* (Leiden: Brill, 1958).

Möndull, the evil helper

In a somewhat unusual turn of events in the fourteenth-century *Gǫngu-Hrólfs saga*, the hero finds himself without a leg to stand on in a literal sense, for his treacherous page Vilhjálmr has chopped off both of his legs. But out of the blue, he promptly receives help, though in this case not from someone good and deserving, but from someone who may be regarded as even more wicked than Vilhjálmr. This someone is Möndull Pattason, who has presented himself at the Danish court and slowly ingratiated himself with Earl Þorgnýr, while slandering Hrólfr's friend Björn and poisoning his wife Ingibjörg so that she loses her mind. Ultimately, Möndull causes Björn to be arrested and has his way with his wife with Björn as a spectator.

When Möndull first arrives at the Danish court, we are not told who he is: "gekk maðr ókunnigr fyrir jarlinn, ok nefndist Möndull Pattason" (a stranger came to the Earl and introduced himself as Möndull Pattason).[10] After the legless Hrólfr has crawled into his friend's house, he sees Ingibjörg, now deformed and blue in the face. Björn arrives, led in fetters by a man "í skarlatsbúnaði ok skarband um enni af gulli gert, hann var lágvaxinn ok miðdigr" (dressed in scarlet and with a golden ennisband, he was short and thick around the waist).[11] Möndull, then, is small and evil, and at this point the likelihood that he will contribute anything positive to the romance is remote, and, indeed, he does not do so of his own free will. It is Hrólfr who turns the tables when he puts his arms around Möndull's throat and threatens to strangle him, no small feat for a man with no legs. Möndull immediately pleads for his life and promises to heal Hrólfr: "hefi ek svá mikil konstr til læknisdóms, at ek má allt heilt vinna, þat lífs er von, innan þriggja nátta; ek vil þér ok kunngera at ek er dvergr í jörðu byggjandi, ok dvergsnáttúru hefi ek á kynstrum til lækidóms ok hagleiks" (I have such an aptitude for healing the sick that I can heal everything that has some life in it within three nights; I would also like to inform you that I am a dwarf from the underground and have plenty of dwarfish nature for wonders of healing and craftmanship).[12]

---

10. Carl Christian Rafn, *Fornaldar sögur Nordrlanda*, 3 vols. (Copenhagen: Popp, 1829–1830), vol. 3, p. 298.
11. Rafn, ed., *Fornaldar sögur Nordrlanda*, vol. 3, p. 307.
12. Rafn, ed., *Fornaldar sögur Nordrlanda*, vol. 3, p. 308.

After this somewhat shocking revelation, Möndull also announces that his aim was to lure noble women to him and that in spite of his evil mission and all the mischief he has caused, he will from now on remain faithful to Hrólfr, for he will never betray someone to whom he owes his life. Hrólfr accepts his offer, even though he suddenly notices that Möndull is "svartr ok ljótr eptir skapan sinni" (black and ugly according to his nature).[13] From this point on, Möndull is commonly referred to as "Möndull dvergr," although it needed his confession to make the other characters realize that he is a dwarf.

Möndull not only heals Hrólfr but also becomes his loyal servant.[14] His supernatural powers make him a very useful aide, and his past crimes are never referred to again. Vilhjálmr the traitor, on the other hand, is unmasked when Hrólfr returns. He tells a rather sad story of his miserable youth and, like Möndull, pleads for his life. Unlike Möndull, however, Vilhjálmr is promptly hanged for his crimes. Clearly, Möndull, as a dwarf, is not regarded as wicked in the same way as Vilhjálmr. In fact, people at the court agree that the dwarf must have been "honum sendr ... til happa" (sent to him ... for good luck).[15]

Having been a powerful adversary, Möndull is now a powerful ally in Hrólfr's expedition to Garðaríki. His short and sturdy appearance is again mentioned, and Möndull himself remarks that he is not exactly valiant in battle. Nevertheless, he proves himself useful by countering the spells of some twelve magicians sent by the evil Grímr the terrible, a demon or magician, to kill Hrólfr and his men. Through the counterspells of the dwarf, the magicians become crazy and kill themselves. Möndull shows little modesty and promptly remarks that Hrólfr would have had few men left, if he had not been there to counter the spells.[16]

In the final battle with Grímr, Möndull again proves his worth. This time he stands on a hill and shoots enemies with his bow, then hands Hrólfr a magic cape, and concludes by walking "tysvar rángsælis kríngum valinn; hann blés ok blístraði í allar ættir, ok þuldi þar forn fræði yfir, ok sagði þann val eigi þeim at meini verða mundu" (twice

---

13. Rafn, ed., *Fornaldar sögur Norðrlanda*, vol. 3, p. 309.
14. This loyalty amazed Jacob Wittmer Hartmann, *The Gǫngu-Hrólfssaga: A Study in Old Norse Philology* (New York: Columbia University Press, 1912), p. 9.
15. Rafn, ed., *Fornaldar sögur Norðrlanda*, vol. 3, p. 314.
16. Rafn, ed., *Fornaldar sögur Norðrlanda*, vol. 3, p. 319.

counter-clockwise around the field, blowing and whispering in all directions and mumbling ancient lore, and then he told them that this field would not harm them).[17] He helps Hrólfr by lending him his coat, which cannot be penetrated by the venom and fire spewed by Grímr; by striking Grímr from the back; and finally by preventing him from cursing Hrólfr in his death throes. Möndull then heals the wounded and is praised by all.[18]

Even when exhibiting his positive side, Möndull cannot be regarded as a good Christian, for his usefulness is based on magic of the same kind as that used by Grímr against Hrólfr. After the battle, he explains to Hrólfr that when Grímr chased him into the ground he was helped by the fact that he had more friends down there than Grímr had.[19] Moreover, he never loses his appetite for noble women, for the sister of Hrólfr's enemy, the king of Garðaríki, disappears, and Möndull is suspected of having abducted her.[20] But according to the moral of the story, supernatural harm done to enemies is very different from supernatural harm done to its heroes. The dwarf has proven to be a loyal and useful helper to Hrólfr, in spite of, or perhaps because of, his wickedness.

If we regard Möndull as an archetypical romance dwarf, his characteristics are as follows:

1. He is small. When Möndull is first introduced, he is described as "lágr á vöxt ok mjök riðvaxinn, fríðr at yfirlitum, utaneygðr var hann mjök" (small in stature and very corpulent, quite good-looking but with very protruding eyes).[21] When Hrólfr first sees him, it is reiterated that he is "lágvaxinn ok miðdigr" (short and thick around the waist). And when he arrives to join Hrólfr on his expedition to Garðaríki, he is once more described as "lágr ok digr" (small and sturdy).[22]

---

17. Rafn, ed., *Fornaldar sögur Nordrlanda*, vol. 3, pp. 328 and 336–37.
18. Rafn, ed., *Fornaldar sögur Nordrlanda*, vol. 3, pp. 343–45.
19. Rafn, ed., *Fornaldar sögur Nordrlanda*, vol. 3, p. 346. Cf. John D. Martin, "Hreggviðr's Revenge: Supernatural Forces in Göngu-Hrólfs saga," *Scandinavian Studies* 70 (1998), p. 321.
20. Rafn, ed., *Fornaldar sögur Nordrlanda*, vol. 3, p. 348.
21. Rafn, ed., *Fornaldar sögur Nordrlanda*, vol. 3, p. 298.
22. Rafn, ed., *Fornaldar sögur Nordrlanda*, vol. 3, pp. 307 and 316. On shortness as an attribute of dwarfs in French romances, see Harward, *The Dwarfs*, pp. 28–32.

2. He can be both good and bad. At first Möndull appears to be no less evil than the demonic Grímr the terrible or the thief and traitor Vilhjálmr. When Hrólfr tries to strangle him and then allows him to live, Möndull becomes loyal to Hrólfr,[23] which, of course, does not necessarily make him good in any moral sense. In fact, he uses the same kind of magic against the demons of the other side as they themselves would use.
3. He possesses all sorts of magical abilities. Möndull himself refers to his craftmanship. He soon turns out to be a remarkable healer, and his magical powers are tested in the war against Grímr the terrible, where he proves to be an extremely powerful magician, maybe more powerful than any Eddic dwarf.[24]
4. He lusts for women who are clearly superior to him. The womanizing aspect of dwarfs is well attested to, especially in *Alvíssmál* and *Sörla þáttr*. In the former, the dwarf Alvíss performs the role of the "unsuitable suitor," a role more often filled by a giant or a berserk. In the latter, dwarfs trade their craftmanship for sexual favors. In both cases, the dwarfs, like Möndull, seem drawn towards women considered too good for them.[25]

Clearly, Möndull is a complex character. He is evil but does good; he equals Hrólfr's formidable adversary, Grímr the terrible, in magical skills; and his shortness does not prevent him from desiring important women. But how does this compare with the image of dwarfs in the Old Norse mythological sources? And how typical a romance dwarf is Möndull?

Defining dwarfs

Keeping in mind that Möndull is somewhat special, all his traits may be perceived as dwarfish in that they are also found in other dwarfs.

---

23. Cf. Margaret Schlauch, *Romance in Iceland* (Princeton: Princeton University Press; New York: American Scandinavian Foundation, 1934), p. 146.
24. See Ármann Jakobsson, "The Hole."
25. On dwarfs and sex, see Paul Acker, "Dwarf-lore in Alvíssmál," *The Poetic Edda: Essays on Old Norse Mythology*, ed. Paul Acker and Carolyne Larrington, pp. 213-27 (New York and London: Routledge, 2002), pp. 215–17; Harward, *The Dwarfs*, pp. 132–35. On the erotic aspect of Möndull, see Davíð Erlingsson, "Fótaleysi göngumanns: Atlaga til ráðningar á frumþáttum táknmáls í sögu af Hrólfi Sturlaugssyni.—Ásamt formála," *Skírnir* 170 (1996), p. 354.

I have argued elsewhere that the dwarfs of Snorri's *Edda* and Eddic poetry (mythological dwarfs, as it were) are first and foremost negative creatures, and that most of their characteristics have something to do with "lack" or "absence." Two of the seven Eddic dwarfs are killers, and one is killed for no reason. The *Ynglingatal* dwarf is instrumental in the demise of a king—or, more accurately, his disappearance and absence. Three Eddic dwarfs may be classified as "reluctant donors," smiths and keepers of great treasures. And Alvíss in *Alvíssmál*, the only Eddic dwarf not in a supporting role, is outsmarted and turned into stone.[26] All in all, there are strikingly few mythological narratives about dwarfs. It is also striking how little information the *Eddas* yield about them and how vague their identities seem to be. They vanish into stones, appear to belong to the night rather than the day, and seem to have a connection with death. They are small in size, have no women, and are usually rather passive, and in the only poem named after a dwarf, the dwarf is the loser in a contest of wits. And even when they appear in considerable numbers, in *Vǫluspá*, there is no clear reason for their presence, a fact that has prompted scholars to regard the dwarf verses as secondary and unimportant to the structure of the poem.[27]

In his recent and excellent study of Old Norse-Icelandic and Germanic dwarfs, Paul Battles evaluates Grimm's ideas about Germanic dwarfs, and although I am not searching for a Germanic *Ur*-dwarf, his careful analysis of the primary traits of dwarfs is extremely useful. Among these is the ability to vanish, which Battles sees as a German rather than Germanic motif,[28] and which I believe is associated with "absence" as a defining feature of dwarfs, a motif that is so clearly present in the Eddic texts that it cannot be regarded as only German. Battles also discusses two old and now rather unpopular theories of the origins of dwarfs that focus on their absence and negativity. One is that the dwarfs were originally spirits of the dead, which Grimm adumbrated but which was more elaborately argued for by Chester Gould, who used dwarf-names as his main evidence.[29] The other is

---

26. Cf. Acker, "Dwarf-lore," p. 219.
27. See Ármann Jakobsson, "The Hole," p. 75, n. 3.
28. Battles, "Dwarfs," pp. 79–80. He discusses Old Norse-Icelandic sources in particular on pp. 36–49.
29. Battles, "Dwarfs," pp. 31–32 and 71–72. Cf. Chester Nathan Gould, "They Who Await the Second Death: A Study in the Icelandic Romantic Sagas," *Scandinavian Studies and Notes* 9 (1926), pp. 167–201, and "Dwarf-Names: A Study in Old Icelandic Religion," *PMLA* 44 (1929), pp. 939–67.

that the dwarfs represent an aboriginal race driven from their lands by invaders and replaced by humans, and that they survive only in memory as mythological dwarfs with unclear meaning.[30] These old theories continue to fascinate scholars and from the point of view of Old Norse-Icelandic literature, they have one merit: the peculiar and lengthy list of dwarf names in Vǫluspá may be important, if it reflects an idea that dwarfs predate humans and then make way for them, and also that their disappearance is somehow fundamental to the survival of humans.[31] But even if the list of dwarf names in Vǫluspá owes something to a notion that dwarfs are spirits of the dead or aboriginal cousins replaced by humans, this view is nowhere apparent in those Old Norse-Icelandic texts where dwarfs actually appear. And yet there are common links: negativity, absence, and lack. Battles also discusses the term *dvergmál* (echo), resounding calls in the mountains that might be interpreted as answers from dwarfs, which also characterizes the dwarfs as absent beings. Like dwarfs, the echo is not really there, it is merely an auditory illusion.[32] Grimm's belief that *dvergmál* had something to do with actual dwarfs in mountains actually fits in very well with his idea that dwarfs may have been spirits, perhaps of the mountain.[33] This is an idea that is possibly reflected in the mythology of Snorri's *Edda*, where four dwarfs hold up the planet.[34] As Terry Gunnell notes, they have parallels in the structure of the pagan hall, suggesting that these narratives may be rooted in religious beliefs.[35] While the tentative link between dwarfs and the elements should not be denied, it is difficult to find tangible evidence for a cult or any actual belief in dwarfs, as Helmut de Boor

---

30. Cf. Battles, "Dwarfs," pp. 72–73, who mentions David MacRitchie and Walter Scott as the proponents of this theory.
31. Ármann Jakobsson, "The Hole," pp. 66–67.
32. Battles, "Dwarfs," p. 80.
33. Battles, "Dwarfs," p. 72. An old and somewhat popular theory is that mythological dwarfs derive from the court midgets of the Middle Ages; see Fritz Wohlgemuth, *Riesen und Zwerge in der altfranzösischen erzählenden Dichtung* (Stuttgart: A. Bonz' Erben, 1906), and Harward, *The Dwarfs*, pp. 21–27). I have previously discussed and argued against this theory in "The Hole," pp. 67–68.
34. Lotte Motz, "The Host of Dvalinn: Thoughts on Some Dwarf-Names in Old Icelandic," *Collegium medievale* 6 (1993), pp. 81–96, is one of few scholars to focus on the four dwarfs, who represent the four main directions (east, west, north and south) and hold up the world.
35. Terry Gunnell, "Hof, Halls, Goðar and Dwarves: An Examination of the Ritual Space in the Pagan Icelandic Hall," *Cosmos* 17 (2001), pp. 3–36.

remarked long ago.[36] There is much more evidence for a belief in the powers of elves, although it can hardly be called exhaustive.[37] This again brings us to the link between elves and dwarfs in the sources, which underlies both Snorri's lack of differentiation between dwarfs and *dökkálfar* (dark-elves) and the fact that many dwarf-names sound more like elf-names.[38] Yet another link between elves and dwarfs is their prowess in the smithy, though in her tireless quest for the origin of the subterranean smith, Lotte Motz shows that it is difficult to demonstrate which of the two was originally most closely connected to the forge.[39] There also remains the problem of whether that particular attribute is a primary or secondary characteristic of dwarfs.

The craftsmanship of the dwarfs is a motif which is present in various types of sources and not least in the romances, along with other attributes that might seem to go hand in hand with it.[40] Battles includes a good discussion of the dwarfish traits that are more prominent in the Old Norse-Icelandic romances than in the *Edda*s. One is the power of healing, wherein Möndull the dwarf's importance to Göngu-Hrólfr lies. Battles argues that Möndull's claim that he has supernatural skills in medicine and that he is a dwarf from the earth is a fair indicator that the two go hand in hand, and that powers of healing are a dwarfish attribute.[41] These powers may, of course, be part of the dwarf's function as an "equalizer" in the romances. Battles takes note of de Boor's study of the "grateful dwarf" episodes in the *fornaldarsögur* (examples of which are discussed below),[42] but he disagrees with de Boor's differentiation between the mythic and the

---

36. de Boor, "Der Zwerg," p. 545. Cf. Ármann Jakobsson, "The Hole," p. 54; Battles, "Dwarfs," p. 77.

37. See Ármann Jakobsson, "The Extreme Emotional Life of Vǫlundr the Elf," *Scandinavian Studies* 78 (2006): 227–254; Terry Gunnell, "How Elvish were the Álfar?" in *The Fantastic in Old Norse-Icelandic Literature—Sagas and the British Isles: Preprints of the 13th International Saga Conference, Durham and York, 6th-12th August, 2006*, 2 vols., eds. John McKinnell, David Ashurst, and Donata Kick (Durham: The Centre for Medieval and Renaissance Studies, 2006), vol, 1, pp, 321–28.

38. Cf. Battles, "Dwarfs," pp. 70–71; Ármann Jakobsson, "The Extreme Emotional Life," p. 236; Lotte Motz, "Of Elves and Dwarfs," *Arv* 29–30 (1973–74), pp. 93–127.

39. See esp. Motz, *The Wise One of the Mountain*.

40. See, e.g., Inger M. Boberg, *Motif-Index of Early Icelandic Literature*. Bibliotheca Arnamagnæana 27 (Copenhagen: Munksgaard, 1966), p. 109.

41. Cf. Battles, "Dwarfs," pp. 74–75.

42. de Boor, "Der Zwerg."

literary aspects, arguing that mythic elements may well have survived in literature centuries after their true meaning was forgotten.[43] It could be added that their function in a romance might then be entirely different from their original significance.

The last dwarfish trait examined by Battles is the desire of the dwarfs for women of other races, which is present both in German and Old Norse-Icelandic tradition.[44] While scholars (influenced perhaps more by *Snow White* than they like to admit) have tended to regard dwarfs as asexual beings,[45] it is nevertheless noteworthy that not only does the motif of dwarfish lust lie at the heart of the frame of *Alvíssmál*, but it is also very prominent in *Göngu-Hrólfs saga*. Both narratives begin with dwarfish lust, but they take different directions. Þórr triumphs over the dwarf and turns him into stone, while Hrólfr uses the dwarf to gain victory over Grímr the terrible.

Möndull resembles the dwarfs of the *Edda*s in various ways. Like Alvíss, he is lustful. Like Fjalarr and Galarr, he is evil. Like Brokkr and Eitri, he possesses skills that prove important to his benefactors. Like the *Ynglingatal* dwarf, he is associated with stone and an enigmatic underground world. However, his role as a supernatural helper also has its unique features. One difference is that unlike Alvíss, his lustfulness is not repressed, and eventually he succeeds in winning his bride.

In spite of these similarities, this particular romance dwarf is a refreshingly novel character. He is forceful and aggressive, vanishes only to reappear twice as powerful and remains with Hrólfr throughout the narrative. While the Eddic dwarf is somewhat ill-defined, in that he is neither good nor bad, more absent than present, more negative than positive, in *Göngu-Hrólfs saga* the dwarf emerges as a trickster, who has a great impact on the narrative and successfully transforms himself from villain to helper.[46] In the *Edda*s, the meaning of the dwarf is

---

43. Battles, "Dwarfs," pp. 75–76.
44. Battles, "Dwarfs," p. 79.
45. Acker, "Dwarf-lore," p. 216; Liberman, "What Happened to Female Dwarfs?" p. 260.
46. I use the word "trickster" more as a metaphor than to suggest that Möndull may have been a mythological figure. In fact, he seems very much to serve a narrative purpose and need not have any cultic significance. Möndull may be regarded more as a knave than an antagonist with trickster-like features such as his double character, his amorality, and trickery, and his status as superhuman and animalistic at the same time. See Amory, "Three profiles," pp. 9–11.

vague. The dwarf's origin, nature, status, and abilities are hard to pin down. Perhaps this is the reason why the dwarf becomes much more prominent in the romances than elves or giants.[47] Unlike, for example, the Eddic *jötnar*, the dwarf is not imbued with Eddic significance and preconceptions. One might speculate that a romance author was allowed to take more liberties with dwarfs as characters than with the more clearly defined anthropomorphic beings. Perhaps it is precisely the vagueness of Eddic dwarfs that makes dwarfs more prominent in the romances.

Proficient ogres

In her *Motif-Index of Early Icelandic Literature*, Inger M. Boberg divides the bulk of her examples of dwarfs into four categories: their appearance, their homes, their characteristics, and their interaction with humans.[48] Examples of all four are to be found in *Viktors saga ok Blávus* (preserved only in fifteenth-century manuscripts and younger), which, unlike *Göngu-Hrólfs saga*, takes place in distant lands rather than the distant past. The dwarf in this saga is a very typical romance dwarf.

Viktors saga ok Blávus tells that knights dress up for a tournament, put on golden helmets, and then compete with each other in every kind of sport.[49] An Icelandic *riddarasaga* hardly get more glamorous than this, though, as Einar Ólafur Sveinsson points out, this glamor is not characteristic of the entire saga.[50] The dwarf of the saga appears when the foster-brothers Viktor and Blávus have challenged the most famous Vikings of the North to a combat but need help. Their wise advisor Kódér leads them to a scruffy island hermit called Skeggkarl, who in turn leads them to his own trusted friend and helper:

---

47. On elves in the romances, see Ármann Jakobsson, "The Extreme Emotional Life," p. 232 On giants in the legendary sagas, see Ármann Jakobsson, "Identifying the Ogre: The Legendary Saga Giants" in *Fornaldarsagaerne: Myter og virkelighed*, ed. Annette Lassen, Agneta Ney, and Ármann Jakobsson (Copenhagen: Museum Tusculanum, 2008).

48. Boberg, *Motif-Index*, pp. 108–11.

49. *Viktors saga ok Blávus*, ed. Jónas Kristjánsson (Reykjavík: Handritastofnun Íslands, 1964), p. 7.

50. Einar Ólafur Sveinsson, "Viktors saga ok Blávus: Sources and Characteristics," in *Viktors saga ok Blávus*, ed. Jónas Kristjánsson (Reykjavík: Handritastofnun Íslands, 1964), p. clxxx.

ganga þeir þa þar til at þeir koma at storum steini heyrdu þeir til barna duergsins ok at þau mælltu at þeim fielli allr ketill j eld ef duergnum fodur þeirra yrdi nockut. Skegg (karl) geingr at steininum ok klappar a lofa sinum ok lykzt wpp steinninn. geingr þar wt duergrinn Dimus. hann var fótlagur ok skamhryggiadr. middigr ok miog baraxladr handsijdr ok hofud mikill

(they walk until they reach a large stone. They hear the children of the dwarf, who remark that they will be destroyed if something should happen to their father, the dwarf. Skeggkarl walks right up to the stone, pats it with the palm of his hand, and then the stone opens. Out walks Dimus the dwarf. He was short in the legs and back, barrel-bellied and skinny-shouldered with long arms and a huge head).[51]

The narrative depicts both a dwarf's abode and his appearance. Like the dwarf that lures King Sveigðir into his rock in *Ynglinga saga*, this dwarf lives in a stone. But unlike any Eddic dwarf, he is graphically described as a monstrous and misshapen being, perhaps even more to be pitied than feared. The concise *Ynglinga saga* narrative of the dwarf and King Sveigðir is eerie, perhaps frightening, but this depiction is close to the comical.[52]

The second description of Dimus in the saga is hardly more flattering: "fylgdi þar med einn undarligr madur ef mann skylldi kalla. hann var j skinn kufli og hafdi jarn staf j hendi. hann war laagr ok læra mikill þunnleitr ok þioa brattr. út eygur ok ennis mióor haals langr ok hofud mikill. handsidr ok herda mior boginn ok barraxladur" (there followed a strange man, if you could call him a man. He wore skins and had an iron staff in his hand. He was short and thick-thighed, with a shallow appearance and a curved ass, wide eyes and a thin forehead, a long neck and a huge head, tiny shoulders and a crooked back).[53] The accuracy of the description is obviously secondary to a need for alliteration, but clearly Dimus is more of an ogre than a human. His

---

51. *Viktors saga ok Blávus*, ed. Jónas Kristjánsson, pp. 18–19.
52. See John Lindow, "Supernatural Others and Ethnic Others: A Millenium of World View," *Scandinavian Studies* 67 (1995), p. 9.
53. *Viktors saga ok Blávus*, ed. Jónas Kristjánsson, p. 43.

ugliness groups him among savages and beasts rather than formidable antagonists,[54] and it is not surprising that the people of India refer to him as an "ouættur" (ogre).[55]

There is nevertheless more to Dimus than meets the eye, for this small and ugly family-man, who lives quietly in a stone, possesses magical powers that make him a useful supernatural helper. He turns out to be the very "duergr klokur ok kyndugur" (clever and skilled dwarf), who made powerful magic weapons for the foster-brothers' chosen adversaries.[56] When Viktor and Blávus first meet him, he is asked to do the same for them. He is a "reluctant donor" until Skegg-karl chastises him, quoting *Njáls saga* almost verbatim.[57] The dwarf is easily subdued by his friend's indignation and not nearly as formidable as Möndull, but he is extremely skillful, providing the foster-brothers not only with clever advice but also aid in battle, in which his physical strength turns out to be impressive. It is further revealed that Dimus is a master of disguise, probably through magic since presumably a dwarf would be easily recognizable.[58] When Dimus and Blávus part, Dimus asks him to mention his name if he is ever in dire need. And indeed, Blávus does need Dimus later in the saga, and when he calls for him all the way from India, the dwarf magically emerges from out of a mountain in the vicinity and is able to help "med sinu kukli" (with his black magic).[59]

Viktors saga ok Blávus gives a conflicting image of the dwarf. Not only is he a reticent creature, who lives a simple life in a stone with his children, but he is also a monstrosity, an aberration from human perfection; and not only is he a skilled craftsman, but he is also strong in battle, a master of disguise, and well versed in all kinds of magic.[60] Moreover, he is a loyal friend. Like Möndull, Dimus is a versatile supernatural helper, who may or may not be good, and while Dimus does not betray his desire for human women or use his skills to satisfy his lust for power, he has in the past made magical weapons

---

54. Cf. Ármann Jakobsson, "Identifying the Ogre."
55. *Viktors saga ok Blávus*, ed. Jónas Kristjánsson, pp. 43–44.
56. *Viktors saga ok Blávus*, ed. Jónas Kristjánsson, p. 14.
57. See *Brennu-Njáls saga*, ed. Einar Ólafur Sveinsson, Íslenzk fornrit 12 (Reykjavík: Hið íslenzka fornritafélag, 1954), p. 298.
58. *Viktors saga ok Blávus*, ed. Jónas Kristjánsson, pp. 21–22 and 25.
59. *Viktors saga ok Blávus*, ed. Jónas Kristjánsson, pp. 28 and 43–44.
60. On dwarfish strength in the romances, see Harward, *The Dwarfs*, pp. 117–19.

for the adversaries of the foster-brothers. As in *Göngu-Hrólfs saga*, the dwarf's magic seems to be available to both good and bad people, but in the end the dwarf sides with the good ones.

Many of the same motifs appear in *Samsons saga fagra*, which may date from the fifteenth century. The thief Kuintelin, a seducer and son of a troll-woman, needs supernatural help after his mother's untimely death. His father directs him to a dwarf in the vicinity:

> skamt burt hiedan j skoginn stendur einn steinn. þar byr j duergr miog klokr er Grelent h(eiter) ... Kuintelin situr vm duerginn. ok eitt sinn getur Kuintelin vigt hann vtansteins ok tekur hann hondum ok ognar honum dauda. duer(gurinn) m(ællti) litil fremd er þier at briota min stuttu bein vil ek helldr leysa mitt líjf. ok giora nockut þat þrek er j.

> (not far from her in the woods stands a stone. Inside it lives a very smart dwarf called Grelent ... now Kuintelin stalks the dwarf and is able to come between him and his stone once. He captures him and threatens him with death. The dwarf says: "There is little glory in breaking my short bones, but I would rather buy my life and accomplish something for you ... ").[61]

This description corresponds well with that given in *Viktors saga*. The dwarf lives in a stone (in this instance in the woods). He is short and ugly (according to some manuscripts), and he is also able to make a wheelcart "med undarligum hagleik" (with wondrous skill), which is used to kidnap the hero's fiancée. She, however, resists, and neither lady nor dwarf wins victory, suggesting that Grelent does not possess superhuman physical strength.

Here again, the dwarf has undergone a conversion. He asks Samson not to kill him, arguing that he was forced, and is allowed to swear allegiance to him.[62] He then helps Samson capture Kuintelin and is sent on a mission with the thief, who has his own agenda, and his story ends in further betrayal and, eventually, his hanging, for a thief

---

61. *Samsons saga fagra*, ed. John Wilson, Samfund til udgivelse af gammel nordisk litteratur 65 (Copenhagen: [n.p.] 1953), pp. 21–22.
62. *Samsons saga fagra*, ed. Wilson, pp. 22–27, 29–31, and 43–45.

can only meet one end in a proper romance. The dwarf, however, does not betray his master, and although Grelent is less impressive than Möndull or Dimus, the similarities among them are obvious: a useful dwarf who is reluctantly drawn into the story does mischief at first but eventually redeems himself.

In *Áns saga bogsveigis*, too, the protagonist gains power over a dwarf by coming between him and his stone ("vígja utan steins"):

> hann sá þar stein einn standa mikinn ok mann hjá einum læk; hann hafði heyrt nefnda dverga, ok þat með at þeir væri hagari enn aðrir menn; Án komst þá á millum steinsins ok dvergsins, ok vígir hann utan steins, ok sagði hann aldrí skulu sínu inni ná, nema hann smíðaði . . . Svá gjörði dvergrinn, sem fyrir var skilit, ok með aungum álögum.

> (He saw a big stone and a man by a creek. He had heard of dwarfs and that they were more skilled craftsmen than other men. Án positioned himself between the stone and the dwarf and prevented him from entering the stone and told him that he would never reach his home, unless he forged items . . . The dwarf did as requested and with no spells).[63]

This dwarf is called Litr, which is also the name of the dwarf who is kicked into the fire during Baldr's funeral in Snorri's *Edda*. Unlike Möndull, Dimus, and Grelent, he does not exhibit many talents; his only role is to be a smith. It is worth noting that the dwarf is here referred to as a human ("enn aðrir menn"), and yet he is clearly not merely a midget, since he possesses an extraordinary talent, if only one. It may be that Án is simply too young to make full use of his dwarf talents.[64]

---

63. Rafn, ed., *Fornaldar sögur Nordrlanda*, vol. 2, p. 327.
64. Cf. Ásdis Egilsdóttir, "Kolbítur verður karlmaður," in *Miðaldabörn*, ed Ármann Jakobsson and Torfi H. Tulinius (Reykjavík: Hugvísindastofnun Háskóla Íslands, 2005), p. 94. Interestingly, in *Nitida saga* King Liforinus gains the services of a dwarf using the same trick, for he wants the dwarf to help him with "kynstri og kuckli" (magic and witchcraft) And like the four dwarfs already mentioned, he is no oathbreaker. See Agnete Loth, *Late Medieval Icelandic Romances*, 5 vols. Editiones Arnamagnæanæ, Ser. B, vols. 20–24 (Copenhagen: Munksgaard, 1962–65); vol. 5, p. 22.

Generally, there seem to be two kinds of dwarfs in the Old Norse-Icelandic romances. The fourteenth-century *Gibbons saga* has both. There is on the one hand the dwarf Lepus, who has been in the service of Queen Greca for a long time and is a loyal and trusted servant. On the other, there is the dwarf Asper, whom Gibbon catches in a wood, and who is extremely ugly: "einn duergr furdv likr sialfum fiandanum ath yfir liti" (a dwarf looking remarkably like the devil himself).[65] However, this demonic creature turns out to be a useful and independent helper, not unlike the trickster Möndull. While Lepus remains a servant, Asper ends up as an earl for his faithful service.

Trollish vengefulness

Whether good or bad, the dwarfs are always helpful. They never break an oath and faithfully serve their masters. Although sometimes they begin by serving evil purposes and are themselves evil, they always redeem themselves.

The examples above suggest that it is sufficient to gain power over the dwarfs or, as in the case of Dimus, shame them into becoming helpers. However, Old Norse-Icelandic romances also provide instances of reciprocity, that is, the narrrative motif of the "grateful dwarf." *Sigurðar saga þögla* (which has been dated to the fourteenth century) tells that while strolling through a forest Sigurðr's son Hálfdan comes to a creek. Close by is a large stone resembling a house ("vaxinn nær sem hus"), where he encounters a strange creature:

> Hann sier þaa ofan fra sier eitthuert kuikuende er honum þotti unndarligt. aa þui uar mannz mynd. þat uar utlima stort og hendur fotsijdar. enn fotleggirnir stuttir suo at eigi uoru þuerar handar. vid þat glotti Half(dan) og uar sem vtan vid lægi augun. Half(dan) tok upp einn steinn og sendi til þessa kuikindis og kom aa kialcann. geck hann j sundur. enn duergsbarn þetta bra vit med suo jllre Raust ath slict þottizt hann eckj sied hafa og þui næst war þat horfit og uissi hann alldre huat af þui uard.

---

65. *Gibbons saga*, ed. R. I. Page, Editiones Arnamagnæanæ, Ser. B, vol. 2 (Copenhagen: Munksgaard, 1960), p. 19.

(He then saw above him a creature he found very strange but it had a human form. It limbs were very large, its hand reached the ground but the legs were shorter than the width of a hand. Hálfdan smiled and its eyes seemed to pop out. Then Hálfdan took up a stone and threw it at the creature and it hit it in the jaw and broke the jaw-bone. But this dwarf-child uttered a cry with such an evil voice that he had never seen the like. And then it was gone and he never knew where it had gone).[66]

The following night, a dwarf appears to Hálfdan in his sleep "og war storum ofryniligur" (and was very menacing). This dwarf, who is larger than the other creature, curses Hálfdan for mutilating his child and strikes Hálfdan with his staff. The prince wakes up with such a headache that he is bedridden all day. His brother Vilhjálmr goes to the same creek and sees the dwarf-child, but he has a very different strategy and presents it with a gold-ring. And indeed, the dwarf appears to him "med blidligu yfirbragde" (with a gentle expression) the following night, promises to relieve Hálfdan of his headache (but not his misfortune), and gives Vilhjálmr the sword Gunnlogi.[67]

The story exhibits well-recognizable folktale elements. One brother meets an Otherworld creature, treats it badly, and pays dearly. The second (or, more often, third) brother is kind to the creature and is rewarded. Clearly, Vilhjálmr is aware of this pattern, for when Hálfdan tells him what happened during his encounter with the dwarf-child, Vilhjálmr predicts that this will lead to misfortune for Hálfdan "þuiat nær aull troll og alfar eru hefnesom ef þeim er misradit e(dur) misbodith. og eigi sijdur leggia þau kapp aa at launa uel ef þeim er uel til gert" (because almost all elves and trolls are vengeful if they have been ill-treated or scorned, and they are also eager to reciprocate in kind if well-treated).[68] The laws of supernatural reciprocity could hardly be stated more clearly.

The fact that Vilhjálmr speaks not of dwarfs but of trolls and elves indicates that dwarfs may be grouped with trolls and elves in the romances, at least when it comes to matters of reciprocity. As noted

---

66. Loth, ed., *Late Medieval Icelandic Romances*, vol. 2, pp. 113–14.
67. Loth, ed., *Late Medieval Icelandic Romances*, vol. 2, pp. 114–17.
68. Loth, ed., *Late Medieval Icelandic* Romances, vol. 2, p. 114.

above, dwarfs and elves are closely linked, though this link is not very prominent in the romances, since elves rarely appear in them. It seems that Vilhjálmr is simply making a statement applicable to all Otherworld creatures, and his use of the terms trolls and elves accentuates a lack of familiarity with dwarfs, although this, of course, does not excuse Hálfdan's behavior towards the dwarf-child.

The motif of the grateful dwarf also appears in *Þorsteins saga víkingssonar* and *Egils saga ok Ásmundar* (both of which are preserved in manuscripts from the fifteenth century). The former tells that Þorsteinn encounters two dwarf-children, male and female, by a creek. No mention is made of their appearance. Þorsteinn bribes the children to fetch their father, Sindri the dwarf. When Sindri arrives, he is cheerful, and although he discourages Þorsteinn from attacking the Viking Ötunfaxi, he gives him a knife and promises him help later, should he need it. Þorsteinn calls on him, when he is in dire need, and Sindri promptly arrives and helps him. The latter, *Egils saga ok Ásmundar*, tells of the equally amicable dealings of Egill with dwarfs. Egill, who has lost his hand in a battle with a jötunn, goes to a creek and sees a dwarf-child fetching water. Egill gives it a golden ring, and in return the child's father heals his hand and makes him an excellent sword.[69]

The motif of a large stone inside the woods appears also in *Hervarar saga ok Heiðreks*, where it is related that King Svafrlami is able to acquire the assistance of two dwarfs when he "vígði þá utan steins" (separated them from their stone). He seems to know not only their names, but also that they are "allra dverga hagastir" (the very best dwarf-smiths), and asks them to make him a magical sword. However, when they part, one of the dwarfs places a curse on the sword that it will be used for horrendous deeds and will kill the king himself.[70] Why the dwarf curses the king is unclear, for elsewhere those who capture a dwarf earn his ever-lasting allegiance simply for not killing him. Yet the same happens in *Völsunga saga*, which relates that when Loki has stripped the dwarf Andvari of all his gold, the dwarf retaliates by cursing the last ring Loki takes from him.[71] This aggressiveness

---

69. Rafn, ed., *Fornaldar sögur Nordrlanda*, vol. 3, pp. 388–89.
70. Rafn, ed., *Fornaldar sögur Nordrlanda*, vol. 1, pp. 414–15 and 514.
71. Rafn, ed., *Fornaldar sögur Nordrlanda*, vol. 1, pp. 152–53.

of the "reluctant donors" of *Völsunga saga* and *Hervarar saga ok Heiðreks* contradicts the image of the dwarf in most of the late medieval romances. Although these dwarfs are, like the others, sought out, the overwhelming majority of romance dwarfs end up aiding the heroes, no matter how ugly or evil they might be at first sight. The single common denominator of these dwarfs is that they are agents of positive events.

The significance of the romance dwarfs

The seven dwarfs of the *Snow White* folktale are not unlike some of the dwarfs in Old Norse-Icelandic romances, although in the former they have moved from stones into comfortable cottages. While the link between the romances and the Disney film seems clear and unbroken, the link between the dwarfs of the romances and the dwarfs of the two *Edda*s is less clear. A brief comparison may be in order:

1. The romance dwarfs live in stones, often in the woods and near a creek or a stream. They have children, and their domestic life is quite similar to that of an Icelandic farmer. No information is given about the abode of the Eddic dwarfs. There is, for example, no mention of a stone when Fjalarr and Galarr invite the giant Suttungr to their home. The dwarf who lures King Sveigðir away lives in a stone but the stone is much more frightening.
2. The small size of dwarfs is specified in both genres, but given less emphasis in the mythological narratives, where it is more often implied than explicitly stated.[72] In the *Edda*s, there is no mention of deformity or ugliness, but the romances are often quite graphic, and the dwarfs are described as being so ugly that they may well appear monstrous or demonic.
3. In some narratives, reciprocity is stressed, but in others it seems to be sufficient for a human to gain power over a dwarf to make him swear allegiance. In *Hervarar saga ok Heiðreks*, the dwarf is his own avenger, but it is much more common for the dwarfs

---

72. Many scholars believe that the stunted growth of dwarfs is an incidental characteristic or a later development; see, e.g., Liberman, "What Happened to Female Dwarfs?" p. 259.

of the romances, who never break oaths, to remain loyal helpers or servants to the end.[73]
4. As evident from *Gibbons saga*, there are two different types of dwarf-helpers in the romances. One is docile and servant-like. The other is independent and has ambitions and aspirations of his own, and this type has some of the characteristics of the trickster.
5. As supernatural helpers, the dwarfs possess various skills. Not only are they excellent smiths, but they also possess extraordinary healing powers and occasionally superhuman strength. They give good advice, are good strategists in battle, and may appear or disappear at will. Not all dwarfs possess all these abilities, and I am reluctant to claim that any particular special skill should be considered an essential skill of dwarfs in the romances. If they have a defining attribute, it is the power of magic, which makes them so useful.
6. The dwarfs are always agents of love. No matter how demonic they look or how wicked they are at the beginning of the narrative, they always end up being supportive in the course of the romance.
7. The assistance which lovers get from dwarfs may seem paradoxical, considering the fact that the dwarfs themselves are not exactly romantic creatures. Yet they marry and have children. Some of them even lust for human women. And one of them ends up with a relationship with a noble lady, though the success of their union remains unknown.

Considering the fact that the dwarfs are unlikely to be the romantic ideal of any audience, one may speculate why dwarfs seem to be essential to Old Norse-Icelandic romances, and why dwarfs serve the romance plot so well. In Old Norse-Icelandic mythological narratives, the dwarfs are defined by their absence. Their common features are all negative: they are small, have no wives, always occupy minor roles. Yet their absence is fraught with meaning—it is a hole which, like Ginnungagap, acquires its significance from its emptiness. The

---

73. Schlauch, *Romance in Iceland*, pp. 145–46, drew attention to this feature.

negative nature of their existence is a reflection of the positive nature of our own existence. The dwarfs are needed as a metaphor for the past, the elusive, and the negative, and their most important role is to vanish, to make way for us.

In the romances, dwarfs gain a new meaning for the medieval Icelandic audience. In these narratives, they are the agents of love. Davíð Erlingsson argues that Möndull may be regarded as Eros:[74]

> Möndull er feiknilegur giljari og ástnautnarmaður. Nafn hans hefur, auk tæknilegu merkingarinnar öxull o.s.frv., einnig merkinguna reður, og frummerking indóevrópsku rótarinnar telst vera að snúa. Læknirinn sem græðir meinið að síðustu er því eiginlega ástarvættur eða-guð, Eros sjálfur, en eðli hans er vitanlega demónískt.
>
> (Möndull is a great fornicator and lover. His name, apart from being the technical term for an axle, can mean penis, and the original Indo-European root would have meant "turn." The physician who finally heals the wound is thus really a love spirit or love god, Eros himself, but his nature is, of course, demonic).

While Möndull is unique in many respects, the most important role of any romantic dwarf is, directly or indirectly, as an agent of love. It is tempting to apply Davíð's observation about Möndull to the dwarfs of the Icelandic romances in general, where a development of dwarfs—partly due to foreign influence—seems to be apparent: from being a mythological metaphor for the negativity of the past, the dwarfs have become a metaphor for love and life itself. The dwarfs may continue to live in stones and be small, but their function is dramatically different. No longer representing Thanatos, they now represent Eros, a strange symbiosis indeed.

Bibliography

Acker, Paul. "Dwarf-lore in Alvíssmál." In *The Poetic Edda: Essays on Old Norse Mythology*. Ed. Paul Acker and Carolyne Larrington. New York and London: Routledge, 2002. Pp. 213–27.

Amory, Frederic. "Three Profiles of the Trickster." *Arv* 44 (1988): 7–25.

---

74. Davíð Erlingsson, "Fótaleysi göngumanns," p. 354.

Ármann Jakobsson. "The Extreme Emotional Life of Vǫlundr the Elf." *Scandinavian Studies* 78 (2006): 227–54.
———. "The Hole: Problems in Medieval Dwarfology." *Arv* 61 (2005): 53–76.
———. "Identifying the Ogre: The Legendary Saga Giants." *Fornaldarsagaerne: Myter og virkelighed*. Ed. Annette Lassen, Agneta Ney, and Ármann Jakobsson. Copenhagen: Museum Tusculanum, 2009. Pp. 181–2000.
Ásdís Egilsdóttir. "Kolbítur verður karlmaður." In *Miðaldabörn*. Ed. Ármann Jakobsson and Torfi H. Tulinius. Reykjavík: Hugvísindastofnun Háskóla Íslands, 2005. Pp. 87–100.
Battles, Paul. "Dwarfs in Germanic Literature: Deutsche Mythologie or Grimm's Myths." In *The Shadow-Walkers: Jacob Grimm's Mythology of the Monstrous*. Ed. Tom Shippey. Tempe, Arizona: Arizona Center for Medieval and Renaissance Studies, 2005. Pp. 29–82.
Boberg, Inger M. *Motif-Index of Early Icelandic Literature*. Bibliotheca Arnamagnæana 27. Copenhagen: Munksgaard, 1966.
Boor, Helmut de. "Der Zwerg in Skandinavien," *Festschrift Eugen Mogk zum 70. Geburtstag 19. juli 1924*. Ed. Elisabath Karg-Gasterstädt. Halle an der Saale: Max Niemeyer, 1924. Pp. 536–57.
Brennu-Njáls saga. Ed. Einar Ólafur Sveinsson. Íslenzk fornrit 12. Reykjavík: Hið íslenzka fornritafélag, 1954.
Davíð Erlingsson. "Fótaleysi göngumanns: Atlaga til ráðningar á frumþáttum táknmáls í sögu af Hrólfi Sturlaugssyni.—Ásamt formála." *Skírnir* 170 (1996): 340–56.
Einar Ólafur Sveinsson. *Um íslenzkar þjóðsögur*. Reykjavík: Ísafold, 1940.
———. "Viktors saga ok Blávus: Sources and Characteristics." In *Viktors saga ok Blávus*. Ed. Jónas Kristjánsson. Reykjavík: Handritastofnun Íslands, 1964. Pp. cix–ccix.
Flateyjarbók. Ed. Guðbrandr Vigfússon and C.R. Unger. 3 vols. Christiania [Oslo]: Malling, 1860.
Gibbons saga. Ed. R. I. Page. Editiones Arnamagnæanæ, Ser. B, vol 2 Copenhagen: Munksgaard, 1960.
Gould, Chester Nathan. "They Who Await the Second Death: A Study in the Icelandic Romantic Sagas." *Scandinavian Studies and Notes* 9 (1926): 167–201.
———. "Dwarf-Names: A Study in Old Icelandic Religion." *PMLA* 44 (1929): 939–67.
Gunnell, Terry. "Hof, Halls, Goðar and Dwarves: An Examination of the Ritual Space in the Pagan Icelandic Hall." *Cosmos* 17 (2001): 3–36.
———. "How Elvish were the Álfar?" *The Fantastic in Old Norse-Icelandic Literature—Sagas and the British Isles: Preprints of the 13th International Saga Conference, Durham and York, 6th-12th August, 2006*. 2 vols. Ed. John McKinnell, David Ashurst and Donata Kick. Durham: The Centre for Medieval and Renaissance Studies, 2006. Vol. 1, pp. 321–28.
Hartmann, Jacob Wittmer. *The Gǫngu-Hrólfssaga: A Study in Old Norse Philology*. New York: Columbia University Press, 1912.
Harward, Vernon. *The Dwarfs of Arthurian Romance and Celtic Tradition*. Leiden: Brill, 1958.
Kalinke, Marianne E. *Bridal-Quest Romance in Medieval Iceland*. Islandica 46. Ithaca and London: Cornell University Press, 1990.
———. "Norse Romance (*Riddarasögur*)." In *Old Norse–Icelandic Literature: A Critical Guide*. Ed. Carol J. Clover and John Lindow. Islandica 45. Ithaca and London: Cornell University Press, 1985. Pp. 316–63.
Liberman, Anatoly. "What Happened to Female Dwarfs?" In *Mythological*

Women: Studies in Memory of Lotte Motz (1922–1997). Ed. Rudolf Simek and Wilhelm Heizmann. Studia Medievalia Septentrionalia 7. Vienna: Fassbaender, 2003. Pp. 257–63.

Lindow, John. Supernatural Others and Ethnic Others: A Millenium of World View." *Scandinavian Studies* 67 (1995): 8–31.

Loth, Agnete, ed. *Late Medieval Icelandic Romances*. 5 vols. Editiones Arnamagnæanæ Ser. B, vols. 20–24. Copenhagen: Munksgaard, 1962–65.

Martin, John D. "Hreggviðr's Revenge: Supernatural Forces in Göngu-Hrólfs saga." *Scandinavian Studies* 70 (1998): 313–24.

Motz, Lotte. "Of Elves and Dwarfs." *Arv* 29–30 (1973–74): 93–127.

———. *The Wise One of the Mountain: Form, Function and Significance of the Subterranean Smith: A Study in Folklore*. Göppingen: Kümmerle, 1983.

———. "The Host of Dvalinn: Thoughts on Some Dwarf-Names in Old Icelandic." *Collegium medievale* 6 (1993): 81–96.

Rafn, Carl Christian, ed. *Fornaldar sögur Nordrlanda*. 3 vols. Copenhagen: Popp, 1829–1830.

Samsons saga fagra. Ed. John Wilson. Samfund til udgivelse af gammel nordisk litteratur 65. Copenhagen: [n.p.], 1953.

Schlauch, Margaret. *Romance in Iceland*. Princeton: Princeton University Press; New York: American Scandinavian Foundation, 1934.

Valdimar Tr. Hafstein. "Groaning Dwarfs at Granite Doors: Fieldwork in Völuspá." *Arkiv för nordisk filologi* 118 (2003): 29–45.

Viktors saga ok Blávus. Ed. Jónas Kristjánsson. Reykjavík: Handritastofnun Íslands, 1964.

Wanner, Kevin. "The Giant Who Wanted to be a Dwarf: The Transgression of Mythic Norms in Þórr's Fight with Geirrøðr." *Scandinavica* 40 (2001): 189–225.

Williams, David. *Deformed Discourse: The Function of the Monster in Mediaeval Thought and Literature*. Montreal: McGill-Queen's University Press, 1996.

Wohlgemuth, Fritz. *Riesen und Zwerge in der altfranzösischen erzählenden Dichtung*. Stuttgart: A. Bonz' Erben, 1906.

Hrólfs saga kraka:
A Tragedy, Comedy, History, Pastoral, Pastoral-Comical, Historical-Pastoral, Tragical-Historical, Tragical-Comical-Historical-Pastoral . . . Romance

JOHANNA DENZIN

Polonius, in *Hamlet*, famously jumbles all the different forms of dramatic verse into one confusing mess;[1] but to be fair to poor Polonius, genre is actually a difficult concept to define. *Hrólfs saga kraka* is one of the most widely-known *fornaldarsögur*, and itself encompasses elements of tragedy, comedy, history, and romance.[2] Traditionally the *fornaldarsögur* ("stories of ancient times") have been loosely defined by their narrative setting, which is typically in a mythic, presettlement period of Icelandic history; and thus these sagas have been descriptively classified as the legendary sagas.[3]

However, Hermann Pálsson and Marianne Kalinke have both defined some of the *fornaldarsögur* as secular romances.[4] In fact, Herman Pálsson and Paul Edwards in *Legendary Fiction in Medieval*

---

1. William Shakespeare, *Hamlet*, ed. Tucker Brooke and Jack Randall Crawford (New Haven: Yale University Press, 1961), 2.2.397–405.
2. *Hrólfs saga kraka ok kappa hans*, in *Fornaldar sögur Norðurlanda*, ed. Guðni Jónsson, 4 vols. (Reykjavík: Íslendingasagnaútgáfan, 1981), vol. 1, pp. 1–105; "King Hrolf and His Champions," in *Eirik the Red and Other Icelandic Sagas*, trans. Gwyn Jones (Oxford: Oxford University Press, 1980), pp. 221–318. All subsequent references are to this edition and this translation.
3. For a standard description of the *fornaldarsögur*, see Hermann Pálsson, "*Fornaldarsögur*" in *The Dictionary of the Middle Ages*, 12 volumes, ed. Joseph Strayer (New York: Charles Scribner's Sons, 1982–89), volume 5, p. 138.
4. Hermann Pálsson and Paul Edwards, *Legendary Fiction in Medieval Iceland*, Studia Islandica 30 (Reykjavík: Heimspekideild Háskóla Íslands and Menningarsjóður, 1970), p. 17; Hermann Pálsson "*Fornaldarsögur*," p. 137. Marianne E. Kalinke, "Norse Romance (*Riddarasögur*)," in *Old Norse-Icelandic Literature: A Critical Guide*, ed. Carol J. Clover and John Lindow, Islandica 45 (Ithaca: Cornell University Press, 1985), pp. 324–7.

Iceland argued that the *fornaldarsögur* function simultaneously as both secular romances and as legendary fiction.[5] How then is this hybrid genre of romance and legend defined? And how does this classification affect our understanding of the *fornaldarsaga*, *Hrólfs saga kraka*? More specifically, for purposes of this article, I would like to analyze how *Hrólfs saga kraka* functions as a romance. To begin, however, I want to examine more closely how Hermann Pálsson defines the *fornaldarsögur* as romances.

Hermann Pálsson points out that the term romance actually encompasses a wide variety of literary texts, and he turns to Northrop Frye's *Anatomy of Criticism* to try to establish a definition of the genre. Frye's study is heavily derived from Aristotle's *Poetics*, and Frye categorizes and then analyzes literary texts around an identification of the central protagonist's *kind* and *degree* of power in relationship to his larger environment. Thus a myth is characterized by a hero who is superior in *kind* to his world, and a romance involves a hero who is superior in *degree* to the other elements in his environment.[6]

Using this very basic definition of romance, as predicated on the nature of the hero, Hermann Pálsson then subdivides the *fornaldarsögur* into hero legends and adventure tales. The heroic legends are characterized by a tragic mode and predominantly center around the death of the hero, and the adventure tales are structured around a series of quests that typically end happily and often involve the themes of love and marriage.[7] Both narrative groups, however, feature a central protagonist who is greater *in degree* than his environment. He is thus always a romance hero, and he operates within the narrative world of the romance. And, although the narratives are often shaped by a masculine warlike ethos and marked by Viking raids, the world of romance mediates this picture—and the Vikings may wear full armor, joust on horseback, or rescue imprisoned maidens.[8] In addition to the trappings of chivalric romance, which can also be reflected in

---

5. Hermann Pálsson and Paul Edwards, *Legendary Fiction*, p. 17.
6. Hermann Pálsson and Paul Edwards, *Legendary Fiction*, pp. 10–2; and Northrop Frye, *Anatomy of Criticism* (Princeton: Princeton University Press, 1957), pp. 33–4.
7. Hermann Pálsson, "*Fornaldarsögur*," p. 138.
8. Hermann Pálsson and Paul Edwards, *Legendary Fiction*, pp. 16 and 22–3.
9. Hermann Pálsson and Paul Edwards, *Legendary Fiction*, pp. 23–4; Hermann Pálsson, "*Fornaldarsögur*," pp. 140–1.

descriptive details of fabulous clothes, food, and sundry objects, there is also the infusion of folkloric motifs.[9]

Hermann Pálsson, quoting Frye, emphasizes the influence of folklore and folkloric motifs on romances in general:

> The hero of romance moves in a world in which the ordinary laws of nature are slightly suspended: prodigies of courage and endurance, unnatural to us are natural to him, and enchanted weapons, talking animals, terrifying ogres and witches, and talismans of miraculous power violate no rule of probability once the postulates of romance have been established. Here we have moved from myth, properly so called into legend, folk tale, *Märchen*, and their literary affiliates and derivatives.[10]

Thus Hermann Pálsson has defined romance by classifying the nature of the hero, by the use of language or images influenced by chivalric romances (perhaps a circular argument), and the strong influence of folkloric motifs. In addition to the obvious role that love, courtship, and marriage would also play in shaping the narrative mode of a story, how do these elements apply to *Hrólfs saga kraka*?

Hrólfs saga kraka represents a fusion of Hermann Pálsson's subdivision of the *fornaldarsögur* into heroic legends and Viking romances. While the saga operates on many levels as a romance (or shows a strong influence of romance elements), the saga which ends with the heroic battle scene and the death of Hrólfr and his men, ultimately remains a tragedy. What I would like to do now, however, is explicate the levels on which the saga does function as a romance, albeit as a tragic romance.

On a very basic narrative level, *Hrólfs saga kraka* relates the stories of five failed romances: King Helgi and Queen Ólöf, Helgi and a mysterious elfin-woman, Helgi and his daughter Yrsa, and the romance of Böðvarr's grandparents and his parents. Also interwoven is a heavy influence from folklore, in particular in the characterization of the elfin woman, the story of Böðvarr's parents and his father's transformation into a bear, in Böðvarr's slaying of the troll-monster at Hrólfr's court,

---

10. Herman Pálsson and Paul Edwards, *Legendary Fiction*, p. 10; Frye, *Anatomy of Criticism*, pp. 33-4.

and even in the journey that Hrólfr and his men make to King Aðils's court to retrieve Hrólfr's treasure, and their subsequent encounters with Óðinn on the journey. There are also several striking instances of the use of descriptive language clearly influenced by chivalric romances. I want to explore all these elements as contributions to the saga's participation in a larger romance paradigm.

The very first section of *Hrólfs saga kraka* (the *Fróða þáttr*) introduces Helgi as a young boy and clearly establishes his bravery and general superiority when he avenges his father's (Hálfdan's) murder. In a comparison to his brother, Hróarr, Helgi is described as: "hermaðr mikill, ok þótti allt meira til hans koma" (p. 13; a great fightingman, and he was thought to be the more important man altogether, pp. 232–33). Thus Helgi has been established as a hero who is greater in degree to his environment, and he is a romance protagonist by the basic definition of romance posited by Frye and Hermann Pálsson. In addition, at the beginning of the second section of the saga, the *Helga þáttr*, Helgi becomes a Viking-lover when he decides that he wants to marry Ólöf, a bellicose and powerful woman who rules Saxland and is remarked to be the best match known in the North. She is described as a warrior maiden who wears a shield, corselet, helmet, and sword. She is moreover, "... væn at yfirliti, en grimm í skapi og stórmannlig" (p. 14; lovely of countenance, but fierce-hearted and haughty, p. 234). Ólöf is thus depicted as a typical *meykongr*, or maiden king.[11] True to the paradigm of maiden-king narratives, she refuses to marry any suitors. The beginning of this story suggests that Helgi and Ólöf will be the protagonists in a typical maiden-king romance in which a proud and fierce, but beautiful, *meykongr* rejects and abuses all suitors, until the male hero outwits her and persuades her to marry him.[12]

It quickly becomes apparent, however, that this paradigm will be subverted. In the usual bridal-quest narrative there is a generic happy ending; the *meykongr* agrees to marry the worthy suitor. There is also the sense, inherent in romance, that the desired woman and the wooer are rare and superior individuals in respect to learning, intelligence, and wit. In *Hrólfs saga kraka*, however, this is true of neither Ólöf

---

11. See Marianne E. Kalinke, *Bridal-Quest Romance in Medieval Iceland*, Islandica 46 (Ithaca: Cornell University Press, 1990), p. 69.
12. Kalinke, *Bridal-Quest Romance*, p. 65.

nor Helgi. While both monarchs are exceptional in many ways (and thus on a basic level function as romance protagonists), they also both exhibit cruel and thoughtless behavior and they both commit acts of violence and betrayal.

Helgi has heard of Ólöf and the queen's arrogance and has decided to enhance his fame by marrying her, whether or not she consents to the marriage. Helgi thus makes no attempt to woo Ólöf's affections. In fact, he surprises her with a large retinue of men before she can collect her own retainers, and proclaims that they will be married immediately. Their conversation reveals Helgi's own arrogance:

> Hún sagði: "Of brátt, herra, þykkir mér at þessu farit, en eigi þykkir mér annarr maðr kurteisligri en þú, ef ek skal þat verða upp at taka at þýðast karlmann, enda vænti ek, at þér vilið þat eigi með svívirðingu gera."
>
> Konungr sagði, at henni væri þat makligt fyrir dramblæti sitt ok stórlæti,—"at vit búum nú bæði saman slíka stund sem mér líkar." (p. 15)

> ("In my opinion, sire," she replied, "that is to proceed over-abruptly. No man alive strikes me as more admirable than you, if I have no opinion but to yield myself to a husband, but I trust you are not proposing to act dishonourably in the matter."
>
> The king replied that what she deserved for her arrogance and pride was that "we spend as much time together as I please." [p. 235])

In this exchange Helgi reveals his aggression and potential violence. While these traits are fitting for a pagan warrior, they are not appropriate in a suitor. Maiden kings are, themselves, often ambiguously characterized. As Kalinke has pointed out, they represent the "quintessence of feminine virtue," but they are also noted for their cruel treatment of all suitors. The male protagonists, however, generally are sincere and honorable in their desire to marry.[13] It is thus unusual to have such a violent proposal of marriage. The characterization of Ólöf as a warrior-maiden, an indigenous Icelandic motif, both constructs

---

13. Kalinke, *Bridal-Quest Romance*, p. 74.

and develops Ólöf's character. Ólöf will be grievously misused by Helgi, but she is a character in her own right, and, like the maiden kings of romance, a strong female figure who is equally capable of exacting revenge.

Helgi becomes too drunk to consummate their nuptials in bed, and to ensure that he will stay asleep, Ólöf sticks him with a sleeping thorn. She also shaves and tars him, sticks him in a leather sack, and has him taken to his ship in disgrace. This physical abuse of a suitor while he is in a deep (induced) sleep is a common motif of the maiden-king romances. In fact, the shaving and tarring, in particular, also occur in two other sagas.[14] By these acts, Ólöf has quite visibly rejected Helgi's offer of marriage. When given the opportunity, she has, like Helgi, also used the element of surprise to gain the upper hand.

Helgi returns to Denmark in disgrace:

Siglir Helgi konungr nú heim í sitt ríki með þessa sneypu ok svívirðing ok unir stórilla ok hugsar oft, hversu hann megi fá á drottningu hefnt. (p. 16)

(King Helgi now sailed back home to his kingdom with this shame and dishonour. He was full of resentment and often studied how he might be revenged on the queen. [p. 236])

Meanwhile, Ólöf's arrogance and tyranny, "ofsi ok ójafnaðr" (p. 17), grow greater than before. Within a short time Helgi returns to Saxland to enact his own revenge. He comes in tatters, disguised as a beggar, and pretends to have discovered a large fortune hidden in the woods. He encounters one of Ólöf's thralls and tells him of the treasure (the thrall then in turn tells the queen). The promise of wealth tempts Ólöf into the woods, alone at night, for she is a "kvenna féágjörnust" (p. 21; most avaricious of women, p. 237), and there she encounters Helgi.

Helgi confronts her and Ólöf admits that she had misused him previously, and she asks him now to arrange their marriage. It is not clear whether this is sincere or a strategic ploy; nonetheless, Helgi refuses to forgive her earlier actions and proceeds to rape her over

---

14. Kalinke, *Bridal-Quest Romance*, pp. 76–7. She cites *Sigurðar saga þǫgla* and *Viktors saga ok Blávus*.

the course of several nights. At this point, what has appeared to be a potential romance turns into a tragedy. Both rulers have been characterized as cruel and selfish individuals. Ólöf's avarice and arrogance and Helgi's violence, in particular, have been emphasized, and neither ruler embodies the traditional qualities of a notable lover.

Ólöf, for her part, returns home pregnant and has a beautiful daughter, Yrsa (named after her dog), whose existence she keeps secret. Yrsa is fostered by peasants and never told of her true parents. On a return trip to Saxland, Helgi, once again disguised as a beggar, discovers Yrsa, who by now is thirteen years old and is tending a herd. Helgi is struck by her beauty, and takes her home to marry, despite her protestations not to do so: "bað hann þat eigi gera" (p. 20). Ólöf hears of the marriage but does not reveal Yrsa's parentage. The narrator comments that she was deceitful and not sincere ("flárað ... ok eigi heilbrjóstuð," p. 20). This horrendous act of omission completes the subverted romance of Helgi and Ólöf. The narrative originally set up the expectation that the two would marry, but instead in a strange inversion, the father and daughter wed. This narrative twist serves in many ways to emphasize the deficiency of Helgi and Ólöf. Both rulers have such fatal flaws (their violence and greed)—that it is impossible for them to become the protagonists of a traditional romance; instead their character flaws precipitate a tragedy.

Helgi and Yrsa, however, live happily together for a period and have a son, Hrólfr. Obviously, despite their happiness, this is not a marriage that fulfills the expectations of a traditional romance; fathers and daughters are not meant to marry, and the romance between Helgi and Yrsa is doomed. Indeed, Ólöf eventually appears and tells Yrsa of her parentage. Shocked, Yrsa leaves Helgi and returns home with her mother. She is later encouraged to marry Aðils, King of Sweden (another disastrous marriage and failed romance).

The third significant "romance" of the saga is Helgi's third relationship with a woman. This relationship occurs after Yrsa has left him to marry King Aðils, and Helgi is alone and despondent. One Yule evening when the weather is miserable, a poor and tattered hag comes to his door asking for shelter. Helgi realizes that it would be "ókonungligt" (p. 27; unkingly, p. 246) not to let her in, and he opens the door. The woman remarks that he has acted well. Helgi then tells her to lie down on some straw and take a bearskin for warmth, but she asks to share his bed, for, as she remarks, "líf mitt er í veði" (p. 28; my very life is at stake, p. 246). Helgi balks at this intimacy, but lets the woman into his bed. This act transforms her back into her true shape, a comely young woman. She then reveals that her stepmother had placed a curse on her that would only be removed when a king had allowed her to share his bed.[15]

It is remarkable that the word "ókonungligt" was used in this conversation. There has been no discussion of Helgi as king in the saga *per se*, and use of "ókonungligt" immediately emphasizes that Helgi is indeed a king, and a certain level of behavior is expected of him as king. In this particular instance, kingly behavior means being kind to a wretched creature despite her appearance. While Helgi does allow the woman to enter and share his bed, he does not maintain the same level of kingly behavior as the episode progresses. When Helgi sees the changed appearance of the woman, he informs her, as he had told Ólöf, "skal nú gera til þín skyndibryllaup" (p. 28; now we must patch up a wedding for you, p. 247), and shows great interest in sleeping with her. Like Ólöf and Yrsa, she resists, but to no avail, and Helgi rapes her.

On leaving, she tells him that because of his lust they will have a child whom he must claim in a year's time or else pay the consequences for it. Helgi neglects to do this, once again failing to act honorably in a relationship with a woman. By using the word "ókonungligt," the narrator reminds the audience that a certain level of behavior is expected of King Helgi, an expectation that he does not fulfill.

This failure is emphasized even more so when the child from his union with the enchanted woman is eventually brought to him. She is a daughter aptly named Skuld, a name that resonates with the notions of 'fault', 'guilt', 'cause', 'debt', and 'responsibility'.[16] Helgi is told that

---

15. Evil stepmothers are a common folkloric motif (see note 20). Inger M. Boberg, *Motif-Index of Early Icelandic Literature*, Bibliotheca Arnamagnæana 27 (Copenhagen: Munksgaard, 1966), p. 249. See T418, "The Lustful Stepmother." There is also the general motif of transformation, and in particular the transformation of the "Loathly Lady." See, Cathalin B. Folks and Carl Lindahl, "Loathly Lady," in *Medieval Folklore*, ed. Carl Lindahl, John McNamara, and John Lindow (Oxford: Oxford University Press, 2002), pp. 142–8; especially pp. 245–6.

16. Kalinke, "Transgression in *Hrólfs saga kraka*," in *Fornaldarsagornas struktur och ideologi*, ed. Ármann Jakobsson, Annette Lassen, and Agneta Ney (Uppsala: Swedish Science Press, 2003), p. 163, n. 5.

he is going to regret not claiming the girl at the appointed time. The theme of betrayal is clear in Helgi's treatment of the enchanted woman and then his daughter by their union. This episode also introduces several folkloric motifs. The motif of the "loathly lady" and the motif of the discrepancy between appearance and reality are evident in the transformation of the elf-woman.

Thus end the disastrous romances of Helgi. Helgi had the potential to be a true romance hero in that he embodied on a basic level great intellectual and physical ability; and yet tragedy intervened. Because the larger *Hrólfs saga* is based on antecedent sources (albeit legendary ones), on one level the saga author was restricted in the ways that he could develop the trajectory of Helgi's character.[17] However, the inclusion of the story of the elfin-woman is a new addition to the story material and could be interpreted as a desire on the part of the author to emphasize Helgi's deficiency as a romance protagonist.

The saga continues to weave in other romance narratives with the inclusion of the stories of the marriages of Böðvarr's grandfather, and also his mother and father. These stories are again new additions to the corpus of the Hrólfr legend, and thus reflect a narrative interest in romance on the part of the saga author. While the larger saga will always function as a tragedy on a meta-narrative level, there is also clearly an authorial interest in exploring the romance dimensions of the legendary material.

The stories told about Böðvarr's family are in some sense self-

---

17. The story of Hrólfr kraki was preserved in oral tradition, but also recorded in written Icelandic sources thought to antedate the saga, namely in Saxo Grammaticus's *Gesta Danorum* (ca. 1218), *Skjöldunga saga* (ca. 1200), Snorri Sturluson's *Skáldskaparmál* (ca. 1220–30) and *Ynglinga saga* (ca. 1220), and in several chronicles including the *Chronicon Lethrense* (1178). Hrólfr is listed as Hrothwulf in the Old English *Widsith* (seventh century) in reference to early Germanic heroes, and in *Beowulf* (seventh to tenth century) where Hroþwulf is named as a nephew of King Hrothgar (Hróar). See: *Saxonis Gesta Danorum*, ed. J. Olrik and H. Ræder (Copenhagen: Munksgaard, 1931–57); *Skjöldunga saga*, in *Danakonunga sǫgur*, ed. Bjarni Guðnason, Íslenzk fornrit 35 (Reykjavík: Hið íslenzka fornritafélag, 1982), pp. 3–38; Snorri Sturluson, *Ynglinga saga*, in *Heimskringla*, 3 vols. ed. Bjarni Aðalbjarnarson, Íslenzk fornrit 26–8 (Reykjavík: Hið íslenzka fornritafélag, 1941–51), vol. 1, pp. 9–83; Snorri Sturluson, *Skáldskaparmál*, in *Edda Snorra Sturlusonar*, ed. Finnur Jónsson (Copenhagen: Gyldendal, 1931), pp. 68–147; *Chronicon Lethrense*, in *Scriptores Minores Historiæ Danicæ*, ed. M. CL. Gertz (Copenhagen: Gad, 1917–18), vol. 1, pp. 34–53; *Widsith*, in *The Exeter Book*, ed. George Phillip Krapp and Elliot Van Kirk Dobbie (New York: Columbia University Press, 1936), pp. 148–49; F. Klaeber, *Beowulf and the Fight at Finnsburg*, 3rd ed. with supplement (Boston: Heath, 1950).

contained narratives, and they are marked by prominent folkloric features, including such folkloric motifs as evil stepmothers, magical transformations, and the use of tripling—of characters, incidents, and objects. Structurally, folktales often begin with a family of three boys, one of whom wants to go out into the world and win renown. The structure of the narrative is then generated by his adventures; and this is the narrative pattern used to tell the story of Böðvarr and his brothers.[18]

The story of Böðvarr begins with the forestory of the bridal quest of Böðvarr's grandfather, King Hringr. King Hringr is widowed, and has been urged to find a new wife. Hringr sends his men on a wooing mission, but their ship is blown off course and they end up in "Finnmark," where they discover a mother and her beautiful daughter who are in hiding. The mother, who is the mistress of the King of the Lapps, and her daughter, Hvít ("white"), are hiding from a suitor she has rejected. Since Lapps are associated in Old Icelandic literature with black magic and sorcery, the Lapp princess forebodes evil.[19] King Hringr ends up marrying Hvít, but he is also an old man who is often out at war, and his young bride turns her attention to her step-son, Björn ("bear"). Amorous step-mothers are also a common motif of Icelandic folktales.[20]

However, Björn loves Bera ("she-bear"), the daughter of a wealthy farmer. Hvít, angry at being rejected by Björn, harshly chastises him:

ok þykkir þér betra, Björn, at spenna heldr karlsdóttur, ok er þér

---

18. Carl Lindahl, "Folktale," in *Medieval Folklore*, ed. Carl Lindahl, John McNamara, and John Lindow (Oxford: Oxford University Press, 2002), pp. 142–8; especially pp. 145–6. See also Max Lüthi, *The European Folktale*, trans. John Niles (Bloomington: Indiana University Press, 1982), pp. 24–36. The story of Svipdagr in the saga also follows this typical structure. Thus, in Sweden a wealthy farmer who was once a great champion has three sons who are strong and handsome. One of the sons, Svipdagr, wants to go out into the world and win renown. Svipdagr first joins Aðils's court, but he then leaves to serve Hrólfr.

19. For example, in a stanza in *Óláfs saga helga*, the skald Sigvatr Þórðarson blames the ineffectiveness of King Óláfr's sword in battle on the spells of Lapp sorcerers—"galdrar fjölkunnigra Finna" (*Óláfs saga helga*, in Snorri Sturluson, *Heimskringla*, ed. Bjarni Aðalbjarnarson, Íslenzk fornrit 26–8 (Reykjavík: Hið íslenzka fornritafélag, 1979), vol. 2, p. 383–4. Hvít's name is also perhaps an ironic commentary on her true nature.

20. Boberg, *Motif-Index of Early Icelandic Literature*, p. 249. See T418, "The Lustful Stepmother."

þat makligt, sem ván er á, ok svívirðiligra en njóta minnar ástar ok
blíðu ... (p. 47)

(You prefer, Bjorn, to embrace a churl's daughter rather, and that is
good enough for you, inferior as it is, and more dishonouring than
to enjoy my love and favours. [p. 264])

In her great anger, Hvít places a spell on Björn that transforms
him into a bear during the day (although he regains his human form
at night). Bera discovers Björn in his transformed bear shape and is
able to recognize him by looking at his eyes; and there is the sense
that Bera and Björn share a great and deep love. Indeed, despite his
transformation, the two lovers live together in a cave, and they share
the nights when Björn again takes the form of a man.

Björn eventually foresees his imminent death and he tells Bera,
who is carrying triplets, that he will be killed in a hunt the following
morning. Presciently, Björn instructs her to avoid eating any of the
bear flesh (his body) that his step-mother will try to force upon her.
Everything goes as Björn predicts, and despite her resistance, Bera is
forced to eat two bites of bear meat. As a consequence, when the children
are born, the first son is an elk from the waist down (Elg-Fróði),
the second son is a dog from the feet down (Þórir Hound's Foot), but
the third son, Böðvarr bjarki[21] is radiant and unspoiled.[22]

As each of the sons reaches maturity, Bera directs them to the cave
where Björn has left each of the boys some treasure, but also a weapon
which corresponds symbolically to their personalities. Reminiscent of
Arthurian romance, embedded in a rock, there are a large sword, an
axe, and a short sword. Elg-Fróði, who is wild and angry by nature,
is upset to find that he can only draw the short sword from the rock.
He takes his gifts and leaves home. He proceeds to build a hut for

---

21. Bjarki presumably derives from the feminine name Björk and in *Hrólfs saga* presumably means "little bear"; Böðvarr derives from *böð*, genitive *böðvar* 'battle,' a word found only in poetry.

22. While this entire tale resonates with the general motif of transformation, Stith Thompson identifies specific folk motifs that involve the marriage to a bear (B601.1), and the eating of the meat of one's bear-lover that then causes the unborn child to have bear characteristics (B635.1.1).

himself to live in, and where he lies in wait for travelers whom he then murders for their riches.

Þórir then goes to the cave to claim his inheritance, and he is able to pull only the axe from the rock. He sets off from home and goes to see his brother Elg-Fróði. When Elg-Fróði recognizes Þórir, he offers him half of his newly accumulated ill-gotten gains, but Þórir refuses them. Elg-Fróði then tells his brother that Gautland is looking for a new king and explains that the Gauts choose their king at an assembly where a chair large enough to hold two men is brought out, and the man who best fits it becomes the new king. Elg-Fróði suggests that Þórir would be a good choice, and Þórir is eventually chosen king by the Gauts because of his great size.

Böðvarr, rather than claiming his inheritance from the cave, instead first asks his mother who his father was. When Böðvarr hears of the horrible machinations of Hvít, he comments that both Elg-Fróði and Þórir should have taken revenge for their father's death (and that Elg-Fróði should leave off murdering travelers for their riches). Böðvarr and Bera then go to see King Hringr, but Bera warns Böðvarr to be careful of Hvít's black magic. Bera then tells King Hringr what had happened to Björn, which does not surprise him, as he had suspected something along those lines. He offers Böðvarr compensation for his father's death and promises him the kingdom when he dies, if Böðvarr refrains from harming Hvít. Böðvarr declares that he has no interest in being king:

> Böðvarr kveðst ekki konungr vilja vera, heldr kvaðst hann vilja með konungi vera ok honum þjóna. "Ertu svá fanginn fyrir þessum óvætti, at þú heldr varla viti þínu né réttum konungdómi, ok skal hún hér aldri þrífast upp frá þessu." (p. 56)

(But Bothvar said he had no desire to be a monarch; he had rather stay with the king, he said, and do him service. "You are so besotted with this monster that you hardly retain grip of your senses or your rightful dominion; but from this day forth she shall not flourish." [p. 273])

Böðvarr proceeds to kill Hvít as vengeance for his father's death. Hringr dies shortly thereafter. Böðvarr rules for only a short period after Hringr's death. He soon convenes an assembly at which he marries his mother to an earl, and then he leaves his kingdom. Böðvarr now goes to claim his inheritance from the cave, and perhaps it is only because he has avenged his father's death that he is able to pull the great sword from the rock, an act his two brothers could not accomplish.[23] This act also clearly establishes him as a hero, and more specifically as a romance protagonist by the definition proposed by Hermann Pálsson and Frye.

Böðvarr then visits his brother Elg-Fróði. Elg-Fróði offers Böðvarr half of his wealth, which Böðvarr refuses (adding that murdering people for money is clearly wrong). Elg-Fróði disingenuously explains that he has often let small and weak men go free and Böðvarr is cheered by this information, but he also reiterates that Elg-Fróði should not kill people in general.

Elg-Fróði then expresses concern about his brother's strength, and before Böðvarr leaves him, Elg-Fróði cuts open his own leg and has Böðvarr drink some of his blood. A variation of this motif occurs when Böðvarr subsequently takes the character Hǫttr under his wing at King Hrólfr's court. This act is also reminiscent of the *Nibelungenlied* material where Sigurðr drinks some of Fáfnir's blood (another corpus of stories that merge legendary and romance motifs and themes).[24]

Before Böðvarr departs, Elg-Fróði tells him to go to Hrólfr's court because he has heard that all the great champions wish to be there:

... því at þar vilja allir vera inir mestu kappar með honum, því at stórlæti hans er miklu meira, rausn ok hugprýði, en allra konunga annarra. (p. 59)

(... for all the foremost champions wish to be where he is, because his munificence, splendour, and courage are greater by far than those of all other kings. [p. 276])

---

23. Like many great swords this sword has certain conditions associated with its use. The sword cannot be drawn without killing someone, it cannot rest under a man's head, or be stood on its hilt, and finally, it can only be used three times in its owner's life. Magic swords or objects are a common folklore (and romance) motif, see Lüthi, *The European Folktale*, pp. 32–3; and Lindahl, *Medieval Folklore*, pp. 145–6. Tripling is also common in folklore, as is the role of the youngest son as the true hero in a tale.

24. The story of Sigurðr is of course told in multiple sources, including the *Poetic Edda*, specifically in the lays *Grípisspá*, *Fáfnismál*, and *Sigrdrífumál*, *Völsunga saga*, and *Das Nibelungenlied*.

This small set description of Hrólfr's court, while not specifically drawn from any romance text, does carry overtones of descriptions from chivalric romances. There is in fact an even longer description of Hrólfr that occurs earlier in the saga. The farmer Svipr also suggests to his son Svipdagr that he should join Hrólfr's retinue:

> Svá er mér sagt frá Hrólfi konungi, at hann sé örr ok stórgjöfull, trúfastr ok vinavandur, svá at hans jafningi mun eigi finnast. Hann sparar eigi gull né gersemar nær við alla, er þiggja vilja. Hann er lágligr at líta, en mikill at reyna og torveldr, manna fríðastr, stórlátr við ómilda, en ljúfr ok hógværr við vesala ok við alla þá, sem ekki brjóta bág í móti honum, manna lítillátastr svá at jafnblítt svarar hann fátækum sem ríkum. Svá er hann mikill ágætismaðr, at hans nafn mun eigi fyrnast, á meðan veröldin er byggð. Hann hefir ok skattgilt alla konunga, þá sem at eru í nánd honum, því allir vilja honum fúsir þjóna. (p. 40)

> (I am told this of king Hrolf ... that he is liberal and free-handed, trustworthy, and particular as to his friends, so that his equal is not to be found. Nor is he sparing of gold and treasures to well nigh all who care to receive them. He is not all that much to look at, but mighty and enduring under pressure; the handsomest of men, harsh towards the oppressor but kindly and gracious to the needy, as to all those who offer him no resistance; the humblest of men, so that he answers the poor as gently as the rich. So great and glorious a man is he that his name will never be forgotten as long as this world is lived in. Further, he has levied tribute on all kings who dwell near him, for all are ready and anxious to do him service. [p. 258])

The chivalric- or romance-inspired vocabulary is even more

---

25. Ármann Jakobsson, "Le Roi Chevalier: The Royal Ideology and Genre of *Hrólfs saga kraka*," *Scandinavian Studies*, 72 (1999), pp. 139–65. Interestingly, however, in the very next scene, Hrólfr contrives underhandedly to force his brother-in-law, Hjörvarðr, to pay him tribute: "Hjörvarðr varð þessu ákafliga reiðr ok verðr þó at láta svá standa, ferr heim við svá búit ok unir illa við sinn hlut, seldi þó skatt Hrólfi konungi eftir því sem aðrir hans undirkonungar, þeir sem honum áttu hlýðni at veita," p. 44; Hjorvarth was incensed by this, but had to let it stand even so. He returned

pronounced in this speech, and this portrayal of Hrólfr, in fact, prompted Ármann Jakobsson to argue that Hrólfr is presented as an ideal chivalric king in the saga.[25]

Before proceeding to King Hrólfr's, Böðvarr visits his brother Þórir (who ends up not being at home). However, Böðvarr resembles his brother so closely that the retainers believe him to be their king, and they place him on the throne and treat him as their ruler. Moreover, he is put to bed nightly with Þórir's wife, although he refuses to share the common blanket—a fact that the queen finds odd until Böðvarr tells her that he is not her husband. Thus, the two spend the nights in conversation until Þórir returns, and Böðvarr reveals his identity to everyone. This bed scene evokes a similar episode in the *Nibelungenlied* material between Brynhildr and Sigurðr.

When Þórir returns he comments that Böðvarr is the only man he would have trusted to share a bed with his wife. Þórir proceeds to offer Böðvarr half of his wealth or retinue, both of which Böðvarr refuses. This small scene serves the larger purpose of establishing Böðvarr's trustworthiness and general moral nature. Interestingly, Böðvarr starts to become the moral compass of this part of the saga. He states very clearly that his father's death needed to be avenged, and then he does it himself. He also forcefully tells Elg-Fróði that he is acting dishonorably. In contrast, Böðvarr himself acts very honorably when he shares a bed with Þórir's wife. At several critical points Böðvarr will subsequently become a moral guide for Hrólfr, so that Böðvarr comes to embody, more than any other character, the qualities of a true hero and a true leader.

Böðvarr leaves Gautland, and the romances proper of the saga have all been told. What continues to operate on the story is a more generalized influence from the world of romances. There are several notable passages where Hrólfr is described with chivalric-inspired language, and the influence from folklore (with its close connection to romance) also continues.

After Böðvarr leaves Gautland, he encounters Höttr's parents and

---

home with this for his pains, and was deeply resentful of his lot. But with it all he paid tribute to king Hrolf, just like those other tributary kings of his who had no choice but to do him homage, p. 261). This contradicts the comment that the other tributary kings on whom he levied tribute "were ready and anxious to do him service."

he learns of their son's plight at King Hrólfr's court. Höttr is being tormented by the warriors at the court who continuously pelt him with bones, so much so, that he has built himself a protective wall of bones to hide behind. Böðvarr's first action at Hrólfr's court is to save Höttr from the horrible game.[26]

Moreover, Böðvarr does not simply rescue Höttr, but he helps bring about Höttr's transformation into a warrior. Böðvarr does this by slaying a "winged creature" that had been plaguing Hrólfr's court, and having Höttr drink the creature's blood, just as Elg-Fróði had Böðvarr drink his blood. Höttr also eats some of the creature's heart and is transformed into a strong and fearless warrior (a scene again reminiscent of Sigurðr and Fáfnir). Böðvarr also arranges to have the creature positioned so that it actually still looks alive and Höttr is able to "slay" it in full view of the court. Böðvarr is consciously trying to erase or neutralize Höttr's previous reputation at the court and wants to establish him as an important warrior. Hrólfr acknowledges this transformation in Höttr, but also suspects Böðvarr's role in it, and Hrólfr renames Höttr, Hjalti, that is, 'hilt,' after Hrólfr's sword, Gullinhjalti, which Höttr had borrowed "to slay" the creature. Hrólfr welcomes Hjalti into his company of warriors.

Böðvarr has gone out of his way first to rescue Höttr, and then to help transform him. The motif of transformation, which reflects a discrepancy between appearance and reality, underlies much of the saga and strikingly so in the Böðvarr story. Böðvarr's father, Björn, is transformed into a bear by his stepmother whose beautiful appearance belies an evil personality. Bera's lowly social status belies her noble nature, which is in part revealed through her ability to recognize Björn in his disguised state, her nobility implying a heightened sense of perception or understanding. Böðvarr is also able to see through Höttr's wretched state and recognize in him a potential warrior.

After Böðvarr joins Hrólfr's court, Hrólfr asks him whether he

---

26. In the process of rescuing Höttr, Böðvarr kills one of Hrólfr's men by catching a bone aimed at Höttr and hurling it back at the warrior who had originally thrown it. Hrólfr forgives Böðvarr for this because he declares that he had told his men previously to stop their cruel game because it has brought dishonor ("óvirðing") to himself and on them "stór skömm," that is, great shame (p. 64). One has to ask whether Hrólfr can be considered a great hero if he allows such "dishonorable and shameful" behavior to occur in his own hall.

knew of any king his equal or ruling over such champions (p. 73); and Böðvarr reminds Hrólfr that he has never claimed his father's patrimony from Aðils who had murdered Helgi (Aðils believing that Helgi wanted to reclaim Yrsa as his wife). Hrólfr replies that Aðils is versed in black magic and that it would be very difficult to go up against him. The conversation between the two is telling, and Böðvarr's role as moral compass is apparent. Böðvarr tells Hrólfr that it is his shortcoming—"Þat skortar yðr" (p. 73)—that he has not attempted to recover his father's patrimony. Hrólfr once more stresses the difficulty of the task, but Böðvarr refocuses the conversation by emphasizing the fittingness—"sómir yðr" (p. 73)—of doing so; in other words, it is proper for a king to behave in such a manner. Hrólfr recognizes the rightness of Böðvarr's position that "eigum vér eftir föðurhefndum at leita ... ok skulum vér á hætta" (pp. 73–4; we have to seek vengeance for our father ... but we will take a chance, p. 288).

It is interesting to compare Hrólfr and Böðvarr. Böðvarr never hesitated to seek revenge for his father's death, and he also confronted Hvít's black magic. In contrast, Böðvarr has to tell Hrólfr twice that it is important for him to claim his father's patrimony. Hrólfr realizes that he needs to avenge his father's death and that he should have done so much earlier. In contrast, Böðvarr refused to claim the treasures left to him by his own father, until he had avenged his father's death. Böðvarr in many ways begins to emerge as the true hero of the story—and some of the narrative tensions in the story between the conflicting legendary and romance strands in the saga seem to be played out in the differing constructions of Hrólfr and Böðvarr. Hrólfr is firmly entrenched in the story as a legendary (and heroic figure) because of the antecedent sources of the story, and yet the story of Böðvarr in many ways eclipses the story of Hrólfr in the saga.[27]

Hrólfr and his champions, his berserkers, and a hundred men eventually begin the journey to Uppsala to confront Aðils. On the way to Sweden they twice meet Óðinn, who is disguised as a farmer who calls himself Hrani. Hrólfr and his entourage stay at Hrani's farm, and on three occasions Óðinn subjects the men to three different tests (a

---

27. I develop the comparison between Böðvarr and Hrólfr in greater detail in my dissertation, "Heroes and Kings in the Legend of Hrolf kraki," (Ph.D. diss., University of Illinois at Urbana-Champaign, 2006).

common folkloric motif) in order to try their mettle before they get to Aðils's court; in this case the testing consists of trying to withstand great cold, great heat, and great thirst (pp. 74–6). All the men fail these tests, with the exception of Hrólfr and his twelve champions. Hrani advises sending everyone else home since "er þá nokkur ván, at þér komið aftr, en engi elligar" (p. 76; there is some hope that you will return, but otherwise none, p. 292). Hrólfr comments, "Mikill ertu fyrir þér, bondi . . . ok þetta skal ráð hafa, sem þú leggr til" (p. 75), which conveys that Hrólfr is impressed by the farmer's good sense, and he thus agrees to take his advice. Hrólfr is capable of appreciating the importance of Hrani's advice, but subsequently he will scornfully refuse a gift of weapons from Hrani, thus angering his host, incurring his fury and later his revenge.

Hrólfr and his champions continue their journey to Aðils's court. The description of their arrival again shows some influence of chivalric romance, or at least chivalric rhetoric:

Eftir þetta ríðr Hrólfr konungr ok kappar hans til hallar Aðils konungs, ok flykkist allr borgarmúgr upp í ina hæstu turna borgarinnar at sjá prýði Hrólfs konungs ok kappa hans, því at þeir váru búnir skartsamliga, ok þykkir mörgum mikils um vert um svá kurteisa riddara. Þeir ríða fyrst seint ok ríkmannliga, en þá er þeir áttu skammt til hallarinnar, þá létu þeir hestana kenna spora ok hleyptu þeim at höllinni, svá at allt stökk undan þeim, sem fyrir þeim varð. (p. 77)

(After this king Hrolf and his champions rode to king Athils's hall, and the entire citizenry of the town crowded up into the town's highest towers to see the brave showing of king Hrolf and his champions, for they were "handsomely arrayed," and many were lost in admiration of such "courtly looking knights." At first they rode slowly and with state, but when they were only a short distance from the hall they gave their horses the spur and galloped to the hall, so that everyone standing before them fled from their path. [p. 292])

The use of the "kurteisir riddarar" (courtly looking knights) to describe the champions is a noteworthy example of the influence of chivalric literature on this mythical-heroic saga. The approach of the knights is "dramatized," as the entire citizenry of the town crowd the ramparts to see the knights who are "búnir skartsamliga" (handsomely arrayed). The drama of the scene is also conveyed through its "staging": Hrólfr and his knights first ride slowly and "ríkmannliga," as powerful men would, up to the castle allowing everyone a good look, and then they spur on their horses to arrive at the door of the hall in a great flourish.

After successfully surviving the traps at Aðils's court and retrieving Hrólfr's treasures, the champions begin their journey home; and they once more encounter Óðinn disguised as Hrani. Hrani comments that the journey turned out much as he had expected, and Hrólfr comments that Hrani was "óreykblindan" (p. 91), not blinded by smoke, that is, not blinded by appearances. Hrólfr is, however, blinded by appearances, for when Hrani offers him some weapons, Hrólfr scornfully refuses them as "ferlig vápn" (p. 91), that is, absurd or monstrous. The narrator does not reveal what it is about the weapons that so offends Hrólfr. Hrani is furious over this gesture of disrespect: "Ekki ertu þér svá hagfelldr í þessu, Hrólfr konungr," sagði Hrani, "sem þú munt ætla, ok eru þér jafnan eigi svá vitrir sem þér þykkizt" (p. 91; You are not so clever in this, king Hrolf, as you may think, said Hrani. Nor are you always so wise as you suppose yourself, p. 305). Indeed, it is a lesson from folktales and romances that it is often dangerous to refuse a gift from a helper-figure.

Böðvarr later realizes Hrólfr's mistake in rejecting Hrani's gift, and he predicts that victory will not be theirs in future battles:

Eftir koma ósvinnum ráð í hug, ok svá mun mér nú fara. Þat grunar mik oss muni ekki allsvinnliga til tekizt hafa, at vér höfum því neitat, sem vér áttum at játa, ok munum vér sigri hafa neitat. (p. 91)

(Fools grow wise after the event, and it is so with me now. I fear we acted not overly-wisely when we refused what we should have accepted—and maybe what we refused is victory. [pp. 305–6])

Hrólfr agrees and concludes that Hrani must have been Óðinn (p. 92). Böðvarr advises Hrólfr to desist from war since he was uneasy as to "hversu konungrinn mundi sigrsæll upp frá þessu, ef hann treysti nokkut á þat" (p. 92; how victorious the king would prove for the future, should he make any trial of this, p. 306). In a gesture of heroic resignation, Hrólfr responds that "Auðna ræðr hvers manns lífi" (Fate rules each man's life) rather than Óðinn, whom he identifies as "sá illi andi" (p. 92; that evil spirit, p. 306).

The descriptive language during the last part of the saga continues to show some influence from romance vocabulary. For example, as Skuld and Hjörvarðr are gathering their troops outside Hrólfr's stronghold in preparation for the final great battle, Hrólfr is depicted as concerned about other things:

> Eigi gaf Hrólfr konungr gaum at þessu. Hugsar hann nú meira á stórlæti sitt ok rausn ok hugprýði, ok alla þá hreysti, sem honum bjó í brjósti, at veita þeim öllum, sem þar váru til komnir, ok hans vegr færi sem víðast, ok allt hafði hann þat til, sem einn veraldligan konungs heiðr mátti prýða. (p. 95)

> (King Hrolf paid no heed to this. He was more concerned now with his munificence and pomp and pride and all that noble valour which filled his breast, with feasting all those who were come there, and that his glory be carried to the ends of the earth; and he had everything to hand which might enhance the honour of a king of this world. [p. 309])

And again in Hjalti's comments on Hrólfr's fighting ability in this last battle:

> Mörg brynja er nú slitin ok mörg vápn brotin ok margr hjálmr spilltr ok margr hraustr riddari af baki stunginn, ok hefir konungr várr gott skap, því at nú er hann svá glaðr sem þá hann drakk öl fastast ok vegr jafnt með báðum höndum, ok er hann mjök ólíkr öðrum konungum í bardögum, því at svá lízt mér sem hann hafi tólf konunga afl, ok margan hraustan mann hefir hann drepit, ok nú má Hjörvarðr konungr sjá þat, at sverðit Sköfnungr bítr, ok gnestr hann nú hátt í þeira hausum. (p. 99)

> (Many a mailshirt is now rent, and many a weapon broken; many a

helm is shattered, and many a gallant knight dashed from his steed. Greathearted is our king, for he is now as happy as when he drank ale deepest, and smites with both hands alike. Quite different is he from other kings in battle, for he appears to me to have twelve men's strength, and many a brave fellow has he slain; and now king Hjorvarth can see that the sword Skofnung bites, and rings aloud in their skulls. [p. 312])

Thus it is seen that Hrólfr does not savagely kill men on the battle field (as Böðvarr will do), but many a gallant knight is dashed from his steed. Bodies are not wounded, but many a mailcoat and helmet is rent and shattered, and many a weapon is broken. Hrólfr is greathearted and has the strength of twelve men. Indeed, he kills many a brave man, not the enemy, with his sword Sköfnungr. As happens in romance, the battle here is a contest between equally brave knights, not a life-and-death confrontation with the enemy. This portrayal of Hrólfr contrasts with that of Böðvarr on the battle field:

> Böðvarr bjarki ruddist nú um fast ok hjó á tvær hendr ok hugsaði nú ekki annat en vinna sem mest, áðr hann felli, ok fellr nú hverr um þveran annan fyrir honum, ok blóðugar hefir hann báðar sínar axlir ok hlóð valköstum á alla vega í kringum sik. Lét hann líkt sem hann væri óðr. (p. 102)

(Bothvar Bjarki now laid about him in earnest. He hewed on either hand, and no other thought than to achieve his utmost before he fell. Now they fell one across the other before him; and he had both arms bloodied to the shoulders, and encircling him on all sides a pile of corpses. It was as though he were mad. [p. 315])

Clearly, both Böðvarr and Hrólfr are presented as heroic fighters, but the language used to describe Böðvarr is much less romantic than that used for Hrólfr. There is, moreover, a constant narrative tension in *Hrólfs saga kraka* between how the legendary king is described and how he actually behaves. Interfacing with this tension is the residue of the earlier analogues which are filtered in the saga on many levels. Hrólfr, the legendary king, was a standard of great heroism, and yet the saga often subverts that reputation. In a discussion of *Hrólfs saga kraka*, Valgerður Brynjólfsdóttir refers to Mikhail Bakhtin's notion of "literary consciousness," where "the contrasting speeches or worldviews of characters demonstrate something that is not specifically stated, but which appears in the conflicts/contrasts in the text."[28] While she specifically links this tension to the burlesque element she sees operating in the saga, she raises an important point in general about the narrative contradictions in the saga. These contradictions seem to result from the fusion of romance elements with the older legendary material, which gets articulated in the contrasting characterizations of Böðvarr and Hrólfr.

Hermann Pálsson has argued that the *fornaldarsögur* function simultaneously as secular romances and as heroic or legendary tales, an observation that seems particularly true of *Hrólfs saga kraka*. There is clearly an interest on the part of the saga author to explore the world of romance within the legend of Hrólfr kraki, which also creates a pronounced narrative tension between the world of romance and the world of the heroic warrior.

Bibliography

Ármann Jakobsson. "Le Roi Chevalier: The Royal Ideology and Genre of Hrólfs saga kraka." *Scandinavian Studies* 72 (1999): 139–65.
Beowulf and the Fight at Finnsburg. Edited by F. Klaeber. 3rd ed. with supplement. Boston: Heath, 1950.
Boberg, Inger M. *Motif-Index of Early Icelandic Literature*. Bibliotheca Arnamagnæana 27. Copenhagen: Munksgaard, 1966.
Bradley [Denzin], Johanna. "Heroes and Kings in the Legend of Hrolf Kraki." Ph.D. diss. University of Illinois at Urbana-Champaign, 2006.
Chronicon Lethrense. In *Scriptores Minores Historiæ Danicæ*. 2 vols. Ed. M. CL. Gertz. Copenhagen: Gad, 1917–18. Vol. 1, pp. 43–53.
Edda: Die Lieder des Codex Regius nebst verwandten Denkmälern. I: Text. Ed. Gustav Neckel, 5th ed. rev. by Hans Kuhn. Heidelberg: Winter, 1983.
Edda Snorra Sturlusonar. Edited by Finnur Jónsson. Copenhagen: Gyldendal, 1931.
Hermann Pálsson. "Fornaldarsögur." In *The Dictionary of the Middle Ages*. Ed. Joseph Strayer. 12 vols. New York: Charles Scribner's Sons, 1982–89. Vol. 11, pp. 328–9.
Hermann Pálsson and Paul Edwards. *Legendary Fiction in Medieval Iceland*. Studia Islandica 30. Reykjavík: Heimspekideild Háskóla Íslands and Menningarsjóður, 1970.

28. Valgerður Brynjólfsdóttir, "A Valiant King or a Coward? The Changing Image of King Hrólfr Kraki from the Oldest Sources to *Hrólfs saga kraka*," in *Fornaldarsagornas struktur och ideologi*, ed. Ármann Jakobsson, Annette Lassen, and Agneta Ney (Uppsala: Swedish Science Press, 2003), p. 145.

Hrólfs saga kraka ok kappa hans. In *Fornaldar Sögur Norðurlanda*. 4 vols. Ed. Guðni Jónsson. Reykjavík: Íslendingasagnaútgáfan, 1981. Vol. 1, pp. 1-105.
Kalinke, Marianne E. "Norse Romance (*Riddarasögur*)." In *Old Norse-Icelandic Literature: A Critical Guide*. Ed. Carol J. Clover and John Lindow. Islandica 45. Ithaca and London: Cornell University Press, 1985. Pp. 316-63.
———. *Bridal-Quest Romance in Medieval Iceland*. Islandica, 46. Ithaca: Cornell University Press, 1990.
———. "Transgression in Hrólfs saga kraka." In *Fornaldarsagornas struktur och ideologi*. Ed. Ármann Jakobsson, Annette Lassen, and Agneta Ney. Uppsala: Swedish Science Press, 2003. Pp. 157-172.
"King Hrólfr and His Champions." In *Eirik the Red and Other Icelandic Sagas*. Trans. Gwyn Jones. London: Oxford University Press, 1961; rpt. Oxford: Oxford University Press, 1980. Pp. 221-318.
Lindahl, Carl. "Folktale." In *Medieval Folklore*. Ed. Carl Lindahl, John McNamara, and John Lindow. Oxford: Oxford University Press, 2002. Pp. 142-8.
Lüthi, Max. *The European Folktale*. Trans. John Niles. Bloomington: Indiana University Press, 1982.
Das Nibelungenlied. Ed. Helmut de Boor. Rev. Roswitha Wisniewski. Wiesbaden: Brockhaus, 1979.
Saxonis Gesta Danorum. Ed. J. Olrik and H. Ræder. Copenhagen: Munksgaard, 1931-57.
Shakespeare, William. *Hamlet*. Ed. Tucker Brooke and Jack Randall Crawford. New Haven: Yale University Press, 1961.
Skjöldunga saga. In *Danakonunga sǫgur*. Ed. Bjarni Guðnason. Íslenzk fornrit 35. Reykjavík: Hið íslenzka fornritafélag, 1982. Pp. 3-38.
Snorri Sturluson. *Heimskringla*. 3 vols. Ed. Bjarni Aðalbjarnarson. Íslenzk fornrit 26-8. Reykjavík: Hið íslenzka fornritafélag, 1941-51.
Valgerður Brynjólfsdóttir. "A Valiant King or a Coward? The Changing Image of King Hrólfr kraki from the Oldest Sources to *Hrólfs saga kraka*." In *Fornaldarsagornas struktur och ideologi*. Ed. Ármann Jakobsson, Annette Lassen, and Agneta Ney. Uppsala: Swedish Science Press, 2003. Pp. 141-56.
Vǫlsunga saga: The Saga of the Volsungs. Ed. and trans. R. G. Finc. London and Edinburgh: Nelson, 1965.
Widsith. In *The Exeter Book*. Ed. George Phillip Krapp and Elliot Van Kirk Dobbie. New York: Columbia University Press, 1936. Pp. 148-9.

"The Best Medicine in the Bitterest of Herbs":

An Eighteenth-Century Moral Tale

M. J. DRISCOLL

1. Introduction

The Icelandic clergyman and poet Jón Oddsson Hjaltalín (1749–1835), known chiefly in his day as a hymnist, was also the author of ten original prose romances (*lygisögur*) and translations or adaptations of a number of other works in prose, principally products of the European Enlightenment, an area in which he appears to have taken a great interest and been reasonably well read for his time.[1] On the last leaves of the manuscript Lbs 893 8vo, one of a number of miscellanies in his hand, there is a list headed "Historiur Lesnar" (stories read), covering the years 1792 and 1793. Alongside works by the Danish authors Johan Herman Wessel (1742–1785) and Peter Frederik Suhm (1728–1798), *Tom Jones* by Henry Fielding (1707–1754), and the *Novelas ejemplares* of Miguel de Cervantes Saavedra (1547–1616)—the latter two both read in Danish translation—there is reference to a work called "Lucian og Gedula." A *Saga af Lucian og Gedulu* is also listed among the works Jón is said to have translated ("útlagt," which can also mean "interpreted") in two unpublished nineteenth-century registers of Icelandic writers, one by Hallgrímur Jónsson djákni (1780–1836), the other by Einar Bjarnason á Mælifelli (1782–1856); the former, writing in 1822, claims to have got this information from Jón himself

---

1. I discuss Jón Oddsson Hjaltalín's life and work at length in *The Unwashed Children of Eve: The Production, Dissemination and Reception of Popular Literature in Post-Reformation Iceland* (London: Hisarlik Press, 1997), especially chapter III, "A parson's pleasure," pp. 75–132.

("eptir hans egin mèr sendri skírslu"), so there seems every reason to accept the attribution.

Texts of a *Saga af Lucian og Gedulu* survive in three manuscripts, the earliest of which, Lbs 638 8vo, is Jón Oddsson Hjaltalín's autograph. The other two manuscripts, Lbs 3021 4to and Lbs 3162 4to,[2] are younger than 638, from 1877 and ca. 1900 respectively, and the texts they preserve of the saga are demonstrably derived from it.

In terms of its style and vocabulary, the *Saga af Lucian og Gedulu* is not unlike Jón's other translations, for example *Sagan af Zadig*, which derives from the earlier of two translations into Danish of Voltaire's philosophical novel *Zadig ou la Destinée*, which Jón appears to have translated some time in the 1790s, or about the same time as he read the original *Lucian og Gedula*.[3]

Lbs 638 is a miscellany, containing, among other things, three sets of Jón's own *rímur* (*Rímur af Sigurði fót og Ásmundi Húnakóngi*, *Rímur af Hreiðari heimska*, and *Fiskimannsríma*), several short texts predominantly on cities of the ancient world (Troy, Nineveh, Babylon, Athens, Tyre, Sidon, and Rome), several short texts on heroic personages (Karlamagnús, Olgeir danski, Skanderbeg, Þiðrik af Bern, Belisarius), Jón's poem *Prastarkviða*, composed in 1809, and the poem *Heimsósómi* by sr. Hallgrímur Pétursson (1614-1674). Also in the manuscript, immediately following *Lucian og Gedula*, we find one of the two surviving texts of Jón's *Sagan af Thómas Jones* (mentioned, as was said, in the list of "Historiur Lesnar" for 1792-93 and also listed among Jón's translations in the registers by Hallgrímur djákni and Einar á Mælifelli), a précis, only some 10,000 words, of Fielding's novel, derived from Hans Jørgen Birch's Danish translation *Tom Jones Historie eller Hittebarnet* from 1781.[4]

---

2. Lbs 3021 4to was written by Grímólfur Ólafsson, who is normally associated with the farms Hrísar and Mávahlíð in Neshreppur on Snæfellsnes; *Lucian og Gedula* is the second of six items, the others being *Starkaðs saga gamla*, *Clarus saga*, *Vilmundar saga viðutan*, *Bergbúaþáttur*, and *Hinriks saga góðgjarna*, and was completed, according to the colophon, on 29 January 1877. Lbs 3162 4to was written around 1900 by sr. Ólafur Ólafsson (1851-1907) í Saurbæjarþingum; *Lucian og Gedula* is the third of six items, the others being *Flóres saga og Blankiflúr*, *Virgilíus saga galdramanns*, *Appolónius saga kóngs af Tyrus*, *Cyrus saga Persakóngs*, and *Adoníus saga*.

3. On Jón's translation of *Zadig* see *Fjórar sögur frá hendi Jóns Oddssonar Hjaltalín* (Reykjavík: Stofnun Árna Magnússonar, 2006), pp. xxx-xxxv.

4. See Driscoll, *The Unwashed Children*, pp. 100, 116-7, 121-4, 127-8.

"The Best Medicine in the Bitterest of Herbs" 233

Jón's *Rímur af Hreiðari heimska,* based on the *þáttur* of the same name,[5] were composed, according to the penultimate verse, in "átián hundrud seýtián" (1817), providing us with a *terminus post quem* for the manuscript as a whole. Assuming that the text of *Saga af Lucian og Gedulu* is indeed by Jón—and there seems no reason not to—the *terminus ante quem* for the manuscript would be 1822, the year in which Hallgrímur djákni lists the saga as among the works Jón himself says he has translated. This agrees with Páll Eggert Ólason's dating of it to "ca. 1820."[6]

A fourth manuscript, JS 631 4to, contains a text entitled "Historia af þeim fræga Lucian og Gedula" written in an unknown hand in the late eighteenth or early nineteenth century.[7] Although the basic storyline is the same as in Jón Hjaltalín's *Saga af Lucian og Gedulu,* there are a great many differences, some quite substantial. In addition, the wording of the two texts is quite different—so much so, in fact, that it does not seem possible that there can be any direct connection between them. The following, taken from the beginning of the story, should suffice to show the extent of the differences between the two texts:

J Flæmingia landi var herramadr nockr ad nafni Prísillanus. Kongvadr[8] var hann, og átti döttr eýna barna er Gedula hét. Hún var yfrid frýd og ad öllu vel mentud því sem fólki af adli þikir sér somi ad nema og æfa. Prísillanus var madr miög rýkr. Átti hann storann herragard og svo mikid jardagóts þar ad auki ad 1200 bændr voru hans landsetar. Hann var madr stoltr og ágiarn og áleit fólk af borgara standi so sem dupt fóta sinna, er eý væri samhæft ad nefnast undir eins og fólk af adli. Prisillanus unni mikid dóttr sinni. Hafdi

---

5. In Björn Sigfússon, ed., *Ljósvetninga saga,* Íslenzk fornrit 10 (Reykjavík: Hið íslenzka fornritafélag, 1940), pp. 245–60; there is one other manuscript of the *rímur,* also an autograph, Lbs 248 8vo, from 1826.

6. Páll Eggert Ólason et al., ed., *Skrá um handritasöfn Landsbókasafnsins,* 3 vols. and supplements 1–4 (Reykjavík: Gutenberg and Félagsprentsmiðjan, 1918–37), vol. 3, p. 124.

7. JS 631 4to is vol. 9 of a 19-volume collection (JS 623–641 4to) of romances of various kinds, written in different hands at different times from the seventeenth to the nineteenth century. Also in this volume are texts of *Trójumannasaga, Mágus saga jarls,* and *Blómsturvalla saga.*

8. This is the form, rather than *kvongaðr,* which is normally used by Jón Hjaltalín, so I have decided to let it stand.

hann látid smýda henni lýtinn vagn til ad aka ý daglega. Lýka hafdi hann tekid heím á sinn herragard eirn bónda son af gótsi sýnu til ad draga vagn hennar og vera henni til skémtunar. Hiet þessi dreingr Lucian. Hann var frýdr ásýndumm, fliótr, snar og eýnardlegr, og svo Gedula hefdi sem mest gaman af dreingnumm hafdi fadir hennar látid klæda hann sem húsara, og ý þessumm búníngi dró hann vagn hennar dagliga, og nefndi hun hann jafnann húsara sinn. (Lbs 638 8vo, ff. 77v-78r)

(In Flanders there lived a certain gentleman named Pricillanus. He was married and had only one child, a daughter, whose name is Gedula. She was very beautiful and well accomplished in the things which the nobility view as being of importance. Pricillanus was a very wealthy man and had a large manor and so much land in addition that 1200 farmers were his tenants. He was a very proud and avaricious man and regarded common people as like the dust of his feet and unworthy of mention in the same breath as the nobility. Pricillanus was very fond of his daughter and had made for her a little cart in which to drive around. He had also taken the son of one of the tenants on his estate and had him pull his daughter's cart and amuse her. This boy's name was Lucian. He was handsome, quick and faithful, and so that Gedula would get the most enjoyment out of him her father had the boy dressed as a hussar, and in this uniform he pulled her about every day in her cart and she always referred to him as her hussar.)

J Flandern biuggu ein luckuleg ektahión sem voru af adle og sem áttu öll þaug jardnesk audæfe sem nokr manneskia kunne ser ad æskia. Þaug áttu fyrer utan 2 storgarda einn ótrúannlegann rikdom af peningum gulle og gérsemum, og til allra þessara storu audæfa attu þaug einn einasta erfinga, nefnelega eina dóttur. Þessi þeira dótter var 6 ára enn einn hussmans sonur þar a þeirra gardi var tilsettur ad keira med þessa dotter i litlum vagne um kring stadenn. Fröjkenenn het Gedula enn dreingurenn, sem henne til glede var klæddur sem husare, het Lucian. Gedula var miög fagurt barn synumm so med öllum rette matte um hana seigia ad hun være natturunnar furduverk. Lucian var ogso fagur asindum og þar hann hafde sifelt frá sinu 8da aldurs are vered a þessum herragarde þa fastheldur eckert almugalegt i fare /:fase:/ hans. Han hafde fagurlega krullad hár, lifleg augu og höfdinglegt yfirbragd. Hann æfer sig so i ad skrifa og reikna ad hann i biriun sins 14da aldurs ars kunne hvorutveggia ágæta vel. (JS 631 4to, f. 147r)

(In Flanders there lived a fortunate couple who were of the nobility and had all the worldly wealth any person could want. They possessed, in addition to two large manor houses, an unbelievable fortune in money, gold, and jewels, and to all this great wealth they had only one heir, namely a daughter. This daughter of theirs was six years old, and the son of one of the smallholders on their estate was set to pull her about the place in a small cart. The girl was named Gedula and the boy, who for her amusement was dressed as a hussar, Lucian. Gedula was a very beautiful child, so that it might rightly be said of her that she was a marvel of nature. Lucian was also very handsome, and as he had been at the manor continuously from the time he was eight years old there remained nothing of the peasant in his demeanor. He had beautiful curly hair, lively eyes, and a noble appearance. He worked so hard at writing and sums that by the start of his fourteenth year he was quite accomplished in both.)

Although essentially the same information is given in both, the actual wording, and in some ways also the focus, is quite different, suggesting that the two Icelandic texts represent independent translations or adaptations of the same original work—but of what work?

Jón Hjaltalín's other translations are all from Danish—the only foreign language, apart from Latin, with which he appears to have been familiar—so the common source of these two texts is most likely also to have been in that language, although whether it was an original Danish work or a work translated into Danish from some other language, German or Dutch, for example, is difficult to say. The vocabulary and syntax of the two texts also reveal considerable influence from Danish, about which more will be said below.

The original is clearly not a work of any great antiquity. The story is set in Flanders at a time when there is a war, according to Jón's text, "milli franskra og keisarans ý Þýskalandi" (between the French and the Kaiser in Germany). If this is meant to refer to an actual historical period (no specific dates or events are mentioned in either text) it is presumably either the Thirty Years War (1618–48) or the War of the Austrian Succession (1740–48), when the southern Netherlands, under Spanish rule until 1713, were administered by Austria. Some of the ideas expressed in the story, in particular its criticism of the assumptions about human nature which underlay aristocratic rule, were scarcely current much before the middle of the eighteenth century, so we are probably looking for a work, perhaps original, perhaps translated, published in Danish sometime between about mid-century and 1793, the year in which Jón says he read the story, a period of at most some forty-five years. In terms of length it is most likely to have been a novella, probably not more than 20,000 words, rather than a full-length novel. Jón's text, like his *Sagan af Thómas Jones*, is clearly a précis, only some 5,700 words; the text of JS 631 is considerably longer—about two and a half times longer, in fact—but still shows signs of having been abridged in places.

Despite many hours spent perusing collections of late eighteenth-century *moralske fortællinger*—and there are many such[9]—and checking short-title catalogues and the like (and in recent years also the Internet), I have not been able to discover the source for these texts. I hasten to add that I am not necessarily saying that the source does not exist, only that, if it does, I have as yet not been able to find it. The present article may, I hope, help to lead me to it.

2. Plot

The plot of the story of Lucian and Gedula, common to both versions, is as follows:

A wealthy Flemish nobleman named Pri(s)cillanus and his wife have a daughter named Gedula. As a child she is attended by the son of one of the tenants on the estate, a handsome and intelligent boy named Lucian. He dresses in the uniform of a hussar and pulls her about the estate in a small cart.

One day, when Lucian is 14 and Gedula about 7, a count/marquis who is visiting Pri(s)cillanus is so impressed by Lucian's manner that

---

9. See Chr. V. Bruun and Lauritz Nielsen, ed. *Bibliotheca Danica: Systematisk fortegnelse over den danske litteratur fra 1482 til 1830*, 5 vols (Copenhagen: Rosenkilde & Bagger, 1961–63), vol. 4, cols. 435–40.

he asks if he can take the boy with him and make something of him in the military, even offering to pay for him. Pri(s)cillanus is, or pretends to be, reluctant to part with the boy, but eventually agrees. Lucian, for his part, declares himself keen to follow the count/marquis, but Gedula is greatly upset at the loss of her "hussar." The count/marquis takes a golden ring set with diamonds from his finger and gives it to Lucian, telling him to present it to Gedula and to tell her that he will first visit her, then ask for her hand, and finally marry her as he advances in rank, a prospect with which Gedula's parents are far from pleased.

In the years that follow, Gedula often wonders what has become of her "hussar," only to be told by her parents that she should forget about him, since he is not of their station. Gedula questions why it is that the nobility should be regarded as so much better than other folk, but is told to keep silent. Nevertheless, she thinks she knows what the truth of the matter is.

One day a letter arrives from Lucian. At first Pri(s)cillanus refuses to tell Gedula what it says, but eventually he reads the letter out. In it Lucian says that has had much success in the military and has already advanced significantly in rank; furthermore he hopes to visit them soon and looks in particular forward to giving Gedula a chance to see her "hussar" again. Pri(s)cillanus and his wife are deeply distressed by this news and decide to put Gedula, very much against her will, into a nearby cloister governed by a very strict abbess/prioress. Initially deeply unhappy there, Gedula is befriended by a young noblewoman named Gyron(n)e, who is also there because she is involved with an officer in the army—called Friðrik in Jón's text and Evfranor in JS 631—of whom her mother does not approve. The two women become inseparable and agree to help each other however they can to get to see the men they love.

At this point the two texts diverge somewhat. In Jón's text it says merely that Lucian writes again to Pri(s)cillanus saying that the count/marquis has died, peace has been established, and that he has advanced even further and now achieved the rank of major and will soon call on them. When he does he is poorly received and not told anything about Gedula's whereabouts. In JS 631 there are several more letters, principally between Evfranor and Gyronne, and a great deal of dialogue, principally between the two women, reporting and commenting on the events outside.

One day two officers arrive at the cloister, one of whom Gyron(n)e recognizes as her fiancé. She asks if the other might be Lucian but is told that it is Captain of Horse Tontrú, Lucian's close friend, Lucian himself being too ill to visit. Gedula, for her part, says that she would not be able to recognize Lucian, not having seen him in so many years. The two men dine with the abbess/prioress, who, having been alerted by Pri(s)cillanus, makes enquiries about Lucian and asks that they not bring him with them on their future visits to the cloister or make it known to him that Gedula is there, to which they agree. While there, the officers are allowed to stroll through the grounds with the young women, and in the weeks that follow the men return repeatedly, dining with the abbess and walking with the young women. During these visits Tontrú's principal topic of conversation is his friend Lucian, in particular the great love he bears for Gedula, which he hopes is reciprocated. At the same time he indicates repeatedly that he wishes he were in Lucian's position, while Gedula, who is not unattracted to Tontrú, finds this wooing by proxy initially confusing and later irritating. One day she receives a package containing a beautiful picture in a golden frame set with jewels which she is told depicts Lucian but, she and Gyronne agree, in fact looks remarkably like Tontrú. The next time the men visit, Gedula asks Tontrú how it can be that he has sent her a picture which is supposedly that of his friend and yet resembles him so completely; is he, she wants to know, Major Lucian, who has under an assumed identity sneaked into the cloister? If this were the case, she says, it would diminish greatly the respect which she would otherwise have for such a famous hero. He replies that he is Master of Horse Tontrú and the image that of Lucian. Even if things were as she suggests, he says, he would hope that Lucian would be forgiven, as his actions would be the result of his great love. Gedula is greatly angered by this and refuses to speak further to any of them. She eventually overcomes her anger, however, and learns that Tontrú and Lucian are indeed one and the same; on their next meeting the two swear their undying love for each other.

Here the two texts again differ somewhat. In JS 631 it is decided that Lucian should continue to pose as Tontrú, and as such he and Gedula are able to secure her parents' permission to wed. Rumors that Tontrú is in fact Lucian reach Pri(s)cillanus's ears, however, and he rushes to the cloister to confront her. It does not help matters that

Lucian is there, without the knowledge of the prioress. Pri(s)cillanus breaks off the engagement and declares that the two may never see each other again. Soon after it emerges that Gedula is pregnant, for which she is expelled from the cloister and brought back to her father's manor in shame. These two incidents are conflated in Jón's text, where Pri(s)cillanus, who has no knowledge of Tontrú, rushes to the cloister upon hearing from the abbess of Gedula's pregnancy.

Gedula is put in a dungeon where she languishes until it is time for her to give birth, attended by an old woman. In the text of JS 631 the old woman herself takes pity on Gedula and asks to be allowed to help her, against the will of Gedula's mother, whereas in Jón's text she is merely set to it by the parents. The birth is difficult and the old woman declares that the child is stillborn. Gedula says that she is lying and, taking the child by the feet, dashes its head against the wall, smashing the skull. She then tells the old woman to take the dead child to her parents and tell them that she has killed it. The old woman does so, relating everything that has happened and swearing that the child was already dead. Gedula's parents refuse to believe her and demand that Gedula be punished for her crime.

From this point on there is a great difference between the two versions. In Jón's text an assembly is called at which Gedula is accused of the murder of her child. She is allowed no defense, we are told, nor would she have accepted any. She is found guilty and sentenced to death. Lucian, meanwhile, has vanished entirely from sight since Gedula's expulsion from the cloister, for which he is greatly criticized.

Three days later Gedula is driven to the place of execution, where the executioner stands ready. Just then fifty armed men arrive, lead by the Kaiser's herald, clutching a writ in one hand. He proclaims in a loud voice that Lucian is to be promoted to general and is to marry Gedula, while Pri(s)cillanus is to pay a fine; he must moreover accept Lucian as his son-in-law and hand over to him full control of all his estates. In addition, Friðrik is to be promoted to major and may marry Gyron(n)e (assuming the approval of her mother can be secured). At that moment Lucian and Friðrik arrive in a coach drawn by six white horses. Gedula is led into the coach, where a joyful reunion with her beloved takes place. Gedula asks to be taken to the cloister where she and Gyron(n)e are joyfully reunited and agree to forgive the abbess.

Lucian and the rest go to Pri(s)cillanus's manor. They are received with scorn, but upon hearing the Kaiser's decree Pri(s)cillanus becomes frightened and agrees to do whatever they say. He and Lucian are reconciled. The following morning Pri(s)cillanus goes to the cloister to see his daughter. Gedula is not at all keen to see him and it takes the others a long time to persuade her. Finally she agrees to forgive him, since he and Lucian have settled their differences. After this there is much joy and celebration.

In the other version, Gedula, having pleaded guilty to the murder of her baby, is initially condemned to death by the jury. The judges are in doubt, however, and the matter is referred to the University. Lucian, meanwhile, sends Evfranor with letters to various people in the court to make sure that his plea is heard by the government. On the day Gedula is to be executed Lucian goes before the authorities and declares that he is equally guilty and should also be punished; he argues his case with great determination and passion, asking not for mercy but for justice. The jury, judges, and other authorities, upon hearing of Pri(s)cillanus's gross mistreatment of Lucian, overthrow their earlier decision; at the same time there comes both an answer from the University in Gedula's favor, and a decree from the government stating that Lucian and Gedula are to be allowed to marry, that Pri(s)cillanus should pay a fine and must accept Lucian as his son-in-law, and that Lucian is to be promoted to *Oberst*. Gedula, who is still imprisoned in her father's dungeon and knows nothing of this, is greatly surprised when the assembled company arrives and tells her what has happened. A celebration follows, after which they all make their way to the cloister, where Gedula is reunited with Gyron(n)e, Pri(s)cillanus informs the prioress that he is fully reconciled with his son-in-law to be, and so on.

It is thought fitting that Gedula and Gyron(n)e should hold their weddings at the same time and there in the cloister, where together they have experienced so much joy and sorrow. In the version preserved in JS 631 there is nothing to stop this from happening, as Evfranor has already gained the consent of Gyron(n)e's mother, who conveniently arrives at the cloister at that moment. In Jón's version, however, this remains to be done, and Lucian offers to accompany Friðrik to seek Gyron(n)e's mother's approval for the wedding.

They leave the following day, taking four retainers with them. Their route takes them through a thick forest, where they are attacked by highwaymen. They are able to kill or rout them but are wounded in the exchange. When they reach the estate of Gyrone's mother she receives them well but becomes alarmed when she sees the blood on their clothing. They tell her what has happened and she praises their courage and thanks them for their great deed. Lucian asks for Gyrone's hand in marriage on behalf of the Major, to which Gyrone's mother, when she hears the Kaiser's will, readily gives her consent. They remain there for three nights while their wounds heal and then return to the cloister, where there is a joyful reunion between mother and daughter.

Both versions end with the double wedding of Friðrik/Evfranor to Gyron(n)e and Lucian to Gedula, after which everyone, with the possible exception of Pri(s)cillanus, lives happily ever after.

3. Names

The names of the characters are for the most part identical in the two versions of the story. *Lucian*, the chief male protagonist, is a common name in many parts of Europe (*Lucien* in French, *Luciano* in Italian, *Luciaan* in Dutch, *Luzian* in German, and so on), the most famous bearers doubtless being the rhetorician and satirist Lucian of Samosata (ca. 120–after 180 A.D.), and the saints Lucian of Antioch (†312) and Lucian of Beauvais (†290).

Gedula, by contrast, does exist as a woman's name, but is far less common. It comes from the Hebrew (גדולה) (*gedula*) and means "greatness" (sometimes also translated as or "largesse" or "grace"). According to Kabbalistic Judaism *gedula* is the first of the five godly forces or emotive attributes within creation,[10] and is regarded as synonymous with חסד (*ḥesed*), "love," the fourth of the ten ספירות (*sefirot*), or divine emanations, through which God reveals himself to man. *Gedula/ḥesed* is seen as paired with גבורה (*gevura*), the Hebrew

---

10. These five forces are listed in I *Chronicles* 29:11: "Yours, O Lord, [is] the greatness, and the might, and the glory, and the victory, and the majesty, for all that is in the heavens and on the earth [is Yours]."

word for "might," also known as דין (*din*), "judgment" or "severity," the fifth of the ten *sefirot* and second of the emotive attributes, the two each acting to temper the other, as it were.[11]

While this would not be an entirely inappropriate name for the female protagonist of our story—and the Kabbalah was certainly known and studied during the Enlightenment—the name could also be a corruption of *Gudula* (itself possibly a pet form of *Gudrun*), after St. Gudula (†712), patroness of Brussels, known in Flemish as *Goedele* and in French as *Gudule*.[12] As the events in our story take place in Flanders, where Gudula/Goedele is a relatively common name, this is certainly the most likely explanation. Interestingly, the feast day of St. Gudula is 8 January, the same day as that of St. Lucian of Beauvais (and the day after that of Lucian of Antioch). This may well be simple coincidence, but it is also possible that the author of the story, looking for names for his protagonists, fell upon these in a calendar of saints' feast days.

Another connection with the Low Countries is found in the name of the man who is responsible for fostering Lucian. In Jón Hjaltalín's text he is called simply "Carl" and is said to be a *greifi* (count); in the other version, however, his name is given as "Spinola," and he is said to be a *margreifi* (margrave or marquis). The name is presumably that of the family of Genoese noblemen including Ambrosio Spínola, marqués de los Balbases (1569–1630), and his younger brother Federico (1571–1603), who distinguished themselves in the Spanish wars in the Netherlands. It is possible that in the original both names were used and that Jón has simply taken the first name and the scribe of JS 631 the surname. There was, in fact, a Carlo Spinola, a Jesuit missionary to China who died a martyr at Nagasaki on 10 September 1622, but there seems no reason why our character should be named for him.

The other names in the story are either so rare or so common as to be of little help in localizing the story. The name of Gedula's father is spelt "Pricillanus" in Jón's text and "Priscillanus" (with Latin declensional endings) or, especially toward the end, "Priscillan" (with Icelandic

---

11. See Gershom Scholem, *The Mystical Shape of the Godhead: Basic Concepts in the Kabbalah*, transl. by Joachim Neugroschel (New York: Schocken Books, 1991), esp. pp. 31–55.

12. See *The Catholic Encyclopedia*, http://www.newadvent.org/cathen/07056b.htm.

endings) in JS 631. Both are presumably corruptions of *Priscillianus*, which was the name of the founder of a sect of Gnostic-Manichaean ascetics in fourth-century Roman Galicia who has the distinction of being the first person in the history of Christianity to be executed for heresy.[13] Although rare, doubtless owing to the severe measures taken by the church to suppress the heresy, the name appears to have survived in Spanish, chiefly in the Philippines, as *Pricillano*. There is also a Saint Priscillianus, a rather shadowy (and thus probably entirely legendary) figure, described simply as a cleric (*clericus*), who was martyred along with Saints Priscus, a priest (*presbyter romanus*), and Benedicta, a laywoman (*femina*), in the persecutions of Julian the Apostate in Rome in 362; their feast day, again probably coincidentally, is 4 January, four days before those of Saints Lucian and Gudula.[14]

The name of the woman who befriends Gedula in the cloister is spelt "Gyrone" in Jón Hjaltalín's text while the form used in the other version is "Gyronne." The former is the name of the principal (male) character in *Gyrone* [or *Girone*] *il Cortese*, a poetical romance by Luigi Alamanni (1495–1556), while the latter turns up as a surname in a number of on-line genealogies, generally with a single hit, a Jeanne Gyronne (1590–1639) of La Rochelle, Charente-Maritime, France,[15] and as a first name, also of a male, in a number of court cases in the State of Arkansas.[16] Curiously, the text of JS 631 parenthetically adds "edur Gudrun" (or Guðrún) the first time the name Gyronne appears; there is unlikely to be any connection between the names Guðrún and Gyronne, although there may be, as was mentioned, between Guðrún and Gedula.

The name of Lucian's friend and fellow officer, and Gyron(n)e's fiancé, is quite different in the two texts; he is called *Friðrik* (written "Fridrich," "Friderich," or "Frederik") in Jón Hjaltalín's text, a common name throughout Europe, but Evfranor (or Evranor—there are nine instances of each) in the other text. This name could be

---

13. H. Chadwick, *Priscillian of Avila: The Occult and the Charismatic in the Early Church* (Oxford: Clarendon Press, 1976); *The Catholic Encyclopedia*, http://www.newadvent.org/cathen/12429b.htm

14. *The Book of Saints: A Dictionary of Servants of God Canonized by the Catholic Church*, 4th ed. (London: MacMillan, 1947), p. 493

15. See e.g. http://www.familysearch.org/, the genealogy website of The Church of Jesus Christ of Latter-day Saints.

16. See e.g. http://courts.state.ar.us/unpublished/2005a/20050616/cr04-554.html.

that of the fourth-century B.C. Greek artist and sculptor Euphranor (Ευφράνωρ) of Corinth, although it is hard to see any reason for the choice.

In Jón's text the two officers, Lucian and his friend Friðrik, both conceal their identities when they visit the cloister, presenting themselves as "Gert" and "Tontrú." In the other text, it is only Lucian who assumes a false identity, as his friend has no need to do so, since, as is spelt out in the text, the prioress knows nothing of his relationship with Gyron(n)e. *Gert*, or *Geert*, is the Low German and Dutch form of *Gerhard* and also found commonly in Scandinavia. *Tontrú*, on the other hand, is a bit of a mystery. It is possible that it is a garbled form of some Flemish or French name, but it is difficult to see what name that might be.

The cloister to which Gedula is sent, unnamed in Jón's text, is referred to repeatedly in JS 631 as "Dórótheu klaustur." The name is presumably that of Saint Dorothy, martyred 6 February 311 at Caesarea, Cappadocia.[17] As the patron saint of horticulture, Dorothy has lent her name to a number of flower shops and florist groups in Flanders, including the Koninklijke Maatschappij Sint-Dorothea, but I am not aware of the existence of any Sint-Dorothea klooster (or a Cloître Sainte-Dorothée in La Flandre française).[18]

Finally, a very minor figure, one of the servants (*þernur*) at the cloister who has no counterpart in Jón's text (where, in fact, there are no servants mentioned at all), is referred to in the text preserved in JS 631 as "Steinunn." One wonders whether there might have been a young woman with this name, and perhaps also one named Guðrún, in the household of the scribe.

4. Style and vocabulary

As was mentioned above, and will have been evident from the passages already cited, the language of both Icelandic texts shows considerable influence from Danish. There is, to start with, a large number of Danish loanwords (for the most part themselves borrowings from

---

17. *The Book of Saints*, p. 184.
18. There is a "Congregation of the Sisters of Saint Dorothy," founded in 1835 by Paula Frassinetti; see http://www.vatican.va/news_services/liturgy/saints/ns_lit_doc_19840311_frassinetti_en.html.

Low German). Words that are found in both texts include *betala* (to pay) and *betaling* (payment), *soddan* (such), *frö(j)ken* (young lady, miss), *or(ð)saka* (to cause), *spursmál* (question), *forakt* (contempt), *skilirí* (a painting, portrait), *ogs(v)o* (also, too), *enn nú* (still, yet), *ekta* (to marry), and *feil* (mistake, ultimately from Latin *fallere*). In addition, there are a great many loanwords from Danish which are found only in one or the other of the two texts. In Jón's text, for example, there are words such as *stumpari* (a poor wretch, from Danish *stymper*[19]), *gunst* (favor, grace(s)), *tukthús* (prison), *testamentera* (will, bequeath, a back-formation from Latin *testāmentum*, from *testārī*), and *eðalmóðugheit* (generosity, magnanimity), while JS 631 has, among many others, *plaga*, in the phrase *plaga að gera e-ð* (be wont to do something), *kompliment*, in the phrase *afleggja sín kompliment* (greet or send one's respects), *innprenta* (impress), *tendens* (tendency), *misbrúka* (misuse), *lumpinn* (of poor quality, cheap, low-class), *óbillegur* (unfair), *foraktanlega* (despicably), *kamers* (room), *lenistóll* ((easy-)chair), *spássera* (stroll), *yfirbevisa* (convince), *begering* (desire, request), *forþéna* (deserve), *yfirtala* (persuade), and *regering* (government). It should be noted that many if not most of these words were already common in Icelandic, some since the late middle ages,[20] and thus need not necessarily be derived from the Danish original. Some almost certainly are, however; *lumpinn*, for example, which is glossed parenthetically in the text as "lítilsverður" (of little worth). It should also be noted that while some of these words can still be used in colloquial/jocular Icelandic, at least by the older generation, the majority of them would not be regarded as possible, or necessarily even understood, by most contemporary native speakers of Icelandic, so effective has been the policy of "language purification" in the last hundred and fifty years or so.[21]

---

19. This delightful word, alas now rather rare in Danish, is defined in *Ordbog over det danske Sprog*, ed. Verner Dahlerup, 28 vols. (Copenhagen: Gyldendal, 1919–1956), vol. 22, cols. 697–99, as a "ringe, ussel, ynkværdig, ynkelig, sølle (mands)person" (lowly, wetched, pitiful, pathetic, shabby (male)person).

20. See, for example, Chr. Westergård-Nielsen, *Låneordene i det 16. århundredes trykte islandske litteratur*, Bibliotheca Arnamagnæana VI (Copenhagen: Ejnar Munksgaard, 1946), and Veturliði Óskarsson, *Middelnedertyske låneord i islandsk diplomsprog frem til år 1500*, Bibliotheca Arnamagnæana LXIII (Copenhagen: Reitzel, 2003).

21. See Kjartan G. Ottósson, *Íslensk málhreinsun: Sögulegt yfirlit* (Reykjavík: Íslensk málnefnd, 1990), esp. pp. 29–50.

The text also contains a number of terms to do with the military, which, although not originally Danish, came into Icelandic through Danish, mostly in the eighteenth century. These include the military ranks *lautenant, kapteinn, majór, óberst,* and *general(l),* this last actually glossed in brackets in Jón's text as "æsti hershöfdingi" (highest commander), as well as *ritmeisteri* (master of cavalry) from Danish *ritmester* (itself from German *Rittmeister*). Finally there is *húsari,* in Danish *husar.* Originally from the Serbian *gussar,* this word came via the Hungarian *huszár* into French, German, and other European languages and was used to refer to a class of light cavalry regiment organized in Hungary in the fifteenth century and subsequently imitated throughout Europe. The appearance of the Hungarian hussars was also copied by those of other nations, being characterized by uniforms of brilliant colors and elaborate ornament—and moustaches: in order to give himself a more military appearance, according to Jón Hjaltalín's version,[22] the young Lucian dons a false pair of *knefelbartar,* a loanword from the Danish *knevelsbart,* which is defined in *Ordbog over det danske Sprog,* vol. 10, cols. 825–26, as "overskæg; moustache; især om stort, svært overskæg (der giver et barsk, martialsk udseende)" (moustache, in particular of a large, heavy moustache (which conveys a harsh, martial appearance)). The Danish word itself derives from German *Knebelbart* (from *Knebel,* gag), which is used to describe the short, pointed beard known in English as a "Vandyke," whereas the Icelandic text makes clear that it is the Danish sense of a large military-style moustache which is meant.

In addition to such obvious loan words, certain usages also show clear signs of Danish influence; *samt,* for example, is used in Jón's text in the Danish sense of "and in addition" rather than the normal Icelandic "still, even though," and both texts have examples of *mikið* (much) used adverbially to mean "very," like the Danish *meget,* as in the sentence "hann lítur mikið vel út" (he is very good looking) and, a particularly good example, "hún fær mikið lítil fríheit" (she is given very little freedom), and of *rétt* (right) to mean "rather" or "quite," as in "hún hefur ekki verið rétt frísk" (she hasn't been terribly well).

---

22. The other text says only that Lucian "leit nú ut sem einn litell stridsmadur" (looked like a little soldier), without mentioning the detail of the moustache.

There are also places, fewer in Jón's text than in JS 631, where the syntax appears to have been influenced by Danish, for example in the word order of genitive constructions, such as "eftir foreldranna beiðni" (at the request of the parents), where it would be more natural in Icelandic to say "eftir beiðni foreldranna" (or "eftir beiðni foreldra þeirra").

It must be said, however, that although the two Icelandic texts in all likelihood both derive directly from a Danish original, it would probably be difficult to prove this on linguistic grounds, since the written Icelandic of the eighteenth century tended generally to show a far greater degree of Danish influence in lexis, style, and syntax than would later be considered acceptable. Of the two texts, Jón's is decidedly the more "Icelandic," and contains many passages in perfectly respectable saga style, albeit of the "post-classical" variety. The text of JS 631, on the other hand, gives the impression of being a fairly raw translation from the Danish, but is certainly not without its moments, not least in the many passages of dialogue.

5. Theme

What is the story of Lucian and Gedula about? That depends, to large extent, on which text of it one reads. In Jón Hjaltalín's version, there is a passage at the end in which the moral implicit in the story is spelt out for the reader:[23]

> Kennir saga þessi mönnum þrýár helstu athugasemdir, sem eru þessar: 1. ad dygd og dugnadur sieu hvöriumm adli dýrmætari; 2. ad grimdarfull og ránglát medhöndlan gétur svo trylt mans gied og synni ad hann af örvæntíng og gremju grýpi til þeírra medala, sem bædi hönumm og ödrumm eru ý ráúninni hrillileg; og 3^{dia} hafi manni ordid það á ad taka stórlega feil er það sýálfs mans skildu og sannri skinsemi samqvæmast ad greida úr því á besta hátt og giöra sem verdur gott úr vondu, því opt er besta lækníng ý beiskustu jurtum. (Lbs 638 8vo, ff. 95v-96r)

---

23. The passage is found in Jón's autograph manuscript and in Lbs 3162 4to, but is lacking in Lbs 3021 4to, where the text goes straight from "undu þau vel sínu ráði og lifðu saman langan aldur" into the standard formula "og endar svo þessi saga."

(This story teaches people three main points, which are these: 1. that virtue and doughtiness are more valuable than any nobility; 2. that cruel and unjust treatment can so transform a person's mind and disposition, that in desperation and anger he resorts to measures that are in truth both to him and others horrible; and 3. if a person has made a serious error it is his own responsibility and most in keeping with duty and good sense to redress it in the best way possible, to make good come out of the bad, for often the best medicine is in the bitterest of herbs.)

This passage is not found in the other version, which ends simply with the statement that Lucian and Gedula lived for a long time and had many children, from whom they derived much pleasure. In the absence of the Danish original, it is impossible to say whether the passage was present there or whether Jón made it up. The points presented in it are easy enough to derive from a reading of the story, so he may well have done. There is, admittedly, nothing specific in either text that would lead one to the last of the points, that it is best to admit to one's mistakes, but then this is the sort of common-sense maxim found in many a piece of public-school-boy fiction, here given the Enlightenment seal of approval by being called "sannri skinsemi samqvæmast" (most in keeping with good sense/true reason); the final sentence, that the best medicine is often to be found in the bitterest of herbs, has the feel of a proverb, but is unknown to me.[24]

The second of the points refers presumably to what for most readers is doubtless the most memorable (not to say shocking) scene in the story, where Gedula dashes the head of her stillborn baby against the wall. The idea that this is an act to which she has been driven by her parents' excessively harsh treatment is in keeping with the ideas of the Enlightenment that people, in particularly those who are to be educated or punished, respond better to rational treatment, the point of which they understand, than to severity (something much of the so-called "Western World" has yet to learn, or at least to implement). There is a passage in JS 631 which seems to point in the same direc-

---

24. "Bitter herbs" ("beiskar jurtir" in Icelandic, "bitre urter" in Danish) are mentioned in several places in the Bible, such as Exodus 12:8, Numbers 9:11, and Lamentations 3:15.

tion. It comes relatively early in the story, when, after Lucian's second letter, Priscillanus has written to the prioress to ask that she ensure that there be no contact between his daughter and Lucian:

Nu huxade Priscillan ad hann hefde utvirkad allt sem einn skinsamur fader kinne ad giöra til ad vardveita sinnar dóttur heidur enn athugade ecke ad þesshattar ordsakar oft þad vesta utfall. (JS 631 4to, f. 153v)

(Priscillanus now thought that he had done everything a prudent father could in order to protect his daughter's honor, not realizing that such things often have the worst consequences.)

It is the first of the points, the idea that virtue is a quality potentially present in all human beings and not restricted to, or necessarily even to be found in, members of the aristocracy, which sets the tone for much of the story. Although this theme is evident in both versions, much greater weight is laid on it in Jón's text than in JS 631. The idea was, of course, one of the basic principles of the Enlightenment, which saw numerous critiques of the arbitrariness and injustice with which distinctions and honors were conferred in society and the idea that the masses were incapable of rational conduct and needed, willy-nilly, to be governed. The worst aristocracies, it was argued, were those in which the mass of people were bound into serfdom by the ruling nobility, as was the case under feudalism.[25] Although the society depicted in the story is not feudal as such, it is made clear enough that Priscillanus regards the people living on his estate more as his possessions than as human beings.

Priscillanus and his wife are described in both texts as excessively proud and arrogant people. In Jón's text this comes at the very beginning, cited above, where we are told that Priscillanus "áleit fólk af borgara standi so sem dupt fóta sinna,[26] er ey væri samhæft ad nefnast undir eins og fólk af adli" (regarded common people as like the dust

---

25. See e.g. J.Q.C. Mackrell, *The Attack on 'Feudalism' in 18th-Century France* (London: Routledge, 1973), in particular chapter V, "Humanitarian objections to 'Feudalism'," pp. 104–32.

26. The phrase "duft fóta sinna/þeirra" is used repeatedly in the Bible, e.g. Matthew 10:14, Luke 9:5, and Acts 13:50–51.

of his feet, who were unworthy of mention in the same breath as the nobility). The arrogance of Priscillanus and his wife manifests itself principally in their complete rejection of Lucian as a possible suitor for their daughter, solely on the grounds that he is not, and therefore never can be, of their class.[27] In the text of JS 631 it says:

> Þesse hjón vóru [...] so stolt ad þaug ecke gatu þolad ad þeinkia um þad sem Margreifenn hafde sagt, þvi þo nu Lucian hefde orded General so hefdu þaug alldrej med gódu gede samþikt þeirra ektaskap, þared hann være fæddur sonur eins litelfjörlegs húsmanns en hun af adle. (JS 631 4to, f. 149r)

(This couple were so proud that they could not bear to consider what the marquis had said [sc. that Lucian and Gedula would one day wed], because even if Lucian became a General they would never willingly agree to the marriage, since he was born the son of a poor freeholder and she was of the nobility.)

They try to make this clear to their daughter, but as she grows up Gedula begins to have her doubts about the legitimacy of the division of mankind into commoner and lord. In Jón's text it says:

> Gedulu þóckti þetta undarlegt og eptir því sem hún tók ad eldast fór hún ad jgrunda þetta betr og spurdi modr sýna þá opt hvad kiæmi til þess ad þetta fólk sem kallad væri af adli væri svo hátt upphafid yfir almúgann, hvört þad væri skapad af dýrmætara efni enn annad fólk. Hún sæe þó ad bædi yrdi þad sýúkt og lýka dæji þad sem adrir menn, ecki heldr hefdi gud gefid því fegri sól, fallegri himinn edr dýrmætara jörd til ábúdar enn ödru fólki. (Lbs 638 8vo, ff. 80v-81r)

---

27. This is also the driving force behind the plot of most products of the Hindi cinema (vulgarly referred to as "Bollywood"): one of the protagonists is prevented from marrying the other because of opposition to the union by one or both of the parents owing to the (perceived) unsuitability—generally on the basis of caste or religion—of the other partner. This applies both to such classic Hindi films as *Awaara* (1951) and *Mughal-E-Azam* (1960) and to modern productions like *Dilwale Dulhania Le Jayenge* (1995) and *Kabhi Khushi Kabhie Gham* (2001). Most Hindi films, at heart, are calls for tolerance. Little would be required, apart from the addition of a few dance numbers, to turn the story of Lucian and Gedula into a fine "Bollywood" film.

(Gedula found this strange and as she grew older she began to wonder more about this and often asked her mother how it had come about that the people who were known as of the nobility were so much more highly favored than the common people, whether they were made of more costly stuff than other people. Yet she could see that they both became ill and died like everyone else; nor had God given them a fairer sun or more beautiful sky or better earth on which to live than other people.)

The corresponding passage in JS 631 is rather shorter; Gedula merely asks "hvort nockur mismunur være a medal manneskianna i fædíngunne, og hvort adalfólk være af annare tegund enn adrar manneskiur" (whether there was some difference between people at birth, and whether the nobility was of a different kind than other people).

The answers she receives are rather different in the two versions. In Jón's text, Gedula's mother, unable to muster arguments against these views, tells her to keep silent, while in JS 631 it says that "uppa þesse og mörg önnur spursmál svarade hennar móder mörgu sem munde ut heimta eina stóra bók ef skrifad være" (to these and many other questions her mother gave many answers which would require a large book if they were written down). Either way, Gedula is unimpressed. In 631 it says that, upon further reflection, she "hélt ad vera þann rettasta dom er hun sialf dæmde" (reckoned the most correct judgment to be the one she herself made), or, according to Jón, "þócktist þó sýá hvad sannast væri" (thought she knew what the real truth was). What this "real truth" was is spelt out in Jón's text, where Gedula tells her mother that "sér sýndist dygd og dugnadr væri sá besti adall, því einginn giæti ad því giördt af hvöriumm hann væri fæddur" (she thought virtue and valor were the best nobility, for one could do nothing about the circumstances of one's birth)—a sentiment repeated almost verbatim in the moral at the end: "ad dygd og dugnadur sieu hvöriumm adli dýrmætari."

In Jón's text there is a yet another statement of this theme, which again has no parallel in JS 631; it comes toward the end of the story, where Pricillanus and Lucian are reconciled. Priscillanus admits that Lucian, despite his humble beginnings, "hefdi hreisti, digd og edalmódugheit framm yfir flesta menn adra" (had strength, virtue and noble-mindedness beyond that of most men). It is interesting, though, that what finally convinces him of this is that when it is time for him to beg Lucian's forgiveness, as stipulated in the Kaiser's writ, Lucian says rather it is he who should ask forgiveness of him. "Þessi géneralsins hógværd," the saga tells us, "kitladi svo þad drambsama sinni Pricillani ad hann fell umm háls Lucians og qvadst med ánægiu antaka hann firir sinn dóttrmann og erfingia" (This modesty on the part of the general so tickled the haughty Pricillanus that he embraced Lucian and said that he would gladly accept him as his son-in-law and heir).

All of these echo something said by the count/marquis near the very beginning of the text of JS 631, that "hraustleike er sa stædste adall" (doughtiness is the greatest nobility). Having said this, the count/marquis then turns to his host and says "edur er þad ecke satt Hr Priscillanus?" (or is that not true, Mr. Priscillanus?), to which the parenthetical remark is added: "enn hann (Priscillanus) var hinn meste heimskinge" (but he (Priscillanus) was a total fool). It is interesting that in JS 631 Priscillanus appears as a rather ridiculous figure. There is, for example, a passage, not found in Jón's version but presumably in the original, describing how Priscillanus is so afraid of being robbed during the war that any time he hears anyone in the street outside he sends someone to look to see who it is, and has all his money and valuables buried in the cellar under a large stone, even though the enemy is many miles away.

Although Jón doesn't use this particular story, perhaps not wanting to make Priscillanus appear as anything other than the excessively stern *pater familias*, there are far more references to Priscillanus's greed—and to money and wealth in general—in his text than in JS 631. The count/marquis, for example, in contradistinction to Priscillanus, is described in Jón's text as "madr gödgiarn og mildr, ör af fie, og gódr sýnumm under lýd" (a good-natured man, kind and generous, and good to his men)—a common way of a describing a king or chieftain in the sagas. The count's generosity in particular to Lucian knows no bounds: we are twice told that the count has given him "stórar summur peninga" (great sums of money) and he leaves his entire fortune to him on his deathbed. Of Lucian too it is said that he "géfur [...] opt fie á tvær hendr, helst þeim fátæku" (often gives money away freely, principally to the poor). None of this is even hinted at in JS 631.

The abbess/prioress, similarly, is only said to be "hörd" (strict) in JS 631, while in Jón's text she is described not only as "vargur ad skaplindi" (with the temperament of a [she-]wolf) but also as "rýk" (rich). Lucian and Friðrik play upon her avarice, giving her fine gifts ("dýrmætar skeinkingar"),[28] with the result that although Jón's text says specifically that once a young woman was inside the cloister any contact with the outside world was impossible, access to the women appears to have been rather easily obtained, once the abbess's palm had been suitably greased. In JS 631 the situation is quite different, with Gedula and Gyronne going to great lengths to conceal from the prioress the fact the two men spend so much time with them. That they should be able to spend any time there at all is carefully explained in 631, where it says:

Það er ad giætandi ad i Flandern eru þar klaustur hvar i adalfolk ma lata sinar dætur an þess þær seu skuldbundnar til ad vera þar alla æfe sidann, þvi þær fá burtfararleife þa þeim bidst nockur sómasamleg gifting. Það er heldur ecke i þeim klaustrum fyrerboded ad kallmenn meige tala vid þær, reika med þeim og borda opennberlega med þeim, enn þó er naquæmlega ad gætt ad soddann friheit ecke seu misbrukud (JS 631 4to, ff. 151r–v)

(It should be noted that in Flanders there are cloisters in which members of the aristocracy can put their daughters without their having to remain there all their lives, for they are allowed to leave when they are made a suitable proposal of marriage. Nor is it in these cloisters forbidden for men to speak to them, walk with them or dine publicly with them, but careful attention is paid that such freedoms are not abused.)

This all makes more sense than what we find in Jón's version, where "Gert" and "Tontrú," openly encouraged by the abbess, spend much of their time at the cloisters, coming and going, as we understand, without hindrance, "stundumm framm á nótt" (sometimes into the night).

---

28. Exploiting avariciousness is a standard trick in the maiden-king romances, for example *Hrólfs saga kraka*; see Marianne Kalinke, *Bridal-Quest Romance in Medieval Iceland*, Islandica 46 (Ithaca and London: Cornell University Press, 1990), pp. 98–99.

This is not the only thing, it has to be said, which simply makes more sense in the text of JS 631 than in Jón's version. The entire *dénouement*, to take the most obvious example, is far more complicated—and believable—in JS 631 than the shameless *deus-ex-machina* of the Kaiser's writ, which in one fell swoop puts right everything that had otherwise appeared to have gone so horribly wrong: the two couples can marry, both Lucian and Friðrik receive promotions (without apparently having done anything to deserve them), the haughty Pri(s)cillanus gets his come-uppance—all's well that ends well, despite Lucian's rather unheroic behavior, disappearing entirely at a time when Gedula most needs him, for which, the text tells us, he is universally censured, even by those who had previously praised him. The explanation for such "factual" discrepancies between the two texts could be that Jón, having read the story in 1793, retold it from memory later, perhaps many years later, and had simply forgotten some of the less important details of the plot.

As noted above, it is, in the absence of the source, difficult—and probably unwise—to say much about which aspects or elements of the two texts may or may not be original. I will say, however, that if and when the source turns up I shall be very surprised indeed if it contains the relatively lengthy episode in Jón's text in which Lucian and Friðrik, seeking the approval of Gyronne's mother for the latter's marriage to Gyronne, travel through a thick forest and are ambushed by a band of highwaymen. Not only does it stand out by being the only episode not told from the point of view of the women, it is also written in a style, with a blow-by-blow description of the encounter worthy of any *lygisaga*, entirely at odds with the rest of the narrative.

I have suggested elsewhere that Jón may have used the texts found in this and several of his other miscellanies as raw material for his sermons.[29] Although the story of Lucian and Gedula would probably have been too long, even in his pared-down version, to be used in a sermon, it seems obvious that it was its moral message that appealed to him. It appears to have been first and foremost the love story, however, that appealed to the scribe of JS 631, who concentrates more on those aspects than on the moral and philosophical ones

---

29. Driscoll, *The Unwashed Children*, pp. 123, 125.

which so dominate Jón's version. The original, one is tempted to think, had an equal measure of both, and so what we have in these two Icelandic texts are two different readings of—two different takes on the same work.

That work, whatever it is, is obviously not a major landmark in world literature. It is, at heart, a romance, and one reminiscent less of the medieval *roman courtois* than of modern romantic fiction of the Mills & Boon variety. Jón seems to want to see it principally as a moral fable. But he also wants it to be a proper story, adhering to the narrative rules of (post-classical) Icelandic fiction. As such, he has had to make certain adjustments, for example the introduction in the very first sentence of the name of Gedula's father, which in 631 comes as a parenthetical remark a couple of hundred words into the story ("so het fader Gedulæ"), and, arguably, the addition of the scene with the highwaymen toward the end—for what's the use of a story with no battles in it? And even as a story can't begin without saying that there was a certain man living in a certain country who had a son, or daughter, named X, so too must any story end, as Jón ends his, with the phrase "og hefur þetta æfintýri svo hier med enda" (and so ends this story).

Bibliography

Björn Sigfússon, ed. *Ljósvetninga saga*. Íslenzk fornrit 10. Reykjavík: Hið íslenzka fornritafélag, 1940.

The Book of Saints: A Dictionary of Servants of God Canonized by the Catholic Church, 4th ed. London: MacMillan, 1947.

Bruun, Chr. V., and Lauritz Nielsen, ed. *Bibliotheca Danica: Systematisk fortegnelse over den danske litteratur fra 1482 til 1830*. 5 vols. Copenhagen: Rosenkilde & Bagger, 1961–63.

The Catholic Encyclopedia. http://www.newadvent.org.

Chadwick, Henry. *Priscillian of Avila: The Occult and the Charismatic in the Early Church*. Oxford: Clarendon Press, 1976.

Driscoll, Matthew James. *The Unwashed Children of Eve: The Production, Dissemination and Reception of Popular Literature in Post-Reformation Iceland*. London: Hisarlik Press, 1997.

———, ed. *Fjórar sögur frá hendi Jóns Oddssonar Hjaltalín*. Reykjavík: Stofnun Árna Magnússonar, 2006.

Kalinke, Marianne. *Bridal-Quest Romance in Medieval Iceland*. Islandica 46. Ithaca and London: Cornell University Press, 1990.

Kjartan G. Ottósson. *Íslensk málhreinsun: Sögulegt yfirlit*. Reykjavík: Íslensk málnefnd, 1990.

Mackrell, J.Q.C. *The Attack on 'Feudalism' in 18th-century France*. London: Routledge, 1973.
Ordbog over det danske Sprog. Ed. Verner Dahlerup. 28 vols. Copenhagen: Gyldendal, 1919–1956.
Páll Eggert Ólason, et al. *Skrá um handritasöfn Landsbókasafnsins*. 3 vols. Reykjavík: Gutenberg and Félagsprentsmiðjan, 1918–96.
Scholem, Gershom. *The Mystical Shape of the Godhead: Basic Concepts in the Kabbalah*. Trans. Joachim Neugroschel. New York: Schocken Books, 1991.

On the Transmission of the Old Norse-Icelandic Legend of Saints Faith, Hope, and Charity

KIRSTEN WOLF

I

The *Martyrologium Romanum* names on 1 August "passio sanctarum virginum Fidei, Spei et Charitatis, quae sub Hadriano principe martyrii coronam adeptae sunt" and, on 30 September, "[i]bidem sanctae Sophiae viduae, matris sanctarum virginum Fidei, Spei et Charitatis."[1] Although no other medieval document testifies to the existence of the three sisters, Faith, Hope, and Charity, and their mother Sophia/Sapientia (Wisdom), a considerable amount of legendary lore has gathered around this family. According to the legend, the widowed Sophia arrived in Rome with her three daughters aged twelve, ten, and nine. She converted many women to Christianity, and for this reason she and her daughters were charged before Emperor Hadrian. The beauty of the three young girls so charmed him, that he offered to marry them to powerful nobles if they agreed to sacrifice to his gods. The girls scorned him, and so he imprisoned and tormented them. Faith was punished, first by being beaten by soldiers, but she remained unharmed. Secondly, he ordered that her breasts be torn off, but out of them flowed milk and not blood. The witnesses cried out against the emperor's injustice, and yet the young girl rejoiced and insulted the emperor. In his anger, the emperor then ordered her to be thrown on a red-hot gridiron and put in a frying pan full of

---

1. *Martyrologium Romanum*, in *Propylaeum ad Acta Sanctorum Decembris*, ed. Hippolyte Delehaye et al. (Brussels: Société des Bollandistes, 1940).

oil, but neither of these measures succeeded in wounding the girl in any way. Finally, he commanded that she be beheaded. Her sister Hope was then summoned but could not be persuaded to abandon her faith either. Accordingly, the emperor first had her beaten with ropes and then thrown into a fiery furnace, but she remained unharmed. Thirdly, he had her placed in a cauldron full of boiling pitch, but the cauldron exploded, and drops from it cremated those who tormented her. Finally, she was killed by the sword. Charity, the third daughter, was encouraged by her mother to follow the examples of her sisters, and she, too, refused to yield to Hadrian's blandishments. In his wrath, the emperor ordered her to be stretched on the rack, but to no avail. Then he had her thrown into a fiery furnace, but flames from it leapt out and killed many spectators while Charity herself walked unscathed in the midst of the fire. Realizing that he had no more options, the frustrated emperor commanded that she be beheaded. Sophia buried the remains of her daughters, and while praying over their bodies she died peacefully at their grave, where she too was interred. As for Hadrian, his body rotted, and he wasted away to death.

No one disputes the existence and martyrdom of the family, but it has so far been impossible to identify them with any certainty. It is generally believed that they were either a family whose members had the Greek names Pistis, Elpis, and Agape, and who were interred on the Aurelian Way, or a family with the Latin names Fides, Spes, and Caritas, and who were buried in the cemetery of Saint Callistus on the Appian Way.[2] The cult of Saints Faith, Hope, and Charity, which did not exist before the sixth century, never became particularly strong and certainly not as widespread as the cult of such virgin saints as Agatha, Agnes, Barbara, Catherine of Alexandria, Cecilia, Lucy, and Margaret of Antioch. Their legend, on the other hand, appears to have enjoyed much popularity. It was translated into several vernacular languages; converted into a play by Hrotswitha, a tenth-century Benedictine nun of Gandersheim in Saxony; and in the thirteenth century it received "canonization," so to speak, by its inclusion in Jacobus de Voragine's (ca. 1230–1298) *Legenda Aurea* compiled between 1252 and 1260.

---

2. Here and in the following, I rely on E. Day, "Faith, Hope, and Charity, SS," in *New Catholic Encyclopedia* 5, 2nd ed. (Detroit: Gale, 2003), pp. 608–9.

II

In Iceland, the situation with regard to the cult and legend of Saints Faith, Hope, and Charity hardly differs from that in the rest of the Eastern and Western worlds in that while there is little or no evidence of a cult of the three sisters and their mother, their legend seems to have been popular, for it is extant in no fewer than four manuscripts.[3] Since there were relics of Saints Faith, Hope, and Charity at the cloister at Eschau, south of Strasbourg, Margaret Cormack speculates that their legend would be likely to be included in hagiographic manuscripts from the Rhineland.[4]

The Old Norse-Icelandic legend of Saints Faith, Hope, and Charity is preserved in full only in AM 235 fol., dated to around 1400. The first four leaves, containing fragments of Saints Hallvard, John the Baptist, Sebastian, and Agnes, are, according to C. R. Unger and Kr. Kålund, from another manuscript.[5] The remaining 64 leaves form a considerable part of what must once have been a comprehensive legendary, which, from the appearance of the manuscript, was heavily used. Arranged according to the liturgical or possibly the calendar year, the leaves contain *Maríu saga egipzku, Magnúss saga Eyjajarls, Jóns saga helga, Pétrs saga postula, Margrétar saga, Mǫrtu saga ok Maríu Magðalenu, Ólafs saga helga, Fídesar saga, Spesar ok Karítasar, Lárentíuss saga erkidjákns, Saga várrar frúar, Ágústínuss saga, Máritíuss saga, Díónýsíuss saga, Flagellatio crucis, Theódórs saga, Marteins saga biskups,* and *Cecilíu saga.* The beginning of *Maríu saga egipzku* and the end of *Cecilíu saga* are missing, and between *Jóns saga helga* and *Pétrs saga postula* there is a lacuna. The

---

3. Margaret Cormack, *The Saints in Iceland: Their Veneration from the Conversion to 1400,* Subsidia Hagiographica 78 (Brussels: Société des Bollandistes, 1994) argues that "there is a good correlation between the saints who are subjects of sagas and those known from other ecclesiastical sources" and notes that "[a]ll but four of the extant saints' sagas correspond to feasts found in the majority of Icelandic calendars" (p. 37). The four exceptions are the legends of the 40 Armenian martyrs, Brendan, Erasmus, and Faith, Hope, and Charity, and Cormack draws attention to the fact that all of them seem to have been well known in Germany.
4. Cormack, *The Saints in Iceland,* p. 38.
5. C. R. Unger, ed., *Heilagra manna søgur: Fortællinger og legender om hellige mænd og kvinder,* 2 vols. (Christiania [Oslo]: Bentzen, 1877), vol. 1, p. vi; Kr. Kålund, *Katalog over den arnamagnæanske håndskriftsamling,* 2 vols. (Copenhagen: Gyldendal, 1889–94), vol. 1, p. 196.

beginning must have contained legends of saints from the first part of the liturgical or calendar year, such as Saints Sebastian (20 January) and Agnes (21 January), who, interestingly, are found on fols. 3–4 of AM 235 fol.[6] The end may have contained legends of saints such as Catherine of Alexandria (25 November), Barbara (4 December), or Lucy (13 December). In the lacuna between Bishop Jón and the apostle Peter, Hallvard (14 May) and John the Baptist (24 June), who are found on fols. 1–2 of AM 235 fol., may have had their place.[7] From marginalia and from notes by Árni Magnússon, it appears that the volume belonged to Skálholt in the sixteenth and seventeenth centuries, though, as noted above, the present first four leaves were obtained from elsewhere. The codex may have been in Skálholt in the first place, but we cannot be certain that it was.

Stock. Perg. 2 fol., which has been dated by Peter Foote to the period ca. 1425–1445, preserves only the latter half of the legend of Saints Faith, Hope, and Charity.[8] The codex now consists of 86 leaves, but is believed to have originally contained 110 or 112. It contains 26 texts, whole or fragmentary, making it the largest collection of saints' lives preserved from medieval Iceland. The legends included are those of Saints Thomas, Martin of Tours, Nicholas, Ambrose, Dionysius, Silvester, Gregory, Augustine, Blase, Stephen the Deacon, Laurence of Rome, Vincent the Deacon, Benedict, Paul the Hermit, Maurus, Mary of Egypt, Martha and Mary Magdalen, Catherine of Alexandria, Barbara, Lucy, Cecilia, Agatha, Agnes, Faith, Hope, and Charity, Flagellatio crucis, and Maurice. The principle of composition is that of hierarchization, and the model seems to be the qualitative ranking of saints of, for example, the litany for Holy Saturday and the *Missale Romanum*.

In AM 233a fol., which has been dated to the third quarter of the fourteenth century, the latter half of the legend of Saints Faith, Hope, and Charity is missing. In its complete state, the codex must have been large and impressive. Only 29 leaves have been preserved, and they contain *Jóns saga baptista, Maríu saga*,[9] *Fídesar saga, Spesar ok*

---

6. Birte Carlé, *Jomfru-fortællingen: Et bidrag til genrehistorien* (Odense: Odense Universitetsforlag, 1985), p. 38.

7. Carlé, *Jomfru-fortællingen*, p. 38.

8. Peter Foote, *Lives of Saints. Perg. fol. nr. 2 in the Royal Library, Stockholm*, Early Icelandic Manuscripts in Facsimile 4 (Copenhagen: Rosenkilde and Bagger, 1962), p. 11.

9. According to Ólafur Halldórsson, *Helgafellsbækur fornar*, Studia Islandica 24 (Reykjavík: Heimspekideild Háskóla Íslands and Menningarsjóður, 1966), p. 1, the last section of this work (fol. 13–14) is from other manuscripts.

Karítasar, Katrínar saga, Mǫrtu saga ok Maríu Magðalenu, Agnesar saga, Agǫtu saga, Margrétar saga, Niðrstigningar saga, and *Inventio crucis*. All the texts are defective with the exception of *Agǫtu saga*, and evidently there are lacunae between *Fídesar saga, Spesar ok Karítasar* and *Katrínar saga*, between *Mǫrtu saga ok Maríu Magðalenu* and *Agnesar saga*, and between *Margrétar saga* and *Niðrstigningar saga*. Ólafur Halldórsson has given weighty arguments that AM 233a was written in the Augustinian monastery at Helgafell (established 1184). Whether it was written for the monastery or for an outside party cannot be ascertained.

In AM 429 12mo, too, the end of the legend of Saints Faith, Hope, and Charity is missing. The codex, which has been dated to ca. 1500, contains the legend of Saint Margaret, a Latin verse in praise of Saints Catherine and Cecilia, the legend of Saint Catherine (fragmentary), a prose and poetic legend of Saint Cecilia, a prose and poetic legend of Saint Dorothy, a Latin verse about and a prayer to Saint Dorothy, the legend of Saint Agnes, the legend of Saint Agatha, the legend of Saint Barbara, and the legend of Saints Faith, Hope, and Charity. Árni Magnússon's note appended to the manuscript, which states that he received it from "Páll á Flókastǫðum," the administrator of the convent land of the convent of Kirkjubær at Síða (founded 1186) from 1681 to 1708 or 1709, makes it reasonable to suggest that the codex was written for the nuns at the convent and used by them. If the dating of the codex to 1500 is correct, it may have been written under the direction of Halldóra Sigvaldadóttir; Halldóra, who was the last abbess of Kirkjubær, was appointed around 1494.[10]

The illustration below gives a rough sketch of which parts of the legend are covered by the four manuscripts:

AM 235 fol. ─────────────────────────────
AM 233 fol.   ──────────
Stock. Perg. 2 fol.   ──────────
AM 429 12mo   ──────────

---

10. Anna Sigurðardóttir, *Allt hafði annan róm áður í páfadóm. Nunnuklaustrin tvö á Íslandi á miðöldum og brot úr kristnisögu* (Reykjavík: Kvennasögusafn Íslands, 1988), p. 63. For a discussion of the codex and its provenance, see my article "Female Scribes at Work? A Consideration of Kirkjubæjarbók (Codex AM 429 12mo)" in *Beatus Vir: Studies in Early English and Norse Manuscripts in Memory of Phillip Pulsiano*, ed. A.N. Doane and

Only AM 235 fol., AM 233 fol., and AM 429 12mo cover the former half of the saga; only AM 235 fol. and Stock. Perg. 2 fol. cover the latter half of the saga. Stock. Perg. 2 fol. and AM 429 12mo share only 4–5 lines of text. And AM 233 fol. and Stock. Perg. 2 fol. do not overlap at all.

In his edition of the legend, Unger (vol 1, pp. 369–376) based the text on AM 233 fol. (called B) as far as it goes (pp. 369–372.15) and noted variant readings from AM 235 fol. (called C) and AM 429 12mo (called D). From where AM 233 fol. ends till Stock. Perg. 2 fol. (called A) begins (pp. 372.15–372.23), the text is based on AM 235 fol. with variant readings from AM 429 12mo. The latter part (pp. 372.23–376) is based on Stock. Perg. 2 fol. with variant readings from AM 235 fol. and AM 429 12mo (as far as it goes). The illustration below shows which three manuscripts cover what sections in Unger's edition:

AM 233 fol.   _____
AM 235 fol.   _____
Stock. Perg. 2 fol.   _____

Unger does not discuss the relationship among the four manuscripts and does not present a stemma, though obviously his A–B–C–D designation implies a hierarchy. Foote, who maintains that the Latin source of the Old Norse-Icelandic legend of Saints Faith, Hope, and Charity was a version of the *passio* presented by *BHL* 2871 (an edition of which is appended),[11] notes on the basis of the (rather selective) variant readings listed in Unger's edition that "the Icelandic text in

---

Kirsten Wolf, Medieval and Renaissance Texts and Studies 319 (Tempe, Arizona: Arizona Center for Medieval and Renaissance Studies, 2006), pp. 265–95.

11. Foote, *Lives of Saints*, p. 28, comments, however, that the incipit is like that given for *BHL* Suppl. 2968b. *BHL* 2871 is represented by two incunables. (1) One appeared in print at Cologne in 1483 as an appendix to another. Its description (from Paderborn) is as follows: Jacobus de Voragine, [*Legenda aurea.*] *Legendae sanctorum per anni circuitum.—Mit Anhang: Historiae plurimorum sanctorum noviter additae.* Daran: Liber, Antonius. Epigramma in laudem urbis Coloniae. (Cologne: Ulrich Zell) 1483. (2) The other is a 1485 Louvain printing, which appears to be a reprint of this 1483 appendix. Its description (from the Paderborn site) is as follows: Jacobus de Voragine. [*Legenda aurea. Teilsausgabe.*] *Historiae plurimorum sanctorum noviter laboriose collecte et prolongate.* Daran: Liber, Antonius. Epigramma in laudem urbis Coloniae. Löwen: Johann de Westfalia (von Paderborn), im Oktober 1485. Here the 1483 text is used.

AM 233a fol. shows now abridgement, now expansion, and variant readings shared by AM 235 fol. and AM 429 12mo or peculiar to one of them are sometimes nearer the Latin." As for the text in Stock. Perg. 2 fol. and AM 235 fol, he argues that it appears to have undergone less revision than that in AM 233a fol. and that readings in Stock. Perg. 2 fol. are generally better than those in AM 235 fol.

On the basis of a comparison of AM 235 fol., Stock. Perg. 2 fol., AM 233a fol., and AM 429 12mo with the Latin original, this article seeks to determine with somewhat more precision the complex relationship among the four manuscripts and to assess Unger's choice of manuscripts for his edition.

III

Stock. Perg. 2 fol. (Unger's A manuscript) can be compared with only AM 235 fol. and AM 429 12mo. A comparison of the texts of the legend in Stock. Perg. 2 fol. and AM 235 fol. shows that the two texts are almost identical. There are very few variant readings, but the ones that can be compared with the Latin original reveal that Stock. Perg. 2 fol. preserves the better readings:

Latin: Filia acquiesce mihi quasi patri (CCCCXLiij[d], 25–26)
Stock. Perg. 2 fol.: heyrdu dottir ok hlyd mer sem fòdur þínvm (85ra31–32)
AM 235 fol.: heyr þu dottir ok hlyd mer fedr þinum (37vb4)

Latin: Et cum intrasset erupit subito flamma de camino et combussit grandem turbam virorum (CCCCXLiiij[b], 19–21)
Stock. Perg. 2 fol.: ok er hvn hafdi j logann gengit. þa springr jsundr allr ofninn ok hleypr siòr gloandi or ofninvm ok yfir mikínn flock manna ok brendi þa alla til bana voveifliga (85va34–37)
AM 235 fol.: ok er hun hafdi i logan gengit. þa springr isvndr ofnin allr ok hlaupa siòr gloandi vr loganum ok yfir mikit folk manna ok brèndi þa alla til bana vofueifliga (38rb6–8)

Latin: Sancta vero deambulabat in igne glorificans et laudans deum (CCCCXLiiij[b], 21–23)

Stock. Perg. 2 fol.: En*n* heilög mær geck j elldín*vm* osaukvt syngiandi *ok* lofandi gud (85va38–39)

AM 235 fol.: en*n* heilög mèr g*eck* ur elldinu*m* osauckut syngíandi o*k* lofandi g*ud* (38rb8–9)

Latin: Qui cum p*r*oximassent ori fornac*is* tres cu*m* ea vider*ent* deam-bula*n*tes (CCCCXLiiij[b], 25–27)

Stock. Perg. 2 fol.: en*n* er þ*eir* gengv ath ofnínv*m* þa sa þeir þria m*enn* ganga m*ed* meyiu*n*ni j loganv*m* (85va41–43)

AM 235 fol.: en*n* er þ*eir* ge*n*gu at elldinu*m* o*k* ofnínu*m* þa sa þ*eir* þria men*n* g*an*ga m*ed* meyiu*n*ni iloganu*m* (38rb11–12).

Since AM 235 fol. cannot be a copy of Stock. Perg. 2 fol., it seems reasonable to assume that AM 235 fol. and Stock. Perg. 2 fol. go back to a common original probably at few or no removes.

The fact that Stock. Perg. 2 fol. and AM 429 12mo (Unger's D manuscript) share only few lines of text, makes it difficult to determine the relationship between the texts of the legends in the two manuscripts. A comparison with the Latin original shows that AM 429 12mo (which is otherwise marred by errors caused by sloppy copying) preserves matter not found in Stock. Perg. 2 fol. (and AM 235 fol.):

Latin: Et exclama*n*s ad d*omi*nu*m* dixit. D*omi*ne Ihesu Chr*ist*e (CCCCXLiij[c], 42–43)

AM 429 12mo: þa m*æ*llti hu*n* *til* guds a þessa lund heyrdu d*r*ottin*n* ih*esus* cr*ist*u*s* (84v12–13)

Stock. Perg. 2 fol.: hun bad *til* g*ud*s o*k* mællti. Heyrdu, drottin*n* mín (85ra1)

AM 235 fol.: hun *til* g*ud*s o*k* mælti. Drottín*n* min*n* (37va12–13)

The addition of "heyrðu" in AM 429 12mo (84v12) suggests a closer affinity with Stock. Perg. 2 fol. than with AM 235 fol. On the other hand, the use of the preposition "á mót" (84v14, as opposed to "í mót") may suggest a closer affinity with AM 235 fol. than with Stock. Perg. 2 fol., though the evidence is only slight.

In the following sentence, AM 429 12mo's "brandreið (ok járn)" seems to be a closer translation of "craticula" than Stock. Perg. 2 fol. and AM 235 fol.'s "járn":

Latin: Horis igitur tribus in craticula transactis cum eam ignis omnino
non maculasset (CCCCXLiij[c], 46–48)

AM 429 12mo: En þriar stundir dags a loganda brandreid ok íarne
ok hafdi elldrínn huergi runít a hana (84v15–17)

Stock. Perg. 2 fol: En þriar stvndir dags var hun æ gloanda járni ok
hafdí hvergí elldr runnit a hana (85ra4–5)

AM 235 fol.: enn þriar stundir dags var hun æ gloanda jarní ok hafdi
huergi elldr runnit æ hana (37va15–16)

There are other examples of AM 429 12mo's having somewhat better readings than AM 235 fol. These include:

Latin: nomine Sophia (CCCCXLiij[a], 16)
AM 429 12mo: Sophía het (81v12–13)
AM 235 fol.: hun het sapientia (36vb19–20)

Latin: Docet enim colendum unum deum et Jhesum filium eius
(CCCCXLiij[a], 25–26)

AM 429 12mo: hun kenir monnum at trua a eínn gud þan er ihesus
heitir (82r1–2)

AM 235 fol.: hvn kennir monnum at trva æ gud þann er ihesus heitir
(36vb26–27)

Latin: Jlle enim in quem spem veram ab infantia posuistis ipse vos
coronabit (CCCCXLiij[b], 15–16)

AM 429 12mo: Sa mun ydr unna er þer laugdud uít ast ok yndi ok
uan fra barnęsku (82v15–16)

AM 235 fol.: Sa man ydr unna sem þer lǫgdud elsku vid allt fra
bernsku (37ra24–25)

Latin: Jmmola magne et sacre Diane. Aspice quam pulcra sit. Vide
quanto decore domina nostra subsistat (CCCCXLiij[c], 13–15)

AM 429 12mo: fęr þu forn míkilli ok heilagri gefíon ok lít huersu
fogr hun er ok huersu faug[r] hasęti hun situr a drotting uor heilog
(84r6–8)

AM 235 fol.: færdu fornir mikilli ok heilagri gefion ok lit huersu fogr
hun er drottíng var heilǫg (37rb26–27)

More often, however, AM 235 fol. has the better readings:

> Latin: Eo tempore mulier quedam nobilis ... cum tribus filiabus suis
> adueniens Romam (CCCCXLiij[a], 15–17)
> AM 235 fol.: A þeire tid kom kona nockr tigin at kyni ok en tignari
> at trv ok godum sidum til roma borgar ... ok þriar dætur hennar
> med henne (36vb18–20)
> AM 429 12mo: en a þeiri tíd kuomu nockurar konur tignar at kyne
> ok en tignare at godum sidum ok at heilagri tru til roma borgar
> ríkís ... ok foru med henne .iíí. dętr henar med henne (81v10–13)

> Latin: exemplo religiose et sobere vite multas ac nobiles mulieres
> conuertit ad fidem veri dei Jhesu Christi (CCCCXLiij[a], 18–20)
> AM 235 fol.: hun feck snvit med fǫgrum dòmum sins lifs ok sidlètis
> mǫrgum gòfgum konum til rettra<r> truar (36vb21–23)
> AM 429 12mo: hun gat snuit med fogro blomi síns sid lętis ok gods
> lifs margum konum gaufugum til heilagrar truar (81v14–15)

> Latin: Post paululum ergo proximius aduocans matrem interrogauit
> (CCCCXLiij[a], 43–44)
> AM 235 fol.: En er hann matti mæla. þa spurdi hann modr þeira
> (37ra3)
> AM 429 12mo: en þegar hann matti męla nockut uit þer męla þa
> spurdí hann (82r14–15)

> Latin: Morantibus autem eis in illa custodia (CCCCXLiij[b], 9–10)
> AM 235 fol.: En medan þèr mædgur voru imyrkua stofnunni
> (37ra18)
> AM 429 12mo: en a medan þer uoru þar (82v10)

> Latin: Saluator noster Jhesus Christus cuius casto eloquio per te
> erudite sumus ipse de celo videns patientiam nostram adornat vos
> et dat ad interrogationem imperatoris responsum (CCCCXLiij[b],
> 24–28)
> AM 235 fol: Gredari vaR ihesus christr man oss styrkia af hans
> hreínu ordi erum ver fyrir þik lærdar. hann siolfr skal mega sío
> oss af himnum med þolinmædi ok hann mun gefa oss gnoga orda
> gnott at svara þessum keisara (37ra30–34)

AM 429 12mo: Grędari uor ih*esus* c*ristus* mu*n* oss styrcía af h*ans* hrei*n*o ordí eru uer lęrd*ar* m*ed* þolin m*e*dí ok þat mu*n* oss gefa noga ordfíme at suara þessu*m* keisara h*ann* síalfr sk*al* oss mega sia or hi*m*num ofa*n* (83r5–9)

As evident from some of the examples above, AM 429 12mo is frequently quite wordy and shows some expansion in comparison with the Latin original and AM 235 fol. This tendency is especially clear in the following two examples:

Latin: Et mater iteru*m* ad eas ait. Agite ut p*ro*mittitis auxiliu*m* nobis ferente do*m*ino ut *et* ego leta de cursu vestro subsequ*atu*r vos (CCCCXLiij[b], 28–32)

AM 235 fol.: Modir þeira suarar. Giorit þer sem þer mælit ok veri s*va* vel at ek mètta m*ed* g*u*ds tra*u*sti koma ept*ir* ydr iuaurn*n* yda*r*ar pislar (37ra34–36)

AM 429 12mo: Mod*ir* þeira s(uarar) gere þ*er sem* þer męlít nu ok óiz eigi ne efíz ok uerít oruggar j g*u*ds traustí er ydr ma*n* alld*r*i bresta ger*a*z s*u*o at ek męttí j g*u*ds augliti ok traustí ept*ir* ydr kom*a* j uaurn yd*a*rra<r> píslar ok kuala (83r9–14)

Latin: Si vero audire co*n*tempseritis iuro p*er* deos me nec etati p*ar*citurum nec g*e*neri nec decori. Sed diuersis vos torme*n*tis excruciatas co*n*suma*m*. *Et* membra vestra p*a*rticulati*m* inscisa canib*us* in escam proicia*m* (CCCCXLiij[b], 40–45)

AM 235 fol.: en*n* ef þér hafn*it* þessu þa sver ek þess v*id* g*u*d min heilaugh at ek sk*al* hu*a*rki hlifa elli ne æsku ok eínungis kyns tign*a*r ne vænleik helldr sk*al* ek ydr t*il* heliar fèra ok kasta hræi ydru vt f*yr*ir dyrr ok hunda (37rb6–10)

AM 429 12mo: en ef þer hafn*i*d ollu þessu þa su*e*r ek þess uít godi*n* mí*n* heilog at ek sk*al* huo*r*tuegía grímr uera elli ok ęsku ok s*u*o kyns tign ok uęnleik ek sk*al* ydr t*il* heliar selía m*ed* ymsum pislu*m* ok saxa hrę ydr f*yr*ir dyr ok hrafn*a* ok hunda (83v4–9)

AM 233 fol. (Unger's B-text), which can be compared with only AM 235 fol. and AM 429 12mo, shares some readings with AM 235 fol. and others with AM 429 12mo, as demonstrated in the following examples:

> Latin: Vnde indignat*us* quida*m* primor*um* vrbis no*mi*ne Antiochus suggestione*m* dedit Adriano ita dice*ns* (CCCCXLiij[a], 20-22)
>
> AM 235 fol.: þa kom t*il* fundar v*i*d keisaran*n* greifi sa e*r* antiochus heit*ir* ok bar vpp vandręđi sin *fyrir* h*o*n*um* ok mælti s*v*a (36vb23-24)
>
> AM 429 12mo: þatan af ko*m* nock*ur* greifi t*il* ro*m*a borg*a*r sa h*e*t antíochus at naf*ní* t*il* fund*ar* u*i*t adrianus ok bar up u*a*ndręđí si*n* ok męllti (81v15-18)
>
> AM 233 fol.: Ok fyrir þ*at* kom eín greifi t*il* romabo*r*g*ar*. sa er antiochus h*e*t t*il* fundar v*i*d adrianu*m*. ok mælti s*v*a (15va16-17)

> Latin: Ingressure *er*go palaciu*m* (CCCCXLiij(a), 39)
>
> AM 235 fol.: En*n* er þèr g*e*ngu in*n* j hollin*n*a (36vb35)
>
> AM 429 12mo: e*n* adr er þ*ę*r uor*u* in*n* leiddar j hollína (82r11-12)
>
> AM 233 fol.: En aðr þær g*e*ngi in*n* i hollina (15va26)

Generally, however, AM 233 fol. shows more of a similarity to AM 429 12mo:

> Latin: nihil loq*ui* potuit (CCCCXLiij(a), 42-43)
>
> AM 235 fol.: h*ann* matti ekki af læta (37ra2)
>
> AM 429 12mo: h*ann* mattí ekki u*i*t þ*ę*r męla (82r14)
>
> AM 233 fol.: h*ann* matti ekki mæla (15va28)

> Latin: Mora*n*tib*us* a*u*tem eis in illa custodia (CCCCXLiij(b), 9-10)
>
> AM 235 fol.: E*n* medan þ*è*r mædgur v*oru* imyrkua stofun*ni* (37ra18)
>
> AM 429 12mo: e*n* a me*d*an þ*ę*r uor*u* þar (82v10)
>
> AM 233 fol.: En meþan þær voru þar (15va42)

A characteristic feature of AM 233 fol. is that it sometimes abridges the text in comparison not only with AM 235 fol. and AM 429 12mo but also the Latin original:

> Latin: Propterea deni*que* vxores nostre here*n*tes illis iam nec ad consortium nec ad cibu*m* nobiscum veniu*n*t (CCCCXLiij[a], 28-31)
>
> AM 235 fol.: fyrir þui suivi*r*dar k*o*nur vor*a*r oss nu ok g*a*nga ept*ir*

hennar fortolum ok vilja eigi koma til rakna med oss ne til borz
eda drykciar ok vilja eigi sia oss (36vb29–31)

AM 429 12mo: fyrir þui suivirda konur uorar oss nu af for tolum
henar ok ganga <í> henne spor ok uilia eíg[i] koma til reck<na>
med oss ne til borz ok eigi til drykíu ok eigi til k[r]asa ok uilia eigi
sía oss um saurgann gard (82r4–7)

AM 233 fol.: ok fyrir hennar kenning ganga fra oss konur varar. ok
gora skilit vid oss bændr sina (15va21–22)

In other instances, AM 233 fol. expands on the Latin original, more so than AM 235 fol. and AM 429 12mo. Especially conspicuous are the amplifications in AM 233 fol., in which reference is made to Norse gods, possibly in an effort to make the text relevant to an Icelandic audience or readership:

Latin: -

AM 235 fol: keisarinn suarar. Sea ma ek giorla at þer munut vera
þrar æ trv yðra ok nenni ek ekki at standa iorda þofi vid konur.
enn þo erum ver eigi skilin at sva bunu (37ra13–16)

AM 429 12mo: G(reifinn) mellti se ek at <þer> munud uera þra
lyndar j tru ydarí ok nenne <ek> eigi at standa j orda þofí uit
konur en skolum traut enn skilín at Suo buno (82v6–8)

AM 233 fol.: Adrianus mælti. þer hafit hrelldan allan róma borgar
lyð. ok konur fra bondum sinum skildar ok sono fra feðrum. en
hafít illyrðt oðin en lastat þór ok balldr en skammat frigg ok freyíu
ok gefion í ordum. ok lastat oll goð uór. ok segít þau onyt. ok eyðit
allri uegsemð þeira ok sieʀ ek giðrla. at þer munit vera þrár æ tru
yðra. ok nenni ek ekki at standa j orða þófui við konur. en uarla
munum ver enn skilín (15va35–40)

Latin: Sacrificate dominatoribus orbis et adopto vos in filias sub
testimonio sacri senatus. (CCCCXLiij[b], 38–40)

AM 235 fol.: blotid drottnum vorum jtarlígum. enn ek skal ydr setia i
enu æstu seti minnar hírðar sva sem detur minar sialfs ok gipta ydr
enum tignuztum aulldungum i minu ʀiki sua sem þer eigid ætt til
(37rb3–6)

AM 429 12mo: blotíd godum ok hlydit drottnum uorum synelegum
ok ítarlegum en ek skal setía ydr j hínu hęsta sęti mínar hallar sem

mínar dętur síalfs ok gípta hínum ríkustum aulldu<n>gum j mínu
ríkí sem þer eigit ętt til (83v1–4)
AM 233 fol.: blotit haleit ok ítarlig goð uór synilig. ok dyrðkit drotna
uara þor ok oðin. skal ek þa uelia yðr hín beztu sæti i minni hirð.
ok gipta yðr hínum tígnuztum hǫfdingium í mínu ríki. sem þer
eigit burði til ok ætt (15vb16–19)

While generally AM 233 fol. seems to be a less faithful rendering of
the Latin original than AM 235 fol. and AM 429 12mo, it should be
noted that on a couple of occasions it preserves the better text:

> Latin: et veni Romam causa filiarum ut eas offeram munus Christo
> (CCCCXLiij(b), 5–7)
> AM 233 fol.: en hingat kom ek til þess at færa dætr minar j forn
> christi (15va34)
> AM 235 fol.: en nu hingat komin fyrir sauk dætra minna. at ek færða
> þær iforn guði almattigum (37ra12–13)
> AM 429 12mo: ok híngat komenn fyrir sakir dętra mínna at fęra þęr j
> forn gudí (82v4–5)

> Latin: Tribus itaque diebus in domo Plaudij exactis (CCCCXLiij(b),
> 32–33)
> AM 233 fol.: En er þær hofðu .iíj. daga j myrkua stofunni uerit ok
> þríar nætr (15vb12–13)
> AM 235 fol.: Enn eptir þria daga (37ra36)
> AM 429 12mo: Eptir þria daga (83r14)

IV

The four manuscripts of the legend of Saints Faith, Hope, and Charity
clearly fall into two groups: (a) a redaction represented by Stock.
Perg. 2 fol., AM 235 fol., and AM 429 12mo; and (2) a redaction
represented by AM 233 fol.

The former redaction presents a fairly faithful rendering of the
Latin original, though some expansion is noticeable. Stock. Perg. 2 fol.
and AM 235 fol. are very closely related. Textually, Stock. Perg. 2 fol.
is superior to AM 235 fol. and so it cannot be a copy of AM 235 fol.
AM 429 12mo, the youngest manuscript, is generally inferior to AM

235 fol., but the fact that on occasion it has better readings than AM 235 fol. reveals that, like Stock. Perg. 2 fol., it is not derived from AM 235 fol. Nor can AM 429 12mo be derived from Stock. Perg. 2 fol., for on one occasion AM 429 12mo preserves matter not found in Stock. Perg. 2 fol. (and AM 235 fol.). The three manuscripts must all go back to a common original, AM 429 12mo possibly at some removes.

The latter redaction is characterized by editorial revisions involving both abridgement and amplification. AM 233 fol., the oldest manuscript, shares characteristics with both AM 235 fol. and AM 429 12mo, but seems closer to the latter than the former. Although in comparison with the Latin original AM 233 fol. is inferior to both AM 235 fol. and AM 429 12mo in that it omits matter preserved in AM 235 fol. and AM 429 12mo, it does on occasion preserve readings closer to the Latin.

While a comparison of the Latin source with Stock. Perg. 2 fol., AM 235 fol., and AM 429 12mo justifies Unger's decision to base the latter part of the legend of Saints Faith, Hope, and Charity on Stock. Perg. 2 fol., a comparison of the Latin source with AM 233 fol., AM 235 fol., and AM 429 12mo does not support his choice of AM 233 fol. as the primary manuscript for the former half of the legend, which should ideally have been based on a conflation of AM 235 fol. and AM 429 12mo.

APPENDIX: BHL 2871[12]

[CCCCXLiij(a)] De sanctis Fide, Spe *et* Caritate vir|⁵ginibus *et* Sophie filiabus.

|⁶ Cvm verbi dei *praedicatio per* totu*m* |⁷ curreret orbe*m* et pietatis docl⁸trina cresce*ns* retraheret |⁹ homi*nes* ab ydolo*rum* cultura *et per* noticia*m* |¹⁰ dei ac baptismi gratia*m* saluare*ntur* inimic*us* |¹¹ *et* corrupto veritatis dyabol*us* no*n* fel¹²rens increme*n*ta fidei *propagari* incital¹³uit a*nim*a*m* Adriani q*ui* tu*nc* Romano*rum* gul¹⁴bernabat imperium ut

---

12. I am much indebted to my colleagues Carole Newlands, John Dillon, and Brian Lush for their help with my edition of this text. Carole Newlands and John Dillon answered several questions, and Brian Lush went over my transcription of the text and made a number of corrections and suggestions.

persecutionem in |¹⁵ Christianam tenderet religionem. Eo tempore |¹⁶ mulier quedam nobilis nomine Sophia |¹⁷ cum tribus filiabus suis adueniens Romam |¹⁸ exemplo religiose et sobere vite multas |¹⁹ ac nobiles mulieres conuertit ad fidem |²⁰ veri dei Jhesu Christi. Vnde indignatus |²¹ quidam primorum vrbis nomine Antiochus |²² suggestionem dedit Adriano ita dicens. |²³ Mulier quedam cum filiabus suis ciuitatem |²⁴ ingressa separauit a nobis matrimol²⁵nia nostra. Docet enim colendum unum |²⁶ deum et Jhesum filium eius nec alter in Christi |²⁷ cultu quisque posse proficere nisi et coniugio |²⁸ et delicijs abstinucit. Propterea del²⁹nique vxores nostre herentes illis iam |³⁰ nec ad consortium nec ad cibum nobiscum |³¹ veniunt. Tunc imperator Adrianus iral³²tus iussit euocari per protectores muliel³³rem et filias eius et introduci in palacium. |³⁴ Erant enim puelle speciose valde et in dil³⁵uinis scripturis erudite. Nam legis et |³⁶ prophetarum et apostolorum scripta memorie |³⁷ commendauerant. Que pudice et honeste |³⁸ quod dedicerant ostendebant pariter et ornal³⁹bant. Ingressure ergo palacium pectus ac |⁴⁰ fontem crucis signaculo munierunt. Et |⁴¹ cum eas vidisset Adrianus stupens |⁴² ad pulchritudinem earum nihil loqui pol⁴³tuit. Post paululum ergo proximius aduol⁴⁴cans matrem interrogauit. Vnde esset vel |⁴⁵ cuius dignitatis. Et additit dicens. Dil⁴⁶scordare sibi fecisti Romanorum ciuital⁴⁷tem separando coniugia et deorum qui orbem |⁴⁸ fabricauerunt abiurando culturam. At tal⁴⁹men nomen tuum edicito. Jlla respondit. [CCCCXLiij(b)] Christiana sum. Adrianus dixit. Nomen |² interrogo non fidei cultum. Jlla respondit. |³ Quod primum et nobile enim Christianum nomen |⁴ est mihi. Secundum carnem vero vocor Sol⁵phia nobilissima Ytalorum genita et |⁶ veni Romam causa filiarum ut eas offeram |⁷ munus Christo. Tunc Adrianus iussit eam cul⁸stodiri interim cum filiabus suis in domo |⁹ Plaudij senatoris. Morantibus autem eis in |¹⁰ illa custodia hortabatur filias mater |¹¹ ad contemptum vite praesentis et ad tolleranl¹²tiam passionum pro Christo dicens eis. Filiole |¹³ mee dominis literis erudite estis; custol¹⁴dite in tempore tribulationis quod didicistis. |¹⁵ Jlle enim in quem spem veram ab infanl¹⁶tia posuistis ipse vos coronabit m[0000] |¹⁷ matri vestre et num prouidebitis gaudium |¹⁸ et ad penas ornabitis vterum meum si fidem |¹⁹ Christi per confessionem piam et tormenta dura |²⁰ seruaueritis. Ad quam filie respondentes |²¹ dicebant. Secura esto domina nostra mater |²² permitte nos ad tribunal imperatoris |²³ istius terreni. Et cognosces fortitudinem |²⁴ confessionis et certaminis nostri Saluator |²⁵ noster

Jhesus Christus cuius casto eloquio per |²⁶ te erudite sumus ipse de celo videns pa|²⁷tientiam nostram adornat vos et dat ad in|²⁸terrogationem imperatoris responsum. Et |²⁹ mater iterum ad eas ait. Agite ut pro|³⁰mittitis auxilium nobis ferente domino |³¹ ut et ego leta de cursu vestro subsequatur |³² vos. Tribus itaque diebus in domo Plau|³³dij exactis iussit imperator adduci eas. |³⁴ Cumque ducerentur puelle subsequebatur mater |³⁵ vt vero ingresse sunt palacium ait ad |³⁶ eas Adrianus. O infantule. Audite me |³⁷ et miserimini etati vestre et senectuti ma|³⁸tris. Sacrificate dominatoribus orbis et |³⁹ adopto vos in filias sub testimonio |⁴⁰ sacri senatus. Si vero audire contempl|⁴¹seritis iuro per deos me nec etati parci|⁴²turum nec generi nec decori. Sed diuersis |⁴³ vos tormentis excruciatas consumam. Et |⁴⁴ membra vestra particulatim inscisa canibus |⁴⁵ in escam proiciam. Ad hec beatae adolescen|⁴⁶tule quasi ex vno ore dixerent. Nobis o |⁴⁷ imperator nec promissiones tue cordi sunt |⁴⁸ nec comminationes terrori. Nos habemus |⁴⁹ patrem qui nos adoptauit ad eternam he[CCCCXLiij(c)]reditatem cuius et comminationes timemus |² quia eterna in illis tormenta sunt. Deceteror |³ si quae supplicia te habere estimas quae fidem |⁴ nostram valeant vincere admoue et cogl⁵nosces Christianorum victores tuis cruciatibus |⁶ fortiores. Tunc furore repletus Adria|⁷nus vocauit matrem earum et dixit. Secundum |⁸ ordinem etatis edicto nomina puellarum |⁹ Que respondens ait. Prima dicitur Fides an|¹⁰ni vero eius sunt duodecim. Secunda Spes quae |¹¹ est annorum decem. Tercia Caritas an|¹²norum nouem. Tunc imperator aduocans |¹³ Fidem dixit ad eam. Jmmola magne et |¹⁴ sacre Diane. Aspice quam pulcra sit. Vi|¹⁵de quanto decore domina nostra subsistat. Sancta |¹⁶ vero Fides respondit. O insipientia et cecitas. |¹⁷ Dimittis illum quem malorum dicis dominum |¹⁸ qui omnia verbo suo ex nihilo fecit et ado|¹⁹ras ligna et lapides arte *bonis et sculp|²⁰tura decoratos. Audiens sermones huius |²¹ Adrianus iussit eam expolia<r>i et virgis ce|²²di donec se polliceretur Diane sacrifica|²³turam. Duodecim itaque centurionibus in pu|²⁴elle corpore mutatis nullus tactus plage |²⁵ apparebat in corpore eius. Ad quam crudeli|²⁶tatem flere ceperant qui praesentes erant et dolen|²⁷tes dicebant. Quid mali fecerunt iste |²⁸ puelle ut tali subiaceant pene. O ma|²⁹lum iudicium. Jniusta sunt praecepta tua o |³⁰ imperator. De loco autem inscisure pro san|³¹guine lac fluebat. Tunc sancta puella dix|³²it

---

*bonis] uncertain

ad regem. Hec sunt ait tote mine tue. |³³ Certe tot centurionibus fatigatis plal³⁴ga in cute mea non comparet. Mammille |³⁵ inscise pro sanguine lac suderunt. Putas |³⁶ scelerate que me istis supplicijs posses |³⁷ separare a deo meo. Quod nunquam omnino obl³⁸tinebis adiuuante me Christo. Et iussit |³⁹ iterum imperator imponi eam super craticulam |⁴⁰ et assari. Jlla autem imposita super craticul⁴¹lam requiescebat super eam quasi natans in tranl⁴²quillo mari non tumultuantibus vndis. Et |⁴³ exclamans ad dominum dixit. Domine Ihesu Christe |⁴⁴ respice super me ancillam tuam ut possim |⁴⁵ resiste tiranno isti et dissoluere temporalem |⁴⁶ eius virtutem. Horis igitur tribus in cratil⁴⁷cula transactis cum eam ignis omnino non |⁴⁸ maculasset iussit illam transferri in sartal⁴⁹ginem et frigi pice cera et bitumine.*Biis | [CCCCXLiiij(d)] quorum ignitis seruescente nimium sartagine |² adolescentula respiciens in celum et inuol³cans omnium nostrorum saluatorem et opificem deum |⁴ et dominum nostrum Ihesum Christum proiecit semet ipl⁵sam in sartaginem. Et sic requiescebat quasi tum |⁶ rore descendente de celo. Cumque nec hoc |⁷ tormento lesa fuisset Adrianus repletus |⁸ ira quia in nullo potue<r>it suadere virgini |⁹ ut immolasset iussit eam gladio percuti. |¹⁰ Quod beata virgo audiens gauisa est et |¹¹ agens gratas Christo et iam matrem precabatur |¹² ut consummationes cursus sui oronibus iuual¹³ret qua possit confessione plena vitam finil¹⁴re. Sorores quibus alloquens ammonebat |¹⁵ ne cruciatibus eius territe Adriani volul¹⁶ptatibus consentirent quo magis eo amplius |¹⁷ vires assumerent quia eam cernerent. Nec |¹⁸ supplicijs superatam. Q[00]nymo ipsam in |¹⁹ tormentis imperatorem vicisse. Post hec oscul²⁰lata matrem et sorores praebuit libens spel²¹culatori ceruicem et ita deciso capite |²² migrauit ex hoc seculo palmam martirij |²³ ferens ad Christum. Exinde Adrianus adl²⁴uocans sequentem matris defuncte sororem |²⁵ blandiebat ei dicens. Filia acquiesce mihi |²⁶ quasi patri et sacrifica sacre Diane ut subl²⁷traharis ab imminentibus penis. Sancta |²⁸ autem puella respondit. Scito imperator que nil²⁹chil proficies inanibus verbis. Soror mea |³⁰ et verbis et exemplo me docuit ut sequar |³¹ mortem eius *filis ei pro bone confessionis tel³²norem. Age quod vis de me quia agnoscas |³³ et carne et mente me illius germanam exisl³⁴tere. Audiens vero Adrianus sermones |³⁵ hos et videns se nihil praeualere

---

*Biis] sic.
*filis] sic.

blanditijs |³⁶ iussit ea*m* expolia*ri et* tondi neruis taul³⁷reis. Et cu*m* dece*m* fuisse*nt* in corp*ore* ei*us* mul³⁸tati ce*n*turiones no*n* potuit a s*an*cto marl³⁹tire obtine*re* co*n*sensu*m*. Mater aute*m* sta*n*s ad |⁴⁰ corp*us* prioris filie orabat dice*n*s. Dom*in*e |⁴¹ Ih*es*u Chr*ist*e. Da tolera*n*tiam *p*aruule ut *et* ipl⁴²sam videa*m* in *con*fessio*n*e integra cursum finil⁴³re sicut *et* priore*m* filia*m*. Et hec *m*atre*m* supl⁴⁴plicit*er* postula*n*te exclamauit adolesce*n*l⁴⁵tula dice*n*s. Dom*in*e d*eu*s me*us* cui milito da |⁴⁶ mihi suffere*n*tiam et victoria*m*. Et co*n*uersa |⁴⁷ ad *im*peratore*m* dicebat. Tyra*n*ne inimice |⁴⁸ veritatis *et* pietatis. Si q*u*od adhuc hal⁴⁹bes torme*n*tum adhibe. Experime*n*to eni*m* [CCCCXLiiij(a)] cognoscas in me dei virtute*m* esse. Jral²tus aute*m* Adrian*us* praecepit eam viuam |³ incendi. Cumq*ue* egrederet*ur* in fornal⁴cem statim flamma extincta est. Jpsa |⁵ v*er*o ibi posita cepit ora*n*s laudare deu*m*. |⁶ Audiens aute*m* voce*m* canta*n*tis Adrial⁷nus iussit ea*m* educi de fornace *et* torquel⁸ri. Cumq*ue* torq*u*eretur de sanctis ei*us* meml⁹bris odor *et* suauissim*us* exiuit *et* hylari |¹⁰ vultu dicebat. Tira*n*ne non sentio pel¹¹nas adiuua*n*te me do*m*ino meo Jh*e*su Chr*ist*o. |¹² Tunc tira*n*nus acrius verbis suis inl¹³flammatus imperauit sibi afferri eneu*m* |¹⁴ *et* mitti in eum pice*m et* adipe*m* et cera*m* et |¹⁵ resina*m* et factu*m* est ita. Cumq*ue* ferue*n*ti |¹⁶ eneo ministri puella*m* lauarent ut ea*m* |¹⁷ ibide*m* mergere*n*t resolutum est eneu*m* |¹⁸ *et* liquo*r et* ferue*n*s excussu*m* incendium exussit |¹⁹ carnifices vsq*ue* ad ossa. Adrian*us* nec |²⁰ tanto miraculo fatigatus iussit ea*m* |²¹ decollari. Jgitur data signa gaude*n*s virl²²go cucurrit ad matre*m* et amplexata*m* |²³ osculata est dice*n*s. Pax tibi mater. |²⁴ Si*m*iliter sororem demulce*n*s osculis rol²⁵gabat ut sine timore accedere*t* ad torl²⁶menta *p*raecipienda q*u*ae exemplo soroum |²⁷ formata nosce*t* no*n* deesse solaciu*m* pro |²⁸ Chr*ist*o patientib*us*. Et inde leuans oculos |²⁹ et manus ad deum dixit. Dom*in*e Jh*es*u |³⁰ suscipe a*n*ima*m* meam q*u*ae in te speraui. |³¹ Et co*n*tinuo *p*ercussa migrauit ad do*m*inum.

|³² Tu*n*c venerabilis mate*r* exclamauit |³³ ad dominu*m* dice*n*s. Dom*in*e d*eu*s ecce iam |³⁴ duas tibi co*n*signaui. Concede mihi |³⁵ ut terciam associes eis. Jpsam etiam pul³⁶ellam videns gaudente*m et* promptam ad |³⁷ martiriu*m* dicebat ad eam. Caritas fil³⁸liola mea eq*u*inimis esto *et* viriliter age |³⁹ quia dominus non deserit sperantes in se. |⁴⁰ Postea Adrian*us* euocans tercia*m* templ⁴¹tabat etia*m* ipsam decipe*re* mollibus verl⁴²bis. Sancta v*er*o et *p*erfecta quasi vera |⁴³ Caritas respondit ei. An ignoras me |⁴⁴ ex eisdem genitorib*us* quib*us* priores |⁴⁵ editam eadem*que* doctrina instructam esse. |⁴⁶ Inferiorem*que* illis me misera*m*

inueniri |⁴⁷ putas quibus sum et genere et educatione |⁴⁸ confidelis. Adrianus auditis Caritatis |⁴⁹ sermonibus magis accensus insania [CCCCXLiiij(b)] iussit eam suspendi et per noua quedam |² argumenta torqueri. Cum parum per mal³chinamenta sua videret se proficere iml⁴perauit eam sic suspensam flagellari. Ad |⁵ quod tormentum cum sancta eleuans ocul⁶los animi ad celum exclamauit dicens. |⁷ Domine Jhesu Christe auxiliare mihi. Et til⁸ranno dixit. Jn uanum laboras. Ego enim |⁹ pro dei amore non sentio cruciatus. Adril¹⁰anus vero turbulenta et terribili voce |¹¹ affatur virginem. Si non vis inquit adol¹²rare deos dic *tum magnae Diana<e> et emitl¹³tam te. Respondit illa. Stulte et insal¹⁴ne quod aduersaris anime mee. Facito quod |¹⁵ vis. Nam hoc a me numquam poterit obtineri. |¹⁶ Ita Adrianus iussit eam in ignem mitti et |¹⁷ cum ipse accessisset ad fornacem et cogeret |¹⁸ ministros ut accederent. Ingressura illa |¹⁹ incendium signauit se in nomine domini. Et cum |²⁰ intrasset erupit subito flamma de camino |²¹ et combussit grandem turbam virorum. Sancta |²² vero deambulabat in igne glorificans et |²³ laudans deum. Tunc Adrianus stupefal²⁴ctus erubuit et praecepit eam de fornace edul²⁵ci per protectores. Qui cum proximassent |²⁶ ori fornacis tres cum ea viderent deambulanl²⁷tes. quorum tamen aspectus sole splendidior erat |²⁸ et territi ad visionem ceciderunt in faciem. Jnl²⁹de recuperato spiritum surgentes humili prece |³⁰ rogabant virginem ut egrederetur. Que |³¹ egressa venit cum protectoribus ad imperatol³²rem. Et ut eam vidit illico iussit occidi. |³³ Audiens sancta dei puella praeceptum regis |³⁴ clamauit ad matrem. Mater memento mei. |³⁵ Et mater ad illam ait. Filiola ora pro me |³⁶ cum sororibus tuis ut et me Christus iubeat |³⁷ ad vos cito venire. Et biis a matre dicl³⁸tis percussa est virgo. Sancta vero Sol³⁹phia mater puellarum collegit corpol⁴⁰ra et condens ea aromatibus imposuit vel⁴¹hiculo et portauit ad octauundecim mil⁴²liarium ab vrbe Roma ibique sepeliuit |⁴³ eas venerabiliter in martirio memoria |⁴⁴ digno. Et reuersa est Romam gratias |⁴⁵ agens deo de exultatione pignorum. |⁴⁶ Post hec abijt ad memoriam filiarum et |⁴⁷ multe cum ea mulieres portantes sil⁴⁸mul aromata ad honorandas reliquil⁴⁹as martirum et cum paenitentibus turbis [CCCCXLiiij(c)] se proiecisset in oratione super sepulchrum fili²arum et cum lacrimis diceret. Filiole accil³pite me ad vos velut sopore pressa quiel⁴uit in pace. Jlle ergo quae cum

---

*tum] possibly tamen

ea vene*ra*nt |⁵ sepelie*ru*nt ea*m* iuxta filias in illo loco |⁶ gaude*n*tes de do*m*ina erga hu*m*anu*m* genu*s* |⁷ electio*n*e. Tyra*nn*us ergo egritudine col⁸arta*tus* est. Na*m* oculi ei*us* excecati sunt |⁹ carnes liq*ue*facte. De ore fleuma in san|¹⁰guine*m* versu*m* vermes excreabat. Ad v||¹¹timu*m* doloris impatie*n*tia vlula*n*s cre|¹²puit medi*us* et dispersa viscea*m* eius vix |¹³ potuerit colligia sepeliri. Finit*ur* mar|¹⁴tiriu*m* s*a*nctaru*m* triu*m* virginu*m* prima die men|¹⁵sis Iulij ad gl*o*riam Chr*is*ti qui regnat cu*m* |¹⁶ pr*ae*terea spi*ri*tu s*a*ncto nu*n*c et semp*er* et pro infinita |¹⁷ secula seculo*rum*. Amen.

Bibliography

Anna Sigurðardóttir. *Allt hafði annan róm áður í páfadóm. Nunnuklaustrin tvö á Íslandi á miðöldum og brot úr kristnisögu*. Reykjavík: Kvennasögusafn Íslands, 1988.

BHL = *Bibliotheca Hagiographica Latina Antiquae et mediae Aetatis*. Subsidia hagiographica 6. Brussels: Société des Bollandistes, 1898–1899; rpt. 1992. *Supplementum*. Subsidia hagiographica 12. Brussels: Société des Bollandistes, 1911.

Carlé, Birte. *Jomfru-fortællingen. Et bidrag til genrehistorien*. Odense: Odense Universitetsforlag, 1985.

Cormack, Margaret. *The Saints in Iceland: Their Veneration from the Conversion to 1400*. Subsidia Hagiographica 78. Brussels: Société des Bollandistes, 1994.

Day, E. "Faith, Hope, and Charity, SS." In *New Catholic Encyclopedia* 5, 2nd. ed. Detroit: Gale, 2003. Pp. 608–9.

Foote, Peter. *Lives of Saints. Perg. fol. nr. 2 in the Royal Library, Stockholm*. Early Icelandic Manuscripts in Facsimile 4. Copenhagen: Rosenkilde and Bagger, 1962.

Kålund, Kr. *Katalog over den arnamagnæanske håndskriftsamling*. 2 vols. Copenhagen: Gyldendal, 1889–1894.

Martyrologium Romanum. In *Propylaeum ad Acta Sanctorum Decembris*. Ed. Hippolyte Delehaye et al. Brussels: Société des Bollandistes, 1940.

Ólafur Halldórsson. *Helgafellsbækur fornar*. Studia Islandica 24. Reykjavík: Heimspekideild Háskóla Íslands og Menningarsjóður, 1966.

Unger, C.R., ed. *Heilagra manna søgur. Fortællinger og legender om hellige mænd og kvinder*. 2 vols. Christiania [Oslo]: Bentzen, 1877.

Wolf, Kirsten. "Female Scribes at Work? A Consideration of Kirkjubæjarbók (Codex AM 429 12mo)." In *Beatus Vir: Studies in Early English and Norse Manuscript in Memory of Phillip Pulsiano*. Ed. A.N. Doane and Kirsten Wolf. Medieval and Renaissance Texts and Studies 319. Tempe, Arizona: Arizona Center for Medieval and Renaissance Studies, 2006. Pp. 265–95.

Arctic Garden of Delights:

The Purpose of the Book of Reynistaður

SVANHILDUR ÓSKARSDÓTTIR

In the late fourteenth century, a curious book was put together in Skagafjörður, Northern Iceland. It was written by a group of scribes, and they rummaged, it seems, through a fair part of the literature available to them in their mother-tongue, copied, excerpted, stitched passages together, and re-organized them. After the initial efforts of these scribes, others added supplementary information on slips that were inserted into the manuscript.[1] The book, therefore, much resembles a "work in progress" and does not have the look of a finished product, as is witnessed by its extraordinary codicological make-up: It consists now of 43 full-sized quarto-leaves, in addition to the inserted slips. The first 31 leaves form two large gatherings within which smaller, irregular gatherings are found. The last part of the manuscript has suffered some damage, leaving five lacunae and making the original collation of leaves difficult to ascertain. The book had begun to disintegrate when Árni Magnússon got hold of it around 1700, for he obtained the best part of it from Skálholt, but additional bifolia came to him from the farm of Gaulverjabær, and one bifolium was later discovered in a different manuscript. The codex from Skagafjörður now bears the shelfmark AM 764 4to in the

---

1. On the working methods of the scribes, see Svanhildur Óskarsdóttir, "Genbrug i Skagafjörður: Arbejdsmetoder hos skrivere i klostret på Reynistaður," in *Reykholt som makt- og lærdomssenter i den islandske og nordiske kontekst*, ed. Else Mundal (Reykholt: Snorrastofa, 2006), pp. 141–53.

Arnamagnæan Collection and is among the manuscripts that remained in Copenhagen after the division of the collection between Iceland and Denmark.

Scholars were long puzzled, if not irritated, by AM 764 4to, and this was due not only to its bizarre physical make-up, but also to its contents, which seemed to be a haphazard collection of encyclopedic text snippets and excerpts from saints' lives and pseudo-historical works thrown together for no apparent reason. But a close study of the contents and composition of the first half of the manuscript has revealed that instead of being a series of disjointed excerpts, it represents an ambitious attempt at compiling a universal history in Icelandic.[2] The book opens with a brief description of the world, and the diverse material that follows is then organized within the framework of *aetates mundi*—the ages of the world—an organizational principle widely used in medieval chronicles. The last age in the Icelandic chronicle is the eighth—which begins after Judgment Day and lasts forever. It does not mark the end of the book, however, for the universal chronicle is followed by more than twenty leaves, containing mainly saints' lives, miracles, and *exempla*. Some of this material is now lost due to the defective status of the manuscript.

Having established that AM 764 4o is not without rhyme or reason—the universal chronicle in the first half of the manuscript shows, on the contrary, an effort on the scribes' part to mould a collection of disparate sources into a structured whole—a natural next step in the inquiry might be to focus on the uses of the book and its intended audience. The preponderance of religious literature indicates that the book was aimed at clerics or cloistered people, rather than laymen, and the numerous sources on which the scribes drew suggest that the manuscript was conceived within an ecclesiastical establishment of some sort where the scribes had access to a considerable library.[3] Paleographic and orthographic analysis has revealed that AM 764 4to belongs to a group of manuscripts associated with the family of Akrar in Blönduhlíð, which had connections to the Benedictine

---

2. Svanhildur Óskarsdóttir, "Universal History in Fourteenth-century Iceland. Studies in AM 764 4to," Ph. D. diss. University of London, 2000.

3. For an overview of the sources used for the compilation of the universal chronicle, see Svanhildur Óskarsdóttir, "Genbrug í Skagafjörður," pp. 145–8.

nunnery at Reynistaður. The convent has therefore been seen as the likely home of a scribal school, which must have produced a considerable number of manuscripts; scholars have been able to assign fifteen extant manuscripts or fragments to members of the school, most of them lawbooks or books of religious texts.[4] As usual, one has to take into account that for each manuscript preserved, several have been lost. Scribes working at Reynistaður would naturally have had access to books owned by the convent, and the episcopal library at Hólar, as well as the monastic libraries of Þingeyrar and Möðruvellir, were not far away. The oldest surviving inventory for Reynistaður was done in 1525. It lists around 35 books, and among them are works which were used as sources for AM 764 4to, that is, *Vitae patrum, Nikulás saga, Martinus saga, Guðmundar saga biskups* and miracles of the Blessed Virgin Mary.[5]

Reynistaður therefore seems to be the place where AM 764 4to was written, and I will from now on refer to the manuscript as the Book of Reynistaður, Reynistaðarbók. But was the nunnery also the place for which the book was intended? Or was it made to order, as one suspects was the case with the three exemplars of the Life of Saint Peter attributed to the same group of scribes? The latter does not seem particularly likely, given the rough and ready physical appearance of the book. At least one of the hands involved in the writing seems to be that of an untrained individual, and the overall impression is of a work in progress, even a draft, rather than a book intended for the market. One might still, of course, suggest that Reynistaðarbók was a prototype for a book that could have been commissioned, but it seems more natural to look for the inception of the work closer to the scribes' home. The manuscript represents a much edited selection of texts. This selection is unique, it seems, not least in the way it endeavors to keep women in focus. In what follows, my aim is to bring

---

4. Peter Foote, ed., *A Saga of St Peter the Apostle. Perg. 4:o nr 19 in The Royal Library, Stockholm*, Early Icelandic Manuscripts in Facsimile 19 (Copenhagen: Rosenkilde and Bagger 1990), pp. 11–65; Stefán Karlsson, "Ritun Reykjarfjarðarbókar. Excursus: Bókagerð bænda," *Opuscula* 4, Bibliotheca Arnamagnæana 30 (Copenhagen: Munksgaard, 1970), pp. 120–40; Ólafur Halldórsson, "Úr sögu skinnbóka," *Skírnir* 137 (1963), pp. 83–105.

5. *DI* IX, pp. 320–322. On the history of the nunnery, see Anna Sigurðardóttir, *Allt hafði annan róm áður í páfadóm: Nunnuklaustrin tvö á Íslandi á miðöldum og brot úr kristnisögu*, (Reykjavík: Kvennasögusafn Íslands, 1988), pp. 85–179.

out the most significant evidence of this focus (it is not possible, in a short article, to treat all the material in the manuscript adequately), and subsequently to discuss the possible uses for which the book may have been intended.

Women in the Old Testament

Let us begin with the first half of the manuscript, the universal chronicle. It is not easy to give a simple overview of the diverse material on which the scribes drew to sketch the history of mankind from the Creation till Judgment Day. The *aetates* scheme divides this linear history into eight parts: the first age begins with Adam, the second with Noah, the third with Abraham, the fourth with Moses, the fifth with King David, the sixth with the Incarnation. The seventh age concerns the indefinite period that elapses between the death of each individual and the Last Judgment. After a description of the coming of Antichrist and Judgment Day, the chronicle ends with a passage on the eternal bliss of the righteous in heaven.

This framework belongs to a long tradition which can be traced back to Saint Augustine and even beyond.[6] Icelanders will have encountered accounts of the *aetates mundi* in the works of Bede, Isidore, and Honorius, and the twelfth-century *Veraldar saga* is an early example of such a work written in the vernacular.[7] A universal history written into the frame of *aetates mundi* is above all the history of salvation, an illustration of the progress of mankind from the Fall to Redemption. Such an illustration inevitably draws on the examples of individuals—good as well as bad—in order to show God's guiding hand at work. Even though the outline of such a narrative is given, and the form prescribed, there is nevertheless room for variation in

---

6. For an overview of universal histories, see Michael I. Allen, "Universal History 300–1000: Origins and Western Developments," in *Historiography in the Middle Ages*, ed. Deborah Mauskopf Deliyannis, (Leiden: Brill 2003), pp. 17–42, and Anna-Dorothee v. den Brincken, *Studien zur lateinischen Weltchronistik bis in das Zeitalter Ottos von Freising* (Düsseldorf: Michael Triltsch, 1957). On *aetates*-schemes, see Roderich Schmidt, "Aetates mundi: Die Weltalter als Gliederungsprinzip der Geschichte," *Zeitschrift für Kirchengeschichte* 67 (1955-6), pp. 288–317.

7. On the development of the genre in Iceland, see Svanhildur Óskarsdóttir, "Um aldir alda: Veraldarsögur miðalda og íslenskar aldartölur," *Ritið* 2005 no. 3, pp. 111–33.

the way the message is conveyed, not least when choosing exemplary characters and anecdotes.

In Reynistaðarbók, the Old Testament provides the backbone for the narrative of the first four ages of the world and well into the fifth. The method used by the scribes is to cull narrative passages from the Bible and link them with genealogies to keep the chronological thread. The line of history is thus maintained through references to a chronology based on counting the generations from Adam and on calculations of the number of years within each age of the world.

The main characteristic of the Reynistaðarbók chronicle is brevity—the scribes do not seem to have room for many anecdotes, and those they include are usually drastically shortened—sometimes the stories are not really told, but merely alluded to. The information on Job may serve as an example:

> Sonarson Esau var Job er mjǫk var freistaðr. *Ymago mundi* segir at hann væri síðan konungr þrjátigi ára. Hann átti sjau sonu ok þrjár dætur, sjau þúsundir sauða ok þrjár þúsundir úlbalda, fjórar þúsundir yxna ok svá mǫrg asna. Þetta var hans eign. (3r$^{27-29}$)[8]

Job is here merely a link in the genealogical chain, and his loss and suffering are not mentioned; it is only said that he was "severely tested." Given these editorial constraints, it is instructive to see what information the scribes chose to retain. It comes as no surprise that they included key passages on Adam and Eve, Noah and the Flood, Abraham, Moses, and David, since these characters or events each signal the beginning of a new *aetas*. In the hexaemeron narrative in the first age, the text is also amplified with a considerable amount of encyclopedic material. Other "standard" narratives, such as the story of Cain and Abel, the building of the tower of Babel, and Jacob's wrestling with the angel are also included. But when one reads these sparse accounts, it is striking how conscious the scribes seem to be of

---

8. In the references to the manuscript I have normalized the orthography. "The grandson of Esau was Job, who was severely tested. *Imago mundi* says he was subsequently king for thirty years. He had seven sons and three daughters, seven thousand sheep and three thousand camels, four thousand cattle and an equal number of asses. That was his property." Cf. *Imago mundi* III.8.

keeping women in the picture. Even though the genealogies are traced through the male line, the scribes usually take care to mention wives, sisters, or daughters of the main Old Testament male characters. This, for instance, is the information on the people in the Ark:

> Þá var Nói sex hundruð vetra er hann gekk í ǫrkina. Kona hans hét Poarpa. Þrír synir hans, Kam, Sem, Jafed, gengu í ǫrkina. Kona Kams hét Katafloa, kona Sem Parphia, kona Jafed Fliva (2v$^{25-27}$).[9]

Later we learn of Sarah, Abraham's wife, Cetora his mistress, and Hagar the servant, who bore Ishmael. The fate of Lot's wife is recounted, we hear of Rebecca, the wife of Isaac, and her giving birth to the twins Esau and Jacob. It is mentioned that Jacob had as wives two sisters, Leah and Rachel, and the fact that Rachel was infertile. The third *aetas* ends with a brief mention of Joseph—which includes his wife, Asenek—and an account of Levi's descendants down to Aron and Moses who, it is said, are the sons of Amram and his wife Joabeth.

The one who stands out—Judith

The fourth age begins with the story of Moses, which ends with a list of the Ten Commandments and is followed by a brief account of Joshua. The scribes then explain that after Joshua and until the reign of Saul the Jews were governed by judges. This information is followed by a few stories set during that time: 1) The rape of the young wife in Gabaon, which sparked the war of the tribes of Israel, a tale which is not scriptural but taken from Honorius' *Speculum ecclesiae*; 2) The death of Abimelech, son of Gideon, at the hands of a woman (Idc 9.5, 53); 3) Samson and Delilah (Idc 15.16-18, 16.4-30); 4) The Ark of the Covenant taken by the Philistines and brought to Asedod (I Sm 4.10-11, 5.1-7); 5) Samuel born to Helkana and Anna, who had been barren (I Sam 1.2, 2.1). Four out of these

---

9. "Noah was six hundred years old when he boarded the Ark. His wife was called Poarpha. Three of his sons, Ham, Shem, Japheth, boarded the Ark. Ham's wife was Chatafloa, Shem's wife was Parphia, Japhet's wife was Fliva." On the tradition of the women's names, see Francis Lee Utley, "The One Hundred and Three Names of Noah's Wife," *Speculum* 16 (1941), pp. 426-52.

five stories involve women, and three concern violent intercourse between the sexes.

Those three stories foreshadow the longest story in the whole chronicle, which appears in the fifth age and is exceptional in that the scribes copied it more or less complete, without major abridgment. This is the deuterocanonical Book of Judith, the story of the pious widow in Bethulia who saves her people by killing Holofernes, the leader of the Assyrian army besieging the town. The fact that the story of Judith is included, almost *in extenso*, indicates the importance attached to it by the scribes or those who commissioned the writing of the manuscript.[10] Wherein lies the appeal of this story for the prospective users of the manuscript? There are no glosses accompanying the text in the manuscript nor any kind of explanatory prose, so one has to deduce the meaning it had for its fourteenth-century Icelandic readers/listeners from the context in which it is put within the book and from the exegetical tradition of the medieval church.

Judith became one of the most celebrated biblical figures in the Middle Ages (and she held a strong attraction for artists and sculptors for much longer, as evident from the numerous works of art that depict her, usually in the act of beheading Holofernes). In medieval exegesis, her chastity was emphasized and juxtaposed with the lustfulness of Holofernes as well as with the frailty of Eve. Judith became the embodiment of virtue and the conqueror of evil—her victory over Holofernes symbolizes the victory of the Christian Church over its persecutors, as well as that of virtue over vice. She was seen as an Old Testament prefiguration of the Virgin Mary, and the image based on Genesis 3.15 of the woman crushing the serpent's head was applied to both of them.[11] Judith differs from Mary, however, in an obvious way, in that she is not a virgin; she had been married and borne a son. In the story, much emphasis is put on her chaste conduct in her widowhood, but the sexual attraction she holds for Holofernes is nevertheless the driving force behind the plot. She is described as being the most beautiful of women, and her allure is sanctioned by

---

10. The text is edited in Svanhildur Óskarsdóttir, "The Book of Judith: A Medieval Icelandic Translation," *Gripla* 11 (2000), pp. 79–124.

11. Marina Warner, *Alone of all her sex: The myth and cult of the Virgin Mary*, 2nd ed. (London: Picador, 1985), p. 55; Margarita Stocker, *Judith: Sexual Warrior. Women and Power in Western Culture* (New Haven: Yale University Press, 1998), p. 11.

God, for it will bring about the downfall of the enemy. Her story is therefore the antithesis to the story of Samson and Delilah, briefly touched on in Reynistaðarbók, where Delilah uses the power she wields over Samson to betray him into the hands of his enemies.

Another important aspect of Judith is her relationship with the elders of her own community. She overrides their decisions, sets off on a different course of action in order to get the siege lifted, and the Jewish leaders are unable to stop her; she expressly forbids the elders to monitor her actions and is accompanied on her mission only by her maidservant. The narrative is often reminiscent of a folk-tale, and here it is a tale with a heroine and her helper who free their people, rather than a hero who in the end wins the princess and half the kingdom.[12] The tale has a well-balanced gallery of characters: on one side there are Judith and her maid and the Jewish people under the leadership of Ozias, on the other Holofernes with his eunuch servant and the Assyrian army. In between comes Achior the Assyrian, who speaks up against Holofernes, is thrown out of the Assyrian camp, and ends up on the Jewish side. The narrative has a chiastic structure and a fair amount of suspense, culminating in the decapitation of Holofernes. Everything is retained in the Icelandic version except prayers and lengthy speeches, indicating a preoccupation with the narrative strand of the text.

The Old Testament books of Esther and Judith were natural texts to turn to when seeking models for medieval women, particularly women of authority. In her study of women's involvement in the production of medieval literature, Joan M. Ferrante points out that women sought to, and were encouraged to, identify with renowned female characters of ancient and biblical history:

> What is particularly striking in the letters and in texts commissioned by women is how much women, even those playing male roles in secular government or rising above sex in their religious lives, are

---

12. On narrative technique in the story see Lois Alonso-Schökel, "Narrative Structures in the Book of Judith" in *Protocol of the Eleventh Colloquy of the Center for Hermeneutical Studies in Hellenistic and Modern Culture* (Berkeley: Center for Hermeneutical Studies in Hellenistic and Modern Culture, 1975), pp. 1–20 ; Toni Craven, *Artistry and Faith in the Book of Judith*, Society of Biblical Literature Dissertation Series 70 (Chico CA: Scholars Press, 1983).

aware of themselves as women and identify with powerful or effective, not oppressed, women in history—with Mary as queen of heaven or mother of God; with Judith and Esther, who saved their people; with the queen of Sheba, who traveled far to hear Solomon's wisdom; with the Christian empresses Helena, who found the true cross, Galla Placidia and Pulcheria, who fought heresy, and queen Clothild, who converted her husband and thereby his people. These are women to be reckoned with, women for a woman in power to identify with.[13]

Ferrante mentions that Hrabanus Maurus dedicated his commentaries on Esther and Judith to the empress Judith, the second wife of Charlemagne's son. The extraordinary virtues of the heroines make them "models for men as well as women, but [their] actions make them particularly apt models for the empress," or so Hrabanus thought.[14]

Judith must have been considered an apt model for members of the religious community at Reynistaður—or her story would not occupy such a central place in the manuscript. One imagines she would have appealed to the nuns on several levels. The traditional exegetical interpretation of her as an example of chastity, where her beauty serves no purpose but the one chosen by God, is obvious in the context of Reynistaðarbók where men and women of the past are used to illustrate sinful or virtuous behaviour. But the sheer amount of space devoted to Judith in the book may also indicate that the text was valued as very entertaining reading, and last but not least the nuns may have appreciated a tale of a woman who was, like many of them, not new in the world—a woman who through widowhood had acquired at least a quasi-independent status, and honor to boot, and consequently could take action when she felt the actions of the men fell short, both in the practical terms of lifting the siege of the enemy, and when it came to obeying and honoring God.

---

13. Joan M. Ferrante, *To the Glory of Her Sex. Women's Roles in the Composition of Medieval Texts*, (Bloomington: Indiana University Press, 1997), p. 7. Ferrante's list is of course selective but we might note that Mary, Judith, Helena and the queen of Sheba are all mentioned in Reynistaðarbók. On Old Testament parallels to Judith cf. Sidnie Ann White, "In the Steps of Jael and Deborah: Judith as Heroine," in *"No One Spoke Ill of Her": Essays on Judith*, ed. James C. VanderKam, Society of Biblical Literature. Early Judaism and its Literature 2 (Atlanta: Scholars Press, 1992), pp. 5–16. For a feminist reading of the significance of Judith, see Stocker, *Judith*, e.g., pp. 12–3.

14. Ferrante, *To the Glory*, p. 55.

Women and visions

The story of Judith is preceded and followed by stories of powerful rulers; the chapter immediately before is taken from the Book of Daniel and contains the famous tale of King Belshazzar and the writing on the wall. After Judith, we find accounts of Alexander the Great, the kings of Britain, and Roman emperors. In the sixth age, the chronicle switches again to biblical and hagiographic sources where the Virgin Mary inevitably enters the scene with the annunciation and the birth of Jesus. The incarnation marks the beginning of the sixth age and it is followed by chapters from the apocryphal *Pseudo-Matthew Gospel* (*De infantia salvatoris*) and further sections from the Gospels. It is noteworthy in this material that Mary is present in most of the passages chosen. She and Joseph naturally play a part in the stories from *De infantia salvatoris*, which depict miracles performed by the baby Jesus on the way to Egypt. Of the Gospel stories, those most extensively related in Reynistaðarbók are the one about Jesus twelve years old in the synagogue and the story of the wedding at Cana. In both cases, the narrative involves a dialogue between mother and son, giving Mary a voice. The chronicle gives a brief summary of Jesus' miracles, ending with a remark on Lazarus and his sisters, Mary and Martha. At that point two miracles associated with Martha are inserted into the Gospel material, both taken from *Marthe saga ok Marie Magdalene*. Christ's crucifixion and ascension are treated in a brief manner, but when it comes to the assumption of the Virgin, the scribes copy a condensed version of Elisabeth of Schönau's vision, a text preserved more fully in *Guðmundar saga biskups* by Arngrímr Brandsson. In Reynistaðarbók, the vision is introduced with these words:

> Sjau árum eptir píning Guðs var sæl mær Maria uppnumin, en þaðan á fertuganda degi tók hon holds upprisu, þat er tveimur náttum eptir Mattheusmessu. Var þat langan tíma mjǫk óvíst fyrir alþýðu, en hversu þat varð ljóst skal hér næst greina (16r[14–17])[15]

---

[15]. "Seven years after the passion of God the Blessed Virgin Mary was assumed [in Heaven], and on the fortieth day thereafter she rose [from death] in the flesh, that is two nights after the feast of St Matthew. This occurrence was for a long time unclear to most people, but we will now relate how it was revealed." The text was edited by Ole Widding

It is explained that the Virgin starts to appear to Elisabeth frequently. On one occasion, instructed by her spiritual father, Elisabeth ventures to ask her whether, God willing, she would tell her whether she had been resurrected in spirit only, or in body as well as in spirit. Elisabeth then adds: "Spyr ek fyrir þá sǫk þessa hlutar þína mildi, at mér er sagt at eigi finnisk skrifat í bókum heilagra feðra af þinni uppnumning" (16r[31-32]).[16] The Virgin answers: "Þat sem þú spyrr máttu eigi at sinni vís verða en þó er þat fyrir ætlat at þessi hlutr skal fyrir þik birtaz ok auðsýnaz" (16r[33-34]).[17] The vision proper then follows a little later on. It is important here that Elisabeth is chosen as the authority through which the knowledge of the Assumption is to be revealed. She gains access to a truth which had eluded the Church Fathers.

The rest of the account of the sixth age is largely taken up by a list of popes and emperors based on Martin of Troppau's *Chronicon pontificum et imperatorum*, to which is added information on other prominent leaders of the church. This account is supplemented here and there by short anecdotes or *exempla* linked in some way to the person in question; the longest of these are attached to Jerome and Gregory the Great.

It was common for universal chroniclers to bring the history down to their own time and stop there, in the sixth age. In the frequent recycling of material that is characteristic of the genre, subsequent writers would continue the thread, tracing the narrative further, to their times. But sometimes the authors had one eye on the world beyond, as it were, and gave some indication of events to come. That is the case in Reynistaðarbók. The chronological thread ends with pope Clement (d. 1270), but before leaving the sixth age the scribes relate how it will eventually come to an end with the coming of Antichrist. They then turn to otherworldly matters with the remark that the seventh age is not in this world—it seems to run concurrently with the first six ages:

---

and Hans Bekker-Nielsen, "Elisabeth of Schönau's Visions in an Old Icelandic Manuscript, AM 764, 40," *Opuscula* 2.1, Bibliotheca Arnamagnæana 25.1 (Copenhagen: Munksgaard, 1961), pp. 93–6.

16. "I ask your kindness about this matter, because I am told nothing is found in the writings of holy fathers concerning your assumption."

17. "That which you ask, you are not yet to know, but it is nevertheless intended that it shall be shown and revealed to you [or: through you]."

each man enters the seventh age on his death as his soul begins the waiting for Judgment Day:[18]

> Af sjaunda heimsaldri kunnum vér fátt at segja því at hann er eigi í þessu lífi heldr í ǫðru sem vér gátum í fyrstu ok byrjaz á dauðastundu hvers manns, þá er sál ok líkami gera sinn skilnat svá sem verǫldinni er vel kunnigt at holdit ferr í mold ok verðr at ǫngu en ǫndin ferr ósýniliga úr þessari verǫld ok í þann stað er hverr hefir sér til verkat. (22r[18–21])[19]

To illustrate the different dwelling places of the souls, the scribes present three short visions. The first one tells of a woman who indulged in carnal sins so that her soul was committed to hell upon death. Her daughter is visited in sleep by a handsome man, who leads her through a valley of horror and disgust. There the daughter sees her mother being immersed in a fiery pit and sucked by serpents. The next story is preceded by a comment on the importance of suffering and the ways in which the living can free souls in purgatory from suffering. The story then recounts the vision of a Roman lady, who is met by a deceased woman describing to her the torments of purgatory. In the final *exemplum*, the daughter of a laborer is led in her sleep through the valley of Paradise, where she meets her deceased father.

The tradition of using visions to illustrate the afterlife goes back to Pope Gregory the Great, one of the "fathers of purgatory." When faced with the problem of how to describe the horrors and delights of the other worlds in his *Dialogues*, Gregory resorted to storytelling. He described the purgation of sins (which he believed would happen in the place where they were committed) through a series of *exempla*. This way of conveying the agonies awaiting sinners set the pattern for descriptions of the Otherworld throughout the Middle Ages.[20] The scribes of AM 764 4to follow this tradition, but their choice of stories

---

18. Such a scheme could be modelled on Bede, cf. Beda Venerabilis, *Opera Pars VI. Opera didascalica 2*, ed. Ch. W. Jones, CCSL 123B (Turnholt: Brepols, 1977), pp. 536–7.

19. "We cannot say much about the seventh age of the world, for it is not in this life but in the other life, as we stated previously, and begins at each man's hour of death, when body and soul part, as is universally known: the flesh is laid in earth and perishes, but the spirit leaves this world invisibly and enters the dwelling place which each man has won for himself."

20. Jacques Le Goff, *La naissance du Purgatoire* (Paris: Gallimard, 1981), pp. 124–8.

nevertheless departs from the line taken by Gregory. For whereas Gregory described the Otherworld as seen through the eyes of men, usually monks or clerics, the main characters in the miracles included in AM 764 4to are women. This is in line with the development of visionary literature. Early examples of the genre centered around men as visionaries, but visions experienced by women became gradually more frequent, and from the thirteenth century onwards the majority of visions were attributed to women.[21]

After having thus outlined the cosmology of the Otherworld, the scribes turn again to the sixth age and Judgment Day. The chronicle ends with a passage on the eternal bliss of the righteous in the heavenly Paradise, based, as are the passages on Antichrist and Judgment Day, on a chapter from *Compendium Theologicae Veritatis* by the Dominican Hugo Ripelin of Strasbourg.[22]

The second half—more *exempla*

Thus far we have seen how *exempla* and other narrative passages are used to enliven the rather dry treatment of world history presented in the first half of Reynistaðarbók, as well as to illustrate virtues, vices, reward, and punishment. In the latter half of the manuscript, *exempla* really come into their own, for narratives of that kind are from then on the mainstay of the text. One might say that they develop the theme introduced in the visions of the seventh age, namely that of the relationship between this life and the other, emphasising the importance of virtuous conduct as a guarantee against torments in the afterlife.

The choice of material here may again offer interesting clues about the intended audience of the book. There are several lacunae in this part of the manuscript, as was mentioned above, so it is not possible to assess the make-up of these sections with complete accuracy. It is nevertheless bound to strike any observer that the material is unusual for an Icelandic manuscript, as several of the texts are not found else-

---

21. Peter Dinzelbacher, *Vision und Visionsliteratur im Mittelalter*, Monographien zur Geschichte des Mittelalters 23 (Stuttgart: Hiersemann, 1981), pp. 226–8.

22. Svanhildur Óskarsdóttir, "Dómsdagslýsing í AM 764 4to," *Opuscula* 10, Bibliotheca Arnamagnæana 40 (Copenhagen: Reitzel, 1996), pp. 186–93. On Ripelin in Iceland, see Ian McDougall, "Latin Sources of the Old Icelandic *Speculum Penitentis*," *Opuscula* 10, Bibliotheca Arnamagnæana 40 (Copenhagen: Reitzel, 1996), pp. 136–85.

where (this is also true of the Judith text discussed earlier). These are texts involving Saints Ursula, Sunnifa, Walburga, Cuthbert, Edward the Confessor, Remigius, and Malcus, all saints whose veneration is not widely attested in Iceland.[23] In addition, we find miracles of Mary and Saint Peter and some other short passages. The last five leaves of the manuscript contain texts of a different kind, annals and genealogies, for example, which will have to be left out of the present discussion.[24]

It is regrettable that the material on Saint Sunnifa has been almost entirely lost due to a lacuna in the manuscript; only the last few lines of a miracle attributed to her have been preserved (fol. 35r[1-16]). Immediately before the lacuna, there are six miracles of Saint Walburga (two of them fragmentary), and it is therefore not unreasonable to assume that the manuscript likewise originally contained a group of miracles connected with Sunnifa, the only Scandinavian female saint before the emergence of the Birgitta cultus in the fifteenth century. The legend of Sunnifa and the saints of Selja was included by Oddr Snorrason in his *Óláfs saga Tryggvasonar* but that text has no parallels with the material in Reynistaðarbók. The legend has obvious similarities with the story of Ursula and the eleven thousand maidens which is retold briefly in Reynistaðarbók (fol. 31v[14-24]). That story has, again, links with Elisabeth of Schönau, who provided the source for Reynistaðarbók's account of the assumption of the Virgin. Elisabeth became associated with the legend when she was asked if she could throw light on the confusing remains of the martyrs—and duly responded with an account of a vision she had experienced. The Ursula-text in Reynistaðarbók does not refer to the vision, but the mention of her in the manuscript is a testament to an interest in the female saint, and provides, like Elisabeth's vision of the Assumption earlier, a connection to the body of legends and religious writings associated with religious women in Germany. That connection also manifests itself in the inclusion of

---

23. Margaret Cormack, *The Saints in Iceland: Their Veneration from the Conversion to 1400*, Subsidia Hagiographica 78 (Brussels: Société des Bollandistes, 1994), p. 35.

24. There will not be room for a discussion on the English saints, Edward and Cuthbert, here. For information on that material, see Christine E. Fell, "Anglo-Saxon saints in Old Norse sources and vice versa," in *Proceedings of the Eighth Viking Congress. Århus 24–31 August 1977*, ed. Hans Bekker-Nielsen, Peter Foote and Olaf Olsen (Odense: Odense University Press, 1981), pp. 95–106.

the miracles of Saint Walburga, one of the Anglo-Saxon nuns who played an important part in Boniface's mission to Germany in the eighth century.[25] Walburga accompanied Saint Lioba when she went to become the first abbess at Tauberbischofsheim, and their connection is hinted at towards the end of one of the miracles in Reynistaðarbók: "Ok er pílargrímr sællar Walburge hafði úti svá skrifaðan atburð gerði Liubila abbadís ok allir þeir er heyrðu [...] margfaldar þakkir hæsta Guði ..." (34r[22-24]).[26] Walburga went on to become an abbess at the double monastery of Heidenheim. Schönau was also a double house, and it has been argued that such establishments were the most conducive to women's learning and book-production.[27] It is therefore not unexpected that material selected to inspire religious women should stem, ultimately, from such an environment.

The women saints, then, are presumably included in Reynistaðarbók because they are women, representing the tradition of the female religious to which the Benedictine nuns at Reynistaður belonged. But what are we to think of the inclusion of Saints Remigius and Malcus? They are, on the face of it, difficult to place in any direct context with Icelandic nuns in the fourteenth century—the one bishop in Rheims, the other a monk, presumably in Egypt. These texts need to be viewed in light of their content and taken into consideration alongside other texts in the manuscript.

Remigius saga is not preserved elsewhere, and a direct source has not been found, but according to the *Handlist* the text consists of material ultimately derived from Remigius' *Vita* by Bishop Hincmar of Rheims.[28] The saga naturally follows the pattern for the life of a confessor; we learn of Remigius' birth and youth, his election as bishop, his exemplary conduct and his miracles. Based on what we

---

25. See Kirsten Wolf, "A Fragmentary Excerpt on Saint Walburga in AM 764 4to," *Gripla* 11 (2000), pp. 209-20, where the text is edited.
26. "And when the end of this event, which we have described, had come for the pilgrim of the Blessed Walburga, abbess Lioba and all those who had heard gave [...] multiple thanks to the highest God."
27. Alison I. Beach, *Women as Scribes: Book Production and Monastic Reform in Twelfth-Century Bavaria*, (Cambridge: Cambridge University Press, 2004), e.g. pp. 2-5.
28. Ole Widding, Hans Bekker-Nielsen, and L. K. Schook, "The Lives of the Saints in Old Norse Prose: A Handlist," *Mediaeval Studies* 25 (1963), p. 331. The saga was edited by C. R. Unger in *Heilagra manna søgur. Fortællinger og legender om hellige mænd og kvinder*, 2 vols. (Christiania [Oslo]: Bentzen, 1877), vol. 2, pp. 222-7.

know of the scribes' treatment of sources we may assume that here, as elsewhere, they used but a selection of passages from the material available to them. In the selection from the Life of Remigius, women seem, again, to be favored. This is evident in the description of the circumstances surrounding Remigius' conception and birth, where the reactions and feelings of his mother Cilinia in particular are dwelt on. And in the sparse collection of miracles one in particular stands out on account of its length—a story describing how Remigius cures a girl possessed by an evil spirit. So although we cannot answer the question why Bishop Remigius rather than someone else should be included in this manuscript, his story seems to have been subjected to the same selective editorial policy as we have seen applied to the biblical material in Reynistaðarbók.

The story of Saint Malchus was perhaps more directly relevant to the Reynistaður community since it concerns the wordly temptations that visit those who have chosen to renounce the world and enter a monastery.[29] The young Malchus enters a community of monks, but after several years the thought of his inheritance begins to prey on his mind and he decides to leave the monastery, much against the advice of his abbot. Before he reaches his old home he is taken captive by heathens, together with a woman, and is forced to live with her in a hut and tend to the sheep. Malchus and the woman agree to live together in chastity, thus deceiving their captors. They manage to escape and Malchus returns to his old abbey while the woman enters a nunnery. The fate of Malchus and his unnamed woman friend found resonance with Abelard and Heloise[30] and could have gone down equally well with Icelanders who had taken vows. The story of Malchus is in Reynistaðarbók atttributed to Saint Jerome, as are some of the other stories of hermits included in the manuscript.[31] Several of these cover similar ground as the story of Malchus. One (25r¹⁴–25v²⁵) describes a young man who enters a monastery but is lured by the devil

---

29. C. R. Unger, ed., *Heilagra manna søgur*, vol. 1, pp. 437–46.
30. Abelard, *The Story of Abelard's Adversities. A Translation with Notes of the Historia calamitatum with a preface by Étienne Gilson*, trans. J. T. Muckle (Toronto: Pontifical Institute of Mediaeval Studies, 1964), pp. 73–4. Cf. Ferrante, *To the Glory*, p. 57.
31. These derive from *Verba seniorum*, the popular collection of tales of religious men, printed among other *exempla* in Unger's *Heilagra manna søgur* under the collective heading of *Vitae patrum*.

to return to debauchery. In another (26v¹⁻²⁸), a hermit in the desert is visited by a woman who was hired by his enemies to seduce him. He resists the temptation by holding his fingers over fire throughout the night. Other *exempla* focus more on virtues central to monastic discipline, such as obedience and humility. Among these is the story of the nun (30v⁷–31r³) who feigns idiocy and is bullied by the other sisters, although she takes on everyone's task. Men are the protagonists in most of these stories, but their message can frequently be directed to nuns as well as monks.

Apart from the tales which directly address the circumstances of people who entered religious orders, the majority of the narratives in the latter half of the manuscript concern the fate of the soul after death. This theme is initiated by the visions in the seventh *aetas*, and it is continued here in more *exempla* of the same type as well as in texts of a slightly different origin, such as the debate between body and soul which is found on fol. 30r⁵–30v⁶. That text is best known in the version contained in the Norwegian *Book of Homilies* and the Reynistaðarbók version is much condensed by comparison. It nevertheless retains the core of the initial speech given by the soul, where it (or she) chastises the body for its various sinful inclinations and lack of concern for the consequences of those vices for the soul herself, who now misses Paradise because of the wrongdoings she blames on the body. The body retaliates and complains that he has merely followed where the soul has led, but that part of the debate is almost entirely omitted in Reynistaðarbók. One wonders if it is because of the unfavorable comparison the body draws between the soul and Eve: "Adamr myndi ok eigi syndgask ef eigi væri ormr ok áeggjan konu, svá eggjaðir þú mik."[32]

The ranting of the soul against avarice, envy and gluttony reverberates in a couple of *exempla*, where the conduct of rich men is criticized. One of them is the popular tale of the rich man who died and whose heart was discovered not in his body, but in his treasure chest. Another well-known anecdote describes how a rich man turns his father out of

---

32. "Also, Adam would not have sinned, were it not for the serpent and the incitement of a woman; thus you egged me on." Ole Widding and Hans Bekker-Nielsen, "A Debate of the Body and the Soul in Old Norse Literature," *Mediaeval Studies* 21 (1959), p. 286. I have normalized the orthography.

the house, but is brought to his senses by his young son, who asks him whether that is the way he expects to be treated when he becomes old and grey.[33] Complementing these illustrations of reprehensible conduct are further visionary *exempla*, including a couple that describe the visions of monks, who are shown the fate of fellow religious.

The uses of the book

It has not been possible in this brief survey to take all the material in Reynistaðarbók into account. Nevertheless, I hope to have shown that the tales included in the manuscript could well have served the needs of a religious community of women. But how was it used? It is possible that the book was intended for the communal reading prescribed in the Rule of Saint Benedict. The heterogenous nature of the material used and the somewhat aggressive editorial policy employed in its compilation means, however, that Reynistaðarbók cannot be considered a typical work of that kind. Much of the material included in the universal chronicle in the first half of the manuscript is not well suited to reading at mealtimes; the narrative thread is often sacrificed for the sake of brevity and factual information takes preference over style. Many passages are hardly more than lists of people or events. The catalogue of popes and emperors has already been mentioned, as have genealogies from the Old Testament. One could also point to a section on the apostles and their fate, lists of Church Fathers and their most important works, a catalogue of the names of the Virgin Mary, and lists of the Ten Commandments and the books of the Pentateuch.

One of the characteristics of these lists is the attention given to information concerning the liturgy—and, to a lesser extent, to the odd article of canon law and morsels of church history. There are a lot of such additions to the list of popes. The reader learns, for instance, that Sixtus I introduced the singing of *Sanctus* at every mass, that Anitius I ordered clerics to wear tonsure, and that Socher I ordered nuns to carry a veil. Even in the sparse account of the first four ages of the world, the scribes occasionally see it fit to link biblical events to liturgical feasts in the church calendar, stating, for example, that

---

33. Cf. Frederic C. Tubach, *Index exemplorum. A Handbook of Medieval Religious Tales* (Helsinki: Academia Scientiarum Fennica, 1969), nos. 2499 and 2001, respectively.

primus dies seculi was the day three nights before the feast of Saint Benedict (1v³⁸⁻³⁹) and that Noah stepped off the Ark two nights before the feast of the apostles Philip and James (3r¹). The reader also learns the circumstances of the composition of the Old Testament canticles *Confitebor, Ego dixi, Exultavit cor meum, Cantemus, Domine audivi* and *Audite coeli quae loquor*. According to the *Breviarium Nidrosiense* these were the canticles to be sung at Lauds during weekdays.[34] Later in the manuscript, an account of the killing of the Innocents in the sixth *aetas* is supplemented by this note: "Tǫlu þessara sveina kunnu vér eigi greina, en sú tala er stendr í níunda responsorio er svá heitir: centum xl iiii milia, heyrir víst eigi til tǫlu barnanna heldr er hon sett in Apocalipsi Iohannis fyrir stórmerkis krapt" (14v³⁴⁻³⁷).[35] The "ninth responsorium" refers to the Feast of the Holy Innocents (*ad vesperam*), where the number 140 is given.[36]

This concern for liturgical matters reminds us that knowledge of the liturgy was an important element of monastic education, in particular for pupils who had decided to enter a monastery as novices.[37] The picture of the uses of Reynistaðarbók could have served gradually becomes clearer. What emerges is a manuscript which attempts to cater to the educational needs of cloistered women. Such books became more frequent as the Middle Ages wore on, as new intellectual and devotional currents spread, and as an increasing number of women took the veil, thus providing a milieu for the development of literary genres or types of books specifically suited for this new audience. The *Speculum virginum* is one such work, which is constructed as a dialogue between the young nun Theodora and the priest Peregrinus. The work was probably compiled in the middle of the twelfth century[38] and is preserved

---

34. Hans Buvarp and Baltzer M. Børsum, *Appendix to Breviarium Nidrosiense*, (Oslo: Børsum, 1964), pp. 70–1.

35. "We do not know the number of these boys, but the number which is found in the ninth responsorio, centum xl iiii milia, does not refer to the number of the children. It is written in Apocalipsi Johannis in expression of powerful events."

36. Lilli Gjerløw, ed., *Ordo Nidrosiensis ecclesiae (Orðubók)* (Oslo: Universitetsforlaget, 1968), p. 161.

37. Susan Boynton, "Training for the Liturgy as a Form of Monastic Education" in *Medieval Monastic Education*, ed. George Ferzoco and Carolyn Muessig (London: Leicester University Press, 2000), pp. 7–20. See also, e.g., Ida-Christine Riggert, *Die Lüneburger Frauenklöster* (Hannover: Hahn, 1996), pp. 218–9.

38. Jutta Seyfarth, ed., *Speculum virginum*, CCCM 5 (Turnhout: Brepols, 1990), pp. 32–7.

in over fifty manuscripts, some of which contain the work translated into a vernacular language; there is, for instance, a Swedish translation made in the fifteenth century at the Birgittine house at Vadstena.[39] The discussion between Peregrinus and Theodora revolves around the various aspects of virginity, chastity, and life under a religious rule, and much attention is given to virtues and vices. To illustrate the virtues, women from the history of mankind are presented, among them the Old Testament heroes Judith and Jael.[40] The most important role model for virgins is, however, the Virgin Mary, and she is accordingly given ample room in the book. The *Speculum virginum* also contains a section on the hexaemeron and the six ages of the world, which is intended to show how the spirit gradually conquers over the flesh, how the virtues gain ground as mankind progresses through history. There are obvious parallels here with Reynistaðarbók, but the form of the two works is very different.

Another twelfth-century work designed for women might provide a closer parallel to Reynistaðarbók, although the Icelandic work inevitably pales by the comparison. This is Herrad of Hohenberg's *Hortus deliciarum*, an astonishing encyclopedic compilation, which was destroyed, sadly, in the late nineteenth century and is known to us only in a reconstruction. It was a large and beautifully illuminated book of over 300 leaves, containing among other things narratives from the Old Testament with allegorical interpretations, Gospel narratives with commentary, material from the Acts of the Apostles, excerpts from the chronicle by Frechulf of Lisieux, passages on virtues and vices, texts dealing with the Church and society, eschatological texts, excerpts from Peter Lombardus' *Sententiae*, a list of popes, calendar, and computus.[41]

Like Reynistaðarbók, the *Hortus* is compiled from many sources

---

39. Matthäus Bernards, *Speculum virginum. Geistigkeit und Seelenleben der Frau im Hochmittelalter*, Forschungen zur Volkskunde 36/38 (Cologne: Böhlau, 1955), pp. 6–13.

40. *Speculum virginum*, p. 105. Judith and Jael are praised for their humility as well as their courage, and so are a string of secular women, e.g., Semiramis and Helena, Constantine's mother, both included in Reynistaðarbók, as is Jael.

41. Herrad of Hohenbourg, *Hortus deliciarum*. Reconstruction. Commentary, ed. Rosalie Green et al. (London: Warburg Institute, 1979). For a list of contents, see Commentary, pp. 2–3. For a thorough study of the work, see Fiona J. Griffiths, *The Garden of Delights. Reform and Renaissance for Women in the Twelfth Century* (Philadelphia: University of Pennsylvania Press, 2007).

(Herrad relies heavily on Honorius who is also very present in Reynistaðarbók), and its overarching subject is the history of salvation, or more specifically "the salvation of the Hohenburg canonesses," as Carolyn Muessig puts it.[42] The canonesses are invited "to increase their knowledge and chances of redemption" through the study of the *Hortus,* which included pagan as well as Christian texts, and where chastity was heavily emphasised.[43] Something similar may have been the purpose behind the compilation of Reynistaðarbók. If so, it gives us an important indication of what someone (the abbess perhaps?) thought should form the body of knowledge for a Benedictine nun in Iceland in the late Middle Ages. The miscellaneous nature of the texts in Reynistaðarbók is a fascinating window through which one sees which works were available in Northern Iceland in the late fourteenth century. But the manuscript does more than that: it gives us a rare insight into the formation of nuns in medieval Iceland.

Bibliography

Abelard. *The Story of Abelard's Adversities. A Translation with Notes of the Historia calamitatum with a preface by Étienne Gilson.* Trans. J. T. Muckle. Toronto: Pontifical Institute of Mediaeval Studies, 1964.

Allen, Michael I. "Universal History 300–1000: Origins and Western Developments." In *Historiography in the Middle Ages.* Ed. Deborah Mauskopf Deliyannis. Leiden: Brill, 2003. Pp. 17–42.

Alonso-Schökel, Lois. "Narrative Structures in the Book of Judith." In *Protocol of the Eleventh Colloquy of the Center for Hermeneutical Studies in Hellenistic and Modern Culture.* Berkeley: Center for Hermeneutical Studies in Hellenistic and Modern Culture, 1975. Pp. 1–20.

Anna Sigurðardóttir. *Allt hafði annan róm áður í páfadóm: Nunnuklaustrin tvö á Íslandi á miðöldum og brot úr kristnisögu.* Reykjavík: Kvennasögusafn Íslands, 1988.

Beach, Alison I. *Women as Scribes: Book Production and Monastic Reform in Twelfth-Century Bavaria.* Cambridge: Cambridge University Press, 2004.

Beda Venerabilis. *Opera Pars VI. Opera didascalica 2.* Ed. Ch. W. Jones. CCSL 123B. Turnholt: Brepols, 1977.

Bernards, Matthäus. *Speculum virginum. Geistigkeit und Seelenleben der Frau im Hochmittelalter.* Forschungen zur Volkskunde 36/38. Cologne: Böhlau, 1955.

Boynton, Susan. "Training for the Liturgy as a Form of Monastic Education."

---

42. Carolyn Muessig, "Learning and Mentoring in the Twelfth Century: Hildegard of Bingen and Herrad of Landsberg," in *Medieval Monastic Education,* ed. George Ferzoco and Carolyn Muessig (London: Leicester University Press, 2000), p. 96.

43. Muessig, "Learning and Mentoring," p. 97.

In *Medieval Monastic Education*. Ed. George Ferzoco and Carolyn Muessig. London: Leicester University Press, 2000. Pp. 7–20.
Brincken, Anna-Dorothee v. den. *Studien zur lateinischen Weltchronistik bis in das Zeitalter Ottos von Freising*. Düsseldorf: Michael Triltsch, 1957.
Buvarp, Hans, and Baltzer M. Børsum. *Appendix to Breviarium Nidrosiense*. Oslo: Børsum, 1964.
Cormack, Margaret. *The Saints in Iceland: Their Veneration from the Conversion to 1400*. Subsidia Hagiographica 78. Brussels: Société des Bollandistes, 1994.
Craven, Toni. *Artistry and Faith in the Book of Judith*. Society of Biblical Literature Dissertation Series 70 Chico CA: Scholars Press,1983.
DI = *Diplomatarium Islandicum. Íslenzkt fornbréfasafn sem hefir inni að halda bréf og gjörninga, dóma og máldaga og aðrar skrár, er snerta Ísland eða íslenzka menn*. Copenhagen and Reykjavík: Hið íslenzka bókmenntafélag, 1857-.
Dinzelbacher, Peter. *Vision und Visionsliteratur im Mittelalter*. Monographien zur Geschichte des Mittelalters 23. Stuttgart: Hiersemann, 1981.
Fell, Christine E. "Anglo-Saxon saints in Old Norse sources and vice versa." In *Proceedings of the Eighth Viking Congress. Århus 24–31 August 1977*. Ed. Hans Bekker-Nielsen, Peter Foote, and Olaf Olsen. Odense: Odense University Press, 1981. Pp. 95–106.
Ferrante, Joan M. *To the Glory of Her Sex. Women's Roles in the Composition of Medieval Texts*. Bloomington: Indiana University Press, 1997.
Flint, Valerie I. J., ed. "Honorius Augustodunensis Imago mundi." *Archives d'histoire doctrinale et littéraire du moyage age* 57 (1982): 7–153.
Foote, Peter, ed. *A Saga of St Peter the Apostle. Perg. 4:0 nr 19 in The Royal Library, Stockholm*. Early Icelandic Manuscripts in Facsimile 19. Copenhagen: Rosenkilde and Bagger, 1990.
Gjerløw, Lilli, ed. *Ordo Nidrosiensis ecclesiae (Orðubók)*. Oslo: Universitetsforlaget, 1968.
Griffiths, Fiona J. *The Garden of Delights. Reform and Renaissance for Women in the Twelfth Century*. Philadelphia: University of Pennsylvania Press, 2007.
Herrad of Hohenbourg. *Hortus deliciarum*. Reconstruction. Commentary. Ed. Rosalie Green et al. London: Warburg Institute, 1979.
Le Goff, Jacques. *La naissance du Purgatoire*. Paris: Gallimard, 1981.
McDougall, Ian."Latin Sources of the Old Icelandic *Speculum Penitentis*." *Opuscula* 10, Bibliotheca Arnamagnæana 40 (Copenhagen: Reitzel, 1996). Pp. 136–85.
Muessig, Carolyn. "Learning and Mentoring in the Twelfth Century: Hildegard of Bingen and Herrad of Landsberg." In *Medieval Monastic Education*. Ed. George Ferzoco and Carolyn Muessig. London: Leicester University Press, 2000. Pp. 87–104.
Ólafur Halldórsson. "Úr sögu skinnbóka." *Skírnir* 137 (1963): 83–105.
Riggert, Ida-Christine. *Die Lüneburger Frauenklöster*. Hannover: Hahn, 1996.
Schmidt, Roderich. "Aetates mundi: Die Weltalter als Gliederungsprinzip der Geschichte." *Zeitschrift für Kirchengeschichte* 67 (1955–6): 288–317.
Seyfarth, Jutta, ed. *Speculum virginum*. CCCM 5. Turnhout: Brepols, 1990.
Stefán Karlsson. "Ritun Reykjarfjarðarbókar. Excursus: Bókagerð bænda." *Opuscula* 4, Bibliotheca Arnamagnæana 30 (Copenhagen: Munksgaard, 1970). Pp. 120–40.
Stocker, Margarita. *Judith: Sexual Warrior. Women and Power in Western Culture*. New Haven: Yale University Press, 1998.
Svanhildur Óskarsdóttir. "Dómsdagslýsing í AM 764 4to." *Opuscula* 10, Bibliotheca Arnamagnæana 40 (Copenhagen: Reitzel, 1996). Pp. 186–93.

———. "The Book of Judith: A Medieval Icelandic Translation." *Gripla* 11 (2000): 79–124.
———. "Universal History in Fourteenth-century Iceland. Studies in AM 764 4to." Ph. D. diss. University of London, 2000.
———. "Um aldir alda: Veraldarsögur miðalda og íslenskar aldartölur." *Ritið* 2005 no. 3: 111–33.
———. "Genbrug i Skagafjörður: Arbejdsmetoder hos skrivere i klostret på Reynistaður." In *Reykholt som makt- og lærdomssenteri den islandske og nordiske kontekst.* Ed. Else Mundal. Reykholt: Snorrastofa, 2006. Pp. 141–53.
The Rule of St. Benedict. The Abingdon Copy. Ed. John Chamberlin. Toronto: Pontifical Institute of Mediaeval Studies, 1982.
Tubach, Frederic C. *Index exemplorum. A Handbook of Medieval Religious Tales.* Helsinki: Academia Scientiarum Fennica, 1969.
Unger, C. R., ed. *Heilagra manna søgur: Fortællinger og legender om hellige mænd og kvinder.* 2 vols. Christiania [Oslo]: Bentzen, 1877.
Utley, Francis Lee. "The One Hundred and Three Names of Noah's Wife." *Speculum* 16 (1941): 426–52.
Warner, Marina. *Alone of all her sex: The myth and cult of the Virgin Mary.* 2nd ed. London: Picador, 1985.
White, Sidnie Ann. "In the Steps of Jael and Deborah: Judith as Heroine." In *"No One Spoke Ill of Her": Essays on Judith.* Ed. James C. VanderKam. Society of Biblical Literature. Early Judaism and its Literature 2. Atlanta: Scholars Press, 1992. Pp. 5–16.
Widding, Ole, and Hans Bekker-Nielsen. "A Debate of the Body and the Soul in Old Norse Literature." *Mediaeval Studies* 21 (1959): 272–89.
———. "Elisabeth of Schönau's Visions in an Old Icelandic Manuscript, AM 764 40." *Opuscula* 2.1, Bibliotheca Arnamagnæana 25.1 (Copenhagen: Munksgaard, 1961). Pp. 93–6.
Widding, Ole, Hans Bekker-Nielsen, and L. K. Schook. "The Lives of the Saints in Old Norse Prose: A Handlist." *Mediaeval Studies* 25 (1963): 294–337.
Wolf, Kirsten. "A Fragmentary Excerpt on Saint Walburga in AM 764 4to." *Gripla* 11 (2000): 209–20.

Love in a Cold Climate—With the Virgin Mary

MARGARET CLUNIES ROSS

There is a wealth of literature devoted to the Virgin Mary and her miracles in Old Norse, most of it Icelandic. Much of it is prose, and a great deal of that has been gathered together in the compendium edited by C. R. Unger as *Mariu saga*.[1] While there have been a number of excellent studies of Marian prose texts,[2] a great deal of research is still needed to trace the sources of these texts, and, above all, to assess how Icelandic authors treated their source material, most of it available from the common stock of Christian Latin or European vernacular literature on the subject of the Virgin and her powers. Just as the Icelandic treatment of foreign sources and vernacular adaptations of European romances has been illuminated in the second half of the twentieth century by Marianne Kalinke, among others, so the voluminous Marian literature of medieval Iceland awaits further investigation, in order to throw light on this literature's role in the expression of indigenous religious devotion and the exploration of the medieval Icelandic psyche through adaptations of well-known miracle stories involving the Virgin's intervention.

---

1. C. R. Unger, ed., *Mariu saga: Legender om jomfru Maria og hendes jertegn efter gamle haandskrifter*, 2 vols. (Kristiania [Oslo]: Brögger & Christie, 1871).

2. Gabriel Turville-Petre, "'The Old Norse Homily on the Assumption and *Mariu Saga*," *Mediaeval Studies* 9 (1947): 131–40, rpt. in his *Nine Norse Studies* (London: Viking Society for Northern Research, 1972), pp. 102–17; Ole Widding "Om de norrøne Marialegender," *Opuscula* 2.1, *Bibliotheca Arnamagnæana* 25.1 (Copenhagen: Munksgaard, 1961), pp. 1–9; Ole Widding, Hans Bekker-Nielsen, and L. K. Shook, "The Lives of the Saints in Old Norse Prose. A Handlist," *Mediaeval Studies* 25 (1963): 294–337

Less well known than Marian prose in Old Icelandic, and certainly less studied, is a group of skaldic poems devoted to the Virgin and her miracles. Although they cannot be dated precisely, most of this corpus of poetry was probably composed in the fourteenth century, while some devotional verse in honor of the Virgin and various saints comes from the fifteenth century. The very late poetry has been edited by Jón Helgason,[3] while the texts of the fourteenth century and possibly earlier date appear in Finnur Jónsson's *Den norsk-islandske skjaldedigtning* (1912–15), E. A. Kock's *Den norsk-isländska skaldediktningen* (1946–50), and now in *Skaldic Poetry of the Scandinavian Middle Ages*, vol. VII: *Poetry on Christian Subjects* (*SkP*, 2007) edited by Margaret Clunies Ross, as well as in several separate editions dating from the ninteenth and twentieth centuries. Schottmann[4] offers the most thorough and systematic analysis of this poetry to date, but there are also important insights into its sources and content in Paasche, Lange, Wrightson, and in *SkP* VII.[5]

The extant Marian poetry in skaldic verse-forms, all of it anonymous, can be divided into two groups. The first and smaller group comprises poems of devotion to the Virgin, which concentrate largely on presenting some of the central Christian liturgical and symbolic expressions of her powers in elevated skaldic diction. To this group belong the elaborate and very clever *Máríudrápa* ("*Drápa* about Mary") as well as *Drápa af Máríugrát* ("*Drápa* about the Lament-of-Mary"). There are also many Christian skaldic poems on other religious subjects, such as lives of the saints and the celebration of the importance of Christ's cross, which include mention of the Virgin and

---

3. Jón Helgason, ed., *Íslenzk miðaldakvæði: Islandske digte fra senmiddelalderen*, 2 vols. (Copenhagen: Munksgaard, 1936–8).

4. Hans Schottmann, *Die isländische Mariendichtung. Untersuchungen zur volksprachigen Mariendichtung des Mittelalters*, Münchner Germanistische Beiträge herausgegeben von Werner Betz und Hermann Kunisch 9 (Munich: Fink, 1973).

5. Fredrik Paasche, *Kristendom og kvad. En studie i norrøn middelalder* (Christiania [Oslo]: Aschehoug, 1914), rpt. in his *Hedenskap og kristendom: studier i norrøn middelalder* (Oslo: Aschehoug, 1948), pp. 29–212; Wolfgang Lange, *Studien zur christlichen Dichtung der Nordgermanen 1000–1200*, Palaestra 222 (Göttingen: Vandenhoeck and Ruprecht, 1958); Kellinde Wrightson, *Fourteenth-Century Icelandic Verse on the Virgin Mary: Drápa af Maríugrát, Vitnisvísur af Maríu, Maríuvísur I-III*, Viking Society for Northern Research Text Series 14 (London: Viking Society for Northern Research, University College London, 2001). Marian poetry in *SkP* VII is edited by Valgerður Erna Þorvaldsdóttir, Katrina Attwood, and Kari Ellen Gade.

her role at Christ's Crucifixion. The second, larger group is a collection of versified Marian miracle stories, most of which can be paired with, and probably derive from, versions of vernacular prose miracles published in Unger's *Maríu saga*. What is interesting about these poems is the extent to which they deviate from the prose texts and the various ways in which the skaldic verse-form and diction are used to present their subjects with particular emphases. The skaldic miracle stories include *Brúðkaupsvísur* ("*Vísur* about a Wedding"), *Vitnisvísur af Máríu* ("Testimonial *Vísur* about Mary"), *Máríuvísur* ("*Vísur* about Mary") *I-III*, and *Gyðingsvísur* ("*Vísur* about a Jew"), the last-named a fragment about a Christian and a Jew, whose narrative cannot be fully reconstituted from what has survived. Of these poems, all but *Vitnisvísur af Máríu* have known sources outside Scandinavia.

Late medieval European vernacular poetry of religious devotion was often characterized by an emotional fervor of great intensity, especially when addressed to the persons of Christ and his mother Mary. Very little of this kind of affective piety appears in the Icelandic Marian miracle poems. However, they display other qualities of equal interest and, it can be argued, they are equally concerned with the range of human emotions that we can call by the shorthand term "love." The figure of the Virgin acts in these narratives as a focus for the exploration of contemporary Icelandic social and, particularly, sexual relations; and the miracles attributed to her express some of the deepest desires of the protagonists of the narratives of which they form a part, desires whose realization was normally impossible in everyday life. Such a role for the Virgin was predicated on the Christian commonplace that she acted as intercessor with Christ for sinful humanity, and that devotion to her could therefore help even the most hardened sinner, as long as he or she prayed to Mary. This situation is dramatized very effectively in *Máríuvísur III*, a poem based on a well known Marian miracle story, often called "Ave on the tongue" or "The drowned sacristan,"[6] in which a fornicating cleric, who is drowned in a raging river after visiting his

---

6. Ole Widding, "Norrøne Marialegender på europæisk baggrund," *Opuscula* 10, Bibliotheca Arnamagnæana 40 (Copenhagen: Reitzel, 1996), p. 93; Kellinde Wrightson, "Marian Miracles in Old Icelandic Skaldic Poetry," in *Treatises of the Elder Tongue: Fifty Years of Old Norse in Melbourne*, ed. Katrina Burge and John Stanley Martin (Melbourne: Department of Germanic and Russian Studies, 1995), pp. 87-99, and Wrightson, *Fourteenth-Century Icelandic Verse*, p. xx

lover, and is about to be claimed by a flock of devils, is saved from Hell by the intercession of the Virgin because he recites the "Hail Mary!" as he drowns, and its first words are found written on his tongue when his case is heard before Christ.

Mary's role as intercessor effectively licensed stories that narrated miracles in which she acted, on behalf of humans or on her own behalf, to explore tabu and socially contested areas of cultural life, partly because she could be represented as championing those who defied social norms, and partly because these same people were often the least powerful members of society. Although the corpus of Icelandic Marian miracles derives for the most part from exemplars known from other parts of medieval Europe, it displays some observable variations and emphases that were almost certainly the expression of local interests and pressures. These characteristics are sometimes more prominent in the poetic versions of the miracles than in their prose counterparts. This may suggest that poets felt they had more freedom within the skaldic verse-form to deviate from their sources, both in terms of their general treatment of themes and in their ability to build particular emphases through the use of kennings and other stylistic devices. Another possibility may be that those skalds who chose Marian miracles as their subjects may have been composing for specific audiences, whose interests influenced the way in which the poets presented their subjects and, indeed, their actual choice of narratives. It has long been suspected that *Máríuvísur I-III* and *Vitnisvísur af Máríu* may have been composed either by the same poet or by different poets working within the same tradition, because they all have the same general structure, all narrate a Marian miracle, and all contain an invocation to Saint Andrew in stanza 2.[7] These similarities suggest that the poet or poets may have been composing for a church or a religious house that was dedicated to both the Virgin and Saint Andrew, of which there were a number in Iceland.[8]

---

7. Bernhard Kahle, ed., *Isländische geistliche Dichtungen des ausgehenden Mittelalters* (Heidelberg: Winter, 1898), p. 17; Hans Sperber, ed. *Sechs isländische Gedichte legendarischen Inhalts*, Uppsala Universitets årsskrift 1910, Filosofi, språkvetenskap och historiska vetenskaper (Uppsala: Akademische Buchdruckerei Edv. Berling, 1911), p. xi; Wrightson, *Fourteenth-Century Icelandic Verse*, pp. xv-xvi; Gade, SkP VII, vol. 2, p. 740.

8. See Margaret Cormack, *The Saints in Iceland. Their Veneration from the Conversion to 1400*, Studia Hagiographica 78 (Brussels: Société des Bollandistes, 1994), pp. 78-80, 126-9, 172-233.

What is certainly true is that many Marian miracle narratives represent her as helping either women or the clergy, both social groups whose interests were often subordinated to those of dominant secular male authorities in medieval Iceland, as in many other parts of Europe. Although the issue of ecclesiastical independence from secular authority was a major point of tension in most medieval European societies, there were some specific issues that affected the clergy in Iceland in particular ways. One of these issues was the ideal of clerical celibacy vis-à-vis the reality of informal clerical marriage or companionship (*fylgilag*), in a society where independence of the Church from secular society was very hard to maintain. Auður Magnúsdóttir has shown how, in the later Middle Ages and right up to the Reformation, priests in Iceland more often than not entered into informal marriage-like relations with women, which were officially opposed by the Church but in practice tolerated.[9] On the other hand, clerical celibacy must have been very hard or even impossible for most ecclesiastics to achieve in such a society, even though it remained an ideal for the Church.

The little-known anonymous skaldic poem *Brúðkaupsvísur* presents a rather revealing dramatization of a young man's inner conflict between his inclination towards a life of celibacy and devotion to the Virgin and the social pressures his relatives bring to bear on him to marry a human bride. Because of the Virgin's intervention, he is able to resist their importunity, even though he comes within a whisker of being married off, and, with the support of a bishop, escapes to the wilderness (its location unspecified) for a life of solitude and devotion to the Virgin. The poem is an Icelandic version of a legend of the Virgin that exists in a number of medieval European collections, both Latin and vernacular. This legend also occurs in several versions in Old Norse, the closest to the poem being the D-version in *Mariu saga*,[10] though some motifs are closer to other Norse versions.[11] The D-version of the prose legend states unequivocally that the young man is a *klerkr*, "a cleric, scholar," whereas the poem is not so clear: in some places he is simply a wealthy young man who has devoted himself to Mary

---

9. Auður Magnúsdóttir, *Frillor och Fruar. Politik och Samlevnad på Island 1120–1400*, Avhandlinger från historiska institutionen i Göteborg 29 (Göteborg: University of Göteborg, 2001).

10. Unger, ed., *Mariu saga*, pp. 118–20

11. Schottmann, *Die isländische Mariendichtung*, pp. 355–6

and spends hours each day singing her praise (sts 3–4), and he is also said to be devoted to book-learning (sts 5–6). It is likely, though, that the poet intended to represent him as a priest, though evidently one whose family expected him to marry.[12] What is certain in the poem is that he was devoted to the Virgin:

> Æstri unni meyju mest
> Máríu siðknár,
> og mætri sig snót
> sjálfan gaf, bóka álmr. (6/1–4)

Prose order: Siðknár álmr bóka unni mest æstri meyju, María, og gaf sjálfan sig mætri snót.

Translation: The well-mannered elm tree of books [MAN] loved most the highest Virgin, Mary, and gave himself to the glorious woman.

Brúðkaupsvísur, which is in the difficult *hálfhneppt* meter, has been preserved in one early sixteenth-century compilation of religious poetry (AM 721 4to) and in three paper manuscripts deriving from it. It was not included by Finnur Jónsson in *Skjaldedigtning,* presumably because he considered it to date from after 1400,[13] but Jón Helgason, who edited it in *Íslenzk miðaldarkvæði* II, was of the opinion that the original poem could be as early as the thirteenth century, pointing to old forms of pronouns, adjectives and verbs.[14] It has been edited for Volume VII of *Skaldic Poetry of the Scandinavian Middle Ages* by Valgerður Erna Þorvaldsdóttir, and I am grateful to her for allowing me to draw on her edition in this discussion. Without denying the existence of the older forms Jón Helgason drew attention to, opinion on the age of the poem has to be balanced by the knowledge that

---

12. A kenning for the protagonist later in the poem (*kennir krossmarks* "knower of the sign of the cross" 12/1–2) suggests that the poet must have thought of him as a priest. Schottmann, *Die isländische Mariendichtung*, pp. 355–6, considered the poet's apparently inconsistent characterisation of the young man as a consequence of his drawing on several prose versions of the story, but it may equally be a reflection of the uncertain marital status of clerics in late medieval Iceland.
13. See also Wrightson, *Fourteenth-Century Icelandic Verse*, p. xv.
14. Jón Helgason, *Íslenzk miðaldakvæði*, pp. 127–36

it also contains some metrical irregularities, misunderstandings of certain kenning types, and uses some items of vocabulary not otherwise attested in Icelandic until after the Middle Ages. In the new edition, the poem has been treated as of fourteenth-century date and normalized accordingly, and the early features Jón Helgason pointed out have been judged to be poetic archaisms.[15]

The plot of the poem hinges on the Virgin's power to support the young man in the teeth of his family's wish to have him get married. Initially, as someone who had promised the Virgin to follow a chaste life (6/5–8) and often "sang beautiful services with love each day" (*saung fagrar tíðir með ástúð hvern dag* 7/5, 8) in her honor, he held out against continual urgings of people (*lýðir* 9/1) to marry, but finally capitulated to a certain unnamed man, "when a very strong wish of his kinsmen then was for it" (*er fíkjum ríkr vili frænda varð um það þá* 9/6–8). He was then betrothed to a wealthy young woman (st. 10) and the poet quickly moves on to describe the bridegroom-to-be and his wedding party (*fúss flokkr rekka*, "an eager party of men" 11/1) setting out for the marriage ceremony itself. However, the young man remembers that he has not performed his customary chanting in honor of the Virgin that day, so he slips into a church to do so, leaving the wedding party outside waiting. During the service he is overcome by drowsiness, brought on apparently by the Virgin herself, and he falls asleep. Mary appears to him in a vision (st. 13) and she is not pleased: "she was seemingly frowning at him" (*hun var ófrýn sýnum við honum* 13/1–2). She upbraids him (sts 15–20) in no uncertain terms, calling him fickle and inconstant for leaving her, to whom he had dedicated himself, and from whom he had obtained favors, for a mere human bride. She states bluntly that he has to make a choice between herself and the human fiancée (st. 18).

The six stanzas of the Virgin's speech are the emotional center of the poem and will be analyzed further below. Their effect on the young man is immediate: he wakes from his sleep (st. 21), takes his vision much to heart, and immediately cancels the wedding feast (st. 22), to the considerable dismay and anger of his men, who fear loss of face, "this journey of men will seem very bad, if you do so" ("*Sjá ferð*

---

15. I acknowledge the advice of my fellow editor, Kari Ellen Gade, in arriving at a plausible date for *Brúðkaupsvísur*.

fíra mun virðaz fráleit, ef þú gjörir svá" 23/5–6). They immediately contact a bishop (st. 24), seeking ecclesiastical authority for their position and expecting the bishop to support them against the young man. Unfortunately for them, after the bishop has asked him why he has broken his promise, and the young man has told him about his earlier vow of devotion to the Virgin, the bishop comes down on his side, encouraging him to "keep every word that you have said to the queen while you are alive" ("*Haltu hvert orð sem hefir mælt við dróttning, meðan ert lífs*" 26/1/2):

> "Betri mun þier vera vitr
> – víst hyggjum það—Krist
> – ástin hennar má mest –
> móðir en hvert fljóð." (26/5–8)

Prose order: 'Vitr móðir Krist mun vera þier betri en hvert fljóð, ástin hennar má mest, hyggjum það víst'.

Translation: 'The wise mother of Christ [= Mary] will be kinder towards you than any woman; her love may achieve the most; we think that for certain.'

The reason for the bishop's change of attitude to the young man, whom he had previously called fickle (*hverforðr* "fickle in words" 25/4), is not clear in the poem, but is explicit in the D version of the prose text, which explains that he is able to demonstrate to the bishop's satisfaction that he had betrothed himself to the Virgin Mary before he was betrothed to his human fiancée, even though his family did not know of his secret vow (Unger, *Mariu saga*, p. 120). For this reason the bishop agrees that he should keep his original promise (*heit*) to Mary and lead a chaste life in this world. He promptly departs for the wilderness, because he wants to be alone and devote himself to Mary: so ends the narrative part of *Brúðkaupsvísur*. In the remaining stanzas (28–33) the poet speaks in his own voice about his love for the Virgin, and how all people should ask for her mercy. He indicates that composing poetry in her honor will most likely bring rewards from her to him and concludes with a conventional prayer for salvation for himself and all men.

Brúðkaupsvísur is not noteworthy for its literary merit, but it is nevertheless a fascinating treatment of a touchy subject, the conflicting claims of spiritual and earthly love. Yet, ironically, both kinds of love are represented in rather similar terms. In the poem earthly love is represented purely in terms of kinship expectations and obligations. The young man comes from a good family and he is expected to marry a woman with good prospects, even though he is both studious, chaste, and devoted to the Virgin Mary. His behavior in jilting the woman, who is never described in any detail, is regarded as shameful by his angry wedding party. That these would have been the social values of medieval Iceland is taken as real, and the bishop's initial response to the young man's behavior is to support social norms. It is only when he discovers that the young man had promised himself to the Virgin before he had been betrothed to his nameless human fiancée that he decides, apparently on the legalistic ground of keeping one's word to the person to whom it had first been promised, that the young man is justified in jilting his fiancée.[16] In addition, but secondarily, the bishop advises the young man that Mary will be kinder towards him than any human woman.

The bishop's last remark, quoted above, highlights a double standard which is unresolved in the poem and perhaps also in medieval life generally. The main reason why the bishop supports the young man against his kin, his prior vows to the Virgin, which amount to a betrothal that takes precedence over his betrothal to his human fiancée, has nothing inherently to do with the main reason why Christians were generally enjoined to love the Virgin, which had to do with her status in the Christian pantheon as the mother of Christ and intercessor with the Godhead for humankind. The Virgin's position was one of power, relative to human women and to humankind in general, although it was itself dependent on her role as Christ's

---

16. A similar legalistic ground is invoked in another miracle of the Virgin told in skaldic verse, *Vitnisvísur af Maríu*, and comparable prose versions in *Maríu saga*. This miracle story has not so far been attested from other European collections and may be indigenous to Iceland. Here a young couple fall in love and pledge their troth in a church before an image of Mary and Christ. Later, the young man becomes powerful and successful and denies his pledge to his girlfriend, who has become impoverished after the death of her father. She tells their story to a bishop, who summons the man to testify in the church before the same image of Mary and Christ. They act as witnesses and confirm the woman's story, whereupon the man confesses, and he and the woman are reunited.

mother, a kinship relationship, as a consequence of her virginity, unstained by sinful concupiscence.

In much medieval European Christian poetry, love between humans and the Virgin was expressed in similar terms to secular love poetry, and in some cases it is difficult to distinguish whether a poem is addressed to a human lover or to Mary herself.[17] In *Brúðkaupsvísur*, the relationship between the Virgin and the young man is also expressed in terms of human heterosexual relations, especially in her long address to her devotee. The bishop's remark that Mary will be kinder to the young man than any woman, "her love may achieve the most" (*ástin hennar má mest* 26/7), may be read out of context as a conventional assertion of Mary's power to save humans in spiritual need, but, as it is expressed in the poem, and in the young man's experience, which is revealed to the audience by means of Mary's direct address to him in a vision in stanzas 15–20 (and which the bishop is not privy to), her very strong love is dramatised as petulant jealousy and bossy control of her devotee, even though it is earlier described more conventionally as mercy (*mildi* 3/5) towards him.

The young man is established in the early part of the poem as resisting the pressures of normal social life to devote himself to the cult of the Virgin and as being learned, chaste and virtuous (stanzas 5–8). As we have established earlier, it is likely that the poet intended to represent him as a cleric, even though the kennings and other phrases used to describe him are not always clear on this point. His behavior, as represented, is typical of someone who wants to devote himself to the contemplative life, with Mary as the focus of his devotion. He rejects both marriage and, later in the poem, human society generally, without that society being characterised as specifically Icelandic. Nevertheless, the one social institution at the heart of the narrative, marriage, comprising betrothal followed by a separate wedding ceremony, is immediately recognizable,[18] and the Virgin, in her address to the young man, is clearly aware of the two necessary parts to a legitimate Icelandic marriage, and uses that knowledge to her advantage.

---

17. Christiania Whitehead, 'Middle English Religious Lyrics', in *A Companion to the Middle English Lyric*, ed. Thomas G. Duncan (Cambridge: D. S. Brewer, 2005), pp. 105–6
18. cf. Jenny Jochens, *Women in Old Norse Society* (Ithaca and London: Cornell University Press, 1995), pp. 20–52

By contrast with the poet's depiction of the young man's fairly conventional asceticism, for which he was largely indebted to his source, his representation of the Virgin herself is unusually lively in terms of a range of human emotions, from possessiveness to jealousy. *Brúðkaupsvísur* goes beyond any of the extant prose versions of this miracle story in the detail of its depiction of the Virgin's reaction to the young man's impending marriage. This poet's Virgin comes across as very much a flesh-and-blood woman facing a situation in which her betrothed has threatened to abandon her for another woman, and not at all as the merciful mother of Christ interceding for a sinful human subject. Although the poet mentions this conventional image of the Virgin at a number of points in the poem, particularly at the beginning and end, they remain at the level of convention, while the angry Virgin of the young man's vision is far more dynamic and confronting.

The vision occupies the central part of the poem, beginning at stanza 13, where the poet describes how Mary appears to the young man as he slept in church, seemingly frowning at him and apparently angry and unhappy (*þótti vera reið og óglöð*, "she seemed to be angry and unhappy" 13/6, 8). The poet's emphasis on her anger and distress here goes well beyond the more decorous description of the D-version of the prose saga, where she is said to be "with the appearance of sorrow" (*með hrygðar yfirbragði* Unger, *Mariu saga*, p. 119). In stanza 14, the young man addresses the Virgin directly to find out why she is so sad and angry, and, from stanzas 15–20, she sets out her grievances. In the first place, she says, she is angry with him (*em eg þier reið* "I am angry with you" 15/4) because he is "fickle and inconstant" (*brigðlyndr og lausgeðr* 15/1, 2), wanting to forsake her company. She judges his offences in stanza 16 as "grievous" (*sárar sakir* 16/2, 3). It is clear that she feels jilted and jealous:

"Væn hugðumz vera þín
vinmær allkær,
báru, en þú bregðz mier
bálruðr, um það mál." (16/5–8)

Prose order: "Hugðumz vera þín væn, allkær vinmær, en þú bregðz mier, báru bálruðr, um það mál."

Translation: "I thought I was your beautiful, very dear beloved maiden, but you deceive me, bush of the flame of the wave [GOLD > MAN], in that matter."

These are the words of sexual jealousy rather than spiritual mercy and grace. The Virgin asserts that she is the young man's true betrothed, and that his proposal to marry a human woman indicates that his love for her is beginning to dissolve (*tekr renna* 17/1). She presents him as ungrateful and guilty of rejection, given that "I caused your prosperity to begin" (*Eg liet þín þrif hefjaz* 17/5). Here, then, the Virgin's generosity towards her devotee is represented as something that should produce a reciprocal obligation of life-long fidelity, interpreted as chastity in human terms, on the part of her worshipper. This notion is of course perfectly consonant with secular ideas of generosity and gift-giving in early Scandinavian society, as we find them articulated in *Hávamál*, for example, but not so easy to accommodate to Christian ideas of spiritual generosity and mercy.

The Virgin goes on to predict that the young man's human marriage will not last and that "affection will come to nothing" (*og ástúð eyðaz* 18/3), which she threatens will also be the case with the love between the two of them unless he gives up his fiancée and remembers her. In stanza 19, she suggests that what she perceives as the cooling of his affection might be due to his blaming her for failing to love him, but she assures him that she "wanted to keep on loving [him] very firmly for ever and ever" ("*Eg vilda að halda ástum við þig allfast um aldr*" 19/5, 8). Her parting shot is to renew her request to him for love and friendship (*elsku og vinlags* 20/2, 4), while the wedding feast is delayed (*meðan boðið dvelz* 20/2), because "a wife will not suit you" ("*Víf mun eigi hæfa þier*" 20/5,6, 7) and no suitable human bride will be found for him, however far he travels. She implicitly recognizes that as long as the wedding feast is delayed, the marriage cannot be concluded and that she still has time to win the young man back to her side. Her strategy certainly works. The young man wastes no time in calling off the wedding, indicating his relief: "My mind has changed quickly, yet I am not sad" ("*skap mitt hefir skipaz skjótt þó e*mka eg dapr*" 22/7–8).

Brúðkaupsvísur projects what a modern reader might consider a double standard towards its subject, in that the spiritual love that the Virgin is conventionally expected to show her human worshippers, expressed as generosity and mercy towards them in connection with the salvation of their souls, is here represented in terms of fidelity in love for her rather than for an earthly woman. Denial of human sexuality is, of course, the ascetic way, which Christianity has always recommended to its most zealous adherents. What is unusual about this miracle poem is that the figure of the Virgin herself is made to invoke secular values of love, loyalty, oath swearing and reciprocity to achieve her ends, and the other religious authority figure, the bishop, is persuaded that the young man should reject his human bride principally because the latter had secretly betrothed himself to the Virgin before his family had engaged him to a woman of their choice. The reasons why the young man is finally permitted to live a life of devotion to the Virgin have therefore everything to do with secular motivations and very little to do with religious fervor, though he himself is said to have been so motivated. Thus clerical celibacy and Mariolatry are sanctioned by secular values applied by two figures of Christian authority, the Virgin herself and the bishop. The secular world, as represented by the young man's family and his wedding party, is disregarded and there appear to be no reprisals for his reneging on his family's marriage plans for him.

This brings us to the point where we can consider the likely appeal of this miracle story to an Icelandic audience. *Brúðkaupsvísur*'s point of view, just like the Icelandic prose versions of the narrative and their non-Scandinavian prototypes, is clearly ecclesiastical. The devout young man's life-style is sanctioned and he evades the social pressures of his kin to get married without suffering any repercussions, even though he gets a dressing-down from the Virgin Mary in his vision and is effectively under her thumb. Furthermore, a love relationship with the Virgin is acknowledged by the bishop to be superior to any relationship with human women, on the grounds that Mary will be better to her devotee than any woman, and will show the strongest kind of love. Thus far it appears that the narrative upholds the desires of celibate male clergy, devoted to Mary, against secular authority.

The concluding stanzas of the poem (28–33) bring the miracle narrative back into the poet's world and that of his audience, just as, in the opening stanzas (1–2), the poet called for God's and Mary's help in composing a praise-poem in her honor. Stanzas 28–31 are addressed to the Virgin herself and focus attention on the poet and his own devotion to her, which he has expressed through his composition of poetry. Taking up the idiom of rewards for services rendered that the miracle story itself deals in, the poet announces that he wants to compose poetry about the Virgin's power and the life of her son more often and indicates that "cheerful women" (*Kát víf* 28/3) shall know this.[19] Although the significance of this reference is unclear, it is possible that the poet is perhaps alluding to a female audience that may have commissioned the poem in the first place.[20] Stanzas 29 and 30 stress the Virgin May's powers to help mankind in need, something that has been demonstrated in respect of one man in the miracle story. The poet writes conventionally: the Virgin is merciful and kind to all men. He then adopts a convention of a slightly different kind, imploring her support for himself, as a sinner, and then strengthening his position by claiming reward for the poem he has just created: "rewards for poems are greatest for a poem [that has been] recited" (*laun ljóða eru mest fyrir kveðinn óð* 31/7–8).

Thus the idiom of reciprocal gift-giving, which was so important a convention in the repertoire of the skalds, is parallel to the values expressed in the miracle story: the young man's attendance at church to sing the Virgin's praises is paralleled by the poet's poem in honor of the Virgin and, by implication, he expects a similar reward: "the beloved one helps me because of the comfort of poems" (*kær hjálpar mier fyrir líkn ljóða* 32/3–4). Thus the miracle narrative and the frame narrative coincide and reinforce one another's values, which are that both secular and spiritual love depend on reciprocity and reward, even if one partner in the relationship is the more powerful. If the poet was himself a cleric, as seems plausible, the thematic reinforcement of frame and miracle narrative would have been even greater.

Bibliography

Auður Magnúsdóttir. *Frillor och Fruar. Politik och Samlevnad på Island 1120–1400*. Avhandlinger från historiska institutionen i Göteborg 29. Göteborg: University of Göteborg, 2001.

Clunies Ross, Margaret, ed. *Skaldic Poetry of the Scandinavian Middle Ages*. Vol. VII *Poetry on Christian Subjects*, Parts 1 and 2. Turnhout: Brepols, 2007.

---

19. Jón Helgason, ed. *Íslenzk miðaldakvæði*, adopted a different reading of this line, *þat skaltu vita, víf* "you shall know that, woman." In both readings, however, there is a direct appeal to a woman or women.

20. If so, did they identify with the powerful figure of the Virgin Mary in narratives of this kind, while recognizing that her love for her devotees was couched in heterosexual terms? Did they disregard the standard kind of anti-feminism expressed in the bishop's statement? Such questions can probably be answered in the affirmative.

Cormack, Margaret. *The Saints in Iceland. Their Veneration from the Conversion to 1400.* Studia Hagiographica 78. Brussels: Société des Bollandistes, 1994.
Finnur Jónsson, ed. *Den norsk-islandske skjaldedigtning.* Vols AI-II (tekst efter håndskrifterne) and BI-II (rettet tekst). Copenhagen: Gyldendal, 1912–15. Rpt. Copenhagen: Rosenkilde & Bagger, 1967 (A) and 1973 (B).
Jochens, Jenny. *Women in Old Norse Society.* Ithaca and London: Cornell University Press, 1995.
Jón Helgason, ed. *Íslenzk miðaldakvæði: Islandske digte fra senmiddelalderen.* 2 vols. Copenhagen: Munksgaard, 1936–8.
Kahle, Bernhard, ed. *Isländische geistliche Dichtungen des ausgehenden Mittelalters.* Heidelberg: Winter, 1898.
Kock, Ernst Albin, ed. *Den norsk-isländska skaldediktningen.* 2 vols. Lund: Gleerup, 1946–50.
Lange, Wolfgang. *Studien zur christlichen Dichtung der Nordgermanen 1000–1200.* Palaestra 222. Göttingen: Vandenhoeck and Ruprecht, 1958.
Paasche, Fredrik. *Kristendom og kvad. En studie i norrøn middelalder.* Christiania [Oslo]: Aschehoug, 1914. Rpt. in his *Hedenskap og kristendom: studier i norrøn middelalder.* Oslo: Aschehoug, 1948. Pp. 29–212.
Schottmann, Hans. *Die isländische Mariendichtung. Untersuchungen zur volksprachigen Mariendichtung des Mittelalters.* Münchner Germanistische Beiträge herausgegeben von Werner Betz und Hermann Kunisch 9. Munich: Fink, 1973.
Sperber, Hans, ed. *Sechs isländische Gedichte legendarischen Inhalts.* Uppsala Universitets årsskrift 1910. Filosofi, språkvetenskap och historiska vetenskaper. Uppsala: Akademische Buchdruckerei Edv. Berling, 1911.
Turville-Petre, Gabriel. "The Old Norse Homily on the Assumption and *Maríu Saga,*" *Mediaeval Studies* 9 (1947): 131–40. Rpt. in his *Nine Norse Studies.* London: Viking Society for Northern Research, 1972. Pp. 102-17
Unger, C. R. ed. *Maríu saga: Legender om jomfru Maria og hendes jertegn efter gamle haandskrifter.* 2 vols. Kristiania (Oslo): Brögger & Christie, 1871.
Whitehead, Christiania. "Middle English Religious Lyrics." In *A Companion to the Middle English Lyric,* ed. Thomas G. Duncan. Cambridge: D. S. Brewer, 2005. PP. 96–119,
Widding, Ole. "Om de norrøne Marialegender." *Opuscula* 2.1. Bibliotheca Arnamagnæana 25.1. Copenhagen: Munksgaard, 1961. Pp. 1–9.
———. "Norrøne Marialegender på europæisk baggrund." *Opuscula* 10. Bibliotheca Arnamagnæana 40. Copenhagen: C.A. Reitzel, 1996. Pp. 1–128.
Widding, Ole, Hans Bekker-Nielsen, and L. K. Shook. "The Lives of the Saints in Old Norse Prose. A Handlist." *Mediaeval Studies* 25 (1963): 294–337.
Wrightson, Kellinde. "Marian Miracles in Old Icelandic Skaldic Poetry." In *Treatises of the Elder Tongue: Fifty Years of Old Norse in Melbourne,* ed. Katrina Burge and John Stanley Martin. Melbourne: Department of Germanic and Russian Studies, 1995. Pp. 87–99.
———, ed. *Fourteenth-Century Icelandic Verse on the Virgin Mary: Drápa af Maríugrát, Vitnisvísur af Maríu, Maríuvísur I-III.* Viking Society for Northern Research Text Series 14. London: Viking Society for Northern Research, University College London, 2001.

Mírmanns saga:
The First Old Norse-Icelandic Hagiographical Romance?

SVERRIR TÓMASSON

Medieval Icelandic writers seem at times to have been fully aware that the boundaries of their texts were not firmly fixed within a rigid historical or generic frame, but could and indeed should be varied according to subject matter. The lives of their chosen saints were not recorded strictly according to the saints' worldly experiences; rather, particularly praiseworthy events were selected and recorded to provide audiences with examples of holy living. A saint's *vita* is, of course, classified as a biography, but its inclusion of miracles that occurred during or after the saint's lifetime also tests the limits of textual boundaries.

I reiterate this common knowledge because there seems to be some confusion among Old Norse-Icelandic scholars and critics regarding the classification of Old Norse-Icelandic hagiographical literature. Some scholars consider, for example, the corpus of sagas of Icelandic bishops to belong to a genre commonly called *biskupa sögur*, a term inherited from Jón Sigurðsson and Guðbrandur Vigfússon, who first edited in two volumes the biographies of Icelandic bishops and *vitae* of Icelandic episcopal saints who lived prior to the Reformation.[1] Jón Sigurðsson and Guðbrandur Vigfússon did not classify these narratives according to literary principles; to them these sagas were of the

---

1. Jón Sigurðsson and Guðbrandur Vigfússon, ed., *Biskupa sögur*, 2 vols. (Copenhagen: Hið íslenzka bókmenntafélag, 1858–1878).

same breed, and in their view it was not necessary to determine the pedigree of these stories more specifically.[2]

More than half a century ago, the British scholar Gabriel Turville-Petre maintained that the oldest translations of Latin legends into Old Norse-Icelandic had greatly influenced the vernacular literature, and that these translations taught the Icelandic/Norwegian authors to express themselves in their own language.[3] In many ways, Turville-Petre's opinions shaped the ideas of other scholars about the earliest attempts to write indigenous biographies, and many scholars took for granted that the native legends were mainly imitations of Latin works. While it is indisputable that the earliest translations could have easily provided Old Norse-Icelandic writers with examples of narrative composition and style, it must be borne in mind that Old Norse-Icelandic authors and translators were educated in ways similar to their colleagues elsewhere in Europe, and that their training at native educational centers, mainly in the private and cathedral schools at Hólar, Skálholt, Haukadalur, and Oddi, helped them compose both in Latin and in the vernacular. Skill in the oral retelling of native tales must also have been a significant asset. Without such a background culture, the Old Norse-Icelandic translations of Latin *vitae* would have been impossible.

The Four Grammatical Treatises, especially the First, display a remarkable tendency to use indigenous terms when discussing grammar and rhetoric.[4] Other literary terms are defined to a lesser degree. Some Old Norse-Icelandic terms demonstrate, however, that the writers were conscious of different types of saints' lives and would have classified the narratives accordingly.

The manuscript AM 624 4to is a priest's manual compiled around 1500. Some parts of it are written by Jón Þorvaldsson, sometime chancellor at the nunnery at Reynistaður in Skagafjörður. The manuscript contains three Icelandic homilies written by him. One of them discusses Saints Mary Magdalen and Martha and is an interpretation

---

2. Cf. Guðbrandur Vigfússon's introduction in *Biskupa sögur*, vol. 1, pp. v–xc.
3. Gabriel Turville-Petre, *Origins of Icelandic Literature* (Oxford: Clarendon Press, 1953), pp. 141–2.
4. On this topic, see my article "Skáldskapur og fræði fyrir stokk innan" in *Frejas psalter. En psalter i 40 afdelinger til brug for Jonna Louis-Jensen*, ed. Bergljót S. Kristjánsdóttir et al. (Copenhagen: Det arnamagnæanske Institut, 1997), pp. 190–2.

of Luke 10:38–42, the account of Jesus visiting the sisters at their home. The homilist takes pains to explain the difference between Mary's and Martha's work:

> Þá gekk Jesús inn í kastala, andlega at skilja, er hann vitraðiz mönnum sýniligr ok lét beraz í heim frá meyju; ok tók kona nokkur hann í hús sitt sú er Martha hét, en hun átti systur er María hét. Tvær systr trúfastar, þær er við drottni tóku, merkja tvenn líf kristins lýðs; þat er *sýslulíf,* ok *upplitningarlíf.* Sýslulíf er at fæða hungraðan, ok klæða nöktan, þjóna sjúkum, ok grafa dauðan ... Upplitningarlíf er at skiljaz við öll fjölskyldu<verk> heims, ok hafna öllum veraldaráhyggjum fyrir ást guðs.[5]

(Then Jesus entered the castle, understood in a spiritual sense, when he appeared to human beings and condescended to be born in this world by the Virgin; he was invited to the home of a certain woman named Martha, who had a sister named Mary. These two faithful sisters, who received Christ, signify the two types of Christian living; that is, *sýslulíf,* the active life, and *upplitningarlíf,* the contemplative life. The active life, *sýslulíf,* is feeding the hungry, clothing the naked, serving the infirm, and burying the dead ... The contemplative life, *upplitningarlíf,* is divorcing oneself from all everyday concerns and rejecting all worldy woes for the love of God.)

Anyone reading these lines knows that behind the words *sýslulíf* and *upplitningarlíf* stand the terms *vita activa* and *vita contemplativa,* which in the later Middle Ages became closely connected with the discussion of the symbolic role of these two sisters. My reason for quoting the passage is that nowhere else in Old Icelandic hagiographic literature—at least to my knowledge—does such an explicit expression of the symbolic significance of the saintly life occur.

The source from which the preacher drew his subject matter remains unknown. The sermon can hardly be a native composition; the Icelandic clergy depended a great deal on foreign, mainly Latin interpretations, as evident from most of the medieval Icelandic

---

5. AM 624 4to, 122v. Cf. Þorvaldur Bjarnarson, ed., *Leifar fornra kristinna fræða íslenzkra: Codex Arna-Magnæanus 677 4to* (Copenhagen: H. Hagerup, 1878), p. 154.

ecclesiastical writings. Þorvaldur Bjarnarson, the editor of this sermon, believed that it was influenced by Bernard of Clairvaux and Gregory the Great,[6] but the discussion of the sisters' role was widespread in the mendicant orders, who saw it as reflecting their own activity, a sort of *vita mixta*, a representation of their double lives as preachers and ascetics.[7]

At the end of the thirteenth century and especially at the beginning of the fourteenth century, Icelandic hagiographers began to change their methods; they incorporated into their *passiones* and *vitae* all sorts of historical details, and their hagiographical narratives took on the character of universal history, with exact chronology and geography alongside traditional interpretations of theological questions. At times, the saint almost vanishes from the scene because of the compiler's historical interests and pedantic vocabulary. No doubt, the compilers believed that this type of writing would further strengthen their readers' faith. The best example of such compositional practice is the twin legend of the apostles John and James (*Tveggja postola saga Jóns ok Jakobs*). As the missions and martyrdoms of the apostles are narrated, historical facts about the reigns of certain pagan tyrants are provided, along with exegetical commentary on fundamental religious elements. When describing how Saint John survives all sorts of torment, the compiler comments:

> Nú er álítanda hvárt þessar greinir samanlesnar í þvingan ok meinlætum Johannis mega eigi *martirium* heita viðrkvæmiliga, meðr því at hinn sæli Gregorius segir at í bindandisdygð ok einni saman pínu holdsins geriz maðr píslarváttr í guðs augliti án allri ofsókn.[8]

(Now it must be considered whether these collected accounts concerning John's sufferings and pain might not appropriately be called *martirium*, since the blessed Gregorius maintains that in the

---

6. Þorvaldur Bjarnarson, ed., *Leifar*, p. x.

7. On this topic, see Katherine Ludwig Jansen, *The Making of the Magdalen: Preaching and Popular Devotion in the Later Middle Ages* (Princeton: Princeton University Press, 2001), pp. 50–1.

8. C. R. Unger, ed. *Postola sögur. Legendariske fortællinger om apostlernes liv deres kamp for kristendommens udbredelse same deres martyrdød* (Christiania [Oslo]: Bentzen, 1874), pp. 610–1.

virtue of abstinence and the torments of the flesh a man becomes a martyr in the sight of God, even without undergoing persecution.)

Tveggja postola saga Jóns ok Jakobs is one of the lives in *Codex Scardensis*, a manuscript produced in the scriptorium at the Helgafell monastery in the latter half of the fourteenth century and most likely commissioned by Ormr Snorrason, a wealthy knight, at Skarð on Skarðsströnd.[9] Another manuscript that was probably commissioned by him, the so-called *Ormsbók*, is a compilation of prose romances. This manuscript now survives only in later paper copies and has been for many years a jigsaw puzzle for Old Norse-Icelandic philologists as they have tried to reconstruct its size and structure from diverse quotations in Swedish lexicographical works dating from the seventeenth century. Desmond Slay has probably come closest to establishing its structure, the order of its sagas, and its original foliation.[10] He proposes that the manuscript was originally about 90 leaves, containing 15 sagas and shorter narratives: *Trójumanna saga, Breta sögur, Mágus saga, Laes þáttr, Vilhjálms þáttr Laessonar, Geirarðs þáttr, Flóvents saga, Bærings saga, Rémundar saga, Erex saga, Bevers saga, Ívens saga, Mírmanns saga, Partalópa saga,* and finally *Enoks saga,* provided the manuscript did not conclude with *Parceval saga,* an adaption of *Le conte du graal* by Chrétien of Troyes.[11]

It is no coincidence that *Ormsbók* begins with *Trójumanna saga*. The saga was placed there on ideological grounds; Ormr Snorrason and other Icelandic noblemen most likely believed that they were descended from the Trojans. According to the medieval understanding of history, the refugees from Troy migrated to Western Europe, and one of their descendants, Brutus, was thought to have settled in Britain. His story usually followed the history of the Trojans, as is the case in *Ormsbók*. One would have expected the next items in *Ormsbók* to

---

9. On the scriptorium at Helgafell, see Ólafur Halldórsson, *Helgafellsbækur fornar,* Studia Islandica 24 (Reykjavík: Menningarsjóður, 1966).

10. See Desmond Slay, "Ívens saga, Mírmanns saga and Ormr Snorrason's Book," in *The Sixth International Saga Conference: Workshop Papers,* 2 vols. (Copenhagen: Det arnamagnæanske Institute, 1985), vol. 2, pp. 953–66.

11. Slay, "Ívens saga, Mírmanns saga and Ormr Snorrason's Book," says in this connection: "Although the seventeenth-century list of contents of OS [i.e. Ormsbók] has 'Partiwals' as its concluding item, no quotation from Parcevals saga has been found in the lexicographical works, and there is no known copy" (p. 954).

be the pseudohistorical narratives of King Arthur and his knights, but the pseudohistorical sequence in the Icelandic manuscript is broken: after *Breta sögur* comes *Mágus saga*, the contents of which are related to *Renaud de Montauban*, a French *chanson de geste*, but the two adaptations of Arthurian romances, *Erex saga* and *Ívens saga*, are far behind in the sequence of stories. The order of the narratives in the manuscript is an indication that they were not merely included for the purpose of tracing the history of the noble origins of Ormr Snorrason and his family, the *Skarðverjar*. *Trójumanna saga*'s pseudohistory is, for example, combined with chivalrous ideals. Some of the sagas in the manuscript must also be labelled as romances with Christian themes, such as *Bevers saga*, *Bærings saga*, *Flóvents saga*, *Rémundar saga* and even *Partalópa saga*, which is probably a translation of the French *Partenopeus de Blois*. The last preserved item, *Enoks saga*, is clearly an exemplum. But how should *Mírmanns saga* be classified?

Mírmanns saga is extant in six versions. They have all been edited diplomatically by Desmond Slay, and in his introduction to the edition he discusses all of the known manuscripts of the saga.[12] Slay calls the version referred to here the D-version. It is preserved in Stock. Papp fol. no. 47, written in the latter half of the seventeenth century by Jón Vigfússon (d. 1692), who copied it from from Stock. Perg 4to no. 6 (dating from the fifteenth century), Stock. Papp fol. no. 17 (dating from the seventeenth century), and *Ormsbók*, which was then the oldest known manuscript of *Mírmanns saga*. Slay considers it very likely that Jón Vigfússon had only two leaves of the saga from *Ormsbók* when he started copying it, and that these leaves contained only the last part of the narrative, about one-fifth or one-sixth. Slay is of the opinion that Jón Vigfússon had inserted some modern words into his copy;[13] this can easily be seen in many places, but on the other hand this version has passages that are lacking in the others, and on the whole Jón Vigfússon does not seem to be as careless a copyist as scholars have maintained.

In his introduction, Slay discusses neither the dating of *Mírmanns saga* nor its literary qualities. Only few scholars have paid any atten-

---

12. *Mírmanns saga*, ed. Desmond Slay, Editiones Arnamagnæanæ, Ser. A, vol. 17 (Copenhagen: Reitzel, 1997), pp. xii–clxi. All subsequent references to *Mírmanns saga* are to this edition.
13. See *Mírmanns saga*, ed. Slay, pp. cxlii-cxliii.

tion to *Mírmanns saga*'s merits. Finnur Jónsson, who acknowledged that the saga was well composed ("godt fortalt"), but expressed reservations about its religious overtones,[14] believed that the saga was an Icelandic work, not older than 1325, and based on outmoded Old French motifs ("afblegede oldfranske minder"), along with some Old Norse-Icelandic ones. In his introduction to the first edition of *Mírmanns saga*, Eugen Kölbing commented on the saga's religious tendency, which he regarded as an attempt to describe the two chivalric worlds, the religious and the secular.[15] Jan de Vries agreed with Kölbing and described it as demonstrating "geistliche Ritterschaft."[16] Jürg Glauser, the last to comment on the saga, argues that it is influenced by the the literature of the crusades.[17]

Mírmanns saga is structured like a romance. The story begins by introducing Mírmann's parents, Duchess Brigida and Duke Hermann, who live in Saxland (Saxony), which was then pagan. Mírmann receives his early education in his native country, but is soon sent to France, where he is fostered by King Hlöðver and further educated. In France, Mírmann is baptized, and King Hlöðver commissions him to christianize his countrymen in Saxland, especially his parents. Mírmann's father is unwilling to accept his son's message. He fights with him in a rage, and the fight ends with Mírmann killing his own father. Mírmann then returns to France and stays with King Hlöðver for some time. Hlöðver's second wife, Queen Katrín, falls in love with Mírmann. Brigida, Mírmann's mother, sends him a letter promising reconcilation, but this turns out to be treacherous, because she gives him a magic drink that causes leprosy. This is the turning point of the saga. Mírmann's role at the court in France is completed, and he undertakes a journey to Italy after hearing of good doctors there.

On this journey, he changes his name to Justinus. The first doctor he seeks is Martin, who cannot cure him, but advises him to go to Sicily to meet a woman named Cecelia, who is famous for her medical skills

---

14. Finnur Jónsson, *Den oldnorske og oldislandske litteraturs historie*, 3 vols. (Copenhagen: Gad, 1920–24), vol. 3, p. 103.

15. Eugen Kölbing, ed., *Riddarasögur* (Strassburg: Trübner, 1872), p. xlv.

16. Jan de Vries, *Altnordische Literaturgeschichte*, 2 vols. (Berlin: de Gruyter, 1964–67), vol. 2, p. 535.

17. Jürg Glauser, *Isländische Märchensagas: Studien zur Prosaliteratur im spätmittelalterlichen Island* (Basel: Helbing & Lichtenhahn, 1983), p. 223.

and able to help him. She diagnoses his illness, telling him that it has been caused by magic, and that a snake has grown in his stomach. She then gives him a magic drink which causes the snake to move into his throat. She calls upon it in the name of Jesus to come out further, and when she and Mírmann place their mouths together, the snake enters her mouth. Mírmann seizes the snake's tail with his teeth and she cuts it in two with a knife and throws the parts into a fire.

Eventually, Mírmann is cured of leprosy and marries Cecelia, though before their marriage she discovers his true identity. After the wedding, Mírmann wants to go back to France, and although Cecelia is hesitant, she eventually grants him permission to visit his friend King Hlöðver. While Mírmann is in France, King Hlöðver dies, and Queen Katrín gives Mírmann a magic drink, causing him to forget Cecelia and marry Katrín. Later Mírmann is defeated by the knight Híringr, alias Cecelia. She brings him back to Sicily, where he lives with her for the rest of his life.[18]

As evident from this synopsis, *Mírmanns saga* does not seem very different from ordinary romances. One may divide the story into four main sections: 1) Mírmann at his parents' house, his studies there, and his education at the court of King Hlöðver in France; 2) his disease, his cure, and marriage to Cecelia in Sicily; 3) his later stay in France, his marriage to Katrín, King Hlöðver's widow, and his subsequent defeat by his former wife, Cecelia, who battles dressed like a man and calls herself Híringr; 4) Mírmann's reunion with Cecelia in Sicily, where he ruled with her for twelve years, after which the married couple entered a monastery and served God. The bipartite structure is, however, obvious: 1) Mírmann's sinful youth and his suffering from the disease, and 2) his life after he has been cured. It may be argued that Mírmann's life is determined by three women: Brigida, Katrín and Cecelia.

I have not found anyone in the Middle Ages bearing the name Mírmann (or Mírmannt as it is written in some manuscripts).[19] It is possible that the name refers to the first part of the Latin word *miracula*, so as to stress that the person is saved by God's mercy, such as those men who are blessed by the intercession of saints. On

---

18. I am indebted to Slay for this summary. He gives an excellent synopsis of the A-text at the end of his edition of *Mírmanns saga*, pp. 196–202.

19. "The name Mírmann," in *Mírmanns saga*, ed. Slay, pp. 191–5.

the other hand, the women's names are all well known saints' names, although Brigida is not well attested in Iceland.[20] Her description in the saga coincides remarkably well with that of Saint Catherine of Alexandria, except that the saint does not kill her clients when they do not behave as she wants. Brigida's virtues are described as follows:

> Kunnosta hennar var með því móti at þat þótti allt sem barnavípr er aðrar konur gjörðu hjá því sem <hun> gjörði. En spektarmál ok veraldarvizka sú er hun hafði numit af heiðnum bókum stóðuz henni eigi hinir beztu klerkar, ok sigraði hun með snilldarorðum kónga ok klerka ef orðaskipti áttu við hana.[21]

(Her knowledge was such that everything that other women did seemed to be children's trifles compared with what she did. The best clerics could not match her in learning and worldly wisdom, which she had studied in pagan books, and she defeated kings and clerics with her rhetorical skill if they disputed with her.)

Saint Catherine, on the other hand, had learned:

> allar þær íþróttir á bókum er *liberalis* heita. Hún kunni og margar tungur að mæla og spakliga að leysa allar spurningar þær er fyrir hana voru bornar... "Til bókar var eg sett. Nam eg yfrið mikið af bókligum íþróttum og veraldligri speki..."[22]

(all of the arts that are named *liberalis*. She had learned to speak many languages and could answer wisely all of the questions she was asked... "I was sent for education. I studied the literary arts and worldy wisdom to a great extent.")

It cannot be mere coincidence that the word *barnavípr* is used when describing Brigida's merits: it clearly refers to Guðrún Ósvífrsdóttir in *Laxdœla saga*.

---

20. Margaret Cormack, *The Saints in Iceland: Their Veneration from the Conversion to 1400*, Subsidia hagiographica 78 (Brussels: Société des Bollandistes: 1994), pp. 86–9.
21. *Mírmanns saga*, ed. Slay, A-text, pp. 1–2.
22. Kirsten Wolf, ed., *Heilagra meyja sögur* (Reykjavík: Bókmenntafræðistofnun Háskóla Íslands, 2003), pp. 124, 126.

At first Queen Katrín is given a favorable description, but later on the image of her changes:

> Svá er sagt frá kóngsdóttur at hun var hverri konu fríðari, mjúk í orðum en mild af fé svá at hun gaf á tvær hendr gull ok silfr, ok varð hun af því þokkasæl við landslýðinn. En í annan stað vánu bráðara tók hun at hyggja at vænleik Mírmanns jarlssons ok atgjörvi er hann hafði, sem fyrr var sagt, um fram aðra menn.[23]

(It is said that the princess was more beautiful than other women, softspoken and openhanded, giving away gold and silver with both hands, and because of that she became very popular among the common people. On the other hand she soon noticed Mírmann's fairness and the virtues that he had beyond other men, as told previously.)

After Mírmann falls ill, Katrín is portrayed less favorably: she speaks of Mírmann being too sick to be at court, and it is remarkable how King Hlöðver rebukes her:

> Katrín drottning kemr at máli viðr kónginn Hlöðver ok sagði honum at hann hefði undarligan sið at hafa þann mann í hirð ok samneyti meðr sér sem at svá væri aumliga yfirkominn í þeim háskasamligasta ok versta sjúkdómi, ok kynni hann sjálfr þar af hina verstu ok óbætanligustu vanheilsu sér sjálfum at brugga. "Þú veizt at ek mæli af réttri elsku ok kærleik viðr þik. Skil þik frá þessum manni at þú hljótir ekki neitt illt af honum." Hlöðver kóngr svarar henni ok segir: "Nú þykki mér öðruvísi háttat í orðum ok atvikum þínum hjá því sem at þá var er hann var heilbrigðr. Þá sýndiz mér svá at þér þótti hann aldregi of nærri þér vera, ... "[24]

(Queen Katrín starts speaking to King Hlöðver and tells him that he had a peculiar custom keeping at court and in his presence a man who so badly overrun by a most dangerous and foul disease, and he himself could be infected by this worst, incurable illness. "You

---

23. *Mírmanns saga*, ed. Slay, A-text, p. 13.
24. *Mírmanns saga*, ed. Slay, D-text, p. 53.

know," she said, "that I speak out of true love and charity toward you. Stay away from this man so that you do not catch anything bad from him." King Hlöðver answers her and says: "Now I find you different in your words and actions from the time when he was healthy. It seemed to me then that you felt as if he were never too close to you ... ")

Later on we are told that Katrín is a *trollkona* and a giantess as well as a very skilful sorceress. Her actions are quite similar to those of Brigida previously. She gives Mírmann and his men a magic potion, causing him to forget the oaths that he had sworn his queen, Cecelia, in Sicily.

The description of Cecelia is in quite a different tone. Although she is not as accomplished as her namesake, Saint Cecelia, she possesses the same healing power as the saint. In one way she is equal to the best of knights. She has trained herself

> við burtreið sem karlar. En þó vissu þat fáir menn því at hun lék í skógi í karlmannsklæðum at fárra manna vitorði, en því gjörði hun svá at Guð er alla hluti veit fyrir, vissi at hun mundi þess þurfa áðr lyki ...[25]

(in tilting, like the men. This, however, was known only to few people, because she practiced it secretly in a forest, dressed in a man's clothes. She did this because God, who foresees everything, knew that she would need this training before everything was over.)

The D-text first describes her countenance as being more beautiful than other ladies in Sicily, and then adds:

> [þ]ar eptir hafi ok farit aðrar hennar listir, því at hun hafi lært allar riddaraligar íþróttir, ok kunnat út at ríða sem hinn besti riddari.[26]

(her other skills were also like this, because she had learned all of the chivalric arts and could ride into combat like the best of knights.)

---

25. *Mírmanns saga*, ed. Slay, A-text, p. 61.
26. *Mírmanns saga*, ed. Slay, D-text, pp. 62–3.

It appears at first glance that Brigida punished her son for killing his father and her husband. One might, however, suspect that this is not the main reason for her actions. In the second chapter of the saga, when Brigida tells her husband that she is expecting a child, he tells her of his dream in which he thought that she had "a snake in [her] chemise; it was surpisingly big and savage, and when [he] wanted to pull it away it bit [him] and [he] had no strength against it."[27] It is also the duke who wants his son to leave and "never come back."[28] The words indicate that something else happened between mother and son, and her remark when she leaves him in her brewery after she has poisoned him supports this notion:

". . . ok þat hlægir <mik> ef hun Katrín kóngsdóttir hefr <ekki slíka> list af ykkar laukagarðsleikum[29] hér eptir sem hingat til."[30]

(it makes me laugh to think that Princess Katrín will no longer enjoy your games in the herbarium as before.)

A person infected by leprosy was in the Middle Ages by some authors considered to have committed a mortal sin;[31] the disease was thought be God's punishment for lust and arrogance.[32] Also, one cannot help but regard the snake as a phallic symbol, and the creature is painted on Cecelia's standard when she conquers Mírmann's army:

---

27. "'Mik dreymdi,' sagði hann, 'at þú hafðir orm einn í serk þér ok þótti mér vera undarliga mikill ok ólmr, en þá er ek vilda hann taka ok kippa honum frá þér, beit hann mik svá at ek hafða ekki afl við honum'" (*Mírmanns saga*, ed. Slay, A-text, p. 2).
28. "ok kvæmi aldri aptr" (*Mírmanns saga*, ed. Slay, A-text, p. 4).
29. The other manuscripts have the variant *augnagaman* (eyes' delight) instead of *laukgarðsleikr* which surely refers to the words Earl Bæringr uses of the relationship between Queen Katrín and Mírmann: "Þér verði hér annat fyrir grönum en kyssa Katrín drottingu í eplagarði sínum" (*Mírmanns* saga, ed. Slay, A and B-text, p. 35; "something else will be closer to your beard than kissing Queen Katrín in her apple garden").
30. *Mírmanns saga*, ed. Slay, D-text, p. 51.
31. Cf. Darrel W. Amundsen, *Medicine, Society and Faith in the Ancient and Medieval Worlds* (Baltimore: The Johns Hopkins University Press, 1996), p. 210.
32. The same motif is also to be found in *Þorsteins saga Víkingssonar* (Carl Christian Rafn, ed., *Fornaldar sögur Nordrlanda*, 3 vols. [Copenhagen: Popp, 1829–30], vol. 2, p. 394); cf. Margaret Schlauch, *Romance in Iceland* (London: Georg Allen & Unwin Ltd, 1934), p. 134; Astrid van Nahl, *Originale Riddarasögur als Teil altnordischer Sagaliteratur* (Franfurt am Main: Peter Lang, 1981), p. 222.

Merki hans [that is, Hírings] var skínandi sem önnur sólarbirti, ok á dregit meðr rauðu gulli, einn jungkæri ok jungfrú, hafandi einn orm hvárt þeirra sér í munni í millum sín sundr deildan með knífi þeim sem at jungfrúin helt á.[33]

(His standard was shining like the other brightness of the sun; it was drawn with reddish gold, a prince and princess, holding in their mouths parts of a snake that had been cut in two with the knife that the princess held in her hand.)

In the battle with Mírmann, the gemstones on Híringr's armor signify his virtues; his saddle is inlaid with an emerald (*smaragdus*), which, according to a translated lapidary, probably Marod's, is "saintly in its nature but more saintly as a token of God's chosen people."[34] On Mírmann's lorica there is a beryl (*berillus*) which is "good for the love of a married couple."[35] The symbolic meaning of those stones must have been known to most of the audience.

As scholars have pointed out, the author of *Mírmanns saga* devotes a great deal of his narrative to God's mercy and kindness; the saga's religious overtones are very prominent. Its historical scenes vary from pagan Saxland to France and south to Apulia in Italy and Sicily. The French are Christianized when Mírmann studies with King Hlöðver, and then the saga's time frame is given:

Í þenna tíma kom hinn helgi Dionisius í Frakkland með umráðum Klementis papa. Ok með því at Hlöðver kóngr var sjálfr góðviljaðr ok sá ok heyrði sannar jarteinir almáttigs guðs ok hans heilagra manna ok þessa hins blessaða byskups er þar var kominn, þá tók hann skírn ok rétta trú, ok allir aðrir þeir sem í váru hans landi, baði ríkir ok fátækir, en Mírmann jarlsson tók trú ok skírn af fortölum Hlöðvers kóngs fóstra síns. En þeir er eigi vildu undir ganga trúna

---

33. *Mírmanns saga*, ed. Slay, D-text, p. 127.
34. "... smaragdus, sá er dýrligr í sínu eðli en dýrligri í jartegn valdra manna guðs" (Kr. Kålund and N. Beckman, ed. *Alfræði íslenzk: Islandsk encyclopædisk litteratur*, 3 vols., Samfund til udgivelse af gammel nordisk litteratur 37, 41, 45 [Copenhagen: Møller, 1908–18], vol. 1, p. 41).
35. "... er góðr hjónum til ástar" (Kålund and Beckman, ed. *Alfræði íslenzk*, vol. 1, p. 79, cf. pp. xxvi, xxix).

stukku ór landi, sumir vestr til Spaníalands. Þar réð fyrir jarl sá er Bæringr hét ... en sumir á hendr Hermanni í Saxland.[36]

(At that time Saint Dionisius came to France at the counsel of Pope Clement. And because King Hlöðver was himself benevolent and saw and heard the truthful miracles of almighty God and his saints and of the blessed bishop who had come there, he was baptized and took the true faith, as did everyone else who stayed in his country, both rich and poor. But Mírmann, the earl's son, took the faith and was baptized at the urging of his foster father, King Hlöðver. Those who did not want to accept the true faith fled the country, some west to Spain, where an earl named Bæringr held power ... and some went to Hermann in Saxony.)

It is not quite clear if by Saint Dionisius the narrator means Dionysius Aereopagate, who in the first century A.D. was sent by Pope Clement to France and martyred there. It is also possible that the person in question was Saint Denis, whom Pope Fabianus sent to France in the third century A.D., where he suffered martyrdom. The sources often confuse the two martyrs. The external time frame of the story could therefore either be in the first or third century. The internal time frame spans only two generations, the lifetime of Mírmann himself and his parents.

No tournament or battle is fought in the saga without prayers for God's assistance; this is a very common topos in the romances[37] and cannot be counted among the peculiarities of *Mírmanns saga*. Neither can the account of Mírmann's Christian mission. Mírmann does not Christianize pagans, but his speeches are repesentative of the type that were people's daily bread at that time. The sermon that he preaches to his father is a good example. In this sermon, he traces almost the entire history of the Jews, from their earliest existence in Paradise until the start of the apostles' missionary work:

Síðan gaf hann postulum sínum vald ok styrk til jartegna slíkra, sem urðu í Rómaborg, þá er Símon hinn illi gekk í móti Petri postula ok gjörði þá sjónhverfing at hann fló í lopti með fjandans krapti. Þá bað

---

36. *Mírmanns saga*, ed. Slay, A-text, p. 15; the C-version gives a more exact chronology and relates that these persons lived during the same age in which Christ himself was born: "... í þeim heimsaldri Kristr var hingat borinn" (p. 15).

37. van Nahl, *Originale Riddarasögur*, p. 156.

Petrus at guð skyldi lægja villu hans ok þá fell Símon ofan ok brast í fjóra hluti ok lauk svá hans ævi.[38]

(Then he gave his apostles the strength and power to perform such miracles, such as those that occurred in Rome when Simon the Evil met Peter the Apostle and made it appear, through the power of the devil, as if he flew in the air. Peter then prayed to God that he should defeat his heresy. Simon then tumbled down and was torn into four pieces and thus ended his life.)

Mírmann's speech is very similar to the historical summaries found in the younger sagas of the apostles, for instance in *Tveggja postola saga Jóns ok Jakobs*. It is also obvious that the author of *Mírmanns saga* knew the older saga of the apostle Peter, since the subject-matter in the above passage is related to that version.[39]

The Christian mission among the pagans is not the main theme of *Mírmanns saga*, and it is difficult to detect in it any relationship to the literature of the crusades. Mírmann is, however, always fighting against pagan knights and Cecelia's suitors. The core of the work is an account of how an earl's son gained worldly power and the nature of his reign. He could only gain worldy power, *gloria mundi*, when living with the widow, Queen Katrín, but this life could in no way be termed *sýslulíf*, for he acquired his power because of Katrín's magic and treachery. When he lost the battle against Híringr, he was not capable of fighting (he was lame), and the story illustrates how he could only get peace of mind by having God's mercy fall upon him. He would then govern in such a way that everyone could see that *gloria Dei* shone over him. This view is stressed at the end of the saga, when the reader is told that:

[þ]au Mírmann kóngr ok Cecelia drotting áttu einn son, ok þann kölluðu þau Hlöðver eftir Hlöðver kóngi í Frakklandi. Hann tók ríki ok kóngdóm eptir þau ok er þeim þótti sitt líf standa meðr hinum bezta blóma, fyrirlétu þau allt veraldarskart ok hégómligt þessa heims líf, ok fóru í einsetu, ok prýddu þar með mannkostum sínar sálir ok líkami til eilífs fagnaðar hjá heilagri þrenningu.[40]

---

38. *Mírmanns saga*, ed. Slay, A-text, pp. 26–7.
39. van Nahl, *Originale Riddarasögur*, p. 156
40. *Mírmanns saga*, ed. Slay, D-text, p. 146.

(King Mírmann and Queen Cecelia had one son and they named him Hlöðver after King Hlöðver in France. He took over the kingdom after them, and when they felt that their life was in its highest blossom, they left all the vain finery of this world and became hermits and thus adorned their souls and bodies with virtues for eternal celebration with the Holy Trinity.)

This ending provides clear evidence that this particular saga was meant to be a romance, a hagiographical romance. The *Skarðverjar* family was accustomed to such literature, and part of their education at Skarð would have been to listen to stories of this kind; later they would also compose them, as evident in the works of Björn Þorleifsson junior, in hagiographical romances such as the *Saga of Saint Christopher* and the *Saga of Gregorius on the Rock*, an Icelandic version of the same material that Hartmann from Aue used in his *Gregorius auf dem Stein*. In the latter, the authors deal with double incest: first a brother and a sister beget a child, and later this child, Gregorius, marries and copulates with his own mother. His marriage with his own mother leads to his worldly power, *gloria mundi*, but through penance he gains peace of mind—the latter part of his story shows that he is living a *vita spiritualis*, and that he is enjoying *gloria Dei*. The concluding sentiment of both *Mírmanns saga* and the *Saga of Gregorius on the Rock* is the same: the *vita carnalis* should be avoided, and the members of the audience should submit to the spiritual power represented by the Church. Only in doing so will their lives be safe. It is quite another matter if the message of hagiographical romances, such as *Mírmanns saga*, was meant to convince women that they could only gain the upper hand or power over men if their married lives ended in hermitage, thus fulfilling the ideal of *vita contemplativa* (*upplitningarlíf*).[41]

---

41. The author wishes to thank Philip Roughton and James Payne for scrutinizing his English.

Bibliography

Amundsen, Darrel W. *Medicine, Society and Faith in the Ancient and Medieval Worlds*. Baltimore: The Johns Hopkins University Press, 1996.
Cormack, Margaret. *The Saints in Iceland: Their Veneration from the Conversion to 1400*. Subsidia hagiographica 78. Brussels: Société des Bollandistes: 1994.
Finnur Jónsson. *Den oldnorske og oldislandske litteraturs historie*. 3 vols. Copenhagen: Gad, 1920–24.
Glauser, Jürg. *Isländische Märchensagas: Studien zur Prosaliteratur im spätmittelalterlichen Island*. Basel: Helbing & Lichtenhahn, 1983.
Jansen, Katherine Ludwig. *The Making of the Magdalen: Preaching and Popular Devotion in the Later Middle Ages*. Princeton: Princeton University Press, 2001.
Jón Sigurðsson and Guðbrandur Vigfússon, ed. *Biskupa sögur*. 2 vols. Copenhagen: Hið íslenzlea bókmenntafélag, 1858–79.
Kålund, Kr., and N. Beckman, ed. *Alfræði íslenzk: Islandsk encyclopædisk litteratur*. 3 vols. Samfund til udgivelse af gammel nordisk litteratur 37, 41, 45. Copenhagen: Møller, 1908–18.
Mírmanns saga. Ed. Desmond Slay. Editiones Arnamagnæanæ, Ser. A, vol. 17. Copenhagen: Reitzel, 1997.
Nahl, Astrid van. *Originale Riddarasögur als Teil altnordischer Sagaliteratur*. Frankfurt am Main: Peter Lang, 1981.
Ólafur Halldórsson. *Helgafellsbækur fornar*. Studia Islandica 24. Reykjavík: Menningarsjóður, 1966.
Rafn, Carl Christian, ed. *Fornaldar sögur Nordrlanda*. 3 vols. Copenhagen: Popp, 1829–30.
Riddarasögur. Ed. Eugen Kölbing. Strassburg Trübner, 1872.
Schlauch, Margaret. *Romance in Iceland*. London: Georg Allen & Unwin Ltd, 1934.
Slay, Desmond. 'Ívens saga, Mírmanns saga and Ormr Snorrason's Book'. In *The Sixth International Saga Conference: Workshop Papers*. 2 vols. Copenhagen: Det arnamagnæanske Institut, 1985. Vol. 2, pp. 953–66.
Sverrir Tómasson, 'Skáldskapur og fræði fyrir stokk innan'. In *Frejas psalter—en psalter i 40 afdelinger til brug for Jonna Louis-Jensen*. Ed. Bergljót S. Kristjánsdóttir et al. Copenhagen: Det arnamagnæanske Institut,1997. Pp. 190–92.
Turville-Petre, Gabriel. *Origins of Icelandic Literature*. Oxford: Clarendon Press, 1953.
Þorvaldur Bjarnarson, ed. *Leifar fornra kristinna fræða íslenzkra: Codex Arna-Magnæanus 677 4to*. Copenhagen: H. Hagerup, 1878.
Unger, C. R., ed. *Postola sögur. Legendariske fortællinger om apostlernes liv deres kamp for kristendommens udbredelse samt deres martyrdød*. Christiania [Oslo]: Bentzen, 1874.
Vries, Jan de. *Altnordische Literaturgeschichte*. 2 vols. Berlin: de Gruyter, 1964–67.
Wolf, Kirsten, ed. *Heilagra meyja sögur*. Reykjavík: Bókmenntafræðistofnun Háskóla Íslands, 2003.

Contributors

Theodore M. Andersson is Professor Emeritus of Germanic at Indiana University. He has specialized in medieval Germanic literature, most recently in Norse/Icelandic literature, especially the sagas. The paper he has contributed to this volume is in line with a long-standing interest in the always problematical dating of the sagas. In his latest book, *The Growth of the Icelandic Sagas (1180–1280)*, published by Cornell University Press in 2006, he has tried to develop criteria for a general chronology of the sagas, and his contribution here is a supplement to the argument proposed in the book.

Ármann Jakobsson, Senior Lecturer at the University of Iceland, is the author of two books on Old Norse royal biographies, *Í leit að konungi* (1997) and *Staður í nýjum heimi* (2002), as well as *Tolkien og Hringurinn* (2003). He is the editor or co-editor of four scholarly anthologies: *Fornaldarsagornas struktur och ideologi* (2003), *Miðaldabörn* (2005), *Kona með spegil* (2005), and *Fornaldarsagaerne: Myter og virkelighed* (2008). Among his interests are Old Norse royal ideology, the portrayal in Old Norse-Icelandic texts of marginal age-groups, supernatural or magical creatures, and the construction of masculinity in texts such as *Njáls saga*. He is currently editing *Morkinskinna* for the *Íslenzk fornrit* series.

Margaret Clunies Ross is McCaughey Professor of English Language and Early English Literature and Director of the Centre for Medieval

Studies at the University of Sydney. She is one of the general editors of the research project *Skaldic Poetry of the Scandinavian Middle Ages* (2007–) and has published widely on Old Norse-Icelandic literature. Among her publications are *Skáldskaparmál: Snorri Sturluson's Ars Poetica and Medieval Theories of Language* (1987), *Prolonged Echoes: Old Norse Myths in Medieval Northern Society* (1994 and 1998), *The Norse Muse in Britain* (1998), and *A History of Old Norse Poetry and Poetics* (2005).

Robert Cook is Emeritus Professor of English at the University of Iceland, having taught at that university from 1990 to 2002. Previously, from 1962 to 1989, he taught English at Tulane University, New Orleans, with guest appointments in Iceland, Copenhagen, and Berkeley. His translation of *Njáls saga* was published in the Penguin Classics in 2001. He has published articles on Icelandic sagas, Old French romances, and medieval English literature, and in 1979 he co-edited *Strengleikar* (together with Mattias Tveitane), translations into Old Norwegian of Old French *lais*. He resides in Reykjavik, and is currently producing a critical edition of the seventeenth-century Icelandic *Einvaldsóður*, a versified world history.

Johanna Denzin, Assistant Professor of English at Columbia College (Missouri), holds a Ph.D. in comparative literature and medieval studies from the University of Illinois at Urbana-Champaign. She works in the areas of Old Norse-Icelandic literature, folklore, and medieval romance.

Matthew James Driscoll is lecturer in Old Norse-Icelandic philology at the University of Copenhagen and curator of the Arnamagnæan Manuscript Collection. He holds degrees from the University of Stirling, Scotland, the University of Iceland, and Oxford University. His research interests include manuscript and textual studies, particularly in the area of Old and early-modern Icelandic; major publications comprise editions and translations of a number of early Icelandic works as well as the monograph *The Unwashed Children of Eve: The Production, Dissemination and Reception of Popular Literature in Post-Reformation Iceland* (1997). He is also involved in a number of projects to do with the digitization and text-encoding of medieval and post-medieval manuscripts.

Margrét Eggertsdóttir, Research Professor at the Árni Magnússon Institute of Icelandic Studies in Reykjavík, holds degrees from the University of Iceland (B.A. 1984, cand. mag. 1989, and Dr. Phil. 2005). She is one of the editors of a complete edition of Hallgrímur Pétursson's works and has written extensively on Icelandic seventeenth-century literature, including a monograph on Hallgrímur Pétursson (*Barokkmeistarinn: list og lærdómur í verkum Hallgríms Péturssonar* (2005)). She is one of the editors of *Gripla*, an international journal that publishes research in the fields of Old Norse-Icelandic philology, literature and history.

Shaun F. D. Hughes is Professor of English at Purdue University, West Lafayette, where he teaches medieval and postcolonial literatures. Among his recent publications are "Elizabeth Elstob (1683–1756) and the Limits of Women's Agency in Early-Eighteenth-Century England" in *Women Medievalists and the Academy* (2005), "The Saga of Án Bowbender" in Medieval Outlaws: Twelve Tales in Modern English Translation (2005), "Late Secular Poetry" in *A Companion to Old Norse-Icelandic Literature and Culture* (2005), and "Was there ever a 'Maori English'?" (2004). For many years, he has had the privilege of participating in the *Urbönuþing*, the Old Norse-Icelandic reading group Marianne Kalinke established at the University of Illinois, Urbana-Champaign.

Jenny Jochens is Professor of History Emerita of Towson (State) University in Maryland, where she taught for about thirty years. In addition to numerous articles, she is the author of *Women in Old Norse Society* (1995) and *Old Norse Images of Women* (1996). She was the president of the Society for the Advancement of Scandinavian Study from 1997 to 1999. Currently, she divides her time among Baltimore, Paris, and Reykjavík.

John Lindow is Professor in the Department of Scandinavian at the University of California, Berkeley, and also teaches in the programs of

Folklore, Medieval Studies, and Religious Studies. His major research fields are Old Norse-Icelandic literature and culture and the folklore of Northern Europe. Major books include *Murder and Vengeance among the Gods* (1997) and *Norse Mythology: A Guide* (2001).

Svanhildur Óskarsdóttir is Associate Research Professor at the Ámi Magnússon Institute in Reykjavík. She received her first degree from the University of Iceland and pursued further studies at the Universities of Toronto, Copenhagen, and London. From the last university she holds a Ph.D. She was lecturer in Icelandic at University College London for six years before her appointment in the Institute. Her main research area is the development of universal history in Iceland, but she is also involved in co-editing the complete edition of Hallgrímur Petursson's works, which is under way at the Institute. In 2003, she received the Outstanding Young Scholar Award from Rannís (The Icelandic Center for Research).

Sverrir Tómasson received his Ph.D. in medieval literature from the University of Iceland in 1988. He has since 1971 worked in the Ámi Magnússon Institute of Icelandic Studies in Reykjavík, where he is now a Research Professor. He has published widely in the field of Old Norse-Icelandic literature. Among his publications are the editions of *Laxdæla saga* (1973), *Íslendinga sögur I–III* (1985–1987), *Sturlunga saga I–III* (1988), *Bósa saga* (1996) and the monograph *Formálar íslenskra sagnaritara á miðöldum* (1988). He is also a co-author of *Íslensk bókmenntasaga* I–II (1992/1993, second edition 2006) and co-editor of *Gripla*. He is currently working on a monograph on Icelandic romances and legends of the fourteenth and fifteenth centuries.

Úlfar Bragason is a Research Professor and Head of the International Department at the Árni Magnússon Institute for Icelandic Studies, Reykjavík. In 1998–2006 he was the Director of the Sigurður Nordal Institute at the University of Iceland. His main areas of research and teaching interest are medieval Icelandic literature and Icelandic emigration to North America. He has published extensively on *Sturlunga saga*, among other topics, and is the editor of *Atriði ævi minnar: Bréf og greinar* by Jón Halldórsson, an Icelandic emigrant to the USA. Úlfar Bragason is currently working on a book on the *Sturlunga* compilation and another on the life of Jón Halldórsson.

Kirsten Wolf is the Torger Thompson Chair and Professor of Old Norse and Scandinavian linguistics at the University of Wisconsin-Madison. From 1988 to 2001, she held the Chair of Icelandic Language and Literature at the University of Manitoba, Canada, and in 1987, she worked as editor of the Amamagnæan Dictionary at the University of Copenhagen. Her primary area of research is Old Norse-Icelandic philology. She has published several editions of medieval Icelandic texts, including *Gyðinga saga* (1995) and *Saga heilagrar Önnu* (2001). Her most recent books are *Daily Life of the Vikings* (2004) and *Beatus Vir: Studies in Early English and Norse Manuscripts in Memory of Phillip Pulsiano* (2006), which she co-edited with A.N. Doane.